Intruders in the Mind

International Perspectives in Philosophy and Psychiatry

Series editors: Bill (K.W.M.) Fulford, Lisa Bortolotti, Matthew Broome, Katherine Morris, John Z. Sadler, and Giovanni Stanghellini

VOLUMES IN THE SERIES:

Maladapting Minds: Philosophy, Psychiatry, and Evolutionary Theory
Adriaens and De Block

Portrait of the Psychiatrist as a Young Man: The Early Writing and Work of R.D. Laing, 1927–1960
Beveridge

Mind, Meaning, and Mental Disorder 2e
Bolton and Hill

What is Mental Disorder?
Bolton

Delusions and Other Irrational Beliefs
Bortolotti

Postpsychiatry
Bracken and Thomas

Philosophy, Psychoanalysis, and the A-Rational Mind
Brakel

Unconscious Knowing and Other Essays in Psycho-Philosophical Analysis
Brakel

Psychiatry as Cognitive Neuroscience
Broome and Bortolotti (eds.)

Free Will and Responsibility: A Guide for Practitioners
Callender

Reconceiving Schizophrenia
Chung, Fulford, and Graham (eds.)

Psychiatry Reborn: Biopsychosocial psychiatry in modern medicine
Davies, Savulescu, Roache, and Loebel

Darwin and Psychiatry
De Block and Adriaens (eds.)

The Oxford Handbook of Philosophy and Psychiatry
Fulford, Davies, Gipps, Graham, Sadler, Stanghellini, and Thornton

Nature and Narrative: An Introduction to the New Philosophy of Psychiatry
Fulford, Morris, Sadler, and Stanghellini (eds.)

The Oxford Textbook of Philosophy and Psychiatry
Fulford, Thornton, and Graham

The Mind and its Discontents
Gillett

Psychiatric Neuroethics: Studies in Research and Practice
Glannon

The Abraham Dilemma
Graham

Is evidence-based psychiatry ethical?
Gupta

Thinking Through Dementia
Hughes

Thomas Szasz: An Appraisal of his Legacy
Haldipur, Knoll, and Luft (eds.)

Dementia: Mind, Meaning, and the Person
Hughes, Louw, and Sabat (eds.)

Talking Cures and Placebo Effects
Jopling

Vagueness in Psychiatry
Keil, Keuck, and Hauswald

Philosophical Issues in Psychiatry II: Nosology
Kendler and Parnas (eds.)

Philosophical Issues in Psychiatry III: The Nature and Sources of Historical Change
Kendler and Parnas (eds.)

Philosophical Issues in Psychiatry IV: Classification of Psychiatric Illness
Kendler and Parnas (eds.)

Philosophy of Psychedelics
Letheby

Discursive Perspectives in Therapeutic Practice
Lock and Strong (ed.)

Schizophrenia and the Fate of the Self
Lysaker and Lysaker

Embodied Selves and Divided Minds
Maiese

Responsibility and Psychopathy
Malatesti and McMillan

Body-Subjects and Disordered Minds
Matthews

Rationality and Compulsion: Applying action theory to psychiatry
Nordenfelt

Diagnostic Dilemmas in Child and Adolescent Psychiatry
Perring and Wells (eds.)

Philosophical Perspectives on Technology and Psychiatry
Phillips (ed.)

The Metaphor of Mental Illness
Pickering

Mapping the Edges and the In-between
Potter

Trauma, Truth, and Reconciliation: Healing Damaged Relationships
Potter (ed.)

The Philosophy of Psychiatry: A Companion
Radden

The Virtuous Psychiatrist
Radden and Sadler

Addiction and Weakness of Will
Radoilska

Autonomy and Mental Disorder
Radoilska (ed.)

Madness and the Demand for Recognition
Rashed

Feelings of Being: Phenomenology, psychiatry, and the sense of reality
Ratcliffe

Experiences of Depression: A study in phenomenology
Ratcliffe

Recovery of People with Mental Illness: Philosophical and Related Perspectives
Rudnick (ed.)

Values and Psychiatric Diagnosis
Sadler

The Oxford Handbook of Psychiatric Ethics
Sadler, Van Staden, and Fulford

Madness and Modernism: Insanity in the light of modern art, literature, and thought
Sass

Disembodied Spirits and Deanimated Bodies: The Psychopathology of Common Sense
Stanghellini

Lost in Dialogue: Anthropology, Psychopathology, and Care
Stanghellini

One Century of Karl Jaspers Psychopathology
Stanghellini and Fuchs

Emotions and Personhood
Stanghellini and Rosfort

Essential Philosophy of Psychiatry
Thornton

The Oxford Handbook of Psychotherapy Ethics
Trachsel, (eds)

Naturalism, Hermeneutics, and Mental Disorder
Varga

The Healing Virtues: Character Ethics in Psychotherapy
Waring

Empirical Ethics in Psychiatry
Widdershoven, McMillan, Hope and Van der Scheer (eds.)

The Sublime Object of Psychiatry: Schizophrenia in Clinical and Cultural Theory
Woods

Alternate Perspectives on Psychiatric Validation: DSM, ICD, RDoC, and Beyond
Zachar, St. Stoyanov, Aragona, and Jablensky (eds.)

Intruders in the Mind

Interdisciplinary Perspectives on Thought Insertion

Edited by

Pablo López-Silva and Tom McClelland

Great Clarendon Street, Oxford, OX2 6DP,
United Kingdom

Oxford University Press is a department of the University of Oxford.
It furthers the University's objective of excellence in research, scholarship,
and education by publishing worldwide. Oxford is a registered trade mark of
Oxford University Press in the UK and in certain other countries

© Oxford University Press 2023

The moral rights of the authors have been asserted

First Edition published in 2023

All rights reserved. No part of this publication may be reproduced, stored in
a retrieval system, or transmitted, in any form or by any means, without the
prior permission in writing of Oxford University Press, or as expressly permitted
by law, by licence or under terms agreed with the appropriate reprographics
rights organization. Enquiries concerning reproduction outside the scope of the
above should be sent to the Rights Department, Oxford University Press, at the
address above

You must not circulate this work in any other form
and you must impose this same condition on any acquirer

Published in the United States of America by Oxford University Press
198 Madison Avenue, New York, NY 10016, United States of America

British Library Cataloguing in Publication Data

Data available

Library of Congress Control Number: 2023940287

ISBN 978-0-19-289616-2

DOI: 10.1093/med/9780192896162.001.0001

Printed in the UK by
Ashford Colour Press Ltd, Gosport, Hampshire

Oxford University Press makes no representation, express or implied, that the
drug dosages in this book are correct. Readers must therefore always check
the product information and clinical procedures with the most up-to-date
published product information and data sheets provided by the manufacturers
and the most recent codes of conduct and safety regulations. The authors and
the publishers do not accept responsibility or legal liability for any errors in the
text or for the misuse or misapplication of material in this work. Except where
otherwise stated, drug dosages and recommendations are for the non-pregnant
adult who is not breast-feeding

Links to third party websites are provided by Oxford in good faith and
for information only. Oxford disclaims any responsibility for the materials
contained in any third party website referenced in this work.

To Geraldine, my inevitable love
PLS

For LJ—an incredible partner in life
TWM

Acknowledgements

My interest in the philosophy of psychopathological phenomena started as a psychology student back in Chile. After that, as a master's and PhD student, Joel Smith and Tim Bayne introduced me to the conceptual complexities of delusional phenomena. I will always be grateful to them for this. Writing a doctoral dissertation on thought insertion made clear the need for further interdisciplinary research on the topic; a need that finally motivated this compilation. Over the past years, my work has been supported by the project FONDECYT initiation in research 'The agentive architecture of human thought' (11160544), the project FONDECYT regular nº 1221058 'The architecture of delusions'—both granted by the Chilean National Agency for Research and Development (ANID) of the Government of Chile, and the Project FACSO 2/2021 granted by the Universidad de Valparaíso Faculty of Social Sciences, Chile. I would like to thank every author who contributed to this compilation, for the time dedicated, the high quality of their contributions, and their patience with our editorial requests. I thank the Universidad de Valparaíso School of Psychology for continuously supporting my research, and George Graham, Bill Fulford, Giovanni Stanghellini, Tim Bayne, Jöelle Proust, Max Coltheart, and Cherise Rosen for supporting the initial book project. I shall also thank Geraldine Ellwanger and Tom McClelland. I met Tom while finishing my doctoral dissertation at Manchester; showing the kindness that characterizes him, he offered thousands of constructive comments on my work; it is certainly a privilege to have him as the co-editor of this compilation. Finally, I would like to thank Oxford University Press for believing in this project and supporting new interdisciplinary approaches to mental phenomena.

Pablo López-Silva, PhD
Professor of Psychology
Universidad de Valparaíso
Chile

Contents

List of Abbreviations — xiii
Editors Information — xv
Intruders in the Mind: Contextualizing Thought Insertion — xxi
    Pablo López-Silva and Tom McClelland

SECTION 1: CHARACTERIZING ALIEN THOUGHTS: REDEFINITIONS AND NOVEL EXPLORATIONS

1. When Is a Thought Mine and When Is It Not? A Personal View on Thought Insertion — 3
   Roberta Payne

2. Delusional Beliefs and Thought Insertion — 7
   Clara Humpston and Matthew Broome

3. Self-Disturbances, Perceptual Anomalies, and Physicality: Towards a Multimodal Model of Thought Insertion — 27
   Aaron Mishara, Pablo López-Silva, Cherise Rosen, and Andreas Heinz

4. Thought Insertion, Mental Affordances, and Affectivity — 43
   Michelle Maiese

5. Soundless Voices and Inserted Thoughts: What Grounds the Distinction? — 59
   Sam Wilkinson

6. On Philosophy and Schizophrenia: The Case of Thought Insertion — 77
   Jasper Feyaerts and Wouter Kusters

SECTION 2: EXPLAINING THE INTRUDED MIND: THE AETIOLOGICAL PROBLEM

7. Thought Insertion and Auditory Hallucinations: Phenomenological and Mechanistic Commonalities — 101
   Catherine Cazimir and Albert R. Powers

8. Schizophrenia and the Error-Prediction Model of Thought Insertion — 113
   Pablo López-Silva and Álvaro Cavieres

9. A Hybrid Account of Thought Insertion — 135
   Kengo Miyazono

10. **Thought Insertion Delusion: A Multifactorial Approach** 151
    Emilia Vilatta

11. **Thought Insertion as a Persecutory Delusion** 171
    Peter Langland-Hassan

SECTION 3: BRAIN, MIND, AND CONTEXTS OF CARE: EXPERIMENTAL AND THERAPEUTIC APPROACHES TO TI

12. **Experimental Approaches to Understanding Thought Insertion** 195
    Elisa Brann, Eamonn Walsh, Mitul A. Mehta, David A. Oakley, and Quinton Deeley

13. **What Can Magic and Science Tell Us About the Experience of Thought Insertion?** 225
    Alice Pailhès, Jay Olson, and Gustav Kuhn

14. **Generalized Internal Model of Mental Representations: Thought Insertion, Mental Agency, and the Cerebellum** 239
    Kentaro Hiromitsu and Tomohisa Asai

15. **Metacognitive Treatment in Patients with Thought Insertion** 253
    Susana Ochoa and Helena García-Mieres

SECTION 4: BEYOND THE PHENOMENON: THOUGHT INSERTION AND THE NATURE OF THINKING

16. **Thought Insertion and Commitment** 273
    Jordi Fernández

17. **Thought Insertion and The Ontology of Thinking** 287
    Johannes Roessler

Index 305

List of Abbreviations

ACM	Alien control of movement
AVH	Auditory-verbal hallucination
BADE	Bias against disconfirmatory evidence
CBT	Cognitive behavioural therapy
DSM	Diagnostic and statistical manual of mental
ESSS	Embodied Sense of Self Scale
fMRI	functional magnetic resonance imaging
FRS	First-rank symptoms
JTC	Jumping to conclusions
MCT	Metacognitive Training
MERIT	Metacognitive Reflection and Insight Therapy
MOSST	MERIT that focused on social skills training
OCD	Obsessive-compulsive disorder
PANSS	Positive and Negative Syndrome Scale
PC	Predictive coding
PE	Prediction error
PET	Positron emission tomography
SAPS	Schedules for the Assessment of Positive Symptoms
SCAN	Schedules for Clinical Assessment in Neuropsychiatry
SMA	Supplementary motor area
SoA	Sense of agency
SoO	Sense of ownership
TF	Two-factor
TI	Thought insertion
ToM	Theory of Mind

Editors Information

Pablo López-Silva is Professor of Psychology at the School of Psychology, and Research Professor at the Institute of Philosophy of the Universidad de Valparaíso, Chile. Pablo López-Silva holds a Licentiate in Psychology, a Professional Qualification as Psychologist, a Postgraduate Diploma in Attachment Theory and Early Care (Pontificia Universidad Católica de Valparaíso), and a Postgraduate Diploma in Higher Education Teaching (Universidad de Valparaíso). Pablo López-Silva holds a Master's in Research and a PhD in Philosophy (University of Manchester, UK). His areas of research are Philosophy of Mind, Philosophy of Psychology, Psychopathology, and Neuroethics.

Tom McClelland is lecturer in the Department of History and Philosophy of Science at the University of Cambridge. He is also a researcher on the Inner Speech in Action project based at UPF Barcelona. Tom McClelland's research explores the philosophy and science of perception, thought, and the self. He is currently working on how mental action is guided by the perception of affordances and how patterns of individual differences in perceptual experience can constitute social injustices. He is interested in how insights from psychology and philosophy of mind can be marshalled to address social problems.

Contributors

Tomohisa Asai is a senior researcher at ATR (Advanced Telecommunications Research Institute International, Department of Cognitive Neuroscience) with Ph.D. (Psychology, The University of Tokyo, 2010). His research interests include the sense of self, schizophrenia, and sensorimotor systems in the brain. His current interest is computational neuroscience using behavioural and EEG/fMRI techniques.

Elisa Brann is a PhD student at King's College London. Her research focuses on understanding the neurophysiological basis of first-rank symptoms of psychosis (hallucinations and delusions), and using hypnotic suggestion to model first-rank symptoms in healthy individuals.

Matthew Broome is Chair in Psychiatry and Youth Mental Health, and Director of the Institute for Mental Health at the University of Birmingham, Distinguished Research Fellow, Oxford Uehiro Centre for Practical Ethics, University of Oxford, and Honorary Consultant Psychiatrist to the East Birmingham Early Intervention in Psychosis Team, Birmingham Women's and Children's NHS Foundation Trust.

Álvaro Cavieres is a psychiatrist and full professor at the Universidad de Valparaíso. He was director of the Department of Psychiatry of the Universidad de Valparaíso and of the

Psychotic Disorders Unit of the Hospital del Salvador. He is the author of a number of published research papers.

Catherine Cazimir, a Miami native, is a third-year medical student at Meharry Medical College. As an esteemed member of Phi Beta Kappa, she graduated with a degree in Biological Sciences and a minor in Chemistry from Florida International University and a Master's in Health Sciences from Meharry Medical College. While working towards her medical degree, Catherine participated in the inaugural Yale–Meharry Summer Research Program. She also has a passion for health equity and community medicine and volunteers her weekends to the homeless community and Meharry's Salt Wagon Clinic.

Quinton Deeley is Senior Lecturer in Social Behaviour and Neurodevelopment at the Institute of Psychiatry, Psychology, and Neuroscience (IOPPN), King's College London. He is also Consultant Neuropsychiatrist in the National Autism Unit and Neuropsychiatry Brain Injury Clinic at the Maudsley and Bethlem Hospitals. Dr Deeley chairs the Maudsley Philosophy Group, and Social and Cultural Neuroscience Group at the IOPPN. Dr Deeley has researched the relationship between culture, cognition, and brain function since his qualifications in Theology and Religious Studies from Cambridge University, and later medicine at Guys and St Thomas' Medical School, London, and psychiatry at the Maudsley and Bethlem Hospitals.

Jordi Fernández is Associate Professor of Philosophy at the University of Adelaide. His teaching and research interests are in philosophy of mind, epistemology, and metaphysics. He is the author of *Transparent Minds: A Study of Self-Knowledge* (2013) and *Memory: A Self-Referential Account* (2019).

Jasper Feyaerts holds a PhD in Clinical Psychology from Ghent University, Belgium. Between 2018 and 2021, he was an FWO postdoctoral research fellow at the Department of Psychoanalysis & Clinical Consulting at Ghent University and the Center for Contextual Psychiatry at KU Leuven. His research interests include phenomenological research on delusions and psychosis onset in schizophrenia spectrum disorders and conceptual research on philosophical issues in psychiatry. He is currently Assistant Professor at the Department of Psychoanalysis & Clinical Consulting at Ghent University, where he pursues phenomenological and philosophical research on psychosis.

Helena García-Mieres Ph.D. is a general health psychologist and postdoctoral fellow at Institut Hospital del Mar de Investigacions Mèdiques (IMIM) in Barcelona, Spain. She received training in the MAS-A scale and MERIT during a research stay with Paul Lysaker. She has many publications regarding the links between personal identity and clinical factors in psychotic disorders. She takes part in collaborations with the MERIT Institute of Dr Lysaker in the form of several ongoing articles and book chapters.

Andreas Heinz, MD, PhD, is Director and Chair of the Department of Psychiatry and Neurosciences, Charité-University Medical Center, Berlin. He studied medicine, philosophy and social anthropology at the Ruhr Universität Bochum, Freie Universität Berlin and Howard University, Washington DC. He is a board-qualified neurologist and psychiatrist. His work focuses on learning mechanisms in mental disorders, intercultural psychiatry and psychotherapy, and the history of racism in schizophrenia theory.

Kentaro Hiromitsu is a post-doc researcher at The University of Tokyo and a neuropsychologist at Tokyo Metropolitan Cancer and Infectious Diseases Centre Komagome Hospital. He completed his PhD at Chuo University in 2019. His research focuses on the disorders of the self in brain-damaged patients and on revealing the mechanisms of the relations between the self and the brain through the approach of neuropsychology, experimental psychology, and neuroimaging.

Clara Humpston PhD, FHEA, is an Assistant Professor in Mental Health at the University of York, United Kingdom, and Honorary Research Fellow at the Institute for Mental Health, University of Birmingham, United Kingdom. Her research interests and experience span from psychopharmacology to cognitive neuropsychiatry to phenomenological psychopathology. She is a strong proponent of inter- and multidisciplinary approaches and values the importance of multiple lines of scientific inquiry in mental health research.

Gustav Kuhn is a Reader in Psychology at Goldsmiths, University of London, where he directs the MAGIC lab (Mind Attention and General Illusory Cognition). The MAGIC lab applies an interdisciplinary approach to studying human behaviour and cognition. Their efforts include but are not limited to using magic to study a wide range of psychological questions, around consciousness, attention, perception, magical beliefs, deception, and free will. The lab strongly encourages an interdisciplinary approach that allows us to bridge the gap between the real-world knowledge acquired by magicians and the sciences.

Wouter Kusters is PhD in linguistics (Leiden University), and an MA in philosophy (Utrecht University). He is the author of several books on the experience and conceptualization of psychosis, or madness as he prefers to call it, of which *A Philosophy of Madness. The Experience of Psychotic Thinking* is the apex. It has been translated from the original Dutch (2014) into English (2020), while Arabic and Chinese translations are due to appear.

Peter Langland-Hassan is Professor of Philosophy at the University of Cincinnati. He is the author of *Explaining Imagination* (OUP, 2020) and co-editor of the anthology *Inner Speech: New Voices* (OUP, 2018).

Michelle Maiese is Professor of Philosophy at Emmanuel College in Boston, MA. Her research addresses issues in philosophy of mind, philosophy of psychiatry, and emotion theory. She has authored or co-authored five books: *Embodied Minds in Action* (co-authored with Robert Hanna, 2009), *Embodied, Emotion, and Cognition* (2011), *Embodied Selves and Divided Minds* (2015), *The Mind–Body Politic* (co-authored with Robert Hanna, 2019), and *Autonomy, Enactivism, and Mental Disorder* (2022).

Mitul A. Mehta is a Professor of Neuroimaging & Psychopharmacology at the Institute of Psychiatry, Psychology & Neuroscience, King's College London, having completed fellowships funded by the Medical Research Council UK, and Wellcome Trust, before his PhD at the University of Cambridge. He is primarily interested in mechanisms of brain modulation, working with psychopharmacological methods and hypnosis, often combined with brain measurement. He chairs the Neuropharmacology group in his department and is co-chair of the Cultural and Social Neuroscience group with Quinton Deeley.

Aaron Mishara is Associated Distinguished Professor at the California Institute of Integral Studies. He holds a PhD in Philosophy and a PhD in Clinical Psychology. He conducted neuropsychological research in Daniel Weinberger's lab (NIMH) and movement disorders in Mark Hallett's (NINDS) lab at the National Institute of Health (NIH). Subsequently, he conducted research in the Departments of Psychiatry, Radiology, and the Clinical Neuroscience Research Unit at the Yale University School of Medicine.

Kengo Miyazono is an Associate Professor of Philosophy at Hokkaido University, Japan. His main research areas are philosophy of mind, philosophy of psychology, and philosophy of psychiatry. He is the author of *Philosophy of Psychology: An Introduction* (Polity, 2021, with Lisa Bortolotti) and *Delusions and Beliefs: A Philosophical Inquiry* (Routledge, 2018).

David A. Oakley is Emeritus Professor at University College London and Honorary Professor at Cardiff University. His earliest research focused on the cortical and subcortical substrates of learning and memory. More recently, he has been interested in hypnosis and suggestion as topics in their own right, as therapeutic techniques, as a means of exploring pain, consciousness and the voluntary control of action, and in the creation of experimental analogues of clinical conditions, such as conversion disorder and functional pain.

Susana Ochoa is a PhD psychologist and she works in Parc Sanitari Sant Joan de Déu since 1997. She has an extensive experience in the field of psychosis, especially in psychological treatments, metacognition and social cognition, validation of instruments and gender issues. She is the PI of more than 20 competitive research projects and author of more than 150 impact factor publications.

Jay Olson is a Postdoctoral Fellow in the Department of Psychology at Harvard University. He did his graduate training at McGill and postdoctoral training at Harvard University. He studies a range of topics across behavioural science and medicine, including placebos, sleep, creativity, and magic.

Alice Pailhès holds a PhD in Psychology and is a scientific consultant. She has pioneered scientific research on magicians' mind control tricks, called forcing techniques. Her research mainly focuses on using magic tricks to study psychological principles such as an illusory sense of agency and freedom over choice, decision-making processes, memory malleability, and placebo effects.

Roberta Payne earned a Batchelor's degree in Classics from Stanford, and a Master's in Italian from UCLA, and a Master's in Romance Languages from Harvard. She also holds a PhD in Comparative Literature from the University of Denver. She has taught English and Latin. In 2013 Roberta published *Speaking to My Madness: How I Search for Myself in Schizophrenia*, an autobiographical memoir narrating her own life and psychopathological experiences.

Albert R. Powers is Assistant Professor at the Yale University Department of Psychiatry and Medical Director of the Yale PRIME Psychosis Research Clinic. He uses psychophysics, in-depth clinical interviews, and neuroimaging to understand the perceptual and neural bases of hallucinations. He has produced the first evidence for a computational model that views hallucinations as an overweighting of Bayesian priors during perception. His ongoing work focuses on applying the computational tools he has developed toward early detection and novel treatment development in psychosis. His clinical work is focused on the treatment of young people experiencing attenuated psychotic symptoms, as Medical Director of the Yale PRIME Psychosis Prodrome Research Clinic.

Johannes Roessler is Associate Professor (Reader) in the Department of Philosophy at the University of Warwick. He has published articles in journals such as *Mind* and *Proceedings of the Aristotelian Society* on issues in epistemology, the philosophy of mind and action, and the philosophy of psychology, and he has co-edited three volumes published by OUP. He is currently working on a monograph on perceptual knowledge.

Cherise Rosen Dr Rosen is a phenomenologist who has conducted extensive research on aspects involving the longitudinal course of psychosis. She is Co-PI of the Chicago Follow-up Study. Her research has focused on the phenomenological constructs of psychosis, hallucinations, delusions, inner speech, felt presence, and self-disturbances. Dr Rosen's research follows quantitative, qualitative, and mixed-methods research designs to elucidate findings that include subjective experience. She has close to 70 peer-reviewed publications and has presented her research nationally and internationally. Her current research emphasis has been on the longitudinal course of hallucinations, delusions, abstraction, and the reframing of voices, other extreme states, and non-consensus realities as meaning-centred experiences.

Emilia Vilatta holds a PhD in Philosophy, a Bachelor's in Philosophy, and Bachelor's in Psychology. She was a Postdoctoral Fellow CONICET (2019–2021). Currently, she is Assistant Professor in Epistemology and Philosophy of Evidence-Based Psychotherapies at the Faculty of Psychology of the National University of Córdoba, Argentina.

Eamonn Walsh is a Reader in Neuroscience Education and Programme Director for the MSc Neuroscience at King's College London. His research explores the effects of verbal suggestion on body representation. He also uses corpus linguistics to identify patterns in assessment that are of educational significance.

Sam Wilkinson is Senior Lecturer in Philosophy at the University of Exeter. His interests are in the philosophy of mental health and well-being, with a specific focus on hallucinations, delusions, psychosis, trauma, loneliness, and inner speech. He also has a general interest in the way that the mind harnesses social and cultural context to enhance and shape cognition.

Intruders in the Mind: Contextualizing Thought Insertion

Pablo López-Silva and Tom McClelland

Delusions have been present among humans since our very beginnings. In ancient Hindi Culture, *Grahi* was regarded as a demon capable of controlling people's bodies causing what we would now regard as epileptic convulsions (Kanner, 1930; Porter, 2003). In the book of Daniel in the Bible, Nebuchadnezzar, King of Babylon, seems to suffer from what we would now call *zoanthropy*, a rare delusion in which the subject believes himself to be an animal (Blom, 2013, 2014). The Persian story of *Laili* and *Majnum* (literally the '*the mad one*') shows how love can drive one to madness, and even death. Clinically relevant delusions have been documented since the 1600s, and, given their strange nature, they have always challenged the notions that philosophers and clinicians have about the normal functioning of our mind. Anticipating a currently dominant idea, in his *Essay on Human Understanding*, Locke (1961) suggests that madness resulted from faulty associations in the process whereby sense data (experiential inputs) were transformed into 'ideas' (beliefs). Porter (2003) suggests that Locke's bottom-up notion of madness as resulting from different impairments in the process of idea formation started to become of the dominant conception of madness in Britain and France around 1700 (p. 127). In fact, the term 'delusion' was first used to refer to mental problems around the same date. Later, for the phenomenological tradition in psychopathology, delusions were considered as the *hallmark* of psychosis, one of the most—if not the most—complex forms of psychological suffering. As Jaspers (1963) claims: '*since time immemorial, delusion has been taken as the basic characteristic of madness. To be mad was to be deluded*' (p. 93). Nowadays, delusions are regarded as one of the most severe symptoms of a number of neuropsychiatric conditions with a higher prevalence in schizophrenia (American Psychiatric Association, 2013; Connors & Halligan, 2020; Harrow et al., 2005; Harrow & Jobe, 2010; Rosen et al., 2016, 2017, 2022).

Delusional phenomena are heterogeneous in structure, theme, phenomenological features, and, arguably, aetiology. Certainly, the understanding of delusional phenomena requires collaboration between different disciplines, such as psychopathology, clinical psychology, neuropsychiatry, philosophy, and phenomenology, among many others (Fulford et al., 2013; López-Silva, 2014; López-Silva & Cavieres, 2021; Kusters, 2021; Humpston, 2022). Among delusions, *thought insertion* is considered as one of the most complex cases (Mullins & Spence, 2003; López-Silva, 2017, 2018; Sterzer et al., 2016). More prevalent in schizophrenia, delusions of thought insertion involve subjects reporting that entities of different nature have introduced thoughts or ideas into their minds (Jaspers, 1963; Mellor, 1970; López-Silva, 2018). Although the subjective structure of the reports on the phenomenon show similarities, the external agents identified by patients are considerably heterogeneous in nature; some of them identify persons (e.g., TV celebrities, relatives; see Frith, 1992), electronic devices (e.g., TVs, radios; see Spence et al., 1997), collective groups (e.g., aliens, the government, secrets societies; see Payne, 2013), and some others refer to surrounding inanimate entities (e.g., houses, trees; see Saks, 2007), among many others. A well-discussed case shows a patient stating that in TI: 'thoughts are put into my mind like "Kill God", it's just like my mind working, but it isn't. They come from this chap, Chris. They are his thoughts' (Frith, 1992, p. 66). In this sense, the particularity of this phenomenon is not that patients have been caused to have certain unusual thoughts (in fact, this can happen all the time in everyday situations, even more saliently when the content of those thoughts is *egodystonic*; see López-Silva, 2015); Rather, the symptom is especially enigmatic because certain thoughts are experienced as not being the patients' but created and inserted by an external agent into their personal space (see Wing, Cooper, & Sartorius, 1974). Self-reporting her own episode of thought insertion, Payne (2013) had the experience of being aware of 'six rules' that had been inserted in her mind by aliens (Payne, 2013, p. 17). This certainly confronts us with an enigmatic type of conscious experience where the boundaries between external and internal reality get blurred.

Intuitively, thought insertion posits a number of questions about how to understand our everyday experience of thinking. However, the symptom has other particularities. First of all, thought insertion is a very rare phenomenon, and it co-occurs over time with a number of other phenomena, such as hallucinations (especially auditory-verbal hallucinations; see Humpston & Broome, 2016), and other delusions (López-Silva et al., 2022). Thought insertion rarely happens alone and, in this sense, it is part of a constellation of symptoms that seem to share certain features, thus making the task of characterizing the phenomenon even more difficult (see Ratcliffe & Wilkinson, 2015). Regarding this, patients do not experience all of their thoughts as inserted (Gallagher, 2004, 2014; López-Silva, 2018), and they only experience certain types of mental states as inserted, such as feelings, emotions, and impulses (Mellor, 1970; Frith, 1992; Sierra & Berrios, 2000; Payne, 2013). This was already observed by Freud (1930), who commented that 'there are cases in which part of a person's own body, even portions of his mental life—his perceptions, thoughts, and feeling—appear alien to him and as not belonging to his own ego' (p. 66). In addition, and very importantly, patients are able to distinguish voices—and other states—from inserted thoughts, which is a relevant issue in light of the phenomenological similarities reported between these two types of phenomena (Sterzer et al., 2016). About this, Saks (2007, p. 29) informs: 'I didn't hear these words as literal sounds, as through the houses were talking and I were hearing them [...] they were ideas I was having. Yet I instinctively knew they were not my ideas. They belonged to the houses, and the houses had put them in my head'.

Inserted thoughts are reported as preceded and accompanied by a number of transformations in the general experience of the subjective, intersubjective, and the physical world of patients (Mayer-Gross, 1932; Conrad, 1958; Fuchs, 2005; Payne, 2013; Rosen et al. 2022; López-Silva et al., 2022; Fusar-Poli et al., 2022). In the phenomenological tradition, the period—that can last from days to months—preceding the emergence of full-blown cases of delusions of thought insertion and other positive psychotic symptoms has been referred to as 'delusional atmosphere' (*Wahnstimmung*; Conrad, 1958). During this period, the world becomes mysterious and puzzling, affording novel meanings (Fuchs, 2005). A case documented by Gross and Huber (1972) shows a patient claiming that, during this period, 'wherever you are looking, everything looks unreal' and that people appeared to be puppets. Another patient claims that 'when you go somewhere, everything seems already set up for you like in a theatre—it's really eerie, and you get terribly frightened' (Fuchs, 2005, p. 134). In the same way, patient BS reports that, during the months preceding her own episode of TI, she experienced a generalized sense of unreality, a general transformation of the social and subjective world: 'I had short periods of time in which I felt like I didn't exist. I had other experiences in which I had to, for instance, touch a coffee table in front of me to make sure it was real' (BS in López-Silva, 2018). The consequence of all this is that patients no longer trust their experience of the world (Fuchs, 2005; Fusar-Poli et al., 2022). Quite importantly, this feeling of general uncertainty not only pervades the general experience of reality, but also specific objects in the field of awareness (Freedman & Chapman, 1973). In consequence, patients start experiencing an increasing oppressive tension, and general feelings of uncertainty, disunity, and lack of control spreads all over their experiences of the physical, intersubjective, and subjective world (Conrad, 1958; Mishara, 2010).

Thought insertion also challenges our intuitions about the apparent boundaries between thinking and sensory states, for it seems to show a cognitive experience reported with variable degrees of *physicality* (Mayer-Gross, 1932; Sterzer et al., 2016). A patient interviewed by Cahill & Frith (1996) reports physically feeling the alien thoughts as they entered his head and claimed that 'he could pin-point the point of entry' (p. 278). This results in patients experiencing a diminished sense of agency with negative connotations. Schneider (1959) reports a patient who experienced thought insertion as a highly physical process imposed with considerable force. Binswanger (1957) describes patients diagnosed with schizophrenia as referring to themselves as mere 'machines' or 'apparatuses' with the only function of registering impressions of the world. This general feeling of alienation from their own experiences seems to be a distinctive feature of psychosis (Fusar-Poli et al., 2022). More recently, and emphasizing the passivity and alienation experienced by patients suffering from thought insertion, Vosgerau and Voss (2014) refer to a patient who claims that: 'It feels like this person is *using* my brain to think his thoughts—just like he is seeing the world through my eyes and interfering with the world through my body. It feels like I am *possessed* by this person (p. 536, our emphasis). Similarly, Sollberger (2014) comments on the case of a patient that suggests: 'others are said to think the thoughts using the subject's mind as a psychological *medium* or "*bucket*"' (p. 590, our emphasis).

It is easy to see why delusions of thought insertion are such an intriguing phenomenon. It blurs our understanding of some of the most fundamental aspects of our mind, and it invites further discussions. In light of its unique features, over the last 20 years both clinicians and philosophers have found in thought insertion a formidable challenge for the way in which consciousness, self-awareness, agency, the nature of beliefs, and a number of other critical concepts have been characterized (Gibbs, 2000; Stephens & Graham, 2000; Billon & Kriegel, 2015; López-Silva, 2016, 2020; Guillot, 2017; Gennaro, 2021; Humpston, 2022; Billon, 2023). However, it is important to note that discussions about thought insertion tend to be featured in the context of philosophical examinations of broader issues in philosophy and psychiatry. On numerous occasions thought insertion has been treated as a footnote to discussions of more prominent topics such as motor agency or the structure of phenomenal consciousness (Frith, 1992; Gallagher, 2014; García-Carpintero & Guillot, 2023). For this reason, discussion of the phenomenon is scattered throughout the literature, making it difficult to keep track of. *Intruders in the*

Mind is an interdisciplinary attempt to bring together high-quality contributions to some of the most fundamental debates arising from the comprehensive study of thought insertion. Making thought insertion its central topic, this compilation gathers a series of essays that, taken as a whole, offer a broad and thoughtful approach to the clinical, phenomenological, conceptual, and experimental aspects of the systematic study of the phenomenon. The compilation is divided into four sections, each of them focusing on a specific set of interrelated debates. In the remainder of this introduction, we will frame each of these sections in order to offer some context for the specific essays featured in each section.

Characterizing Alien Thoughts: Redefinitions and Novel Explorations

One of the first challenges of trying to explore delusions of thought insertion is the notorious scarcity of clinical reports. This is fundamental for this task because, without a clear description of the phenomenon, it is virtually impossible to establish the adequate *explananda* for a plausible explanatory theory for it (López-Silva, 2014, 2018). As Pickard (2010, p. 56) points out, when discussing phenomena such as thought insertion: 'the same patient reports are used again and again, and they do not fully capture the phenomenon'. The challenge is made still more pressing by the fact that even the few existing descriptions of the symptoms are surrounded by a number of descriptive disagreements. An anecdotal passage reveals that this trouble is not exclusive of our project. When trying to compile cases for his *Compendium of Psychiatry*, Emil Kraepelin found many difficulties in accessing clinical reports. As Bentall (2003) observes, this was one of the main reasons why Kraepelin finally moved from Heidelberg to Munich in 1902. that the difficulties with finding specific and well-described cases of psychopathological phenomena are not new and suggest that better-coordinated forms of collaboration are needed among researchers on the field. Trying to address this difficulty, Chapter 1 of this volume offers a first-person description of what it is like to experience thought insertion. This succinct contribution is replete with insights that only lived descriptions on the phenomenon can offer. The importance of bringing forward the voices of those who suffer from this type of delusion is something that has been highlighted in the recent literature (Fusar-Poli et al., 2022). This is certainly an important step for researchers to become more aware of the nuances and complexities associated with the experience of thought insertion.

Once we have accessed reports of the experience of patients, one of the next key issues is the problem of how thought insertion should be *characterized*. The goal of this debate is to provide an account of the structure of the delusion that allows us to later explain it. This *sense* need not be exhaustive, but it needs to offer an alternative for the question about what thought insertion *consists of*. In Chapter 2, Clara Humpston and Matthew Broome ask whether delusions of thought insertion can be characterized as a type belief. By using resources coming from the phenomenological tradition in psychiatry, the authors compare thought insertion with other co-occurrent phenomena in psychosis in order to offer a more nuanced conceptualization of the symptom. Their proposal emphasizes the paradoxicality and perplexity with which experiences of thought insertion are reported and locate the experience of the patients at the centre of the discussion. The guiding idea behind this contribution is that without patient experience on the central stage, neither philosophical nor empirical investigations will possess real benefit—not even to the theorists or researchers.

In Chapter 3, Aaron Mishara, Pablo López-Silva, Cherise Rose, and Andreas Heinz take a similar approach. Gathering elements from the history of psychiatry, they focus on an often-neglected feature of inserted thoughts, namely, its *physicality*. Very commonly, approaches to the characterization of thought insertion use negative and positive strategies. While the negative strategy examines what the thought reported as inserted lack, and how the lack of a certain specific phenomenal feature would prove their externalization, the positive strategy consists in examining what features inserted thoughts have that everyday thoughts do not (for examples of negative strategies see Frith, 1992; Campbell, 1999, 2002; Zahavi, 2005; Bortolotti & Broome, 2008; Martin & Pacherie, 2013; Gallagher, 2014; for examples of positive strategies, see Synofzik, Vosgerau, & Newen, 2008; Sollberger, 2014; Billon & Kriegel, 2015). Transcending this dichotomy, the authors of Chapter 3 suggest that thought insertion is better-characterized as a multimodal experience involving a disruption to the inner connectedness of thoughts by a 'becoming sensory' of the thoughts experienced as inserted. After clarifying some of the main elements of their proposal, the authors explore the way in which predictive coding and Bayesian inference—an approach currently popular within cognitive neurosciences—may provide a framework capable of linking the neurobiology of psychosis with its clinical phenomenology.

Considering the *relational* and *situated* nature of the human mind, in Chapter 4 Michelle Maiese brings together the resources of ecological psychology, enactivism, and phenomenology. Maiese suggests that we ordinarily have a sense that our thoughts are afforded or solicited by aspects of our environment, or by our existing mental states. In cases of thought insertion, thoughts would not be experienced as afforded. As a consequence, thoughts in psychosis seem so foreign and alien that subjects claim that they have been inserted in their mind by another source. Maiese claims that thought insertion can be characterized as cases where the disclosure of affordances for certain mental actions is disrupted. The novel suggestion of the author is that affectivity is central to the disclosure of affordances and that a disruption to *affective framing* plays a central role in thought insertion. In this way, Chapter 4 is able to add an additional layer to the analysis of the experience of thought insertion, namely, the connection between cognition and affectivity.

In Chapter 5, Sam Wilkinson strengthens the analysis of the experience of thought and focuses on its co-occurrency with auditory-verbal hallucinations. In the context of this discussion, it has been suggested that inserted thoughts and soundless voices might belong to the same type of phenomenon. Wilkinson pulls apart the two meanings of this claim. On the one hand, it seems to refer to the existence of similar etiological mechanisms; on the other hand, it seems to refer to the existence of similar experiential features. The author asks why advocates of the latter claim fail to account for why soundless voices and inserted thoughts get described so differently if they have similar experiential features. By isolating the different experiential features that are likely to lead to an experience being reported *as a voice* as opposed to *as a thought*, the author ends up questioning whether it is plausible that these are underpinned by the same mechanism after all. In this way, the authors of Chapters 3 and 4 are able to stablish a fruitful connection between discussion about the phenomenological features of thought insertion in psychosis with examinations of the potential faulty mechanisms underlying it.

As mentioned before, delusional experiences such as thought insertion connect psychiatry with some of the deepest aspects of human existence. Strongly rooted in the type of being we are, psychosis seems to push us to an existential understanding of mental illness, and how this 'too human' phenomenon relates to other aspects of our anthropology and practices. Opposing overly restrictive approaches to the characterization problem, in Chapter 6 Jasper Feyaerts and Wouter Kusters take a deep dive into the experience of thought insertion and suggest that philosophy and schizophrenia (as the main clinical conditions in which thought insertion is reported) share a basic kind of attitude towards ordinary life viz. *preoccupation with* and *reflection on*. The authors suggest that, in both cases, subjects deal with the contradictions and paradoxes that unavoidably arise as a *result* of such preoccupations. However, while the philosopher attempts to get a clear theoretical view on what he already possesses, the schizophrenic individual seeks to existentially regain what they are acutely aware of as having lost. In other words, while the philosopher tries to penetrate to the most fundamental layers of self-experience in order to acquire knowledge about them, the schizophrenic individual is thought to be spontaneously confronted with them through their imminent disintegration or erasure. This proposal connects the often-neglected field of the psychology of philosophy with the study of psychopathological phenomena, thus broadening our comprehension of not only thought insertion but also the anthropological nature of philosophical enquiring.

As can be seen, taken as a whole the essays contained in the first part of this compilation will introduce the reader to a well-developed discussion of some of the most fundamental disagreements that emerge when philosophers and clinicians jointly attempt to characterize our target phenomenon.

Explaining Thought Insertion: The Aetiological Problem and the Nature of Thinking

Once we have characterized thought insertion and identified its main features, the next challenge is to offer an account of how this phenomenon is produced. Any candidate explanation should be consistent with patients' phenomenological reports and the currently available empirical evidence. While the former will establish clear *explananda* for the proposed theory, the latter will provide independent support for it. Certainty, understanding how thought insertion is produced is a complex matter due to the general complexity of human cognition and the specific rarefied context in which delusions of thought insertion arise. In the first chapter of this section (Chapter 7), Catherine Cazimir and Al Powers further explore issues surrounding co-occurrence. They consider not only phenomenological, but also mechanistic and neural commonalities in the aetiology of thought insertion and auditory-verbal hallucinations. For a long time, such similarities have motivated the idea of a common genesis in both types of symptoms. In fact, in opinion of the authors, the current evidence available in the literature seems to suggest that these delusions of thought insertion and auditory-verbal hallucinations would be connected conceptually and mechanistically. However, they also argue that neither phenomenon is sufficiently understood to reach this conclusion with certainty, leaving room for future contributions to our understanding.

In Chapter 8 Pablo López-Silva and Álvaro Cavieres target the so-called prediction-error model of the aetiology of thought insertion. Focused on the neuropsychiatry of thought insertion, they establish a number of conceptual, phenomenological, and empirical issues faced by this model. This neuropsychiatric model of delusions is an application of the idea that, in creating our conscious experience of reality, our brain uses prior learned predictions to infer the causes of incoming sensory data. A number of authors have suggested that such a process can be formalized as a type of Bayesian inference where probabilistic predictions are combined with observed sensory data to compute, and with this, neurocomputational psychiatry might be able to offer a plausible understanding of the brain in psychosis. This has been called the predictive coding framework and it conceives of the brain as a hierarchy aiming at maximizing the evidence for its model of the world comparing prior expectations with incoming sensory data. When predictions match sensory data, the brain's model of the world is reinforced, thus improving our general understanding of reality. However, when incoming signals do not match our predictions, the brain uses those prediction-errors to update the model, allowing new learning. The model suggests that, in psychosis, decreased precision in the encoding of prior beliefs about sensory data would lead to maladaptive inferences. In turn, prediction problems result in the attribution of salience to otherwise irrelevant stimuli, leading to delusional mood (Sterzer et al., 2016), and producing positive symptoms of schizophrenia such as delusions and auditory-verbal hallucinations (Notredame et al., 2014; Sterzer et al., 2018).

Over the past years the predictive coding model has been gaining explanatory traction due to the way in which it brings together insights from neurosciences, computational psychiatry, and phenomenological psychopathology (some of them also explored in Chapter 3). The authors of Chapter 8 suggest that the model is able to offer a more complete and contextualized explanation for thought insertion formation due to the inclusion of the delusional mood into its explanatory proposal. However, at the same time, they suggest that the error-prediction model cannot completely account for the bizarre nature of the external attributions that characterizes our target phenomenon, and for this reason the chapter motivates further discussion on the mechanistic underpinnings of the symptom. Now, it is plausible to think that a single theory might not be able to deal with the complexities of our target phenomenon. Taking this into consideration, in Chapter 9 Kengo Miyazono suggests that the error-prediction model can be hybridized with another popular neuropsychiatric model, namely, the two-factor model. According to this theory, delusion production is explained by the interplay between two distinct neurocognitive factors that play different explanatory roles (Coltheart, 2010). On the one hand, experiential alterations (factor–1) would explain the content of the delusion, while, on the other hand, cognitive alterations (factor–2) would explain why such content is finally endorsed by the patients and why delusions persist despite counterevidence. Opposing an implicit rivalry between these two approaches, the author of this chapter claims that a hybrid account would be able to explain many important features of thought insertion, and with this, it opens an interesting path for further research.

Taking a similar open-minded and collaborative approach to the examination of the aetiology of thought insertion, Emilia Vilatta stresses the need for a multifactorial model in Chapter 10. Vilatta focuses on how two different ways of understanding the production of delusions can work together. On the one hand, the so-called *deficit approaches*—such as the ones characteristic of neuropsychiatry—posit that delusions are the result of a number of sensory and cognitive alterations that affect the process of belief acquisition or evaluation. According to these approaches, the delusional content does not seem to have any relevant causal role and the description of the deficits is carried out at a functional or subpersonal level. On the other hand, motivational approaches consider that the process of delusion formation is caused by the psychological benefits that delusions confer to the subject. According to this view, delusions are characterized as an active psychological response to an internal threat or an external psychological stimulus. This approach is usually tied to what is called *the content view* of delusions (Ratcliffe & Wilkinson, 2015, p. 4), namely, a perspective that considers that a subject fails to recognize a thought as her own because of an aversion to the thought-content (Cf. López-Silva, 2015). In this chapter Vilatta claims that appealing to the content of delusions of thought insertion cannot explain its aetiology entirely, but, at the same time, it suggests that content is still relevant to understand it. This type of insightful exercise is totally necessary if we want to build bridges between traditions that have been separated by a long time.

In the final chapter of this section (Chapter 11) Peter Langland-Hassan explores a completely different path to understand delusions of thought insertion. After examining some of the main problems that two-factor models of delusions face, this chapter explores thought insertion as a form persecutory delusion. This idea seems to have not only important conceptual consequences, but also practical ones. Specifically, it predicts that clinical interventions for persecutory delusions may also be successful for thought insertion. This chapter is a clear example of how careful philosophical examination can help to enrich the understanding of the psychotherapeutic treatment of delusions. The idea behind this exploratory chapter is that some clinical diagnostic tools would create the appearance of deep differences between symptoms such as thought insertion and persecutory delusions where there are none. In order to make his case, Langland-Hassan reviews first-person reports and evidence for considerable volatility in the type of delusions that patients present with over time. By doing this, Chapter 11 is able to go beyond the traditional ways in which thought insertion has been conceptualized enriching our understanding of its complex and multi-layered nature.

Taken as a whole, the essays contained in the second part of this compilation will introduce the reader to an up-to-date and open-minded discussion of some of the most fundamental challenges that emerge when philosophers and clinicians jointly attempt to explain the aetiology of thought insertion.

Experimental and Therapeutic Approaches to TI: Brain, Mind, and Contexts of Care

The study of pathological and non-pathological conscious states needs to be in constant dialogue with experimental research. Psychopathological phenomena not only reveal important things about human anthropology works, but about the architecture of cognition and how the brain underpins such architecture. The type of control over different variables that experimental research allows is central for informing evidence-based approaches to the treatment of different conditions such as schizophrenia. However, the study of delusions such as thought insertion is hard to approach experimentally.

The guiding idea behind Chapter 12 is that experimental approaches to investigating alterations in experience complement phenomenological approaches such as descriptive psychopathology, which characterize the content of experience. Elisa Brann, Eamonn Walsh, Mitul A. Mehta, David A. Oakley, and Quinton Deeley propose that experiments might be able to produce alterations in experience under controlled conditions which, when accompanied by measurement of brain activity, can help identify underlying brain processes. Importantly, experimentally produced alterations in experience resembling symptoms of psychopathology can provide insights into relevant brain processes. The main problem in this context is that thought insertion is almost untouched by experimental methods. As a preliminary step for the creation of experimental models of thought insertion, this chapter focuses on discussing some of the main challenges and limitations of investigating thought insertion experimentally and suggest how effective experimental paradigms can be designed. Even though the creation of an experimental approach to delusions of thought insertion seems to be a very difficult task, this chapter offers a clear examination of what such model should look like.

Now, it is important to note that the study of culturally embedded practice can offer a novel window into how the mind works and how experimental models of consciousness can be produced. In Chapter 13 Alice Pailhès, Jay Olson, and Gustav Kuhn offer a novel approach to the complementary connection between philosophy and experimental research by focusing on the ways in which a popular anthropological practice informs the understanding of delusions such as thought insertion, namely, *magic*. The authors of this chapter suggest that magicians have developed a wide range of psychological tricks that allow them to manipulate their audiences' experience of the world. Some of these tricks consist of manipulating people's thought processes. Certainly, this latter process is of particular interest for the understating of thought insertion for it involves a person—the magician—inserting thoughts into people's minds. After outlining some of the main principles that magicians use to perform acts of thought insertion into the spectator's mind, the authors examine the benefits of using magic to mimic delusions of thought insertion in non-clinical populations and discuss results from novel paradigms using magic as a tool to provide the illusion of a thought-inserting machine. Such a novel approach to the experimental exploration of delusions seems to be able to connect the neurocognition of delusions with anthropologically common practices, which, in turn, helps us to produce a wider understanding of psychopathological phenomena.

Scientific approaches to thought insertion need clear identification of brain structures to inform plausible experimental models. In Chapter 14, Kentaro Hiromitsu and Tomohisa Asai focus on the role that the *cerebellum* plays in the production of delusions of thought insertion, advancing our understanding of the neurobiological underpinnings of this type of delusion. The authors suggest that the human mind possesses internal systems that can *regulate* the interaction with any type of stimulus if certain representations about the relation between the self and that stimulus are learned as a model. In turn, this learned model will serve to predict certain aspects of reality, and our interactions with it. A typical example of this is motor control, a model largely discussed in the context of the aetiology of thought insertion that suggests that our brain *controls* our own body. Here, the learned representation (the relationship between the motor outflow and the sensory inflow) is called the internal model, which further includes coupled submodules, that is, the inverse and forward models for each representation. The authors examine the neurocognitive mechanisms and the role of the cerebellum in the production of three types of conscious experiences, namely, mental agency among healthy persons, thought insertion in psychosis, and the aftereffects of cortical lesions. An exploration of the shared mechanism between these populations seems to indicate that the generalized theory of thought insertion would be associated with the production of certain internal models, and, in this sense, *thought insertion* would be a form of learning disorder that generates an atypical agency experience. Likely, further explorations on how the cerebellum behaves in different populations could aid the study of the neurocognitive mechanisms underlying thought insertion.

In the final chapter of this section (Chapter 15) Susana Ochoa exemplifies how conceptual discussions of psychopathological phenomena can inform therapeutic approaches. A number of symptoms of schizophrenia suggest the existence of dysfunctions of metacognitive abilities in this population. In simple terms, metacognition can be understood as 'thinking about thinking'. This ability includes *monitoring—the* capacity to observe one's own cognitive processes—and *control*, the ability to modify these cognitive processes (Flavell, 1979; Nelson & Narens, 1990). In the particular case of thought insertion, they would exist an impairment in the process of self-monitoring one's own cognitive processes and disruptions of integrative functions of cognition. Therefore, thought insertion can be characterized as a malfunction of cognitive abilities. Taking this idea into consideration, Chapter 15 examines two psychotherapeutic approaches focused on metacognition that have shown empirical efficacy for the treatment of thought insertion: *Metacognitive Training*, developed by Steffen Moritz and Todd Woodward, and *Metacognitive Reflection and Insight Therapy*, developed by Paul Lysaker and his team. By becoming aware of thinking processes and obtaining a more complete experience of being in the world, patients using such approaches would produce a richer and more coherent sense of the self and personal narrative, which would allow important improvements in their quality of life and mental health.

The chapters in this section introduce the reader to the ways in which sciences and philosophical thinking can inform experimental and therapeutic approaches to thought insertion. From this, it is clear that further research on the matter is needed, not only to improve our understanding of the ways in which consciousness breaks down, but also to improve our prospects of helping those who suffer from psychiatric conditions.

Beyond the Phenomenon: Thought Insertion and the Nature of Thinking

Thought insertion provokes complex discussions about descriptive, clinical, neurocognitive, and explanatory elements associated to the understating of consciousness and cognition. As already mentioned, thought insertion has also attracted the attention of philosophers due to the ways in which it defies some fundamental tenets about the very architecture and ontology of thinking, one of the least understood aspects of consciousness in the philosophy and sciences of the mind. The last section of our compilation aims at analysing the ways in which thought insertion can inform our understanding of the way in which thinking works.

A number of philosophers over time have suggested that being aware of having a certain mental state and being aware of that mental state *as one's own* is one and the same thing. Others claim that this idea is undermined by thought insertion delusion, as subjects report having thoughts which are not theirs. For such subjects, being in a particular mental state and owning that mental state seem to have been pulled apart as separate components of their experience. In Chapter 16 Jordi Fernández claims that we can only understand thought insertion by first understanding what's involved in experiencing a conscious state as one's own. By drawing on the philosophical literature on self-knowledge, this chapter suggests that the experience of owning a conscious state is the experience of being *committed* to that state. By accepting this idea, the author tries to account for the disownment of thoughts characterizing thought insertion. In this sense, thought insertion would be an example of a more general phenomenon; the phenomenon of lacking the experience of commitment for mental states to which we should be committed when we become aware of them. In the author's opinion, thought insertion involves missing the experience of being committed to the thoughts that they disown (i.e., the inserted thought). In order to clarify his proposal, the author describes how the championed proposal can also be applied to other mental disorders in which subjects disown some of their conscious states such as disowned memory and anarchic hand syndrome.

Taking a similar philosophical stand in the analysis of delusions, in Chapter 17 Johannes Roessler challenges a popular interpretation of thought insertion, namely, the No Subject view. This view characterizes thought insertion as an awareness of a thought—conceived as an event in one's stream of consciousness—without being aware of oneself as thinking that thought.

Roessler argues that this view rests on some problematic ontological assumptions regarding the nature of thoughts and that it ultimately fails to explain the phenomenon. He then places these concerns within the wider context of the conflict between two different movements in the philosophy of psychopathology, which he labels post-Heideggerian phenomenological psychopathology and post-Davidsonian philosophy of mind. This leads him to challenge the assumption that an adequate thought insertion is one that *makes sense* of the subject's experiences.

Taken together, the last two contributions of our compilation open up a number of questions about how psychopathological phenomena can encourage illuminating distinctions that enable us to better understand the structure and ontology of conscious thinking.

Final Remarks

The study of psychosis is an invitation to explore some of the most fundamental aspects of the type of being we are. In the same way, the study of delusions takes us to some of the deepest recesses of the human mind. Delusions lead us to reflect on the link between self and reality. The case of thought insertion is an enigmatic one, for it shows how fragile the boundaries of our (supposedly) private space are. It shows how complex cognition is, and how consciousness relates to the brain and our intersubjective reality. But more importantly, thought insertion is an examination of the lives of people who suffer. The reasons why thought insertion attracts the attention of philosophers are crystal clear. However, before all that, thought insertion is something that happens to people; it is something that is suffered by people. This matter should not only motivate further conceptual and empirical research, but also remind us to be humble when we take psychopathological phenomena as a target of enquiry. The risk of over-intellectualizing the investigation of this type of phenomenon by offering interpretations that only written words can sustain is high. The risks of offering inflexible views just to respect certain schools of thought are high. The risk of becoming hypnotized by the complexity of the technical terms used in examining the phenomenon is high.

The study of thought insertion is an opportunity for philosophy to become central in the discussions of issues that affect not only our intellectual life, but also our mental health. Every approach to the study of any aspect of the phenomenon should be penetrated by a recognition that, behind these analytic exercises, there are persons. The study of thought insertion is an opportunity for philosophers to go beyond their intellectual glass castles and engage embodied and embedded phenomena. For a long time, philosophical analysis focused on disembodied pictures of mental phenomena. The study of thought insertion is an opportunity to overcome this by creating inter and multidisciplinary frameworks; common places where different traditions and knowledges can converge in order to produce holistic pictures of the human condition. *Intruders in the Mind* attempts to provide a space of this nature. By gathering contributors from different continents and disciplines, the compilation is an invitation for the community to explore collaborative paths of research. Certainly, no compilation will be able to cover every debate emerging from the discussion of these specific delusions; however, *Intruders in the Mind* should serve to introduce the reader to the complexities of the philosophical analysis of psychopathological phenomena and the human mind.

References

American Psychiatric Association (2013). *Diagnostic and Statistical Manual of Mental Disorders* (5th ed.). Arlington, VA: American Psychiatric Publishing.

Bentall, R. (2003). *Explaining Madness*. England: Allen Lane.

Billon, A. (2023). What is it like to lack mineness? In M. García-Carpintero and M. Guillot (Eds.), *Self-Experience: Essays on Inner Awareness* (pp. 314–340). Oxford: Oxford University Press.

Billon, A., & Kriegel, U. (2015). Jaspers' dilemma: The psychopathological challenge to subjectivities theories of consciousness. In R. Gennaro (Ed.), *Disturbed Consciousness* (pp. 29–54). USA: MIT Press.

Binswanger, L. (1957). *Schizophrenie*. Germany: Neske.

Blom, J. D. (2013). Klinische zoantropie. *Tijdschrift voor Psychiatry, 55*(5), 359–368.

Blom, J. D. (2014, March 4). When doctors cry wolf: A systematic review of the literature on clinical lycanthropy. *History of Psychiatry, 25*(1), 87–102.

Bortolotti, L., & Broome, M. (2008). Delusional beliefs and reason giving. *Philosophical Psychology, 21*(3), 1–21.

Cahill, C., & Frith, C. D. (1996). A cognitive basis for the signs and symptoms of schizophrenia. In C. Pantelis, H. E. Nelson, & T. Barnes (Eds.), *Schizophrenia: A Neuropsychological Perspective*. New York: John Wiley and Sons.

Campbell, J. (1999). Schizophrenia, the space of reasons, and thinking as a motor process. *The Monist, 82*(4), 609–625.

Campbell, J. (2002). The ownership of thoughts. *Philosophy, Psychiatry & Psychology, 9*(1), 35–39.

Coltheart, M. (2010). The neuropsychology of delusions. In A. Kingstone, & M. B. Miller (Eds.), *The year in cognitive neuroscience 2010* (Vol. 1191, pp. 16–26). (Annals of the New York Academy of Sciences; Vol. 1191). Wiley-Blackwell, Wiley. https://doi.org/10.1111/j.1749-6632.2010.05496.x

Connors, M. H., & Halligan, P. W. (2020). Delusions and theories of belief. *Conscious Cognition, 81*, 102935.

Conrad K. (1958). *Die beginnende Schizophrenie*. Stuttgart, Germany: Thieme Verlag.

Flavell, J. H. (1979). Metacognition and cognitive monitoring: A new area of cognitive-developmental inquiry. *American Psychologist*, 34(10), 906–911.

Freedman B, & Chapman LJ. (1973). Early subjective experience in schizophrenic episodes. *Journal of Abnormal Psychology*, 82, 46–54.

Freud, S. (1930). *Civilization and its Discontents*. UK: Martino Fine Books.

Frith C. (1992). *The Cognitive Neuropsychology of Schizophrenia*. Hove, UK: Erlbaum.

Fuchs, T. (2005). Delusional mood and delusional perception. A phenomenological analysis. *Psychopathology*, 38, 133–139.

Fulford, K., Davies, M., Gipps, R., Graham, G., Sadler, G., Stanghellini, G. & Thorton, T. (Eds.) (2013). *The Oxford Handbook of Philosophy and Psychiatry*. Oxford: Oxford University Press.

Fusar-Poli, P., Estradé, A., Stanghellini, G., Venables, J., Onwumere, J., Messas, G., et al. (2022). The lived experience of psychosis: A bottom-up review co-written by experts by experience and academics. *World Psychiatry*, 21(2), 168–188.

Gallagher, S. (2004). Neurocognitive models of schizophrenia. A neurophenomenological critique. *Psychopathology*, 37, 8–19.

Gallagher, S. (2014). Relations between agency and ownership in the case of schizophrenic thought insertion and delusions of control. *The Review of Philosophy and Psychology*, 6, 865–879.

García-Carpintero, M. & M. Guillot (Eds.) (2023). *Self-Experience: Essays on Inner Awareness*. Oxford: Oxford University Press.

Gennaro, R. 2021. Inserted thoughts and the higher-order thought theory of consciousness. In P. A. Gargiulo, & H. L. Mesones-Arroyo (Eds.), *Psychiatry and Neurosciences Update*: Vol 4 (pp. 61–71). Dordrecht: Springer.

Gibbs, P. (2000). Thought insertion and the inseparability thesis. *Philosophy, Psychiatry, & Psychology*, 7(3), 195–202.

Gross, G., & Huber, G. (1972). Sensorische Störungen bei Schizophrenien. *Archiv für Psychiatrie und Nervenkrankheiten*, 216, 119–130.

Guillot, M. (2017). I me mine: on a confusion concerning the subjective character of experience. *Review of Philosophy and Psychology*, 8, 23–53.

Harrow, M., Grossman, L. S., Jobe, T. H., & Herbener, E. S. (2005). Do patients with schizophrenia ever show periods of recovery? A 15-year multi-follow-up study. *Schizophrenia Bulletin*, 31(3), 723–734.

Harrow, M., & Jobe, T. H. (2010). How frequent is chronic multiyear delusional activity and recovery in schizophrenia: A 20-year multi–follow-up. *Schizophrenia Bulletin*, 36(1), 192–204.

Humpston, C. S. (2022). Paradoxes in a prism: reflections on the omnipotent passivity and omniscient oblivion of schizophrenia. *Philosophical Psychology*, 1–14. https://doi.org/10.1080/09515089.2022.2078187.

Humpston, C. S., & Broome, M. R. (2016). The spectra of soundless voices and audible thoughts: Towards an integrative model of auditory verbal hallucinations and thought insertion. *Review of Philosophy & Psychology*, 7, 611–629.

Jaspers, K. (1963). *General Psychopathology* (7th ed.). Manchester: Manchester University Press.

Kanner, L. (1930). The names of the falling sickness. An introduction to the study of the folklore and cultural history of epilepsy. *Human Biology*, 2(1), 109–127.

Kusters W. (2021). *A Philosophy of Madness*. Massachusetts, MA: MIT Press.

Locke, J. (1961). *An Essay Concerning Human Understanding*. London: J.M. Dent & Sons Ltd.

López-Silva, P. (2014). La relevancia filosófica del estudio de la esquizofrenia. Cuestiones metodológicas y conceptuales. *Revista Colombiana de Psiquiatría*, 43(6), 168–174.

López-Silva, P. (2015). Schizophrenia and the place of egodystonic states in the aetiology of thought insertion. *The Review of Philosophy & Psychology*, 7(3), 577–594.

López-Silva, P. (2016). The typology problem and the doxastic approach to delusions. *Filosofía Unisinos, 17*(2), 202–211.

López-Silva, P. (2017). DSM-V and the diagnostic role of psychotic delusions. *Archives of Clinical Psychiatry, 44*(6), 162–163.

López-Silva, P. (2018). Mapping the psychotic mind: A review on thought insertion. *Psychiatric Quarterly, 89*(1), 957–968.

López-Silva, P. (2020). Atribuciones de Agencia Mental y el Desafío desde la Psicopatología. *Kriterion, 61*(147), 1–19.

López-Silva, P., & Cavieres, A. (2021). *La Realidad Transformada: Hacia una Recalibración de la Psicopatología Contemporánea*. Santiago: SONEPSYN.

López-Silva, P., Harrow, M., Jobe, T. H., Tufano, M., Harrow, H., & Rosen, C. (2022). 'Are these my thoughts?': A 20-year prospective study of thought insertion, thought withdrawal and thought broadcasting and their relationship to auditory verbal hallucinations. *Schizophrenia Research*. doi: 10.1016/j.schres.2022.07.005.

Martin, J-M. & Pacherie, E. (2013). Out of nowhere: Thought insertion, ownership and context- integration. *Consciousness and Cognition, 22*(1), 111–122.

Mayer-Gross, W. (1932). Psychopathologie und Klinik der Trugwahrnehmungen. In O. Bumke (Ed.), *Handbuch der Geisteskrankheiten. Band I. Allgemeiner Teil I*. Berlin: Verlag von Julius Springer.

Mellor, C. S. (1970). First rank symptoms of schizophrenia. *The British Journal of Psychiatry, 117*, 15–23.

Mishara, A. L. (2010). Klaus Conrad (1905–1961): Delusional mood, psychosis and beginning schizophrenia. Clinical Concept Translation-Feature. *Schizophrenia Bulletin, 36*, 9–13.

Mullins, S., & Spence, S. (2003). Re-examining thought insertion. *British Journal of Psychiatry, 182*, 293–298

Nelson, T. O., & Narens, L. (1990). Metamemory: A theoretical framework and new findings. *Psychology of Learning and Motivation, 26*, 125–173.

Notredame, C. E, Pins, D., Deneve, S., & Jardri, R. (2014). What visual illusions teach us about schizophrenia. *Frontiers in Integrative Neuroscience, 8*, 63.

Payne, E. (2013). *Speaking to my Madness*. USA: CreateSpace.

Pickard, H. (2010). Schizophrenia and the epistemology of self-knowledge. *European Journal of Analytic Philosophy, 6*(1), 55–74.

Porter, R. (2003). *Madness: A Brief History*. Oxford: Oxford University Press.

Ratcliffe, M., & Wilkinson, S. (2015). Thought insertion clarified. *Journal of Consciousness Studies, 22*(11–12), 1–25.

Rosen, C., Harrow, M., Humpston, C. S., Tong, L., Jobe, T. H., & Harrow, H. (2022). 'An experience of meaning': A 20-year prospective analysis of delusional realities in schizophrenia and affective psychoses. *Frontiers in Psychiatry, 13*, 940124.

Rosen, C., Jones, N., Chase, K. A., Gin, H., Grossman, L. S., & Sharma, R.P. (2016). The intra-subjectivity of self, voices and delusions: A phenomenological analysis. *Psychosis, 8*(4), 357–368.

Rosen, C., Jones, N., Chase, K. A., & Sharma, R. P. (2017). The phenomenological construct of self, voices, and other extreme states. *Schizophrenia Bulletin, 43*(1), S96–S97.

Saks, E.R. (2007). *The Centre Cannot Hold: My Journey Through Madness*. New York: Hyperion.

Schneider, K. (1959). *Clinical Psychopathology* (trans. By M.W. Hamilton). New York: Grune & Stratton.

Sierra, M., & Berrios, G.E. (2000). The Cambridge Depersonalization Scale: A new instrument for the measurement of depersonalization. *Psychiatry Research, 6*(93), 153–164.

Sollberger, M. (2014). Making sense of an endorsement model of thought insertion. *Mind and Language, 29*(5), 590–612.

Spence, S. A., Brooks, D. J., Hirsch, S. R., Liddle, P. F., Meehan, J., & Grasby, P. M. (1997). A PET study of voluntary movement in schizophrenic patients experiencing passivity phenomena (delusions of alien control). *Brain, 120,* 1997–2011

Stephens, G. L. & G. Graham. (2000). *When Self-Consciousness Breaks: Alien Voices and Inserted Thoughts.* Cambridge, MA: MIT Press.

Sterzer, P., Adams, R. A., Fletcher, P., Frith, C., Lawrie, S. M., Muckli, L., Petrovic, P., Uhlhaas, P., Voss, M., & Corlett, P. R. (2018). The predictive coding account of psychosis. *Biological Psychiatry, 84*(9), 634–643.

Sterzer, P., Mishara, A. L., Voss, M., & Heinz, A. (2016). Thought insertion as a self-disturbance: An integration of predictive coding and phenomenological approaches. *Frontiers in Human Neuroscience, 10,* 502.

Synofzik, M., Vosgerau, G., & Newen, A. (2008). Beyond the comparator model: A multifactorial two-step account of agency. *Consciousness and Cognition, 17*(1), 219–239.

Vosgerau, G., & Voss, M. (2014). Authorship and control over thoughts. *Mind & Language, 29*(5), 534–565.

Wing, J. K., Cooper, J. E., & Sartorius, N. (1974). *Measurement and Classification of Psychiatric Symptoms* (9th ed.). Cambridge, UK: Cambridge University Press.

Zahavi, D. (2005). *Subjectivity and Selfhood: Investigating the First-Person Perspective.* Cambridge, MA: The MIT Press.

SECTION 1
CHARACTERIZING ALIEN THOUGHTS

Redefinitions and Novel Explorations

1

When Is a Thought Mine and When Is It Not?

A Personal View on Thought Insertion

Roberta Payne

I'm not at all certain I know what 'thought insertion' is. Does the term imply my recognition that something is literally being inserted into my mind? And does that something have to be recognized by me as an actual thought—someone else's—taking up space in my mind? Here, I am, of course, using a standard metaphor with those last six words. Standard metaphors are a somewhat satisfactory way for a person to express her psychosis, which, for the most part, can't be expressed well in unadorned standard language.

I've had schizophrenia for more than 50 years now. Overall in that time, there has been much inside of my head that isn't mine—unwished for, disliked, and out of my control. These powerful phenomena have, at times, pressed me against the edges of my mind so that I've felt myself to be only a minimal, marginalized part of it. I've been—in episodes of the schizophrenia—a prisoner of thoughts in my mind, thoughts that aren't my own. Is hearing voices an example of thought insertion? I do hear voices from time to time, usually coming out of my apartment's air conditioner in the summer and its heater in the winter. Voices are more 'three-dimensional' than thoughts, because voices have a strong physical (auditory) presence that thoughts do not. The voices I hear are metallic, urgent, cunning, magical, extremely attractive, and masculine; and they persistently call me 'evil'. The metallic, magical, and attractive aspects remind me aesthetically of the effects of LSD, which I imprudently took when I was 21, the year before I became mentally ill. My voices take up room inside my mind and, at the same time, outside of it. Sometimes they sound external (as voices out in the hall) or just outside my head and behind it; but they are always so personal that they belong to my mind alone. They are real, and I have no control over them. Because they're so attractive, they remind me of the songs of the Sirens calling Odysseus in the *Odyssey*; I'm oddly fond of them and wonder what will happen to them when I die.

Similarly, I don't know if thought broadcasting is categorized by psychiatry as thought insertion. I've experienced two types of broadcasting. First, many years ago, while I was psychotic, I took walks outdoors during which I experienced talking to neighbourhood dogs through rays from my head, silently commanding the dogs to start or stop barking. I did this of my free will and took pleasure in having this special power. They were thoughts—not voices—coming out of my head in the form of invisible rays. The dogs seemed to obey me, which I enjoyed. The second type of broadcasting was the converse of the first. During that same period, I was aware of my television set sending out messages to me that resembled invisible rays about my then-excessive drinking, and one evening forcing me to watch—broadcast especially for me—a movie about alcoholism titled *Days of Wine and Roses*. I remember the TV station sending out rays that I was 'evil': I could tell they were angry at me and revolted by me at the same time. I was terrorized by the movie but unable to turn the TV off or even leave the room to go to the bathroom. These events were entirely real and compelling, even though I realized that such broadcasting was technically impossible.

Another time, a set of 'Rules' appeared in my mind. I assumed they came from somewhere or something with intelligence, since the Rules had logic and were in language. There were ten of them, governing every aspect of my behaviour. I became conscious of them as a whole, as a numbered list. They were specific: I was able to write them down literally, Rule by Rule, word by word. The first was fairly innocuous, telling me how I should take individual steps and what I could and could not touch with my feet. The Rules were progressively more demanding. Rule Nine said that I had to become completely insane; Rule Ten stated that I was to kill myself. Rule Eight ordered me not to show any of them to anyone. But within days the Rules threatened to overwhelm me. So I wrote them down, folded the piece of paper up tightly, and put it under my psychiatrist's lamp base, begging him not to look at it. The Rules were all-powerful. They could not have been more real to me unless they had been spoken, that is, unless they had been hallucinations. I must add that, during much of that period of time, I was also having the experiences of depersonalization (being distinctly aware that I didn't exist) and derealization (feeling that people and walls and furniture in front of me were two-dimensional, like wallpaper).

Soon thereafter, Space Aliens became part of my life. They came from a huge, eerily silent spaceship. I was aware of the spaceship hovering above me, to the front; it was silver and shiny, like a dirigible. I can't tell you the means by which I saw it; it was not with my eyes. It was more like imagination, but without my mind making any effort. The Space Aliens put the idea in my mind that I was 'evil' and furthermore that I had to put on my bathrobe (I was in bed; it was about midnight), go down the elevator of the apartment building, cross over to a back alley, and walk through it in the dark until I was murdered by someone out there at that hour. I followed these directions on two separate occasions, walking many blocks through the alley each time; fortunately, I was never harmed. I recall distinctly that I offered no mental or emotional resistance to these orders. It was like being in a mild but all-powerful trance; I remember remarking upon that fact to myself as I walked. The Aliens' orders were precise, and all were entirely within my head. No hallucinations were involved, even though I could describe the spaceship visually.

All of these phenomena—the voices, the broadcasting, the Rules, the Space Aliens—were completely real to me. No one could talk me out of owning memories of them. At the same time, I realize they were not real to any other being that I know about. I have heard this called 'double awareness', and I think that that is an accurate way to put it in words. I want to make the point here that double awareness is a comfortable state of being when I'm psychotic. (Whenever I lecture medical students on the subject of schizophrenia, I invariably find that this simultaneous awareness is unfathomable to most of them. I tell them that they may simply need to take my word about its existence.)

From the beginning of my illness at age 22, I knew that all this was abnormal and so unnatural that it might well be consternating to others, even condemned. As a result, I've been reluctant to disclose any of it, except when clearly appropriate. It wasn't until last year (2018) that I was able to tell anyone about my auditory hallucinations. Thus, I wonder about the relationships between stigma and paranoia. I also wonder whether thought insertion bridges the phenomenon of delusion and the phenomenon of hallucination.

So, when is a thought mine and when is it not? Because thoughts are often expressed in words, and grammar and vocabulary are largely received from society, it's hard to see exactly what's mine. But through the years, I've observed that if the thoughts inside my mind are kindly towards me and towards the rest of the world, they're usually mine. If the thoughts inside my mind are obsessed with 'evil' and 'bad' and cause me psychological pain that can't be reconciled logically with real events, they're usually not mine.

Also, I've come to see—with the passage of time since these particular phenomena occurred—that many (or all, really?) of them have a relationship to events in my actual life. My being ordered by a television station to watch a movie about alcoholism: Was that really me telling myself I needed to come to the realistic conclusion that I had a drinking problem? The Rules: Was their source somehow the rules for her family's behaviour that my harsh mother taped to walls when I was a child? And the Space Aliens devising for me a death walk at night: Was this actually me denying responsibility for a suicide wish? Recently I made up a metaphor for the thoughts that schizophrenia has brought me over the years. Schizophrenia is like a backroom embezzler, working silently in the back of my head, screwing up the bookkeeping of my mind and issuing false or misleading and potentially harmful facts and figures to me. Staying on guard for them is everything.

2
Delusional Beliefs and Thought Insertion

Clara Humpston and Matthew Broome

2.1. Introduction

Imagine a sudden interruption in your thinking process. Imagine a thought that is present in your mind, yet it is so alien that it cannot possibly be your own, and of which you have no recollection of how it connects to prior thoughts. You are certain that you did not think such thoughts and therefore they cannot be yours. Such thoughts are so real—almost visceral, as if it is felt by your entire being—yet extremely strange at the same time. This uncanny, almost indescribable experience naturally calls for an urgent explanation, for it threatens the very integrity of your mind and of yourself. All this may sound like the product of science fiction to the vast majority of individuals; indeed, most people will never wonder, let alone doubt, whether the thoughts in their head and minds are truly theirs. In fact, most people would not even question what makes a thought *theirs* in the first place. This seemingly obvious insight is the Cartesian certainty—thinking leads to existence and thus links to self. Any breach to this certainty directly challenges ideas of selfhood and existence. It is exceedingly hard to imagine what it might be like to 'find' thoughts in your head that are not yours because to most, it is simply nonsensical to even begin considering such a possibility.

However, to some individuals, such a feeling is not only a possibility but a truth held with absolute conviction. This bizarre experience is called thought insertion (henceforth TI). TI is defined as the experience of thoughts that do not have the feeling of familiarity, of being one's own, but have been put into one's mind without one's volition (Mellor, 1970). Not surprisingly, TI is widely regarded as a psychiatric symptom. Even less surprisingly perhaps, it is a psychiatric symptom that characterizes a psychotic illness such as schizophrenia (a first-rank symptom), and acts as the one of the most significant and sinister hallmarks of a break from consensual reality. It is impossible to fathom the experience of TI because doing so would require us to relinquish our sense of self-autonomy, the most central and sacred evidence of being an independent and free agent. By merely beginning to imagine the loss of control over one's thinking processes, or having thinking take place that is not part of the activity of the self, it strikes the deepest forms of fear and anxiety by attacking our notion of having a self and unified consciousness, hence those who report these experiences must be 'mad' and cannot be trusted or even treated as 'one of us normal people'. Nothing seems to signal madness more than the claims of TI; to most clinicians, it simply has to be a delusion that needs to be corrected with pharmacological and psychotherapeutic interventions. Clinicians may not have the capacity (or interest, in some cases) to dig deeper into the experiences of TI, for the fear of reinforcing the patients' delusions. A potential consequence of this active dismissal of the realness of TI from the patients' subjective point of view is the loss of nuance and, eventually, rapport.

Here we offer an examination of the experience of TI from the angle of phenomenological psychopathology and question the meaningfulness and usefulness of always assuming that TI is a delusional belief in research and practice. We will evaluate whether TI qualifies as a belief and further, as a *delusional* belief; our aim is to present an argument for a better understanding and more nuanced conceptualization of TI, with patients' subjective experience at centre stage.

2.2. Defining Delusional Beliefs

2.2.1. Delusional beliefs in schizophrenia-spectrum psychoses

One of the most commonly accepted views of delusions is the doxastic view (i.e., delusions as beliefs). In the *Diagnostic and Statistical Manual of Mental Disorders*, Fifth Edition (DSM-5; American Psychiatric Association, 2013, p. 819), delusions are defined as follows: 'A false *belief* based on incorrect inference about external reality that is firmly held despite what almost everyone else believes and despite what constitutes incontrovertible and obvious proof or evidence to the contrary. The belief is not ordinarily accepted by other members of the person's culture or subculture (i.e., it is not an article of religious faith).' This consolidates the belief-based conceptualization of delusions for most clinicians. Given their pivotal role in the diagnosis of psychotic disorders including schizophrenia, delusions are seen as incorrigible, inconceivable, and often incomprehensible. In the DSM-5 definition, delusions are beliefs derived from incorrect *inference* about, and not simply a fundamental break from, external reality. This implies some sort of basis in consensual reality upon which false inferences are constructed, and also alludes to a deliberative process (Baker et al., 2019)—patients with delusions somehow arrived at the delusional belief because they made wrong inferences about events in the outside world. Indeed, cognitive theories of delusion formation focus on the inferential process of anomalous experiences perceived to be arising from the external world and align with principles of cognitive neuropsychiatry. In other words, it follows the 'normal' pathways of belief formation, also called 'belief-positive' models of delusion (for a very comprehensive overview, see Bell et al., 2006). These models are most useful when evaluating monothematic delusions; however, these are not as common in, say, schizophrenia, compared to organic psychoses where clear causal factors may be identified.

Delusional beliefs in schizophrenia tend to be more systematized and polythematic and pose their own unique challenges when it comes to theorizing. This latter category sometimes calls for 'belief-negative' models of delusion formation, where the belief formation process itself is pathological (such as a perceived tendency towards irrationality and impulsivity when forming inferences). A typical example of this may be a hallucination leading to delusion formation. In this case, the trigger or precursor to delusion formation is not based in external reality, yet something faulty about the patient's inferential process itself compelled the patient to 1) become convinced that the hallucination is real; and 2) become convinced that the hallucination comes from a malicious other, giving rise to a persecutory delusion (see Section 2.3.1.). Of course, this is not the only pathway. Persecutory delusions do not by any means have to arise from negative or emotion-laden hallucinations; instead, unlike some of the more bizarre experiences seen in schizophrenia, persecutory delusions are far more transdiagnostic and can sometimes be found in nonclinical populations, albeit in milder forms such as magical thinking and conspiracy theories (Freeman, 2006). It is unlikely that there will ever be a specific subtype of delusion that sufficiently indicates a diagnosis of schizophrenia, at least not any judgement based on delusion content. Rather, it is often the *form* (the how and not the what) of delusional thinking that imbues a schizophrenic psychosis from other psychotic and non-psychotic disorders.

2.2.2. Delusional beliefs and first-rank symptoms

Schneiderian first-rank symptoms (FRS) remain a contentious topic in psychiatry, perhaps at least partly due to a loss of the nuanced approach first adopted by Schneider in contemporary diagnostic systems (Broome et al., 2012; Heinz et al., 2016; Moscarelli, 2020). FRS are traditionally conceived as characteristic of schizophrenia and may aid differential diagnosis. However, despite recent evidence showing a higher prevalence of FRS in the schizophrenia spectrum (e.g., Humpston et al., 2020), others have found practically no clinical utility for FRS (e.g., Peralta & Cuesta, 2023). A moderate approach may be to acknowledge the higher prevalence of FRS in schizophrenia-spectrum disorders while refraining from inferring diagnosis specificity (Shinn et al., 2013), as even the most bizarre FRS hardly act as the sole criterion for a diagnosis of schizophrenia in practice.

Arguments about clinical utility aside, the nature of FRS also stimulates fascinating debates. Most FRS, including TI, involve a profound alteration in one's ego boundary. In other words, the boundary between what is self and what is other is not only blurred, but also severely damaged (yet never truly absent). Patients may report feelings of passivity, such as they are under the control of an alien force like an automaton or a replacement of will (Hirjak et al., 2013). Thoughts, emotions, and even actions may no longer possess first-person authority, for they are not perceived as willed by the patient themselves (i.e., 'made' impulses and 'made' volitional acts). Many FRS challenge the tight connection between first-person experience, selfhood, and agency—yet the miracle is that, despite this, patients can function in other ways and non-alienated and non-passive experiences still occur, and this sustained ability to function perhaps challenges our default Cartesian assumptions. Nevertheless, there is something that grants the experience of TI a special status, as compared to other thought interference symptoms such as thought withdrawal, broadcast, or echo. Perhaps it is because in the latter cases, no matter how distressing the experience, the thoughts in question remain the patients' own thoughts. There is a striking difference between the statement of 'these thoughts are *not* mine' and 'other people can hear *my* thoughts', or '*my* thoughts are being taken away from me'. Among all the FRS, TI in this sense is clearly the closest to 'qualifying' as a delusional belief ('delusion of TI'), perhaps with the exception of aforementioned passivity phenomena (Section 2.4.2 of this chapter), which are also referred to as 'delusions of control' in many cases. Nevertheless, as we will argue later, TI and other associated FRS are far more than just delusional beliefs and do not necessarily require a delusional aspect *or* belief status to take hold in a patient's mental space.

2.2.3. From thoughts to beliefs to *delusional* beliefs

Whether the belief formation process itself is intact, explaining delusions under a purely doxastic framework has its own shortcomings. A prominent example against the doxastic account is the observation that many delusions do not lead to action in accordance to the delusional content ('double-bookkeeping') and are sometimes so amorphous and indiscrete in nature that they lack the basic qualities of even non-pathological beliefs (Gerrans, 2013). On the other hand, a fully non- or anti-doxastic account also fails to capture for example the level of conviction and, in some cases, the action-guiding quality of delusions. Delusions are clearly not just some random thoughts. Contemporary theorists have defended a kind of 'modest doxasticism', arguing for complexity and nuance (Bortolotti, 2012). However, perhaps a more pertinent question to ask is when does a random thought become a belief and when does this belief become delusional? There is certainly no easy answer; as mentioned previously, by using the word 'become', it already implies a (meta-)cognitive and deliberative process. Maybe thoughts do not have to 'become' beliefs and certain beliefs do not have to 'become' delusional—it is neither a linear nor a 'filtering' process where only some of the thoughts in a patient's mind end up as (delusional) beliefs. While none of these features directly diminishes the explanatory power of the doxastic account, they do encourage us to look at the bigger picture especially in a specialized case such as TI.

2.3. TI: Always a Delusional Belief?

2.3.1. TI and persecutory delusions

Persecutory delusions are the most severe forms of paranoid ideation and are considered as 'threat beliefs' (Freeman, 2016); they are frequently associated with significant distress, preoccupation, and affective disturbances such as high levels of anxiety and low mood. The most widely accepted explanation for persecutory delusions used to be one of cognitive bias with regard to attributional style (i.e., externalizing bias), yet more recently theories about their aetiology have shifted from the cognitive to the negative affective domain, including a strong focus on the role of stress, self-esteem, and trauma (Hardy et al., 2016). Persecutory delusions may also arise as a consequence of anomalous sensory and perceptual experiences such as hearing critical voices attacking the individual. The individual may form the belief that the voices come from their neighbours who are gossiping behind their back, which can lead to arguments, litigative claims and, in some extreme cases especially when there is severe distress, violence against the perceived persecutor (Ullrich et al., 2018).

The relationships between TI and the 'prototypical' paranoid delusional belief of persecution are complex and understudied. To date has been no systematic comparison between the two symptoms. However, one striking similarity is the external agency and sometimes personification of the source of the patient's strange belief/experience. In TI, the thoughts do not belong to oneself and in persecutory delusions, someone else is causing harm. Still, the alien agency may also be a differentiating factor. Neither persecutory delusion nor TI necessarily *require* a fully personified 'other', whether it is the persecutor or the source of one's alien thoughts. Both may occur as the end result of sensory abnormalities and experiences of passivity in thinking, affect, and volition. Just like persecutory delusions sometimes arise following hallucinations (especially those of a negative or abusive nature), TI does not usually manifest 'out of nowhere' either; despite some well-cited counterexamples claiming that patients simply 'discover' alien thoughts in their mind out of the blue (e.g., Mullins & Spence, 2003), the lack of causal coherence in contrast to the patient's 'own' stream of thoughts does not always automatically lead to them believing the thoughts come from someone else, especially when the thoughts are less emotion-laden than those often associated with persecutory delusions. That said, some inserted thoughts can be extremely unpleasant and can force the individual to act upon such thoughts. Indeed, the formation of persecutory delusions may well be one endpoint of repeated episodes of TI, although this link has not yet been studied empirically.

2.3.2. TI and other thought interference symptoms

As mentioned previously, TI differs from other thought interference symptoms (thought withdrawal, broadcast, echo—which are all considered FRS) in that TI is an ego-boundary permeation phenomenon (i.e., permeability of the barrier between the individual and their environment; see Sims, 1993) where both the agency and possession (ownership) are perceived as alien, 'not one's own' (see Table 1 in Mullins & Spence, 2003). Again, how well TI 'sits' within the range of thought interference symptoms has not been properly profiled; however, it does seem that the alien thought possession (as opposed to thought agency) is the differentiating factor. TI also differs from unsolicited, 'influenced' thinking or even the kind of spontaneous thoughts we all have where, although in both cases the direction of ego-boundary permeation is inwards, in influenced or unbidden thinking the thoughts themselves still remain as the patient's own—it's just that they are 'made to think' (i.e., the problem lies with thought agency only). On the other hand, the direction of ego-boundary permeation in thought withdrawal and broadcast is outwards and the thoughts involved are the patient's own; the difference between thought withdrawal and broadcast is that in withdrawal, the thought is taken away from the patient from without whereas in broadcast, the thought not only diffuses outwards but is also accessible to other people. In this sense, thought echo would be audible thought broadcast (also a type of hallucination) and thought withdrawal would be reverse TI. We have argued elsewhere that ego-boundary permeation, combined with various 'levels' of external accessibility and perceptualization (e.g., audibility), are best viewed as forming a spectrum or even multiple spectra where experiences can shift and morph between one another, especially in schizophrenia (omitted for review).

Another pertinent question is whether thought interference symptoms are delusional beliefs. If they are indeed all delusional beliefs, then TI as one subtype of these symptoms must also be a delusion. A further question is whether being a delusion *defines* the experience of TI in its entirety, for example through accounts of delusion based on 'faculty psychology' or even the DSM which often refers to TI as '*delusions of TI*' or 'a common delusion in schizophrenia' (e.g., Gibbs, 2000). Framing TI and related thought interference symptoms as mainly, if not purely, 'false beliefs' severely undermines the reality of such experiences and further feeds into the epistemic injustice to which many patients with schizophrenia are subjected (i.e., everything the patient says is situated in a delusional milieu and therefore not to be trusted). We consider such an approach far too simplistic, if not damaging, and does not at all capture the nuance and intricacies involved, especially when taking into account patients' subjective experiences when these symptoms occur. Yet there are clearly cases where delusional beliefs even by the strictest definitions have taken hold in patients who report TI; next, we offer some suggestions as to how we can potentially reconcile the clinical and phenomenological differences between these cases.

2.3.3. TI *with* delusions versus TI *as* delusions

One way to differentiate between the various mental states during and after episodes of TI is the detailed investigation of first-personal experiences as reported by the patient; however, an added layer of complexity is that individuals who have such unusual experiences often speak in metaphors, because common language cannot possibly convey their true meaning—let alone what it actually 'feels like'. The Schedules for Clinical Assessment in Neuropsychiatry (SCAN; Wing et al., 1990) instrument, for example, separates 'replacement of will' (i.e., passivity symptoms of thought including TI) from delusions and requires the former to possess a primary generative experience first. It is this kind of deep and intricate investigation that is necessary to truly disentangle the patients' subjective experiences: instead of grouping all reports of TI as delusional beliefs, it is perhaps more accurate and clinically useful to say there are TI *with* secondary delusions regardless of the belief status. We do not think this is merely a game of lexicon; the label of 'delusion' can have powerful consequences for the patients' self-identity, sometimes leading to persistent doubt about the 'abnormality' of one's own mental state even if it is just an everyday unbidden thought that the patient is having.

In a sense, the label of delusion may not even be applicable to most cases of TI, even though delusions can often manifest in patients who report TI. Again, this is not just a difference in language use. TI as an experience itself is frightening, confusing, and disorientating; a delusional elaboration could just be the desperate measure the patient's mind calls out for in order to reduce the instability and anxiety caused by losing control over one's thinking processes. Delusion formation can act as a long-awaited yet erroneous revelation ('apophany'; see Mishara & Fusar-Poli, 2013; Broome et al., 2012, p.178) so full of meaning and significance that fits perfectly within the structure of consciousness, becoming something so intrinsic to the patient's being that the mind just cannot let go of it. As long as the original generative experiences persist, the secondary delusion will be 'called upon' repeatedly, leading to consolidation and maintenance. Although not all experiences of TI will inevitably result in delusion formation and not all delusions are the consequences of aberrant sensory or motoric perception, reports of TI should never be straightforwardly dismissed as 'delusional beliefs'—at least not until there is clear evidence of the latter. The words patients use may sound as if they fully believe in the veracity of their experiences and there can still be delusions involved; TI in this case however is best framed as a duplex phenomenon consisting of the generative/experiential alteration first and foremost, before any foundation for delusional beliefs can be constructed.

2.3.4. The belief status of TI

Are the experience of having inserted thoughts and the act of ascribing them to another agent beliefs, even though they might not always lead to delusion formation? William James (1889) defined belief as 'the mental state or function of cognizing reality', and that 'belief will mean every degree of assurance, including the highest possible certainty and conviction' (p.21). He went on to argue that 'The true opposites of belief... are doubt and inquiry, not disbelief' (p. 22). In this sense, the experience of TI will almost certainly lead to a very curious state of mind: one of doubt and inquiry *and* one of conviction and certainty. Patients reporting TI do not usually begin with a strong conviction that their thoughts are definitely not generated or possessed by themselves (but by another agent); rather, it is akin to a profound sense of *dis*orientation or uncanniness—'are these thoughts mine?'—which calls for the eventual *re*orientation and in some cases delusional elaboration as an attempt to answer this urgent and debilitating existential question. The delusions that form from TI are qualitatively different from those arising as a consequence of, for example, traumatic brain injury where delusions tend to be monothematic and fit better with the traditional definitions of 'belief' (Stone & Young, 1997). To us, TI exemplifies the paradoxical nature of many symptoms of schizophrenia that are distinct from symptoms of organic or even other non-organic (e.g., affective) psychoses. As we mentioned in the Introduction, the mere act of questioning whether the thoughts in one's mental space (which does not have to be a physical demarcation of inside/outside the head) are one's own in the literal sense indicates a kind of subtle change in a person's subjectivity that cannot be easily explained away by whether one believes in it or not. Sometimes a person does not need to actively believe in something for it to bear truth or *feel* real. This in-between state of reality and falsehood, doubt and conviction shapes if not defines the mental state of a person with schizophrenia, where language used to convey shared human experiences breaks down; they are at the mercy of an interfering 'other' while being 'othered' by those around them. TI is an extremely isolating symptom associated with a very lonely illness that reaches far beyond common sense or what is humanly possible; as such, what most people would usually consider as beliefs also fall short when trying to examine experiences like TI.

2.4. TI and Transformations of Self-Consciousness

2.4.1. Ego-boundaries and their permeability

The very concept of 'ego-boundaries' is complex, contentious, or even elusive, and is one that has largely faded out of medical education and symptom-based psychiatric diagnoses. However, ego-boundaries and their disturbances play a pivotal role in the psychopathology of schizophrenia (and perhaps less in other disorders), at least historically. Almost all the forefathers of psychiatric theory and nosology (e.g., Kraepelin, Bleuler, Minkowski, Schneider) have written about the profound alterations in (and in the most severe cases, loss of) unity, coherence, and integrity of self-consciousness. Such alterations often arise from a kind of permeation, diffusion, or perforation of ego-boundaries: the demarcation between self and other, the 'innate' ability to differentiate what is an inner and what is an outer (mental) space. In schizophrenia, this demarcation is damaged to the extent of dissolution or distorted into something unusable and unrecognizable. But this may all sound like a grand metaphor, as there is still no neurobiological 'hard evidence' supporting the existence of a fixed ego-boundary, where it is located, or how it is constructed. All we know seems to be derived from philosophical investigation and patients' self-report, which (wrongly, in our view) do not carry much weight in contemporary 'evidence-based', biologically centred psychiatry.

In a recent account, Gipps (2020) rejects both the metaphysical and the epistemological conceptualizations of ego-boundary; the former refers to the ego-boundary as akin to a cellular membrane able to undergo some kind of ontological osmosis, which in turn renders the whole concept unnecessarily obscure and practically impossible to study, whereas the latter focuses too much on one's explicit self-knowledge and its failings in recognition. Both approaches 'objectify' the ego-boundary, as if it was a measurable and quantifiable 'thing' like a physical membrane, and at the same time (perhaps paradoxically) makes it too mysterious to be intelligible. Moving away from cognitivist accounts of symptoms such as TI, Gipps instead offers an enactivist approach, where ego and its boundaries are continuously constituted by a transcendental self, amenable to its interactions with the world and other inhabitants in it. This notion is supported by empirical research on disturbances in bodily representation and peripersonal space in schizophrenia (e.g., Costantini et al., 2020).

We too reject the (purely) epistemological account of self-acquaintance and are sympathetic to Gipps' enactivist approach; ego-boundary is not unchangeable or concretized a priori. Nevertheless, we think there is some value in the analogy with the metaphorical cell membrane—metaphorical being the key word here—the process of 'ontological osmosis' does not have to be static either and can indeed be actively modifying itself given the external and internal circumstances. We admit this may appear elusive, yet to us schizophrenia is characterized (if not defined) by ontologically impossible experiences and the distorted metaphysical dimensions of self cannot be fully understood in commonsensical or even interpersonal terms.

2.4.2. TI, passivity phenomena, and auditory-verbal hallucinations

Analogically speaking, TI is to thinking what passivity phenomena are to action and volition; both involve fundamental and substantial transformations in how one's minimal selfhood is constructed and embedded in the wider environment and not just what one (consciously or unconsciously) acknowledges as self-generated. In fact, some theorists argue that TI is in fact a form of passivity phenomenon but ascribed to thoughts (Henriksen et al., 2019). The authors consider TI 'a cognitive experience of a thought content that the patient claims is not his own' (p.4). It breaches almost everything an individual takes for granted about first-personal authority and the privileged nature of what they think and perceive, but is it really only a cognitive experience and does the patient need to 'claim' anything for the said experience to be not theirs? Gray (2014) puts forward the argument for a third factor in delusion formation in relation to passivity experiences (including TI), namely one where the subject needs to make a judgement about whether a thought is theirs or not, i.e., the necessity for identification. However, the need for identification (which is normally absent) for a thought that is first-personally accessible does not have to lead to a delusional elaboration either. After all, the subject might just conclude that thought is still theirs. If the first-personal authority and awareness of the taken-for-granted presence of 'for-me-ness' over one's thoughts cannot be challenged, then it may follow that the awareness of *absence*, i.e., the thoughts are not willed by self, cannot be disputed either.

We argue that this awareness of absence is not about the thoughts themselves (it is extremely rare that TI can fully 'replace' the patient's own thinking), but about the first-person givenness of thoughts that exist and are accessible within one's mind. One's stream of consciousness does not always need to be accessed through active introspection; rather, it is the 'becoming sensory' of some thoughts that drive them towards an absence of wilfulness and being experienced as inserted from an external source or agent (Sterzer et al., 2016). It must be pointed out that this 'becoming sensory' does not necessarily lead to auditory-verbal hallucinations (AVH), which are far more transdiagnostic and are by no means specific to the schizophrenia spectrum. Thoughts 'becoming sensory' cannot be simply heard through one's auditory capacities but are absorbed into the very basis of their self, with an immeasurable level of immediacy and salience. These 'soundless voices' (Ratcliffe & Wilkinson, 2015) might actually be more clinically useful than 'actual' AVH as indicators of schizophrenia, as they precisely capture the paradoxical, unstable, and unsustainable 'in-between' states of thought, perception, and volition that lie at the core of the experience of a schizophrenic (rather than broadly psychotic) disorder.

2.4.3. What makes TI so different?

We have already alluded to the observation that TI differs from other thought interference symptoms as well as 'prototypical' delusional beliefs in psychosis, such as persecutory delusions. As mentioned earlier, in TI the 'diffusion' through a permeable ego-boundary is inwards only, as opposed to outwards (thought broadcast and withdrawal) or in some way bidirectional (thought echo, where the thoughts are 'reflected' back at the individual). This means an added layer of invasion and violation of one's inner psychological space and may possess a higher propensity to 'require' an explanation. Sometimes (but not always), TI arises as part of ego-dystonic states situated within an all-encompassing affective disturbance which might be an indication of subconscious rejection of certain intolerable thought contents and the associated distress or anxiety (López-Silva, 2016). In other cases, TI is preceded by depersonalization and derealization as well as other subtle perceptual changes, which is consistent with recent empirical findings suggesting detachment and dissociative symptoms 'travel' along similar trajectories with FRS over time (Humpston et al., 2020).

Still, there are widespread debates and disagreements between explanationist and endorsement accounts of TI (Sollberger, 2014; López-Silva, 2018); while we tend to be more sympathetic to the explanationist view (i.e., delusions in TI form as an attempt to make sense of the anomalous experiential component rather than framing TI as a delusion in its entirety), we do consider TI to hold a special status in psychopathology that even a delusional elaboration can only serve as a mere *attempt* to explain its influence which can sometimes fail. In this sense, we are very supportive towards the potential meaningfulness of FRS in the differential diagnosis of schizophrenia and view the apparent lack of clinical specificity over 'other' delusions and hallucinations as likely due to the progressive deviation from their original conceptualization. A thorough understanding of Schneider's FRS is supposed to offer a rare glimpse into the subjective worlds of patients with schizophrenia, with all the rawness, richness, and immediacy of the psychopathological experience. It should not come as a surprise that a nuanced view of TI as an FRS possesses inherent utility for carrying out highly focused investigations into schizophrenia.

2.4.4. Ontologically impossible experiences in schizophrenia

TI is one example of the kind of 'ontologically impossible' experiences that typify schizophrenia, and in our view is more entrenched and impactful than any (delusional) belief. This extensive breakdown of first-person authority originates from a sense of detachment from commonsensical reality in the most ineffable, enigmatic, and literal manner that nothing short of a delusional construct will help to calm the mind undergoing such detachment and transformation. For the patient with schizophrenia, in order to reintegrate with the 'real' world and protect the fragile equilibrium between the two 'worlds', self-disturbances may seem a petty or even worthwhile price to pay (Ratcliffe & Broome, 2012). However, to articulate their delusional-hallucinatory world also carries the heavy burden of the intrinsic shortfalls of everyday language, which is evolved to convey *humanly possible* experiences (even imaginations are confined by what is *imaginable* in the first place). Of course, gaining 'access' to a separate ontological dimension never makes the sufferer of schizophrenia less human; if anything, it makes them *more* aware of a form of reality that has to run parallel to the shared social reality. Any cross-contamination or entanglement between the two would lead to a collision with disastrous consequences, including the paralysis of self.

Nevertheless, the effort to navigate between the two worlds and the attempt to keep them parallel often mean that the sufferer is stuck between the two. Unable to fully detach from or participate in either reality, the mind inflicted with schizophrenia sinks deeper into the void as the delusional-hallucinatory world begins to encroach upon the commonsensical one. This is where 'double-bookkeeping' fails to protect either reality. Thoughts and percepts may be merging with one another like molecules diffusing and reacting in a suspension in thin air; volition *feels* alien and painful. There is no need to judge or identify their source because there is simply no tangible source to be found in *this* world. Yet such disintegration does not need to arise from a florid state of psychosis—perhaps it is more accurate to describe it as an existential ailment *in addition to* psychotic symptoms—but is something that has been there at the centre of the patient's self for a very long time, eating its way outwards rather than being invaded from without (Parnas et al., 2021). The patient is plagued by an unspeakable solitude that is paradoxically imbued with significance and meaning from the non-existent 'other'; a deep sense of being fundamentally different in the very essence of what it means to be human ('*Anderssein*'). The patient is isolated by consciousness itself. Perhaps this is why schizophrenia is such an 'othering' disorder: ontologically impossible experiences are quite physically beyond what the intersubjective world can accommodate.

2.4.5. Heterogeneity in the experience of TI

Despite being treated as a unitary concept (a delusion) in many cases, TI can possess significant heterogeneity especially in the way it is described by patients with schizophrenia or psychosis. Perhaps some of the controversies in the theory and research of TI come from this apparent lack of first-person accounts; only a handful of perhaps outdated vignettes are quoted again and again (such as the infamous Eamonn Andrews example; Mellor, 1970). In a survey by Gunn (2016), users from multiple mental health online forums shared their experiences of TI openly under pseudonyms. Some even opted to use the term TI in a very clinical sense and stated that they had insight to realize the bizarreness of their experiences. However, their insight was not about the truth or falseness of TI—the user went on to describe in some detail how the government, aliens, chips in their head, and psychic powers were the sources of the inserted thoughts in spite of their 'insight' telling them these were bizarre ideas.

Another user asked the question, 'Is it still regarded as thought insertion if you don't know who is doing the inserting?' (p.563) which supports our argument of TI being a duplex phenomenon: there is clearly a strong sensory-perceptual component followed by a delusional elaboration or the rejection of another agent being the source ('doing the inserting'). However, this does not render their experience of TI less real, perplexing, or frightening. Just as a patient reported on these forums, 'I'm aware the thoughts that come to mind are NOT from external people, but I do believe my thoughts are not from me—but from something else in my mind, like the voice that speaks to me, for example' (p. 564). To us, this quote illustrates both the difficulty in differentiating thought from perception and the strange 'in-between' state characteristic of schizophrenia that is almost impossible to be captured by common language use.

2.5. Theoretical and Clinical Implications

2.5.1. Reviving phenomenological psychopathology in research and practice

Current diagnostic systems and intervention strategies largely focus on the identification and treatment of mental illness at a symptom level; even in psychological therapy, the aim is mostly to reduce distress and 'correct' anomalous thinking patterns. This is particularly true for psychotic disorders, where the breakdown in the shared perception of reality means that 're-integrating' patients into consensual reality carries the most weight when devising treatment plans. In terms of research, there has been a tremendous amount of investment into the neurobiological underpinnings and cognitive mechanisms of psychosis without a deeper analysis of the experiential aspect. As we have outlined in this chapter, patients with schizophrenia are very unlikely to be totally oblivious of commonsensical reality or fully 'believe' in their delusional-hallucinatory worlds; rather, they are plagued by the awareness of more than one world or reality. Phenomenological psychopathology has taught us that the deficit in schizophrenia does not lie entirely within impairments in 'reality testing', but in choosing which reality is more inhabitable. In many cases, it is chosen *for* the patient even before any deliberative or willed action—the delusion simply 'fits perfectly' within the structure of one's self-consciousness or calls for a radical restructuring of one's existing perceptions of the world (Sips et al., 2020).

To be able to grasp the complexity, impact, and meaning of experiences such as TI, researchers and clinicians ought to familiarize themselves with the richness of experiential data and cannot just focus on images of the brain. Neuroscience and phenomenology should never antagonize each other and should form the kind of 'inseparable unity' between the soma and the psyche of which Jaspers spoke (Humpston & Broome, 2020). Even self-disturbances may have developmental roots (Poletti & Raballo, 2019), which complement neurobiological frameworks.

2.5.2. The open-minded and inquisitive clinician

It needs to be borne in mind that most patients with schizophrenia find it almost impossible to describe the actual feelings associated with TI—or even psychosis in general. Patients risk not being believed by their clinicians (by using phrases like 'as if'), yet if they show too much conviction they will be labelled as delusional. It is therefore the clinician's role to elicit and explore the finer experiential nuances beyond face value, even when the patient articulates their symptoms in a very literal sense. For example, someone experiencing prodromal psychosis might report an overwhelming sense of dread, uncanniness, and unease (delusional atmosphere) accompanied with sensitivities to environmental stimuli (e.g., lights becoming brighter, sounds louder), but it is not often likely that they will use any of these terms. Instead, the patient might just say 'things don't feel right' or 'I can't think straight', showing behavioural aversion to the lighting in the room or asking the clinician to speak more quietly. All these signs should be picked up before establishing firm symptomatology. In the case of TI, again patients are unlikely to say in the first instance, 'I believe have inserted thoughts' or 'someone is inserting thoughts into my mind'; rather, they might seem perplexed and report thoughts that do not 'feel' like theirs (yet they may or may not recognize cognitively that said thoughts are still their own).

To us, we are not so interested in the judgements of agency or ownership when it comes to TI—in a way, judging TI as one's own or attributing to an external agent makes little difference to the underlying *experience*—the vital aspect is the raw feeling and basic sense of a breach in one's first-person authority, which is often indescribable. An attempt to articulate such an experience can by itself give the appearance that it holds some sort of belief status, and the further the patient 'formulates' their experience in commonsensical terms, the more deluded the patient will sound to the one doing the clinical assessment. We do not at all suggest that concepts such as delusions and hallucinations should be abolished; we urge clinicians to stay open-minded in their own judgements, as words like 'delusion' or 'hallucination' carry strong epistemic weights to the patient.

2.5.3. Delusional beliefs, truth, and reality

We are strong advocates of the view that although the patients' thoughts and perceptions about the external world can be utterly false, they cannot make mistakes about what is *real*. Reality is constructed and experienced through first-personal terms, whereas truth is built upon a shared and intersubjective foundation. Something that is true (e.g., colour) in the world might not be real to the individual (e.g., colour-blindness), and something that is real to the individual (e.g., inserted thoughts and hallucinated voices) might not be true in the physical world. However, physicality is only one such building block of the world. If everyone suddenly became colour-blind, would colour still exist as truth? Similarly, if everyone hallucinated simultaneously, would that hallucination be considered a real percept? We are cautious to not paint ourselves in a naïvely idealistic light; these are merely thought experiments. Still, to the patients with schizophrenia these are more than just curious experiments or uninvited imaginations. They represent a reality that is ontologically impossible, paradoxically inescapable, yet never pathologically incomprehensible. One would think that the world would still exist even if humans became extinct, but no one can hold this view with absolute certainty. Delusional beliefs, on the other hand, are usually held with more certainty than what 'normal people' might all take for granted—do they still carry less truth by definition? We encourage clinicians and researchers to reflect on their own truth and reality before 'jumping to the conclusion' that patients with schizophrenia are epistemically inferior.

2.6. Conclusion

In this chapter, we have presented an account of TI from the perspective of phenomenological psychopathology that is largely non-doxastic; however, this is not to say that (components of) TI cannot *become* doxastic. Instead, we have argued for the conceptualization of TI as a duplex phenomenon with elements of both frameworks. We have resisted a purely cognitivist account of TI and focused on the paradoxical and ontologically impossible qualities of schizophrenia, as opposed to other disorders in the wider psychosis spectrum. We consider TI and related passivity symptoms (i.e., most FRS) as fundamental violations in an individual's ego-boundary and such transformations in self-consciousness may indeed have higher clinical utility in the diagnosis of schizophrenia. Further, these symptoms raise fascinating (and in many ways, disturbing) questions against principles that are frequently taken for granted in Western philosophy and in daily life: what if the unity of selfhood and its perceived links to first-personal givenness are nothing more than a historical, social trend, and the so-called ontologically impossible experiences are actually true? What if the seemingly causal relationship between thinking and the existence of self is merely an illusion? We have no doubt that debates around the nature of TI will continue; our hope is that we have geared the arguments towards a more patient-centred approach. Without patient experience on the centre stage, no amount of philosophical investigations or empirical studies will possess real benefit—not even to the theorists or researchers. In sum, we view TI not purely as a delusional belief nor a sensory experience in its entirety, but as a prime example of the paradoxicality and perplexity that are at the core of the schizophrenia syndrome.

References

American Psychiatric Association (2013). *Diagnostic and Statistical Manual of Mental Disorders (DSM-5®)*. Washington, DC: American Psychiatric Publishing.

Baker, S. C., Konova, A. B., Daw, N. D., & Horga, G. (2019). A distinct inferential mechanism for delusions in schizophrenia. *Brain, 142*(6), 1797–1812.

Bell, V., Halligan, P. W., & Ellis, H. D. (2006). Explaining delusions: a cognitive perspective. *Trends in Cognitive Sciences, 10*(5), 219–226.

Bortolotti, L. (2012). In defence of modest doxasticism about delusions. *Neuroethics, 5*(1), 39–53.

Broome, M. R., Harland, R., Owen, G. S., & Stringaris, A. (Eds.). (2012). *The Maudsley Reader in Phenomenological Psychiatry*. Cambridge: Cambridge University Press.

Costantini, M., Salone, A., Martinotti, G., Fiori, F., Fotia, F., Di Giannantonio, M., & Ferri, F. (2020). Body representations and basic symptoms in schizophrenia. *Schizophrenia Research*. https://doi.org/10.1016/j.schres.2020.05.038.

Freeman, D. (2006). Delusions in the nonclinical population. *Current Psychiatry Reports, 8*(3), 191–204.

Freeman, D. (2016). Persecutory delusions: a cognitive perspective on understanding and treatment. *The Lancet Psychiatry, 3*(7), 685–692.

Gerrans, P. (2013). Delusional attitudes and default thinking. *Mind & Language, 28*(1), 83–102.

Gibbs, P. J. (2000). Thought insertion and the inseparability thesis. *Philosophy, Psychiatry, & Psychology, 7*(3), 195–202.

Gipps, R. G. (2020). Disturbance of ego-boundary enaction in schizophrenia. *Philosophy, Psychiatry, & Psychology, 27*(1), 91–106.

Gray, D. M. (2014). Failing to self-ascribe thought and motion: Towards a three-factor account of passivity symptoms in schizophrenia. *Schizophrenia Research, 152*(1), 28–32.

Gunn, R. (2016). On thought insertion. *Review of Philosophy and Psychology, 7*(3), 559–575.

Hardy, A., Emsley, R., Freeman, D., Bebbington, P., Garety, P. A., Kuipers, E. E., et al. (2016). Psychological mechanisms mediating effects between trauma and psychotic symptoms: the role of affect regulation, intrusive trauma memory, beliefs, and depression. *Schizophrenia Bulletin, 42*(suppl_1), S34–S43.

Heinz, A., Voss, M., Lawrie, S. M., Mishara, A., Bauer, M., Gallinat, J., et al. (2016). Shall we really say goodbye to first rank symptoms?. *European Psychiatry, 37*, 8–13.

Henriksen, M. G., Parnas, J., & Zahavi, D. (2019). Thought insertion and disturbed for-me-ness (minimal selfhood) in schizophrenia. *Consciousness and Cognition, 74*, 102770.

Hirjak, D., Breyer, T., Thomann, P. A., & Fuchs, T. (2013). Disturbance of intentionality: A phenomenological study of body-affecting first-rank symptoms in schizophrenia. *PLoS One*, *8*(9), e73662.

Humpston, C. S., & Broome, M. R. (2020). Thinking, believing, and hallucinating self in schizophrenia. *The Lancet Psychiatry*, *7*(7), 638–646.

Humpston, C., Harrow, M., & Rosen, C. (2020). Behind the opaque curtain: A 20-year longitudinal study of dissociative and first-rank symptoms in schizophrenia-spectrum psychoses, other psychoses and non-psychotic disorders. *Schizophrenia Research*. https://doi.org/10.1016/j.schres.2020.07.019.

James, W. (1889). The psychology of belief. *Mind*, *14*(55), 321–352.

López-Silva, P. (2016). Schizophrenia and the place of egodystonic states in the aetiology of thought insertion. *Review of Philosophy and Psychology*, *7*(3), 577–594.

López-Silva, P. (2018). Mapping the psychotic mind: A review on the subjective structure of thought insertion. *Psychiatric Quarterly*, *89*(4), 957–968.

Mellor, C.S. (1970). First-rank symptoms of schizophrenia. *British Journal of Psychiatry*, *117*, 15–23.

Mishara, A. L., & Fusar-Poli, P. (2013). The phenomenology and neurobiology of delusion formation during psychosis onset: Jaspers, Truman symptoms, and aberrant salience. *Schizophrenia Bulletin*, *39*(2), 278–286.

Moscarelli, M. (2020). A major flaw in the diagnosis of schizophrenia: What happened to the Schneider's first rank symptoms. *Psychological Medicine*, *50*(9), 1409–1417.

Mullins, S., & Spence, S. A. (2003). Re-examining thought insertion: Semi-structured literature review and conceptual analysis. *The British Journal of Psychiatry*, *182*(4), 293–298.

Parnas, J., Urfer-Parnas, A., & Stephensen, H. (2021). Double bookkeeping and schizophrenia spectrum: divided unified phenomenal consciousness. *European Archives of Psychiatry and Clinical Neuroscience*, *271*(8), 1513–1523.

Peralta, V., & Cuesta, M. J. (2023). Schneider's first-rank symptoms have neither diagnostic value for schizophrenia nor higher clinical validity than other delusions and hallucinations in psychotic disorders. *Psychological Medicine*, *53*, 2708–2711. https://doi.org/10.1017/S0033291720003293.

Poletti, M., & Raballo, A. (2019). Uncanny mirroring: A developmental perspective on the neurocognitive origins of self-disorders in schizophrenia. *Psychopathology*, *52*(5), 316–325.

Ratcliffe, M., & Broome, M. (2012). Existential phenomenology, psychiatric illness and the death of possibilities. In S. Crowell (Ed.), *Cambridge Companion to Existentialism* (pp. 361–382). Cambridge: Cambridge University Press.

Ratcliffe, M., & Wilkinson, S. (2015). Thought insertion clarified. *Journal of Consciousness Studies*, *22*(11–12), 246–269.

Shinn, A. K., Heckers, S., & Öngür, D. (2013). The special treatment of first rank auditory hallucinations and bizarre delusions in the diagnosis of schizophrenia. *Schizophrenia Research*, *146*(1–3), 17–21.

Sims, A. C. P. (1993). Schizophrenia and permeability of self. *Neurology, Psychiatry and Brain Research*, *1*, 133–135.

Sips, R., Van Duppen, Z., Kasanova, Z., De Thurah, L., Teixeira, A., Feyaerts, J., & Myin-Germeys, I. (2020). Psychosis as a dialectic of aha-and anti-aha-experiences: a qualitative study. *Psychosis*, *13*, 47–57.

Sollberger, M. (2014). Making sense of an endorsement model of thought-insertion. *Mind & Language*, *29*(5), 590–612.

Sterzer, P., Mishara, A. L., Voss, M., & Heinz, A. (2016). Thought insertion as a self-disturbance: an integration of predictive coding and phenomenological approaches. *Frontiers in Human Neuroscience*, *10*, 502.

Stone, T., & Young, A. W. (1997). Delusions and brain injury: The philosophy and psychology of belief. *Mind & Language, 12*(3-4), 327-364.

Ullrich, S., Keers, R., Shaw, J., Doyle, M., & Coid, J. W. (2018). Acting on delusions: the role of negative affect in the pathway towards serious violence. *The Journal of Forensic Psychiatry & Psychology, 29*(5), 691-704.

Wing, J. K., Babor, T., Brugha, T. S., Burke, J., Cooper, J. E., Giel, R., et al. (1990). SCAN: schedules for clinical assessment in neuropsychiatry. *Archives of General Psychiatry, 47*(6), 589-593.

3

Self-Disturbances, Perceptual Anomalies, and Physicality

Towards a Multimodal Model of Thought Insertion

Aaron Mishara, Pablo López-Silva, Cherise Rosen, and Andreas Heinz

'It thinks in me; it is not I who thinks.'

3.1. Introduction: Thought Insertion as 'Physical Force'

Thought insertion (TI) is regarded as a complex and severe symptom of psychosis considered to be a transdiagnostic phenomenon with a higher prevalence in people diagnosed with schizophrenia but also found in brief psychosis, schizoaffective disorders, and some drug-related experiences (Heinz et al., 2016; Mullins & Spence, 2003; Rosen, et al., 2011; López-Silva, 2018). Clinical data indicate that TI is a multimodal sensory phenomenon in which rich meaning is given to the experience (Rosen et al., 2022). Despite the well-documented prevalence of TI, we know little about its underlying mechanisms. A number of current approaches often focus their analysis on specific constructs such as the sense of ownership (SoO) and the sense of agency (SoA) (López-Silva, 2021). One problem with current models of TI is that there is a dearth of studies that examine TI and related disturbances on the level of granularity required to advance the field. In this chapter, we apply phenomenological analysis to examine self-disturbances (*Ichstörungen*)—such as TI—as developed by the Early Heidelberg School of Psychiatry (Beringer, 1927; Gruhle, 1915; Mayer-Gross, 1928; Mayer-Gross, 1932). In TI, the inner connectedness of thoughts and experiences is disrupted by a 'becoming sensory' of those thoughts experienced as inserted (e.g., by external agency).[1] For the Early Heidelberg School of Psychiatry, self-disturbances are 'explained' by a neurobiological process the mechanisms of which are largely unknown.[2]

In this chapter, we propose that careful phenomenological examination suggests that TI experiences are not merely verbally expressed but contain a 'physicality' from the multimodal perceptual processing of bodily self in the experience (even if this bodily self is passively experienced as mere object). For this reason, verbal descriptions of SoA and SoO may actually obscure the phenomenology on the level of analysis required. As we explore next, predictive coding and Bayesian inference may provide a framework able to link the neurobiology of psychosis with its clinical phenomenology (Sterzer et al., 2018).

The complexity and lack of clear definition make TI the target of far-reaching philosophical, diagnostic, and empirical debates (Campbell et al., 2005; Gallagher, 2015; Martin & Pacherie, 2013; Stephens & Graham, 2000; Sterzer et al., 2016). Individuals who experience TI report that certain thoughts are experienced as alien and have been placed in their minds by agents of varying kind, such as persons (Frith, 1999), magical agents (Napo et al., 2012), electronic devices (Spence et al., 1997), collective groups (Payne, 2013), and inanimate entities (Saks, 2007). Notably, the meaning given to the experience often maps onto the cultural values and mores at the time. The phenomenological psychiatrist Binswanger (1957) observed that individuals with schizophrenia may sometimes refer to themselves in the most inhuman, thing-like terms', e.g., as a 'machine', 'computer', or 'apparatus' whose sole function is to 'register' impressions (Binswanger, 1957). This concretization of metaphors of self is nevertheless an implicit way of preserving a (minimal) self in its now compromised ability to transcend the present perspective (Mishara, 2007). On the other hand, a psychotic patient in Mali experienced inserted thoughts caused by 'witches' living in his belly, thus evincing the cultural malleability of explanations provided for this experience (Napo et al., 2012).

In TI, a sense of permeability, diminished ego boundaries, or lack of mental privacy can pervade the individual's experience of reality, others, and self. Some foreign agents violate the individual's boundaries by means of intrusion

---

[1] As reviewed in (Sterzer et al., 2016, p. 4): 'Mayer-Gross is the herald of what later came to be known as the "perceptual anomalies" approach to the positive symptoms of schizophrenia, the view that low-level perceptual anomalies play a critical role in the positive symptoms of schizophrenia, including thought insertion and other self-disturbances'. Mayer-Gross described a "'becoming sensory" (Versinnlichung) in the sensory representation of thoughts. The phenomenological psychiatrists Matussek, Conrad and Binswanger later developed this view'.

[2] For discussion of Husserl's and Jaspers' diverging approaches to the phenomenological method, the unconscious, and automatic processing, see: Mishara and Fusar-Poli (2013); see also Mishara (2010a), Giersch and Mishara (2017a), Giersch and Mishara (2017b), and Mishara (1990) on Husserl, Freud, and the unconscious.

into the person's most intimate sphere of personal existence (Straus, 1949; Straus et al., 1958). The individual often reports these experiences to be highly physical, imposed with considerable force, including 'being sexually raped' from a distance (Schneider, 1939). That is, the individual is barred from 'negotiation concerning the conditions under which the patient remains at the disposal of others' (Kendler & Mishara, 2019). The self-disturbances (including TI) often involve a relationship of one-sided power, disrupting the individual's so-called power-sphere of the self (Machtsphäre) (Mishara & Zaytseva, 2019).

3.2. Imaginary Physicality: An Oxymoron?

There is growing recognition that hallucinations may occur in multiple modalities (Pienkos et al., 2019; Williams & Montagnese, 2020). TI are not hallucinations. They are not experienced as 'voices' heard in the surroundings or in a person's head (Jaspers, 1946). Nevertheless, we propose that multimodal perceptual anomalies also occur in thought disturbances, precisely because 'thoughts' in TI lose their character as thoughts and behave more like objects (as in the case of the lattice fence described next). We hypothesize that TI is not experienced as thinking but as a 'physical process' that is no longer experienced as thoughts but as multimodal sensory-like occurrences. The phenomenological psychiatrist, later to become philosopher, Karl Jaspers (1963) observes: 'It is extremely difficult to imagine what the actual experience is with these 'made thoughts' (passivity thinking) and these thought withdrawals. We just must accept the account as outsiders relying on the descriptions, we are given ...' (Jaspers, 1963). What may seem to the observer as impassive forbearance may be very painful for individuals with psychosis, who may feel unable to share their experiences.[3]

In this regard, Birchwood and colleagues (2000) provide a cognitive model which 'assumes that the same cognitive mechanisms in everyday social cognition (e.g., evolutionary rank theory, social comparison, etc.) remain intact in psychosis (Birchwood et al., 2000). However, a detailed study of the phenomenology of the experience of the hallucination's omnipotence (sometimes also present in TI) may indicate that the experience of power in psychosis may be different than the disparity of power in everyday social cognition' (Mishara & Zaytseva, 2019). Chadwick and Birchwood (1994) describe the patient's 'omnipotence appraisals' as a one-sided relationship attributed to the voices (or

---

[3] In this chapter we use the word 'physicality' and related terms to document the individual's subjective experience. That is, the 'physicality' is real for the individual experiencing psychosis.

other 'power relationships') (Chadwick & Birchwood, 1994). They propose that the discrepancies in power that patients with schizophrenia experience with regard to their voices (or self-disturbances generally) reflect the discrepancies they experience in actual social relationships. Alternatively, it is also possible that feelings of omnipotence may compensate for the experienced lack of power or refer to a tipping point when helplessness regarding psychotic phenomena flips into imaginary experiences of control. Birchwood et al. (2000) claim that the distress arising from the voices can be understood by reference to the individual's relationship with the voices (or self-disturbances) rather than the voice content, or illness characteristics alone (Mishara & Zaytseva, 2019; Rosen et al., 2016).

While Chadwick and Birchwood (1994) and Birchwood et al. (2000) present a compelling approach, there is much that remains unexplained (Birchwood et al., 2000; Chadwick & Birchwood, 1994). We present an alternative phenomenological approach as first developed by the Early Heidelberg School of Psychiatry. This is coupled with our own general efforts to apply this work to contemporary issues in the field, and specifically, to the analysis of thought insertion. As indicated here, adherence to certain theoretical formulations may actually obscure the underlying phenomenology by imposing overly speculative categories to psychopathological phenomena. For contemporary discussions of these topics, see (Billon & Kriegel, 2015; Gallagher, 2012; Gallagher, 2015; Zahavi, 2005).

3.3. The Early Heidelberg School of Psychiatry: The Phenomenology of Thought Insertion as Self-Disturbance (Ichstörung)

The origin of the term self-disturbances (*Ichstörungen*) is sometimes attributed to Jaspers. Jaspers (1913) describes phenomena related to self-disturbances (e.g., passivity thinking, being 'influenced', inserted and withdrawn thoughts) (Jaspers, 1913). Nevertheless, he neither systemizes the different self-disturbances nor uses the concept. It was discovered only recently—as far as we know—that it was Jaspers' Heidelberg colleague Gruhle (1915) who first coined the term self-disturbances in application to schizophrenia (Gruhle, 1915; Kaminski et al., 2019; Mishara et al., 2016; Sterzer et al., 2016). Gruhle, and other members of the Early Heidelberg School of Psychiatry, especially Mayer-Gross and Beringer, described and developed the 'self-disturbances' concept in schizophrenia. Specifically, they proposed that TI involves a disruption to the inner connectedness of thoughts and experiences by means of a 'becoming sensory' of those thoughts experienced as inserted. This includes how thinking is anticipated moment-to-moment as continuous (Giersch &

Mishara, 2017a; Giersch & Mishara, 2017b). Moreover, as indicated in healthy individuals, the interconnecting of thoughts need not be conscious (Giersch & Mishara, 2017a; Giersch & Mishara, 2017b; Mishara, 1990; Sterzer et al., 2016). Kurt Schneider (1939) later incorporated many of the self-disturbances in his first-rank symptoms (Kendler & Mishara, 2019).

Gruhle reports a person with schizophrenia who experiences TI. She is about to place soup on the stove. She has performed this same action innumerable times before. This time, however, she is absolutely certain that a foreign agent inserted the thought into her mind. Despite the absence of any obvious difference in content from other thoughts, the individual knows precisely which thoughts are inserted. When asked how she knows this, she responds: 'I can't explain. I just know it' (Kaminski et al., 2019). In TI, the inner connectedness of thoughts and experiences is disrupted by a 'becoming sensory' of those thoughts experienced as inserted (e.g., by an external agency). Unable to find continuity with his/her previous life history, the individual experiences a radical change in personality (Jaspers, 1963; Jaspers, 1910; Jaspers, 1913; Mishara & Fusar-Poli, 2013). In the self-disturbances of schizophrenia, one's own cognitive automatic processing appears to function *independently* from self or its volition. This means the automatic processing is experienced as acting on its own, which can be disturbing for individuals with self-disturbances (Mishara et al., 2016; Sterzer et al., 2016; Uhlhaas & Mishara, 2007). Moreover, changes in sensory and perceptual experience in the early course of schizophrenia are often 'incomparable', or 'unlike anything experienced before' (Mayer-Gross, 1928; Mayer-Gross, 1932; Mayer-Gross & Stein, 1926; Sterzer et al., 2016; Sterzer et al., 2019). The phenomenological psychiatrist Blankenburg (1984) applies Jaspers' opposition of *explanation vs. understanding* to the 'loss of common sense' that he claimed to characterize experiences in schizophrenia. It was claimed that the '*context blindness*' of reduced common sense is reflected in a diminished relatedness to others (*Intersubjektivitätsbezogenheit*) (Blankenburg, 1984; Blankenburg & Mishara, 2001; Mishara & Fusar-Poli, 2013). These alterations are fundamental to understanding the type of multisensory alteration characterizing TI. We explore this idea in the following section.

3.4. The Multimodal Physicality of TI (and Other Self-Disturbances)

We have suggested that TI and related self-disturbances involve the multimodal becoming sensory of thought (Mayer-Gross, 1928; Mayer-Gross, 1932; Sterzer et al., 2016). In his description of TI and related thought disturbances,

Jaspers (1963) remarks that such a *group of phenomena involves disruptions of context for the individual* (Jaspers, 1963). He suggests that:

> The thought arises and with it a direct awareness that is it not the patient but some external agent that thinks it ... Just as patients find their thoughts are *'made' for them* so they feel that these are being *withdrawn*. A thought vanishes and there arises the feeling that this has come about from an outside action. A new thought then appears without context (*ohne jeden Zusammenhang*). That too is made from outside. (Jaspers, 1963, pp. 122–123, our insertion).

In a similar vein, Kusters (2014, p. 105) indicates that: 'During madness, thoughts are more like inspirations or epiphanies coming from outside, that are experienced as strange and for which the mad person is not responsible' (Kusters, 2014). He rather feels like the thoughts present themselves to him rather than that he thinks them. Gruhle also reports that some individuals are 'surprised' by their own thoughts. Gruhle describes an individual with schizophrenia who insists that the inserted thoughts he is experiencing are not a form of thinking: 'Sometimes, it is the thoughts of others who pass through. I cannot do anything about it. It is something different than hearing, and it is not like thinking' (Jaspers, 1963; Kendler & Mishara, 2019, p. 981).[4] Blankenburg makes the interesting observation that thought withdrawal (TW)—similarly to TI—is frequently experienced in connection with *abnormal bodily sensations* especially those that are *experienced as made' from outside* (Blankenburg, 1973). Along similar lines, Pawar and Spence (2003) observe that some individuals are able to report the exact point that an inserted thought enters their minds (Pawar & Spence, 2003). The TI enters their minds but is experienced as alien. Along similar lines, Pawar and Spence (2003) observe that some individuals are able to report the exact point that an inserted thought enters their minds (Pawar & Spence, 2003). Pawar and Spence cite an individual experiencing thought broadcasting (*Gedankenausbreitung*) 'whose thoughts are perceived as leaving the subject's head and mind' (Pawar & Spence, 2003, p. 289).

---

[4] Gruhle's complete citation is as follows: 'The one thing I have to deal with all the time is this dragging through me. I cannot express it any better than this. Sometimes this lasts the entire day, sometimes more forceful, sometimes less ... Sometimes, it is pulled through me from a department store, at other times, a mass grave and a falling to one's doom, or from Siberia, through the entire night. I no longer know the words. There is no tone or sound, just a passing through, sometimes greater, sometimes less. Someone tells something—but one does not hear it—it is just drawn through the head ... Sometimes, it is the thoughts of others that pass through ... I cannot do anything about it. It is something different than hearing, and it is not like thinking.' (Kendler & Mishara, 2019, p. 981)

The Austrian psychiatrist Berze (1913) describes the following case report: 'Using electricity, a certain P. [living in Leipzig] triggered these jerky movements in me ... I know that he is a prophet through his transmittal of thoughts ... He acts as if I could hear what he has to say, but I do not hear; nevertheless, I know it. He comes directly into my brain as a thought. P also imposes these jerky movements ... I am merely an instrument, helpless, an automaton' (Kendler & Mishara, 2019).

3.5. The Case of A. the Locksmith (Mayer-Gross)

Mayer Gros reports the following case: While attempting to sleep, A., a 39-year-old locksmith hears talking about a locksmith from the street below. After 3 weeks the occurrence disappears. The voices return one year later, but now something *new* occurs. He hears a man's voice speaking continuously to him. *Nevertheless, he is unable to report back a single word of what is said to him*. He does not recognize the voice but has the impression that it is a man's voice. Moreover, the person seems completely preoccupied with the locksmith. 'When I grasp a thought, it becomes a topic of discussion. If I happen to look in some direction and see something, I get it said back to me that this something is about this or that.'

Still, A. is not able to think what he wants but only thinks what is predetermined for him. When he reads the newspaper, he is redirected to whatever the voice decides no matter whether he wants to or not. The voice is not any proper voice. It pursues him day and night, even in his dreams. *He is unable to sustain longer connected, interrelated thoughts (zusammenhängend denken) since the inserted thoughts interrupt his own. The thoughts are unpleasant because they are disruptive, not because of content*. He hears things that make him laugh, despite the fact that he does not want to laugh. Anything more than this, he cannot say. He is in no position to discern what the voice has just whispered to him. This voice is quite different from the previous ones. 'At that time, the voices would actually call out to him. *Now, it is a thought which is directly inserted into his mind. With all this going on, he cannot process his own thoughts*' (Mayer-Gross, 1928) our translation, paraphrasing, and emphases, p. 453).

The following observations can be made regarding concerning A's (the locksmith's) report:

(a) Difficulty thinking (*Denkerschwerung*): A. is unable to report back what is said to him. This is accompanied by continuous interruptions made by the external agent (TI).
(b) Passivity: A. is not able to think what he wants, but only thinks what is predetermined by foreign agency.
(c) Becoming amnestic: The thoughts are withdrawn precisely the moment of having them.
(d) Difficulty in distinguishing thought from images: One cannot say how much one is still thinking and how much the idea is imaginary (or entered a world of the 'imaginary').
(e) The thoughts are often unpleasant because they are disruptive, (not because of their content).

Note that in the course of illness, A. first experienced hallucinations, which then shifted to TI. This observation is in direct opposition to the views of Mayer-Gross' colleagues Schröder and the celebrated neuropsychiatrist Wernicke. The latter both claim that TI is often the precursor in the course of illness to thoughts becoming loud (*GLW*, Gedankenlautwerden), and to *AVHs*, i.e., Auditory Verbal Hallucinations (see Sterzer et al., 2016; Mishara & Zaytseva, 2019). They argue (1915, 1921a, b, 1926, 1928) that *GLW*, *AVHs*, *TI*, and 'the made thoughts and experiences' (Wernicke's autochthonous ideas), are not based on a perceptual disturbance but strictly on a verbal-linguistic one (i.e., 'phonemes') occurring in a predetermined sequence. Despite his insistence on phonemes, Schröder maintains that what is critical is a 'feeling of foreignness' (Fremdheitsgefühl). According to Mayer-Gross, however, what makes the inserted thought stand out from the patient's other thoughts is not a 'feeling of foreignness', but rather the experience of individual thoughts becoming sensory (Sterzer et al. 2016). This involves a transformed sense of what is experienced as perceptual according to a 'functional transformation' (Mayer-Gross & Stein, 1926).

3.6. The Early Heidelberg Mescaline Experiments and TI

In the 1920's, Heidelberg psychiatrists Beringer (1927), and Mayer-Gross (1928, 1932) conducted a phenomenological study of the effects of mescaline in healthy participants to model self-disturbances and psychosis (Beringer, 1927; Mayer-Gross, 1928; Mayer-Gross, 1932). The participants included psychiatrists and medical students with the goal of becoming more able to empathize with or understand those experiences of individuals with psychosis that Jaspers (1913) had labelled as non-understandable. As indicated by Mayer-Gross, and his Heidelberg colleagues, Beringer and Gruhle, the difficulty in distinguishing thought from images becomes evident in psychosis. Moreover, *one's thoughts become objects in the various sensory modalities*. In psychosis and mescaline intoxication, Mayer-Gross describes a merging between the subject and experience. Beringer reports on the experience of one of the healthy controls undergoing mescaline intoxication:

> One believes one hears sounds and sees faces and yet, *I cannot tell whether I am hearing or seeing* ... I hear scratching, harsh trumpet blasts, which are all a painful gnashing. I am the music, I am the lattice-work, *whatever I see, hear, smell ... everything which I attempt to grasp in thinking I see* ... *I saw one of my thoughts catapult out of me and merge into the lattice-work. This is not a simile but the sensation that something has left my body, which at the same time is optical* ... The strange sounds are at the same time visual perceptions, jagged and angular, jagged lightning, oriental ornaments, all turning into this horrid yellow. My body is ransacked and is, at the same time, itself. All these things I did not think but experienced, felt, smelled, saw, and my movements were also like this. I felt, tasted, smelled the tone ... The same occurred when I merely thought about my hands. I saw, felt, tasted my hands. Everything was so clear and certain. All critical thinking is nonsense in the face of the direct experiencing of the impossible. (Beringer 1927; our translation and emphases added, p. 497)

As the subject reports, the 'body is ransacked'. Sensory modalities and thinking collapse into one another: 'The same occurred when I merely thought about my hands. I saw, felt, tasted my hands.' The objects change as soon as they are co-perceived in another mode of sensory processing (Kaminski et al., 2019). Mayer-Gross observes similar multimodal bodily experiences in the Heidelberg mescaline studies as a model psychosis of self-disturbances (including TI).

3.7. Phenomenology and the Neurocomputational Modelling of Psychosis

In their 'predictive coding account of psychosis', Sterzer and colleagues (2018) write: 'predictive coding and Bayesian inference may provide a framework, linking the neurobiology of psychosis with its clinical phenomenology

(Sterzer et al., 2018). Anticipating the focus of predictive coding accounts on perceptual inference, and in line with phenomenological observations, early theories of psychosis emphasized altered perception', for example, Mayer-Gross. During psychosis, Bayesian predictive coding suggests that prior beliefs are imprecise in comparison to sensory input-driven posteriors (Sterzer et al., 2016). Accordingly, there is a weaker influence of perceptual priors built up at previous encounters with the same visual information. The mismatch between imprecise prior and newly constructed posterior knowledge will create prediction errors that adjust prior knowledge accordingly. Due to the continuing imprecision of prior knowledge, though, sensory input-driven posteriors will keep deviating from priors, thus repeatedly shifting knowledge generation towards sensory input. This hypothesis is in line with the well-known finding of reduced susceptibility to some visual illusions in schizophrenia, pointing to reduced precision of prior beliefs at low hierarchical levels (Adams et al., 2013a).

Dopamine release can be triggered to reduce complexity by increasing the signal-to-noise ratio. If increased dopamine synthesis and turnover is indeed contributing to salience attribution by otherwise irrelevant cues (Heinz, 2002; Kapur, 2003), then increased dopamine release should not only impair encoding of reward prediction errors but also promote misattribution of salience to otherwise irrelevant events including one's own cognition, thus contributing to delusional mood (Heinz, 2017, p. 99).

Delusional mood is an early stage of delusion formation (Conrad, 1958; López-Silva, 2016; Mishara, 2010b), when the world appears to be full of signs that carry an as-yet undeciphered meaning for the afflicted person. The seemingly unusual and surprising representations of external events may then be explained top-down by systematic delusion formation, a process that reduces complexity at the price of forming rigid belief systems (Heinz et al., 2019). So once their meaning is finally deciphered, the afflicted person discovers that they are in fact highly important to a powerful 'Other'. This 'Other' observes their every step and manipulates the environment (as we observed earlier in The Case of A., the Locksmith). However, the price of this attention is often a feeling of being controlled and persecuted, it means standing in the centre of attention, permanently exposed to the encircling social environment. In this regard, Binswanger, (1957) describes a 'delusional theater or stage' (Wahnbuehne) (Binswanger, 1957; Uhlhaas & Mishara, 2007).

The attribution of salience to otherwise irrelevant stimuli does not explain why environmental perceptions are imbued with specific meaning centred around the person with psychosis. Dopamine-associated, stress-triggered, or chaotic salience attribution to inner speech may help explain why certain thoughts can appear to be alien, or why certain 'verbalized' thoughts may change their sensory quality, as in TI. Nevertheless, this does not fully explain why unexpectedly salient thoughts are attributed to an outside agent who apparently controls them, or why acoustic hallucinations appear to focus on the afflicted person. Indeed, this failure to self-ascribe thoughts, as well as aberrant self-relevance attribution to environmental stimuli both point to a dysfunction of the self, which can also be observed in transcultural studies of schizophrenia (Pankow et al., 2016).

A report by a patient in Mali (recorded 2008) shows how TI may be related to other phenomena of external control/passivity, auditory hallucinations, and thought broadcasting:

> I have witches in my belly. It hurts and is full of wounds. They often talk. When I eat and want to take a fifth spoon, they say no. Sometimes when some of them annoy me, the others tell them to stop. They use my thoughts. It happens that I think, but the thought does not belong to me. I notice this because of the way I think in such moments. But often I think the way the witches think. They also take my thoughts away when someone addresses me from the outside. And when I am in my village, the witches can communicate with the villagers. When I read a book, it is not me, it is them who read the book. If I want to read myself, I have to say very loudly: 'I want to read!' It is all because of them. When you touch your belly, a human can become afraid. There is a direct connection between the human and the belly.

3.8. Phenomenology of Everyday Cognition, Bias, and the Study of Self-Disturbances

The practice of philosophic phenomenology (as developed by Husserl) is based on methods used to reduce bias and/or attachment to one's preferred abstract concepts and other types of bias. Phenomenology employs a method of 'bracketing' our current experience by suspending our assumptions that (often unconsciously) bias thinking and experience. However, even the disciplined phenomenologist cannot completely rid oneself of bias. In fact, bias is often necessary and adaptive as hermeneutic theory indicates, and in Bayesian accounts, it is reflected in prior knowledge that necessarily structures all sensory experience (Adams et al., 2013b; Heinz et al., 2019). One uses a *phenomenological method to bracket the naïve realism of our experience as a default self-perspective* in one's situated habitual world

(Mishara & Fusar-Poli).[5] We examine the application of phenomenological methodology and related approaches to the study of self, self-disturbances, and schizophrenia in another publication. In a strong programmatic statement, Woods et al. (2014) indicate that the phenomenology of hallucinations can be applied in an interdisciplinary context. Jaspers' own phenomenological approach (1910) to psychopathology also recognizes the urgency of applying both humanistic and scientific approaches to the complexity and diversity of subjective data (see Mishara & Fusar-Poli, 2003, 2013; Woods et al., 2014). In this chapter, we have attempted to apply this approach to the study of thought insertion.

3.9. Final Remarks

In this chapter, we discuss the work of the Early Heidelberg School of Psychiatry (namely Gruhle, Mayer-Gross, and Beringer) and how this work applies to the current debate about how to make sense of delusions of thought insertion. In TI, the inner connectedness of thoughts and experiences is disrupted by a 'becoming sensory' of those thoughts experienced as alien and inserted (e.g., by an external agency). Current approaches often make the focus of their analysis specific terms such as the SoO and the SoA (López-Silva, 2021). Verbal descriptions of SoA and SoO may actually obscure the phenomenology on the level of analysis required. In support of this view, *we found that the TI experiences contain a 'physicality' in the multimodal perceptual processing of bodily self in the experience (even if this bodily self is passively experienced as mere object).* In their 'predictive coding account of psychosis', Sterzer and colleagues (2018) propose that 'predictive coding and Bayesian inference may provide a framework, linking the neurobiology of psychosis with its clinical phenomenology ... (Sterzer et al., 2018). Anticipating the focus of predictive coding accounts on perceptual inference, and in line with phenomenological observations, early theories of psychosis emphasized altered perception', for example, Mayer-Gross. Moreover, as we also indicate in this chapter, phenomenological approaches dovetail nicely with the neurocomputational modelling of psychosis.[6] Beringer and Mayer-Gross observe

---

[5] For a discussion of phenomenological method as it informs clinical practice, see Mishara (2010a). Jaspers writes "we live uncritically ... in an immediate world", (Jaspers, 1920, our translation) a world given to us naïvely and effortlessly. We remain blind to the interpretive lens through which we experience this "immediate" world, the product of implicitly functioning, unnoticed biases (Jaspers, 1920)'.

[6] As we document elsewhere (Kaminski et al., 2019; Sterzer et al., 2016), Mayer-Gross is herald of the 'perceptual anomalies' approach to schizophrenia, the view that low-level perceptual anomalies play a critical role in self-disturbances.

similar multimodal bodily hallucinatory experiences in the Heidelberg mescaline studies as a model psychosis of self-disturbances. We have indicated in this chapter how different approaches come together in the study of thought insertion. We feel that this is an excellent opportunity to bring together future further research in these areas.

Acknowledgements

PLS collaboration was supported by the project FONDECYT regular n° 1221058 'The architecture of delusions' granted by the Chilean National Agency for Research and Development (ANID) of the Government of Chile and the Project FACSO 2/2021 granted by the Universidad de Valparaíso, Chile. The funding bodies had no other contribution to any part of the article.

References

Adams, R. A., Stephan, K. E., Brown, H. R., Frith, C. D., & Friston, K. J. (2013a). The computational anatomy of psychosis. *Frontiers in Psychiatry, 4*, 47.
Adams, R. A., Stephan, K. E., Brown, H. R., Frith, C. D., & Friston, K. J. (2013b). The computational anatomy of psychosis. *Frontiers in Psychiatry, 4*, 47.
Beringer, K. (1927). *Der Meskalinrausch: Seine Geschichte und Erscheinungsweise* (Monographien aus dem Gesamtgebiete der Neurologie und Psychiatrie). Berlin: Springer, pp. 978–973.
Billon, A., & Kriegel, U. (2015). Jaspers' dilemma: The psychopathological challenge to subjectivity theories of consciousness. In R. J. Gennaro (Ed.), Disturbed Consciousness: New Essays on Psychopathology and Theories of Consciousness (pp. 29–54). Oxford: The MIT Press.
Binswanger, L. (1957). *Schizophrenie*. Neske.
Birchwood, M., Meaden, A., Trower, P., Gilbert, P., & Plaistow, J. (2000). The power and omnipotence of voices: Subordination and entrapment by voices and significant others. *Psychological Medicine, 30*(2), 337–344.
Blankenburg, W. (1973). *Lexikon der Psychiatrie: Gesammelte Abhandlungen der gebräuchlichsten*. Herausgeber: Müller, C. (Hrsg).
Blankenburg, W. (1984). Unausgeschöptes in der Psychopathologie von Karl Jaspers. *Nervenarzt, 55*(9), 447–460.
Blankenburg, W., & Mishara, A. L. (2001). First steps toward a psychopathology of 'common sense'. *Philosophy, Psychiatry, & Psychology, 8*(4), 303–315.
Campbell, T., Chamberlin, J., & Carpenter, J. L., H.S. (2005). American Association of Community Psychiatrist (AACP): AACP ROSE: Recovery Oriented Services Evaluation. Measuring the Promise: A Compendium of Recovery Measures. Available at: https://www.hsri.org/publication/measuring-the-promise-a-compendium-of-recovery-measures-volume-ii/
Chadwick, P., & Birchwood, M. (1994). The omnipotence of voices: A cognitive approach to auditory hallucinations. *The British Journal of Psychiatry, 164*(2), 190–201.

Conrad, K. (1958). *Die beginnende schizophrenie [Beginning schizophrenia]*. Cambridge: Cambridge University Press.

Frith, C. (1999). How hallucinations make themselves heard. *Neuron, 22*(3), 414–415.

Gallagher, S. (2012). What is phenomenology? In S. Gallagher (Ed.), Phenomenology (pp. 7–18). London: Springer.

Gallagher, S. (2015). Relations between agency and ownership in the case of schizophrenic thought insertion and delusions of control. *Review of Philosophy and Psychology, 6*(4), 865–879.

Giersch, A., & Mishara, A. (2017a). Disrupted continuity of subjective time in the milliseconds range in the self-disturbances of schizophrenia: convergence of experimental, phenomenological, and predictive coding accounts. *Journal of Consciousness Studies, 24*(3-4), 62–87.

Giersch, A., & Mishara, A. L. (2017b). Is schizophrenia a disorder of consciousness? Experimental and phenomenological support for anomalous unconscious processing. *Frontiers in Psychology, 8*, 1659.

Gruhle, H. W. (1915). Selbstschilderung und einfühlung. *Zeitschrift Für Die Gesamte Neurologie Und Psychiatrie, 27*(1), 148–231.

Heinz, A. (2002). Dopaminergic dysfunction in alcoholism and schizophrenia-psychopathological and behavioral correlates. *European Psychiatry, 17*(1), 9–16.

Heinz, A. (2017). *A New Understanding of Mental Disorders: Computational Models for Dimensional Psychiatry*. Oxford: MIT Press.

Heinz, A., Murray, G. K., Schlagenhauf, F., Sterzer, P., Grace, A. A., & Waltz, J. A. (2019). Towards a unifying cognitive, neurophysiological, and computational neuroscience account of schizophrenia. *Schizophrenia Bulletin, 45*(5), 1092–1100.

Heinz, A., Voss, M., Lawrie, S. M., Mishara, A., Bauer, M., Gallinat, J., Juckel, G., Lang, U., Rapp, M., & Falkai, P. (2016). Shall we really say goodbye to first rank symptoms? *European Psychiatry, 37*, 8–13.

Jaspers, K. (1910). Eifersuchtswahn. Zeitschrift Für Die Gesamte Neurologie Und Psychiatrie, *1*(1), 567–637.

Jaspers, K. (1913). *Allgemeine psychopathologie, ein leitfaden für studierende, ärzte und psychologen*. Berlin: Springer.

Jaspers, K. (1920). Die Zusammenhänge des Seelenlebens: I. Die verständlichen Zusammenhänge. In K. Jaspers (Ed.), *Allgemeine Psychopathologie für Studierende, Ärzte und Psychologen* (pp. 170–232). Berlin: Springer.

Jaspers, K. (1946). Die Stellungnahme des Kranken zur Krankheit. In K. Jaspers (Ed.), *Allgemeine Psychopathologie* (pp. 345–356). Berlin: Springer.

Jaspers, K. (1963). *General Psychopathology*, trans. Hoenig J., & Hamilton, M. W. Manchester: Manchester University Press.

Kaminski, J. A., Sterzer, P., & Mishara, A. L. (2019). 'Seeing Rain': Integrating phenomenological and Bayesian predictive coding approaches to visual hallucinations and self-disturbances (ichstörungen) in schizophrenia. *Consciousness and Cognition, 73*, 102757.

Kapur, S. (2003). Psychosis as a state of aberrant salience: a framework linking biology, phenomenology, and pharmacology in schizophrenia. *American Journal of Psychiatry, 160*(1), 13–23.

Kendler, K. S., & Mishara, A. (2019). The prehistory of Schneider's first-rank symptoms: Texts from 1810 to 1932. *Schizophrenia Bulletin, 45*(5), 971–990.

Kusters, W. (2014). Filosofie van de waanzin. *Tijdschrift Voor Psychiatrie, 56*(10), 669–670.

Lopez-Silva, P. (2016). The unity of consciousness in pre-psychotic states. A phenomenological analysis/La unidad de la conciencia en estados pre-psicóticos. Un análisis fenomenológico. *Estudios De Psicología, 37*(1), 1–34.

López-Silva, P. (2018). Mapping the psychotic mind: A review on thought insertion. *Psychiatric Quarterly, 89*(1), 957–968.

López-Silva, P. (2021). Atribuciones de agencia mental Y el desafío desde la psicopatología. *Kriterion: Revista De Filosofia, 61*, 835–850.

Martin, J., & Pacherie, E. (2013). Out of nowhere: Thought insertion, ownership and context-integration. *Consciousness and Cognition, 22*(1), 111–122.

Mayer-Gross, W. (1928). Zur Struktur des Einschlaferlebens. *Zbl.Ges.Neurol.Psychiat., 51*, 246.

Mayer-Gross, W. (1932). *Die Klinik der Schizophrenie*. Berlin: Geisteskrankheiten HD.

Mayer-Gross, W., & Stein, H. (1926). Über einige abänderungen der sinnestätigkeit im Meskalinrausch. *Zeitschrift Für Die Gesamte Neurologie Und Psychiatrie, 101*(1), 354–386.

Mishara, A., Bonoldi, I., Allen, P., Rutigliano, G., Perez, J., Fusar-Poli, P., & McGuire, P. (2016). Neurobiological models of self-disorders in early schizophrenia. *Schizophrenia Bulletin, 42*(4), 874–880.

Mishara, A. L. (1990). Husserl and Freud: Time, memory and the unconscious. *Husserl Studies, 7*(1), 29–58.

Mishara, A. L. (2007). Is minimal self preserved in schizophrenia? A subcomponents view. *Consciousness and Cognition, 16*(3), 715–721.

Mishara, A. L. (2010a). Autoscopy: Disrupted self in neuropsychiatric disorders and anomalous conscious states. In D. Schmicking, & S. Gallagher (Eds.), Handbook of Phenomenology and Cognitive Science (pp. 591–634). Dordrecht: Springer.

Mishara, A. L. (2010b). Klaus Conrad (1905–1961): Delusional mood, psychosis, and beginning schizophrenia. *Schizophrenia Bulletin, 36*(1), 9–13.

Mishara, A. L., & Fusar-Poli, P. (2013). The phenomenology and neurobiology of delusion formation during psychosis onset: Jaspers, Truman symptoms, and aberrant salience. *Schizophrenia Bulletin, 39*(2), 278–286.

Mishara, A., & Zaytseva, Y. (2019). Hallucinations and phenomenal consciousness. In G. Stanghellini, M. Broome, A. Raballo, A. V. Fernandez, P. Fusar-Poli, & R. Rosfort (Eds.), The Oxford Handbook of Phenomenological Psychopathology (pp. 484–508). Oxford: Oxford Handbooks Online.

Mullins, S., & Spence, S. A. (2003). Re-examining thought insertion: Semi-structured literature review and conceptual analysis. *The British Journal of Psychiatry, 182*(4), 293–298.

Napo, F., Heinz, A., & Auckenthaler, A. (2012). Explanatory models and concepts of West African Malian patients with psychotic symptoms. *European Psychiatry, 27*(S2), S44–S49.

Pankow, A., Katthagen, T., Diner, S., Deserno, L., Boehme, R., Kathmann, N., Gleich, T., Gaebler, M., Walter, H., & Heinz, A. (2016). Aberrant salience is related to dysfunctional self-referential processing in psychosis. *Schizophrenia Bulletin, 42*(1), 67–76.

Pawar, A. V., & Spence, S. A. (2003). Defining thought broadcast: Semi-structured literature review. *The British Journal of Psychiatry, 183*, 287–291.

Payne, R. L. (2013). *Speaking to My Madness: How I Searched for Myself in Schizophrenia*. Scotts Valley, CA: CreateSpace.

Pienkos, E., Giersch, A., Hansen, M., Humpston, C., McCarthy-Jones, S., Mishara, A., Nelson, B., Park, S., Raballo, A., & Sharma, R (2019). Hallucinations beyond voices: a conceptual review of the phenomenology of altered perception in psychosis. *Schizophrenia Bulletin, 45*(Supplement_1), S67–S77.

Rosen, C., Jones, N., Chase, K. A., Gin, H., Grossman, L. S., & Sharma, R. P. (2016). The intrasubjectivity of self, voices and delusions: A phenomenological analysis. *Psychosis, 8*(4), 357–368.

Rosen, C., Grossman, L. S., Harrow, M., Bonner-Jackson, A., & Faull, R. (2011). Diagnostic and prognostic significance of Schneiderian first-rank symptoms: A 20-year longitudinal study of schizophrenia and bipolar disorder. *Comprehensive Psychiatry, 52*(2), 126–131.

Rosen, C., Harrow, M., Tong, L., Jobe, T., Harrow, H. (2022). An experience of meanings': A 20-year prospective analysis of delusional reality in schizophrenia and affective-psychosis. In review.

Saks, E. R. (2007). *The Center Cannot Hold: My Journey Through Madness*. London: Hachette UK.

Schneider, K. (1939). *Psychischer befund und psychiatrische diagnose*. Leipzig: Thieme.

Spence, S. A., Brooks, D. J., Hirsch, S. R., Liddle, P. F., Meehan, J., & Grasby, P. M. (1997). A PET study of voluntary movement in schizophrenic patients experiencing passivity phenomena (delusions of alien control). *Brain: A Journal of Neurology, 120*(11), 1997–2011.

Stephens, G. L., & Graham, G. (2000). *When Self-consciousness Breaks: Alien Voices and Inserted Thoughts*. Oxford: The MIT Press.

Sterzer, P., Adams, R. A., Fletcher, P., Frith, C., Lawrie, S. M., Muckli, L., Petrovic, P., Uhlhaas, P., Voss, M., & Corlett, P. R. (2018). The predictive coding account of psychosis. *Biological Psychiatry, 84*(9), 634–643.

Sterzer, P., Mishara, A. L., Voss, M., & Heinz, A. (2016). Thought insertion as a self-disturbance: An integration of predictive coding and phenomenological approaches. *Frontiers in Human Neuroscience, 10*, 502.

Sterzer, P., Voss, M., Schlagenhauf, F., & Heinz, A. (2019). Decision-making in schizophrenia: A predictive-coding perspective. *NeuroImage, 190*, 133–143.

Straus, E. (1949). Die Ästhesiologie und ihre Bedeutung für das Verständnis der Halluzinationen. *Archiv Für Psychiatrie Und Nervenkrankheiten, 182*(3), 301–332.

Straus, E. W., Straus, E. W., & Morgan, B. T. (1958). Aesthesiology and hallucinations. In R. May, E. Angel, & H. F. Ellenberger (Eds.), *Existence: A New Dimension in Psychiatry and Psychology* (pp. 139–169). London: Basic Books/Hachette Book Group.

Uhlhaas, P. J., & Mishara, A. L. (2007). Perceptual anomalies in schizophrenia: Integrating phenomenology and cognitive neuroscience. *Schizophrenia Bulletin, 33*(1), 142–156.

Williams, D., & Montagnese, M. (2020). Bayesian psychiatry and the social focus of delusions. [Preprint]. DOI:10.13140/RG.2.2.27852.23683.

Woods, S. W., Walsh, B. C., Addington, J., Cadenhead, K. S., Cannon, T. D., Cornblatt, B. A., Heinssen, R., Perkins, D. O., Seidman, L. J., Tarbox, S. I., Tsuang, M. T., Walker, E. F., & McGlashan, T. H. (2014). Current status specifiers for patients at clinical high risk for psychosis. *Schizophrenia Research, 158*(1–3), 69–75. ISSN 0920-9964. https://doi.org/10.1016/j.schres.2014.06.022

Zahavi, D. (2005). *Subjectivity and Selfhood: Investigating the First-person Perspective*. Oxford: MIT Press.

4

Thought Insertion, Mental Affordances, and Affectivity

Michelle Maiese

4.1. Introduction

The notion of affordance is a theoretical concept introduced by J. J. Gibson (1979) that emphasizes the complementarity of the animal and the environment and the link between perception and action. What the environment affords are 'what it *offers* the animal, what it *provides* or *furnishes*, either for good or ill' (Gibson, 1979, p. 237). Which actions a particular object affords is specified *relationally*. An object is graspable by virtue of its physical properties together with an animal's bodily structure and ability to grasp that object. In recent years, some theorists have utilized the notion of affordance to shed light on the dynamics of various mental disorders. Gallagher (2018), for example, maintains that disorders such as schizophrenia reorient a subject's concerns, interests, and abilities and thereby alter her affordance space. Likewise, de Haan and colleagues (2013) argue that the various symptoms of depression can be understood in terms of an apparent shrinking or constriction of the affordance field. These theorists have focused primarily on possibilities for motor engagement and bodily action and the disruptions to bodily agency that occur in mental disorder. However, as McClelland (2019) points out, in addition to experiencing affordances for bodily actions (such as grasping and climbing), human subjects experience affordances for mental actions (such as imagining, attending, and deliberating). I propose that we build on these ideas to gain a better understanding of cases of thought insertion among subjects with schizophrenia.

Ordinarily, possibilities for mental action (such as thought) are disclosed as relevant against the backdrop of environmental conditions together with a subject's existing mental states. However, in cases of thought insertion, this disclosure process is disturbed, resulting in disruptions to the subject's senses of agency and ownership. Although the thoughts are first-personally accessible via introspection, they seem so foreign and alien that subjects claim that they have been inserted in their mind by another source. To make sense of how affordances ordinarily are disclosed, and how this commonplace experience is disrupted in cases of thought insertion, I appeal to the enactivist notion of solicitation, McClelland's (2019) conception of 'mental affordance', and some observations about the phenomenology of affordance-responsiveness. I argue that affectivity is central to the disclosure of affordances and that a disruption to *affective framing* plays a central role in thought insertion.

4.2. Affordances, Solicitations, and Mental Action

Gibson maintains that 'an affordance is neither an objective property nor a subjective property; or it is both, if you like' (Gibson, 1979, p. 129). He further suggests that an affordance is 'both physical and psychical', and that it points both to the environment and to the observer; thus, an affordance concerns both properties of the animal and properties of the environment taken in reference to each other. The basic idea is that the environment dynamically offers various possibilities for interaction and engagement, but only in relation to an organism with particular capacities. The primary goal of perception is not the construction of internal images of the surrounding world, but rather the effective control of action. Perception is understood as a kind of dynamic sensorimotor activity that involves goal-oriented exploration of the environment.

To make sense of the relational nature of affordances, some theorists have looked to the enactivist approach in philosophy of mind. Enactivism emphasizes that meaning is constituted dynamically via a living animal's ongoing, active, embodied engagement with their environment (Thompson, 2007). According to Varela, Thompson, and Rosch (1991), the various forms of cognition emerge as a result of coupled interactions between an organism with specific sensorimotor capacities and the environmental features to which it is sensitive. The sort of bodily intelligence and 'informational sensitivity' (Hutto & Myin, 2012) highlighted by some enactivists fits well with ecological psychology's non-representational view of perception and the notion that perception does not require internal mental states to be matched with some pre-existing external state of affairs. Instead, perception is relational, dynamic, organism-centred, and goal-directed. Many enactivist theorists also look to phenomenology for guidance: lived experience tells us that perception and action are deeply interrelated, that a central function of perception is to control action, and that action serves to guide perception.

Both ecological psychology and enactivism emphasize that perception and action are inseparable; but whereas Gibson's ecological account treats perception as central, some enactivist theorists have turned the primary focus to agency and the question of which factors shape whether an available affordance *solicits* action. Rietveld and Kiverstein (2014) maintain that an affordance becomes a solicitation 'when it is relevant to our dynamically changing concerns', takes on a 'demand character' and becomes manifest at the bodily level in a state of 'action readiness' (p. 342). Along similar lines, Gallagher describes a solicitation as 'an affordance that draws an agent to action due to its relevance, or the way that it stands out in the perceptual field' (Gallagher, 2018, p. 722). This focus on solicitations reflects many enactivist theorists' emphasis on phenomenology, and 'on the point of the view of the organism itself, understood as an intentional center of meaningful behavior' (Ramstead et al., 2016, p. 3).

Once we turn the focus to *solicitations*, we see that an object invites action not just because of its features and what abilities the animal possesses, but also because of that animal's particular goals, concerns, and sociocultural context. Along these lines, Rietveld and Kiverstein (2014) and Ramstead et al. (2016) distinguish between a landscape of affordances and a field of affordances. While the *landscape* (or 'total ensemble') of affordances is comprised of the entire set of affordances that are available to a particular agent in a given environment at a specific time, the *field* of affordances consists of the relevant possibilities for action that a particular individual is responsive to in a concrete situation (Ramstead et al., 2016, p. 5). This field can be understood as the 'situation-specific, individual 'excerpt' of the general landscape of affordances' (de Haan et al., 2013, p. 7) that stand out as relevant for a particular agent in a specific context. When an agent explores the environment, the information and affordances she detects are apprehended in relation to her goals and interests. Thus, many action-possibilities will not be 'seen', and will lack a demand character, because they are irrelevant to the agent given her specific goals and concerns.

Insofar as the affordance field shifts as the needs and interests of an agent change, it is clearly subject-dependent (Dings, 2018, p. 684). Among the subjective factors that constitute an agent's field of affordances are that agent's body scheme, concerns, habits, and past experience. Whether affordances solicit action is a thoroughly dynamic process in which specific action-possibilities become more or less inviting over the course of a day. This raises an important question about 'what makes it the case that a skilled individual is solicited by one affordance rather than another' (Rietveld & Kiverstein, 2014, p. 340) at a particular time. Since subjects encounter an environment 'overflowing with affordances', they need some way of singling out just those ones that are relevant to their interests, preferences, and needs (Rietveld & Kiverstein, 2014, p. 341). Rietveld and Kiverstein (2014) point to the way in which agents become increasingly sensitive to the specific demands of a given situation and to the success of their own performance. Likewise, some earlier Gestalt psychologists (Lewin, 1936; Koffka, 1935) have suggested that the 'demand character' of something in the environment is bestowed upon it in experience, according to the needs of the observer. But just *how* do agents gauge which affordances are relevant and become attuned to the demands of concrete situations in the here and now? How do they come to experience a 'weighted menu of options' (McClelland, 2019) for action so that they can select from a shortlist of the most promising or relevant options, rather than having to consider *all* the available possibilities?

Ramstead et al. (2016) highlight how the world we inhabit is 'disclosed as a matrix of differentially salient affordances with their own structure or configuration'; a particular animal encounters this broad ensemble of affordances and evaluates them, 'often implicitly and automatically' for relevance' (p. 4). The notion that 'demand character' is spontaneously *bestowed* or *disclosed* points to a pre-reflective interpretive activity on the part of the animal as agent. Note that a key claim made by many affordance theorists, including Gibson, is that we are perceptually sensitive to affordances, so that we see a chair's property of being sit-able or a set of stairs as being climb-able. But it seems clear that affordance-detection and the selection of one action-possibility rather than others goes beyond sensory perception, where perception is understood as picking upon information for the purposes of behavioural discrimination (Scarantino, 2003, p. 953). An agent could perceive invariants and disturbances in the optic or acoustic array in just the way that Gibson describes, but it would mean little for the animal as agent unless these affordances were somehow deemed *relevant*. Solicitations are not simply perceived, but rather *appraised*. For example, we do not simply see a chair as sit-able with our eyes, but rather gauge its sit-ability as relevant in our current situation, given our concerns and interests. Such appraisal often is not deliberate or explicitly attended to, but rather more spontaneous, intuitive, and pre-reflective.

This process whereby some affordances are disclosed as demanding or inviting has an integral affective dimension. Relevant affordances solicit an agent by 'beckoning certain forms of perceptual-emotional appraisal and readiness to act' (Ramstead et al., 2016, pp. 4–5); and 'the phenomenon of being attracted or drawn by a solicitation can be understood as an emotional perturbation' (Rietveld, 2012, p. 213). Those affordances which become relevant are those with affective significance, and the way in which things appear significant to a particular agent has much to do with her concerns and interests. A specific action-possibility 'solicits action (i.e. calls me to act) only when I am responsive to act (i.e. concerned)' (Dings, 2018, p. 687). A pizza affords eating, but only draws me to act when I am interested in eating. A shoe affords throwing, but only draws me to act when I am feeling angry. This suggests, once again, that affordances are not simply perceived via the senses; rather, they are gauged or selectively attended to, and this process of selective attention relies heavily on affectivity. A subject's affective attunement to a particular situation, informed by her concerns and interests, helps to determine which available affordances solicit action.

To make sense of how this sort of selective attention works, we need not appeal to mental representations or propositional content. Instead, it appears that human agents possess some kind of pre-theoretical, non-intellectual understanding of where to direct their attention in a given context, which is built up through learning and mediated by past experience. As individuals navigate through the world, they do not sequentially process all the information that is potentially available to them, but instead focus on certain very specific things rather than others. Affect operates as the 'allure' of consciousness and implies a 'dynamic gestalt or figure-ground structure' whereby some objects emerge into affective prominence, while others become unnoticeable (Thompson, 2007, p. 374). What I call *affective framing* is a spontaneous, pre-reflective, bodily way of attending selectively to our surroundings in accordance with *felt importance* and *what matters to us*. While the brain certainly plays a crucial role, the provision of affective and motivational colour or tone to events and situations is not simply a neural achievement. Affective framing is best understood as distributed over a complex network of brain and bodily processes, including metabolic systems, endocrine responses, musculoskeletal changes, and cardiovascular responses. A subject's way of framing things also is embodied partly in her facial expressions, gestures, posture, movements, and overall bodily comportment. Bodily feelings help to determine the focus of both action and perception and thereby carve out a field of relevant action-possibilities. The way in which the world is disclosed to the subject, including what she attends to in perception, and what she strives for in action, are shaped and contoured by bodily feelings of caring.

This basic mode of pre-reflective attention undergirds sense perception and plays a crucial role in gauging the relevance of environmental stimuli. At the moment when a subject sees a face, for example, she frames that face as friendly or hostile, and this value-apprehension is bound up with bodily feeling and an affective response (Schlimme, 2013, p. 107). The subject experiences whatever object she encounters as having a particular quality and as affording particular actions, and the process of focusing her attention and gauging which action-possibilities are relevant and inviting is guided and prescribed by that subject's specific pre-reflective interests and concerns. An affective frame thereby operates as an affective mode of presentation 'whereby significant events or states of affairs [are] disclosed through diffuse, holistic bodily feelings' (Slaby, 2008, p. 447); a particular bodily condition is lived through in the very process of gauging the relevance of things in one's environment. Such framing determines subjects' attentive focus, right down to the most fine-grained levels, and thereby fixes precisely which features of their surroundings become salient for them. Some affordances emerge into affective prominence, while others become unnoticeable, and this allows the agent to become attuned to the action-possibilities that matter to her. If subjects did not rely on affective framing, they would be faced with a potentially endless array of possible behavioural options.

Accounting for affordance 'perception' in terms of affective framing helps to make sense of how the demand character of an affordance is bestowed and highlights that this disclosure process is fundamentally bodily-affective. Which action-possibilities are framed as live options is partly a matter of what exists in the world and what an agent's bodily structure and capacities actually are, and also partly a matter of *what matters to him*. An agent's built-up affective frames have been shaped by his past learning and experience and help to determine 'what shows up as relevant for him and her in this specific situation' (Rietveld, 2012, p. 219). Specific affordances become solicitations against the backdrop of an agent's enduring concerns and overall perspective.

The claim that affordances and solicitations are *disclosed*, rather than simply perceived, is supported when we consider the phenomenon of mental affordances. McClelland (2019) rightly notes that there has been fairly little discussion of affordances for mental action, possibly due to a belief that there is no such thing as mental action. However, it would be difficult to deny that like bodily acts, cognitive operations frequently have an intentional or purposive structure. It is true that while bodily acts require overt movement, mental acts can be performed covertly; however, this hardly disqualifies them as actions. Covert mental acts include not just covert counterparts to overt action (such as inner speech), but also mental acts that may have no direct link to bodily action (such as abstract contemplation). In addition to experiencing possibilities to walk and kick, we experience possibilities to attend, imagine, and deliberate (McClelland, 2019, p. 170). And just as have a sense of ourselves as agents of bodily action, we have a sense of ourselves as agents of mental action. Objects and situations afford specific imaginative acts, and when we look at a visual scene, our attention is drawn to (and solicited by) some items over others.

McClelland notes that unlike bodily actions, many of our mental actions are not directed toward physical objects, but instead toward things in our mind. For example, an unprompted thought that I should train to become an astronaut might afford imagining what it would be like to do a spacewalk (p. 172). Mental images, in turn, can solicit thoughts or acts of reflection. However, this apparent fact that mental items can afford mental actions is at odds with the claim that affordances are perceptible properties (p. 172); after all, mental items are not perceived. Indeed, although the very title of Gibson's book (*The Ecological Approach to Visual Perception*) makes it clear that his primary focus is on sensory perception (and affordances that are visually perceivable), the disclosure of mental affordances often does not involve sensory perception. Again, it would be more accurate to say that possibilities for mental action are *disclosed*, and I have argued that the process whereby particular affordances are disclosed as inviting or demanding is fundamentally affective. In the case of thought, this means that which possibilities are appraised as relevant (and which possible acts of thinking actually are solicited) depends partly upon an agent's interests, concerns, and overall affective attunement. Affective framing allows for the sort of 'automatic proto-assessment' (McClelland, 2019, p. 166) whereby we select from a shortlist of the options for mental action that we feel, in-and-through our bodies, are more relevant or inviting. Only a fraction of possible thoughts will be solicited.

4.3. The Disclosure of Mental Affordances in Thought Insertion

I have argued that affective framing allows for selective attention and enables a subject to appraise the relevance of available affordances. Ordinarily, as we encounter the world, we gauge things as important or significant to us in relation to open possibilities, upcoming items of interest, or our goals for the future. Acting 'appropriately' and moving toward 'optimal grip' on available affordances 'requires that a complex and particular situational context is taken into account by the individual's motor intentional activity' (Rietveld, 2012, p. 215). Engaging effectively includes being responsive to opportunities for action offered by the material environment, to opportunities for social engagement, and to opportunities for various kinds of cognitive engagement, such as thinking. Adaptive agency then 'can be understood as an agent's having a grip on a rich, dynamic, and varied field of relevant affordances' (Ramírez-Vizcaya & Froese, 2019). Affective framing allows the agent to gauge what sorts of actions a situation calls for given her goals and interests, and to carry out fine-grained adjustments to her activity in order to achieve such goals.

As noted in the introduction, some theorists have looked to the notions of affordance and solicitation to make sense of the disruptions to agency that occur in various sorts of mental disorder. It appears that subjects suffering from various disorders often find it difficult to gain 'optimal grip' on available action-possibilities. Building upon these ideas, I argue that many mental disorders centrally involve some sort of disruption to agency and that such disruptions are fruitfully understood in terms of a diminished ability to engage effectively with available affordances. Crucially, the difficulty is not simply that someone's sense organs are malfunctioning; rather, the agent faces challenges with respect to gauging the relevance of available affordances and being solicited appropriately. A subject who engages inappropriately in a recurrent, patterned manner fails to gauge relevant action-possibilities and exhibits behaviour that is insufficiently grounded in her situation (de Haan, 2017). Disruptions to agency that occur in cases of depression, for example, can be understood in terms of a constriction of the affordance field, so that many available action-possibilities are experienced as closed off. In the case of obsessive-compulsive disorder (OCD), there is a narrowing and rigidification of the affordance space 'as the subject finds herself limited to one repetitive action, or one set of specific actions, and unable to move beyond that' (Gallagher, 2018, p. 723). Presented with a hammer, she is unable to refrain from picking it up and using it.

Disruptions to agency also can occur in the event that subjects are solicited by irrelevant affordances (Rietveld, 2012, p. 219). For example, consider the language disturbances sometimes found among subjects with schizophrenia. The ability to speak a sequence of words in a sentence is made possible by the ability to inhibit possible associations for each separate word. In order to inhibit the production of 'irrelevant' words in their speech, subjects must have some way of gauging which possible words are relevant given the situation at hand and what they wish to communicate. However, because subjects with schizophrenia are deficient in these inhibition mechanisms and find it difficult to focus their attention on salient contextual features, they are highly susceptible to irrelevant word associations. Consider the following example from Saks (2007): 'I'm just kidding around ... Kidding has to do with sheep.

I'm sheepish. Have you ever killed anyone? I've killed lots of people with my thoughts' (p. 215). In such instances of 'word salad', single elements of language lose their function as carriers of intentional meaning and stand out separately from the background (Fuchs & Rohricht, 2017, p. 132) of affective framing. The individual is solicited to speak by language affordances that are not relevant given her interests and the surrounding context. Is it possible to build upon these insights, together with this paper's earlier discussion of mental affordances and affective framing, to shed light on thought insertion?

Subjects with schizophrenia sometimes describe various thoughts as alien and not their own despite their recognition that these thoughts occur within their own minds. That is, they appear to think or believe particular things while claiming that these mental states are not theirs. Fernandez (2010) calls this 'awareness without ownership'. What makes thought insertion seem so bizarre is that it appears to involve 'the divorce between first-personal awareness of the content of a thought, and the possibility of self ascribing that thought' (Bortolotti & Broome, 2009, p. 214). This points to one way in which the disclosure of affordances can be pathological: Dings (2018) characterizes a solicitation's 'mineness' as 'the extent to which an affordance is experienced as being close to "who I am" or, more precisely, "who I take myself to be"' (Dings, 2018, p. 691.) While Dings maintains that this sense of 'mineness' is connected to the fact that the experienced solicitation fits into an individual's psychobiography or personal narrative, I believe that we also have a pre-reflective, pre-narrative sense of the extent to which a solicitation meshes with desires and interests. Via my account of affective framing, I have argued that our concerns and interests form a backdrop for sense perception and our appraisal of significance. Our various enduring projects and commitments involve built-up patterns of bodily responsiveness, felt concerns, and habits of attention (affective framings) that help to shape which action-possibilities become relevant for us. Mental actions, such as thoughts, are solicited against this backdrop of affective framing, (together with background perceptual and situational conditions, the subject's background beliefs and knowledge, and the content of her preceding thoughts). Because trains of thoughts ordinarily are focused and guided by built-up patterns of affective framing and bodily attunement, they do not seem to appear out nowhere.

In schizophrenia, however, the patterns of attention and bodily orientation that ordinarily serve as the backdrop for thought are severely attenuated. Even in the event that a subject recognizes some of these thoughts as being quite similar in content to those she ordinarily would be think, the thoughts are not guided and focused by way of affective framing. That is, because these solicited thoughts do not arise against the structure-giving backdrop of a person's desiderative feelings, her concerns about the future, or her current needs and desires, they seem alien and out of context; subjects attempt to *recontextualize* them by attributing them to some other source (Martin & Pacherie, 2013). Note that this is quite different from unbidden thoughts that a subject regards as undesirable or do not mesh with her self-conception. It also is distinct from the disruption to the disclosure of mental affordances that occurs in OCD. Subjects with OCD experience themselves as being unable to resist particular thought patterns and have a sense that these compulsive thoughts are forced upon them. However, although they take these thoughts to be in tension with their self-conception, they do not deny that the thoughts are their own. Inserted thoughts, in contrast, are not just unintended or forced, but also *alien*. This experience of alienness, and the subject's sense that the thoughts that have been solicited are not hers, results from attenuated affective framing. That is, what remains more intact in OCD, but is deficient in thought insertion, are built-up affective framings. Without some framework in which particular mental affordances can take on relevance and significance, the thoughts that occur come to be experienced as distant and object-like, divorced from one's sense of self. The experience of thinking may lose its intentionality, its desiderative tone, and its world-directedness. Once thinking loses its sense of naturalness and transparency, subjects may adopt an objectifying, hyper-reflective stance (Sass & Parnas, 2001), making even the most ordinary, mundane thoughts (e.g., 'It's about time for dinner') seem foreign.

4.4. Agency, Ownership, and Entitlement

Conceptualizing thought insertion in terms of a disruption to the disclosure of mental affordances (due to attenuated affective framing) allows us to accommodate some of the core insights of several prominent accounts of thought insertion.

First, my proposed account acknowledges that thought insertion involves a loss of a sense of agency. Along these lines, Stephens and Graham (2000) maintain that when a subject says that a thought that occurs in her mind is not her own, what she means is that she experiences that thought as '*subjectively*, but not *agentically*' her own' (p. 153). Ordinarily, mental affordances are elicited automatically and pre-reflectively, and we experience ourselves as being drawn or solicited to think particular thoughts in light of our surroundings and current mental states. When we experience affordances, we 'thereby implicitly experience ourselves as agents able to engage with our environment' (McClelland, 2019, p. 160). That is, our experience of ourselves as mental agents is reflected in the experienced field of mental affordances, and I have maintained that this field is carved out by way of bodily attunement and affective framing. But in cases of thought insertion, because this background of affective attunement is diminished, the thoughts that are solicited are not experienced as arising against this backdrop. As a result, the subject does not have a sense that she is the causal source of the thought.

Second, this account acknowledges that thought insertion also involves a disordered sense of ownership and that 'the subject affected by thought insertion is often radically alienated from the thought she reports' (Bortolotti & Broome, 2009, p. 208). I have proposed that these solicited thoughts lack a full sense of 'mineness' due to attenuated affective framing; this hypothesis is supported by the fact that subjects with schizophrenia commonly encounter a loss of bodily attunement and an eroded sense of self. Along these lines, Sass (2004) describes how subjects experience 'a fragmented and alienated sense of the lived body' and a loss of bodily transparency, which produces a sense of disharmony and artificiality that can disrupt the flow of motor activity (p. 134). The quasi-affective sensations and bodily states that subjects experience include 'sensations of movement or pulling or pressure inside the body or on its surfaces; electric or migrating sensations; awareness of kinaesthetic, vestibular, or thermic sensations; and sensations of diminution or enlargement of the body or its parts' (Sass, 2004, p. 135). Because their framework of bodily attunement is diminished, subjects begin to experience sensations that are dissociated from their ongoing sense of self, lack a sense of personal relevance, and are experienced as free-floating rather than being meaningfully directed toward the world. As a result of this 'ipseity disturbance' (Sass & Parnas, 2001) and loss of tacit self-awareness, subjects commonly report a sense of self-detachment, or of observing their own mental processes from the outside.

Bodily alienation and attenuated affective framing also contribute to an impaired capacity for practical and cognitive engagement with one's surroundings. Subjects with schizophrenia experience what some theorists have called 'unworlding': there is a sense of strangeness about external objects that ordinarily would seem familiar and subjects find themselves less capable of engaging with and 'grasping' their surroundings. Insignificant details of the surrounding environment become conspicuously salient, commonplace objects seem to lose their familiar meaning and recognizable significance, and the cognitive or perceptual world undergoes a kind of fragmentation. A chair, for example, might appear not as something to sit in, but rather as a 'thing' that has lost its function and meaning. Minkowski and Targowla (2001) describe this phenomenon as 'pragmatic weakening' and a loss of vital contact with reality.

An appeal to affordances helps to explain why these losses of 'grip' on both one's self and one's world go hand in hand. When affordances are disclosed, this disclosure process reveals something about the subject and her capabilities, in addition to revealing something about the environment. Due to the loss of bodily attunement associated with attenuated affective framing, subjects have an erroneous sense of their own abilities and capacities and their experience of affordances is distorted. The background bodily framework that ordinarily undergirds the sense of self and serves as the backdrop for cognitive and practical engagement is seriously attenuated. Objects and people in their surroundings seem to be stripped of their recognizable affordances, and subjects also lose their 'grip' on available possibilities for mental action. This conceptualization of thought insertion, as one of several disownership symptoms associated with schizophrenia, highlights how the disclosure process (whereby affordances are framed as relevant and inviting) has been disrupted.

Third, an appeal to affordances and affective framing helps to explain why subjects lack a sense of entitlement to the thoughts in question (Bortolotti & Broome, 2009), do not experience being committed to them (Fernandez, 2010), and do not endorse their content. Note that in Stephens' and Graham's account, a person denies that she is the agent of a thought because she finds she cannot explain its occurrence in terms of her theory or conception of her intentional psychology (Stephens & Graham, 2000, p. 162). In cases where a subject finds the thoughts inexplicable by reference to her self-conception, she is unlikely to regard them as agentically her own. Pointing to attenuated affective framing allows us to make sense of this. Because the disclosure of affordances and solicitations does not take place against the backdrop of affective framing, the relevant thoughts seem not to be attributable to her. However, my proposed account is far less intellectualistic. It says that prior to a subject's considering whether thoughts conform to her 'theory' of what she is like (Stephens & Graham, 2000, p. 163) and what she is likely to do, she has some basic, pre-reflective sense of whether these thoughts 'fit' with her surroundings and with the rest of her beliefs, desires, interests, and concerns. I have suggested that affective framing provides the backdrop for the disclosure of mental affordances; when this backdrop is attenuated, the thoughts that are solicited seem to come out of nowhere.

Fourth, my proposed account explains why subjects with schizophrenia encounter difficulties with affordance engagement across a wide range of domains. This includes selective attention deficits that impact their ability to process linguistic stimuli, remember events, engage interpersonally with others, and exhibit executive control. For example, some subjects experience deficits in perceptual grouping, so that objects do not stand together in an overall context and instead appear as meaningless details. They also have difficulty excluding distracting visual, auditory, and tactile input when trying to concentrate on selected parts of the environment (Maher, 2003, p. 14). All these tasks require the inhibition of irrelevant information and the ability to focus one's attention on relevant considerations. However, among subjects with schizophrenia, there is a notable discrepancy between the amount of attention something deserves and the amount that it receives. Like bodily alienation, disturbed self-experience, and 'unworlding', thought insertion is bound up with an impaired ability to appreciate salience.

4.5. Conclusion

I have argued that thought insertion should be understood in terms of a disruption to the disclosure of mental affordances that results from attenuated affective framing. Subjects find it difficult to focus their attention on what matters and to disregard considerations or details that are irrelevant or unimportant. Because things in both their inner and outer world are no longer apprehended against the backdrop of desiderative bodily feelings, the cognitive or perceptual world undergoes a certain fragmentation; even possibilities for thought begin to lack recognizable significance and relevance. My proposed account makes sense of how thought insertion involves a diminished sense of agency and ownership, and also links it together with experiences of bodily alienation and 'unworlding'. If this account is roughly correct, then the loss of 'grip' encountered by many subjects with schizophrenia reflects a general disruption to selective attention and an impaired ability to gauge the relevance of action-possibilities. Note that this account resonates with the 'aberrant salience hypothesis' (Kapur, 2003), according to which a dopaminergic dysfunction causes insignificant details of one's environment to become salient and captivate attention. However, in line with the enactivist approach, my proposed account emphasizes the role of the *whole living body* in gauging salience; and as I have shown, the notion that there is a disruption to the disclosure of affordances helps us to make sense of many of the characteristic symptoms of schizophrenia.

References

Bortolotti, L., & Broome, M. (2009). A role for ownership and authorship in the analysis of thought insertion. *Phenomenology and the Cognitive Sciences, 8*(2), 205–224.

de Haan, S. (2017). The existential framework in psychiatry. *Mental Health, Religion, and Culture, 20*(6), 528–535.

de Haan, S., Rietveld, E., Stokhof, M., & Denys, D. (2013). The phenomenology of deep brain stimulation-induced changes in obsessive-compulsive disorder patients: An enactive affordance-based model. *Frontiers in Human Neuroscience, 7*, 1–14.

Dings, R. (2018). Understanding phenomenological differences in how affordances solicit action. An exploration. *Phenomenology and the Cognitive Sciences, 17*(4), 681–699.

Fernandez, J. (2010). Thought insertion and self-knowledge. *Mind & Language, 25*(1), 66–88.

Fuchs, T., & Rohricht, F. (2017). Schizophrenia and intersubjectivity: An embodied and enactive approach to psychopathology and psychotherapy. *Philosophy, Psychiatry, and Psychology, 24*(2), 127–142.

Gallagher, S. (2018). The therapeutic reconstruction of affordances. *Res Philosophica, 95*(4), 719–736.

Gibson, J. J. (1979). *The Ecological Approach to Visual Perception*. Boston, MA: Houghton Mifflin.

Hutto, D., & Myin, E. (2012). *Radicalizing Enactivism: Basic Minds Without Content*. Cambridge, MA: MIT Press.

Kapur, S. (2003). Psychosis as a state of aberrant salience: A framework linking biology, phenomenology, and pharmacology in schizophrenia. *American Journal of Psychiatry, 160*(1), 13–23.

Koffka, K. (1935). *Principles of Gestalt Psychology*. New York: Harcourt Brace.

Lewin, K. (1936). *Principles of Topological Psychology*. New York: McGraw-Hill.

Maher, B. (2003). Schizophrenia, aberrant utterance, and delusions of control: The disconnection of speech and thought, and the connection of experience and belief. *Mind and Language, 18*(1), 1–22.

Martin, J., & Pacherie, E. (2013). Out of nowhere: Thought insertion, ownership, and context-integration. *Consciousness and Cognition, 22*, 111–222.

McClelland, T. (2019). Representing our options: The perception of affordances for bodily and mental action. *Journal of Consciousness Studies, 26*(3–4),155–180.

Minkowski, E., & Targowla, R. (2001). A contribution to the study of autism: The interrogative attitude. *Philosophy, Psychiatry, and Psychology, 8*(4), 271–278.

Ramírez-Vizcaya, S., & Froese, T. (2019). The enactive approach to habits: New concepts for the cognitive science of bad habits and addiction. *Frontiers in Psychology, 10*, 301.

Ramstead, M., Veissiere, S., & Kirmayer, L. (2016). Cultural affordances: Scaffolding local worlds through shared intentionality and regimes of attention. *Frontiers in Psychology, 7*, 1090.

Rietveld, E. (2012). Bodily intentionality and social affordances in context. In F. Paglieri (Ed.), *Consciousness in Interaction: The Role of the Natural and Social Context in Shaping Consciousness* (pp. 207–226). Amsterdam, Netherlands: John Benjamins Publishing.

Rietveld, E., & Kiverstein, J. (2014). A rich landscape of affordances. *Ecological Psychology, 26*, 325–352.

Saks, E. (2007). *The Center Cannot Hold: My Journey Through Madness*. New York: Hachette Books.

Sass, L. (2004). Affectivity in schizophrenia: A phenomenological view. *Journal of Consciousness Studies, 11*(10–11), 127–147.

Sass, L., & Parnas, J. (2001). Phenomenology of self-disturbances in schizophrenia: Some research findings and directions. *Philosophy, Psychiatry, and Psychology*, 8(4), 347–356.
Scarantino, A. (2003). Affordances explained. *Philosophy of Science*, 70(5), 949–961.
Schlimme, J. (2013). Depressive habituality and altered valuings: The phenomenology of depressed mental life. *Journal of Phenomenological Psychology*, 44, 92–118.
Slaby, J. (2008). Affective intentionality and the feeling body. *Phenomenology and the Cognitive Sciences*, 7, 429–444.
Stephens, G.L., & Graham, G. (2000). *When Self-consciousness Breaks: Alien Voices and Inserted Thoughts*. Cambridge, MA: MIT Press.
Thompson, E. (2007). *Mind in Life: Biology, Phenomenology, and the Sciences of the Mind*. Cambridge, MA: Belknap Press.
Varela, F., Thompson, E., & Rosch, E. (1991). *The Embodied Mind: Cognitive Science and Human Experience*. Cambridge, MA: MIT Press.

5
Soundless Voices and Inserted Thoughts

What Grounds the Distinction?

Sam Wilkinson

5.1. Introduction

Two primary symptoms associated with diagnoses of schizophrenia are auditory-verbal hallucinations (a.k.a. hearing voices), on the one hand, and inserted thoughts (sometimes referred to as delusions of thought insertion) on the other. Although some theorists are tempted to say that these are fundamentally the same thing (e.g., Frith 1992), to many this does not seem plausible—after all, one is apparently clearly auditory, whereas the other is not.[1] Nevertheless, there is an increasing recognition of the existence, and moderate prevalence, of voice-hearing experiences that are described as *soundless voices* (e.g., Stephens & Graham, 2000; Woods et al., 2015, Ratcliffe & Wilkinson, 2016; Wilkinson, 2019). In contrast to voice hearing that is experienced as auditory, soundless voices have been deemed by several theorists (e.g., Stephens & Graham, 2000; Langland-Hassan, 2008; Wu, 2012; Ratcliffe & Wilkinson, 2015) to be the same phenomenon as thought insertion, simply described by the experiencing individual in a different way. For example, consider this quote from Wu (2012, p. 90, fn.5): 'I am inclined to say that hallucinations are always perceptual (e.g., auditory) states and that with soundless voices, we have an intrusive *thought* phenomenon.' Similar statements are made by Stephens and Graham (2000, pp. 99–100), and several others.

The idea that the same phenomenon might be described differently by different individuals carries with it important insights. First of all, language is a relatively blunt instrument to capture experience at the best of times, and it is hampered still further when the experiences are strange, unfamiliar, and there is a deep gap in common-ground with the interlocutor (see Deamer,

---

[1] See Jones (2010) and Wilkinson (2014), for the suggestion that different subtypes may involve different mechanisms.

2022). On such a view, inserted thoughts and soundless voices are simply different attempts to grapple with a hard-to-express unfamiliarity (Ratcliffe & Wilkinson, 2015; Ratcliffe, 2017).[2] My aim in this paper is not to criticize the position that inserted thoughts and soundless voices are the same phenomenon. I think that this holds important insights. However, I think there is still something to be gained from trying to clarify this claim as much as possible, and to examine precisely in what sense it might be true. In particular, my central question in this paper is as follows:

Suppose that inserted thoughts and soundless voices are the same phenomenon described differently; what is it about the phenomenon that makes an individual describe it in one way as opposed to another? One answer might be that there are no clear patterns to be observed; it's simply different interpretative styles that inevitably vary across individuals. These in turn could be affected by cultural factors (see, e.g., Luhrmann et al., 2015), or even something as contingent as their first interactions with clinicians or clinical narratives, that might provide them with the expressive tools for experiences that that are otherwise very hard to describe. This could be the correct answer, and I suspect that, though it is not (to my knowledge) the answer explicitly given, it is what many of these theorists would accept or assume. This also explains why they wouldn't ask themselves my central question in the first place, since it doesn't have an interesting answer. In spite of this, I think it is worth asking ourselves if there are detectable reasons for reporting something as a voice rather than a thought or *vice versa*. These would, I suggest, be in addition to the aforementioned socio-cultural factors.

I proceed as follows. I start by disambiguating the claim that they are 'the same phenomenon'. This could be interpreted as a mechanistic claim or an experiential claim. The mechanistic claim, though more plausible, is less interesting for our purposes here. After all, we are interested in why individuals describe experiences in one way rather than another. As a result, I go on to dissect the experiential reading and isolate three different senses in which we

---

[2] Other than the expressive inadequacies of language, there are more subtle distortions that arise from verbal report (not to mention the repetition, over and over, of these reports in clinical literature (Ratcliffe & Wilkinson, 2015)). To illustrate this, consider the following observation. Soundless voices are often deemed experiential, whereas thought insertion, though also, at heart, experiential is often deemed to be delusional (unlike soundless voices). The very idea that someone could put thoughts into my head is deemed so farfetched as to be delusional, whereas hearing voices is less of an infringement of the laws of consensus reality—even if they are soundless. And yet these could be two different ways of reporting on exactly the same phenomenon. To develop this further, note how the statement 'I am hearing a soundless voice' is a claim about experience, whereas 'Someone is putting thoughts into my head' is not. And so, whereas both can be asserted with full doxastic force, the experiential framing of the former provides a sort of buffer, an illusory doxastic distancing. Again, this is just a distortion in how they are reported: both could be uttered in the context of doxastic responses to anomalous experiences that are taken at face value.

might talk of the same (or similar/different) experience. I then make some general observations about the phenomenology of thinking, and then enumerate different options for what might lead someone to report something in terms of a voice rather than a thought. Finally, I gesture towards future directions for thinking about underlying mechanisms that may account for some of these differences.

5.2. Disambiguating the Sameness Claim

To say that they are 'the same phenomenon' can be interpreted in two quite different ways, namely, either as mechanistic sameness, or experiential sameness. Let's examine these more closely.

5.2.1. Mechanistic sameness

The 'same phenomenon' could simply mean that the same kind of thing is going on, mechanistically speaking. So, for example, they might both involve mechanisms that generate imagery or memories, or they may involve episodes of inner speech that have been misattributed in some way. Whatever your preferred account of voices hearing, most relevantly soundless voices, the basic idea would be that the same applies to thought insertion.

In Wilkinson (2014), I proposed that there are at least three subtypes that can be understood within the predictive processing framework, namely, hypervigilance, memory-based, and inner speech-based hallucinations. These are three different phenomena in the mechanistic sense. Indeed, any superficial and coarse-grained experiential similarity there might be (leading to all three being called 'hearing voices') is masking deep and important underlying differences. On closer inspection, the different subtypes yield (and are hypothesized in response to) more fine-grained experiential differences. For example, memory-based hallucinations are more likely to feature content that is directly related to past events, inner-speech-based subtypes are more likely to be reported as soundless, and so on. Interestingly, misattributed inner speech is the candidate mechanism that is most commonly taken to explain both soundless voices and inserted thoughts (*locus classicus*, Frith, 1992).

In what follows, I'll assume that the mechanism of interest is misattributed inner speech, and it is this subtype that is a plausible candidate as an account of both phenomena.

5.2.2. Experiential sameness

Having said this, even within one broad, mechanistic subtype, there may be experiential differences. As a result, to interpret 'the same phenomenon' experientially is a stronger claim. The claim that both soundless voices and inserted thoughts both implicate inner speech is interesting, and relatively plausible, but it does not amount to the claim that they are the same experiences. Just as your mental imagery, or episodic memories can vary enormously from instance to instance, so can your inner speech (McCarthy-Jones & Fernyhough, 2011).

To say that soundless voices and inserted thoughts are reported in response to the same experience is to say that they are the same from the first-person perspective, that undergoing them is the same. But what does this mean?

5.3. Disambiguating Experiential Sameness

When we talk about experiential sameness (or indeed similarity, or difference) we might be talking about three quite different things, what I will here call, narrow, moderate, and broad senses of experiences.

5.3.1. The narrow sense

When we say that two experiences are the same, similar, or different, we might be talking about the de-contextualized sensory features. For a visual experience, for example, this would be the 'mental paint' so to speak, and you would get analogues in other sensory modalities, most relevantly for our purposes, the auditory qualitative features of loudness, pitch, and timbre. In this sense, you might say that inserted thoughts and soundless voices are the same in that they are both soundless. But this seems to point to a lack of sensory qualities; it tells us what they are not, not what they are. What qualities can be pointed to in order to explain what these experiences *are* like?

5.3.2. The intermediate sense

The intermediate sense goes beyond the sensory, but remains decontextualized. It is about the here-and-now, but extends beyond the sensory to include emotional and affective aspects of experiences, and (although its existence as a *sui generis* form of phenomenology is highly contested (see Bayne & Montague, 2011)), cognitive phenomenology.

Of course, one may question whether the time-slice considerations of experience, as in the narrow and intermediate senses are actually intelligible. Nevertheless, even from this position, we can in principle talk about two experiences and talk about their similarities and differences in these narrow and intermediate senses. We might, for example, compare two voice-like experiences and note, for example, that one was loud, aggressive, and accompanied by a sense of fear, while the other was soundless, gentle, and accompanied by a sense of comfort. Notice that, though narrow and decontextualized, this is still much broader than the merely sensory.

5.3.3. The broad sense

As phenomenologists have always (i.e., since Husserl founded the discipline) been at pains to point out, experience doesn't occur in a vacuum, but as part of the dynamic flow of life. But can these contextual factors play a constitutive (rather than merely causal role) in making the experience the experience that it is? I think there are good reasons for thinking that this is the case.

Let us stipulate that there are two qualitatively identical experiences of fear, except that one is in the context of watching a horror movie, whereas the other, hits you from nowhere, while you are cleaning your teeth. The latter, I suggest, would be far more troubling. We don't only experience things, react to things, we also have expectations about our experiences of and reactions to things. Ultimately, experiences can be the same (narrow/intermediate sense) and yet different (broad sense) to the extent that they fit or fail to fit into the coherent, smooth flow of life, and the overarching contexts in which they make sense. This would clearly apply to episodes of inner speech and their experiential accompaniments.

This broader notion goes beyond the qualitative features of the here-and-now and includes not only relatively short-term retention and protension (see Miller, 1984 on Husserl's phenomenology of time consciousness), but also a longer-term and overarching sense of coherence, of what one is currently in the process of doing (relaxing, getting ready for bed, mid-way through a football match, etc.).

5.4. The Phenomenology of (What We Call) Thinking

What we are interested in here is whether there are features of experiences (in all three senses: narrow, intermediate, and broad) that lend themselves to being described in terms of thoughts rather than in terms of voices.

In order to ascertain this, we need to reflect first, not so much on what thinking is per se (the word gets used in so many different ways for different kinds of thing) but on what makes particular experiences encourage us, as those who have them, to call them episodes of thinking.

Let us examine explicitly verbal thinking. This is overwhelmingly thought to be, if not co-extensive with inner speech, at least conducted *in* it, or engaged in *with* it. (Notice that this is not wedded to the claim that all thinking involves inner speech, only that some of it does.) With this in mind, our question is: Suppose you experience an episode of inner speech. What is likely to make you call that thinking?

A canonical example of what we call thinking involves being engaged in inner speech acts, not mere acts of inner speaking (this distinction between 'inner speech acts' and 'mere acts of inner speaking' I borrow from Roessler 2016). This becomes clear when we consider the sorts of episodes of inner speech that emphatically do not count as thinking. For example, you might count to ten in your head, or engage in mental rehearsal of speech, or silent reading. These are all mere acts of inner speaking, rather than inner speech acts. What is the difference? Well, inner speech acts are authentic expressions of one's state of mind. You assert, 'That's nice' in inner speech because you've judged something to be nice, you ask yourself, 'What did I come upstairs for?' because you are genuinely trying to remember what you came upstairs for. With a mere act of inner speech, what you say is not an expression of your state of mind, and relevant variations in the latter do not entail variations in the former. When you rehearse in your head, reprising King Lear, 'How sharper than a serpent's tooth it is to have a thankless child!' you are not expressing your state of mind.

One interesting feature of these canonical examples of linguistic thought, of inner speech acts, is that they are world-directed, and so often go unnoticed. However, sometimes when you reflect on your thinking, it becomes very explicit that you are saying something in inner speech: you become aware of the exact words that you are using in thought, you may even become aware of specific patterns of stress in your conscious thinking ('Why did *she* say that?' and 'Why did she say *that*?' are different thoughts, the former expressing surprise at the sayer, the latter at what was said).

I don't think that this is a 'refrigerator light' phenomenon, namely, that the thinking is in fact non-linguistic, but only gets put into language on reflection (by analogy, you might erroneously think that the light in the fridge is on even when the door is closed). I think a more plausible account of this is simply the transparency and absorption of world-directed activity. This kind of absorption has been noted by thinkers in both Anglo-American and Continental traditions. Consider this quote from Gilbert Ryle:

> Of course an agent can, from time to time, if he is prompted to do so, announce to himself or the world 'Hallo, here I am whistling "Home Sweet Home".' His ability to do so is part of what is meant by saying that he is in that particular frame of mind that we call 'being alive to what he is doing'. But not only is his actually making such announcements not entailed by the fact that he is concentrating on whistling this tune, but his concentration would be broken each time he produced such a commentary. (Ryle, 1949, p. 159)

A very similar point is made by Jean-Paul Sartre:

> If I count the cigarettes in that case [...] It is very possible that I have no positional consciousness of counting them. Then I do not know myself as counting. Yet at the moment when these cigarettes are revealed to me as a dozen, I have a non-thetic consciousness of my adding activity. If anyone questioned me, indeed, if anyone should ask, 'What are you doing there?' I should reply at once, 'I am counting'. (Sartre, 1943/2013, pp. 19–20)

By analogy, I think in language through my inner speech acts, even though I may only become aware of that when I am prompted to reflect on it. Just as Ryle's whistling, or Sartre's counting, is not brought into existence by the reflective act, it was there all along, the same goes for my inner speech acts, my act of linguistic thinking.

And so, typical examples of inner speech that we naturally call thinking are internalized versions of what Ryle calls 'unstudied utterances': 'That's a nice car!', 'What's for lunch?', 'That can't be right', and so on. They are, as it were, explicit and authentic expressions of states of mind. Interestingly they sometimes spill out into overt private speech (where we speak out loud to ourselves). In such situations, I would say, we are quite literally thinking out loud (most people seem to think that 'thinking out loud' is non-literal, but I think we learn a lot from thinking of it as entirely literal).

To clarify, I am perfectly happy to accept that there are many forms of imagistic, spatial, non-linguistic thinking. All I am saying is that there are some forms of linguistic thinking, and that this occurs in inner speech. If you grant me this, all I am saying is that reflecting on why some inner speech intuitively counts as thinking and other inner speech does not, may shed light on the difference between inserted thoughts and soundless voices. In particular, one might hypothesize that mere acts of inner speech are less likely to be described as thoughts, and hence more likely to be described as voices. Having said that, inner speech acts may well be described in either way. So the question arises, within this category of inner speech acts, are there other features that might serve as grounds for the distinction?

5.5. Candidate Grounds for the Voice vs. Thought Distinction

In the narrow, intermediate, or broad sense, what differences might there be in two experiences of inner speech acts that could serve as grounds from one being described as an inserted thought, while the other might be described as a soundless voice? Let's run through some options. None of these are likely to be law-like regularities: there will be exceptions. What we are looking for instead are the sorts of considerations that may bias reports in one direction over another. Note also that I am listing these in an exploratory manner. Some of these we will discard as candidates, but that we end up doing so is interesting in itself.

5.5.1. Linguistic vs. Imagistic experiences

Before looking at clear examples of inner speech acts, I'd like to address a very obvious dimension of phenomenological difference. There are well-documented differences in people's 'inner lives'. Some individuals have lots of inner speech, others less so (McCarthy-Jones & Fernyhough, 2011). Some people report 'thinking in language' while others report 'thinking in pictures'. Now, pictures are unlikely to be reported as voices, but they might be reported as thoughts. We see this in one of the stock examples of thought insertion (that arguably gets over-used):

> I look out of the window and I think that the garden looks nice and the grass looks cool, but the thoughts of Eamonn Andrews come into my mind. There are no other

thoughts there, only his … He treats my mind like a screen and flashes his thoughts into it like you flash a picture. (Mellor, 1970, p. 17)

Contrast this with the following example of soundless voices:

It's hard to describe how I could 'hear' a voice that wasn't auditory; but the words used and the emotions they contained (hatred and disgust) were completely clear, distinct and unmistakeable, maybe even more so that if I had heard them aurally. (Ratcliffe & Wilkinson, 2016, p. 53)

Of course, this goes some way towards explaining why certain non-linguistic thoughts aren't reported as voices, because they can't be. What about linguistic instances of inserted thoughts? In a rich source of first-person reports, Rachel Gunn (2016) presents material from various online forums.

Yes, I get thought insertion all the time. [...] I get thoughts directly from the government, and sometimes even alien beings from another world. There were times that it was very severe. Sometimes it is scary because they *tell me things and what to do*. (Gunn, 2016, p. 562, emphasis added)

Here is another fascinating example:

I truly do have unwanted thoughts that are forced into my head from somewhere [...] I mean I will have a thought saying my grandmother is a bitch. I would never ever think of my grandmother as a bitch. She is one of the greatest women I know and I adore her. (ibid., p. 563)

Note the turn of phrase: 'I will have a thought *saying*'. Is this literal, linguistic saying, or is it a way of capturing content after the fact that was initially experienced non-linguistically? We may never know, but let's suppose that it's the former. If that is correct, and there are linguistic forms of thought insertion, why might they be reported as thoughts that are inserted, rather than as silent voices that are 'heard'? We clearly need to appeal to different considerations, beyond linguistic vs. non-linguistic, in order to ground the distinction.

5.5.2. Type of speech act

As we've seen, when you think in language, in inner speech, you don't simply experience a string of words in your head: they are speech acts, acts of wondering, questioning, asserting, and so on. Might certain speech acts lend themselves to being described as thoughts, while others as voices?

This doesn't seem to clearly distinguish voices and thoughts. As we've just seen, inserted thoughts can be reported for assertions ('My grandmother is a bitch') and commands ('they tell me what to do'). There are reports of soundless voices making assertions and commands, too.

5.5.3. Direct vs. indirect mode of address

Episodes of inner speech, like speech in general, can have direct or indirect modes of address, which is to say that they can be directly, explicitly directed at the recipient ('I'm such an idiot!'/'You can do it!'/'What did I come upstairs for?'), or they can be indirectly directed ('That's nice'), where it is for the benefit of the recipient without being explicitly directed at them.[3]

The rule doesn't seem to be strict, but one might think that, all other things being equal, a direct mode of address is more likely to be interpreted as a voice ('Do this!', 'Your granny is a bitch!'), whereas an indirect mode of address is more likely to be interpreted as a thought ('The grass looks nice'/'Granny is a bitch').

5.5.4. Transparency/opacity

If you think of language as a lens through which the world is presented, you can either experience it as transparent, something you see through to the world, or you can experience the language as opaque, where you focus on the words themselves.

Again, it seems like a transparent episode of inner speech is more likely to be described as thought-like (the focus is on what you came upstairs for, or whether Granny is a bitch, not on the words that were spoken), whereas an opaque episode of inner speech is more likely to be described as a voice (recall: 'the words used, and the emotions they contained' (Ratcliffe & Wilkinson, 2016, p. 53)).

---

[3] Notice how explicitly self-directed speech can be either in the first or second person: 'I can do it!' vs. 'You can do it!'

5.5.5. Contextual coherence

Related to this notion of transparency, is the notion of contextual coherence. This is also where the broad notion of experiential sameness/similarity becomes especially relevant. Some episodes of inner speech are coherent with context, while others are not. What do we mean by context? This can be what I am doing, perceiving etc. but it can also be how I feel, as well as the kind of person that I am. The latter is sometimes treated separately as 'egodystonic' thinking, but my self-conception can also be seen simply as a more long-term context.

To see the incoherence of short-term context, consider the following quote:

> Often, in a quiet place, and all the time at night when I am alone, I experience thoughts that do not 'feel' like my own. It's like they come out of a part of my brain that is not the part that controls my 'normal' thoughts and into my awareness from there. It is hard to describe. These 'false thoughts' are usually about random subject matter and usually make little sense, but are extremely distracting. (Gunn, 2016, p. 562)

As for egodystonic thinking, recall: 'I would never ever think of my grandmother as a bitch.' What we seem to have heard is an intrusive thought that is disowned, and hence attributed to an external source. What does this have to do with voices? Well, a voice is often experienced as another agent speaking (represented with varying degrees of richness (see Wilkinson & Bell, 2016)), and so the idea that the voice (the agent behind the voice) might say something that is incongruent, or not in keeping with one's self-image wouldn't come as a surprise. Of course the voice wouldn't say something that is in keeping with my personality, because it's not me. In contrast, it seems like an inserted thought is sometimes experienced as a thought, and subsequently (even if immediately) disowned. Hearing a voice (soundless or otherwise), in contrast, might not need to be disowned, because it was never 'owned' in the first place.

5.5.6. Agentive representation

Does more agency increase likelihood of something being deemed a voice? (Note, as Wilkinson and Krueger (2022) point out, 'a voice' sometimes means an agent, rather than an experience, auditory or otherwise, as in the question,

'How many voices do you hear?') Perhaps, but, in two stock examples of thought insertion (from Frith (1992) and Mellor (1970)), there is very specific agentive attribution. It's not simply: 'Feels weird. Not me.' Rather it's: 'It's this guy, Chris' (Frith, 1992, p. 66), or 'The thoughts of Eamon Andrews' (Mellor, 1970, p.17). However, in many less well-known examples, this is not the case. Indeed, consider this example from Gunn where there is an explicit awareness of a lack of agentive attribution:

> I feel as though some thoughts that pop up in my mind are definitely not mine, and that they are being put there by someone else but I can't identify who. Is it still regarded as thought insertion if you don't know who is doing the inserting? (Gunn, 2016, p. 563)

Having said this, as Wilkinson and Bell (2016) point out, there is huge amount of variety among voices in terms of agency attribution/representation: some are only very sparsely represented. Perhaps, however, the sparsely represented ones that are described as hearing voices are an auditory subtype. Whether a soundless voice that wasn't experienced as agentive would be called a voice, rather than a thought, is something potentially worth exploring.

5.5.7. Condensation vs. expansion

Although we have encountered examples of inserted thoughts that seem linguistic, that involve thoughts 'saying something', that doesn't necessarily mean that there is a focus on the exact words used. In contrast, soundless voices seem to involve knowledge of the exact words used. Indeed in Wilkinson (2019), I argued that one way of understanding soundless voices was that certain kinds of information were being received in the absence of the kinds of information that typically accompany them. More precisely, this means that those who hear soundless voices can typically answer the question 'What words were used?', but not questions about loudness, pitch, and timbre (somewhat analogous to how in monochromatic vision, you can answer questions about shape and shade, but not colour).

Now, one hypothesis might be that inserted thoughts are like soundless voices, but stripped down still further: you can't say (or at least didn't experience) the exact words used, but you do know the exact content conveyed. So here you might ask: Did the thought 'say', 'Your grandmother is a bitch', 'Your granny is a bitch' or 'My granny is a bitch', or what exactly? If this hypothesis is correct, the person might say: it's indeterminate, at least in terms of what

I experienced, but I knew the exact content, I knew what was being said and that it was about that individual that I call 'granny'.

But would this not go against the idea that inner speech is involved in both soundless voices and inserted thoughts? Surely on this account it's only plausible as an account of the former. Well, not if, like Fernyhough (2004), you are a Vygotskian, because then you postulate varying degrees of 'condensation' and 'expansion' for inner speech.

To explain this, all-too-briefly, Vygotsky thought that inner speech is the end point in a developmental trajectory that starts with the capacity for social speech, for external dialogue. Then, what emerges is overt private speech, namely, speech that is only produced for the benefit of the speaker (e.g., for the purposes of reasoning, attentional focus, emotional regulation, etc.). Then, inhibitory capacities develop, and it becomes 'internalized', first in fully expanded form, and then becomes condensed. This 'condensation' occurs since, as individuals become skilled at, and accustomed to, inner speaking, they can leave parts of the inner speech out (phonology, syntax, etc.) and getting ever closer to what Vygotsky called 'thinking in pure meanings' (Vygotsky, 1934).[4] This is represented in the following diagram (Fig. 5.1) from Fernyhough (2004).

In Fernyhough's (2004) model, the default form of adult inner speech is condensed: it gets expanded in conditions of stress or cognitive load. An interesting upshot of this might be that, if we think of soundless voices in terms of expanded inner speech, and inserted thoughts in terms of condensed inner speech, soundless voices could tend to be experienced in conditions of relative stress or cognitive load, compared to inserted thoughts, which are condensed. Either way, the hypothesis that reports of soundless voices correspond to experience of inner speech that are more 'expanded' and that reports of thought insertion correspond to the more condensed variety, is worth considering. Furthermore, reflection on what tends to lead to expansion and condensation in these contexts, may prove illuminating.

5.5.8. Taking stock

The picture we are left with is (perhaps inevitably) messy. There are various factors that may play roles, but none are decisive. At best, there are various features that constrain and bias rather than dictate, and they can combine in various ways, tipping the interpretative scales one way of the other. Granted,

---

[4] There is debate among those who broadly accept the Vygotskian story, whether 'thinking in pure meanings' is ever really achievable.

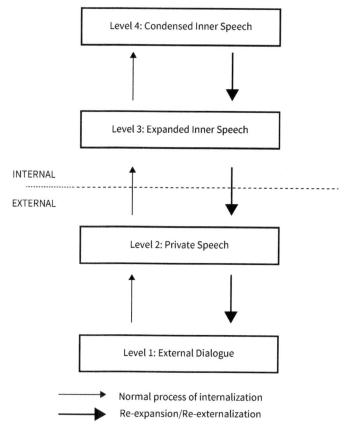

Figure 5.1 Stages of internalization.

there are some things that you can't readily describe as voices, others that you can't describe as thoughts, but many appear in the middle as describable as both. This is in keeping with Humpston and Broome (2016) who claim that there is a spectrum between soundless voices and inserted thoughts. It is also very much in keeping with Ratcliffe's (2017) insight that what we often call hallucinations are not, as mainstream assumptions suggest, unambiguous sensory-perceptual states, but are rather unfamiliar intentional states, in-between perceiving and thinking.

5.6. Clues About Underlying Mechanisms?

We put questions about underlying mechanisms to one side, and, for the sake of argument, accepted the hypothesis that both soundless voices and inserted thoughts involve misattributed inner speech. However, the potential experiential differences that we have explored may provide more fine-grained clues about differences in underlying mechanism. We can even stick with the inner speech-based hypothesis, while making more fine-grained predictions about why an individual might report a soundless voice rather than an inserted thought. In the best-case scenario, this may inform differential diagnosis and treatment pathways. So, for example, if we felt that contextual issues were important, we might hypothesize issues with context-integration and binding (Martin & Pacherie, 2013). If we think that agentive representation is an important factor, we might look at hyperactive agency attributions (Raihani & Bell, 2017). This is all extremely speculative and preliminary, but the idea would be to move from the observation of subtle experiential in these differences to the question: Why might they be there, mechanistically speaking?

5.7. Summary and Conclusion

In this paper I have explored potential differences in the experiences that get respectively called inserted thoughts and soundless voices. While accepting the claim of other theorists that these two experiences may be the same, I started by disambiguating three senses of sameness of experience. First, there is the narrow sense of the intrinsic qualitative features of the core aspects of the experience. Second, there is the intermediate sense that includes other peripheral phenomenological accompaniments, such as emotional or interpretative features. Third, there is the broad and most demanding sense, which includes contextual features: how that experience, in the first and second sense, fits into the general flow of life. This includes what is currently going on, what you are currently in the business of doing, but also more long-term and stable contextual features such as your own self-image. An experience can be in keeping, disruptive, and many things besides.

For two experiences to be the same experience in all three senses, then, is setting the bar very high. The two experiences would need to have the same intrinsic features, accompanying features and contextual features. Of course, claims of 'sameness' can be stripped back to claims of similarity: they will be similar to the extent that they share these features. This disambiguation frees up the possibility that, in spite of a core similarity between experiences that are reported as inserted thoughts and soundless voices, there is scope for many dimensions of difference, some of which may shed light on why they are reported in one way or the other. I explored the following, which I do not take to be exhaustive: whether the experience is linguistic or imagistic; the type of speech act; the mode of address; the transparency or opacity of the experience; contextual coherence; degree and agentive representation; and the degree of 'condensation' or 'expansion' of the inner speech experience. It has been very exploratory and speculative, but I hope at least to have shown how digging deeper into these more fine-grained and nuanced distinctions can yield clues for future investigation.

References

Bayne, T. & Montague, M. (eds.) (2011). *Cognitive Phenomenology*. Oxford: Oxford University Press UK.

Clark, A. (1996). Linguistic anchors in the sea of thought? *Pragmatics and Cognition*, 4(1), 93–103.

Deamer, F. (2022). Bridging the gap in common ground when talking about voices. In A. Woods, B. Alderson-Day, & C. Fernyhough (Eds.), *Voices in Psychosis: Interdisciplinary Perspectives*. Oxford: Oxford University Press.

Fernyhough C. (2004). Alien voices and inner dialogue: Towards a developmental account of auditory verbal hallucinations. *New Ideas in Psychology*, 22, 49–68.

Frith, C. (1992). *The Cognitive Neuropsychology of Schizophrenia*. London: Psychology Press.

Gunn, R. (2016). On thought insertion. *Review of Philosophy and Psychology*, 7(3), 559–575.

Humpston, C. S., & Broome, M. R. (2016). The spectra of soundless voices and audible thoughts: Towards an integrative model of auditory verbal hallucinations and thought insertion. *Review of Philosophy and Psychology*, 7(3), 611–629.

Jones, S. R. (2010). Do we need multiple models of auditory verbal hallucinations? Examining the phenomenological fit of cognitive and neurological models. *Schizophrenia Bulletin*, 36(3), 566–575.

Langland-Hassan, P. (2008). Fractured phenomenologies: Thought insertion, inner speech, and the puzzle of extraneity. *Mind and Language*, 23(4), 369–401.

Luhrmann, T. M., Padmavati, R., Tharoor, H., & Osei, A. (2015). Hearing voices in different cultures: A social kindling hypothesis. *Topics in Cognitive Science*, 7, 646–663.

Martin, J.-R. & Pacherie, E. (2013). Out of nowhere: Thought insertion, ownership and context-integration. *Consciousness and Cognition*, 22(1), 111–122.

McCarthy-Jones, S. R., & Fernyhough, C. (2011). The varieties of inner speech: Links between quality of inner speech and psychopathological variables in a sample of young adults. *Consciousness and Cognition*, 20, 1586–1593.

Mellor, C. S. (1970). First rank symptoms of schizophrenia. 1. The frequency in schizophrenics on admission to hospital. II. Differences between individual first rank symptoms. *British Journal of Psychiatry*, 117, 15–23.

Miller, I. (1984). *Husserl, Perception, and Temporal Awareness*. Oxford: MIT Press.

Raihani, N.J., & Bell, V. (2017). Paranoia and the social representation of others: A large-scale game theory approach. *Scientific Reports*, 7, 4544 (2017)

Ratcliffe, M. (2017). *Real Hallucinations: Psychiatric Illness, Intentionality, and the Interpersonal World*. Cambridge, MA: MIT Press.

Ratcliffe, M., & Wilkinson, S. (2015). Thought insertion clarified. *Journal of Consciousness Studies*, 22(11–12), 246–269.

Ratcliffe, M., & Wilkinson, S. (2016). How anxiety induces verbal hallucinations. *Consciousness and Cognition*, 39, 48–58.

Roessler, J. (2016). Thinking, inner speech, and self-awareness. *Review of Philosophy and Psychology, 7*(3), 541–557.

Ryle, G. (1949). *The Concept of Mind.* London: Hutchinson & Co.

Sartre, J.-P. (1943/2013). *Being and Nothingness: An Essay on Phenomenological Ontology.* London: Routledge.

Stephens, G. L., & Graham, G. (2000). *When Self-Consciousness Breaks: Alien Voices and Inserted Thoughts.* Oxford: MIT Press.

Vygotsky L. S. (1934/1987). *Thinking and Speech. The Collected Works of Lev Vygotsky* (Vol. 1). New York, NY: Plenum Press.

Wilkinson, S. (2014). Accounting for the phenomenology and varieties of auditory verbal hallucination within a predictive processing framework. *Consciousness and Cognition, 30,* 142–155.

Wilkinson, S. (2019). Hearing soundless voices. *Philosophy, Psychiatry, and Psychology, 26*(3), 27–34.

Wilkinson, S., & Bell, V. (2016). The representation of agents in auditory verbal hallucinations. *Mind & Language, 31*(1), 104–126.

Wilkinson, S., & Krueger, J. (2022). The phenomenology of voice-hearing and two concepts of voice. In A. Woods, B. Alderson-Day, & C. Fernyhough (Eds.), *Voices in Psychosis: Interdisciplinary Perspective* (pp. 127–133). Oxford: Oxford University Press.

Woods, A., Jones, N., Alderson-Day, B., Callard, F., & Fernyhough, C. (2015). Experiences of hearing voices: Analysis of a novel phenomenological survey. *The Lancet Psychiatry, 2,* 323–331.

Wu, W. (2012). Explaining schizophrenia: Auditory verbal hallucination and self-monitoring. *Mind and Language, 27*(1), 86–107.

6

On Philosophy and Schizophrenia

The Case of Thought Insertion

Jasper Feyaerts and Wouter Kusters

> When we do philosophy, we should like to hypostatize feelings where there are none. They serve to explain our thoughts to us.
> **Wittgenstein, Investigations, 598**

6.1. Introduction

The relation between philosophy and schizophrenia is intimate and complex (Sass, 1992; Strassberg, 2014; Kusters, 2020). On the one hand, it seems that schizophrenia, perhaps more than other forms of psychopathology, entails a form of experience in which traditional philosophical issues can become the explicit object of questioning perplexity and existential concern (Blankenburg, 1971; Humpston & Broome, 2016). This is apparent, for example, in the often ontological, cosmological, or metaphysical cast of the delusions that are considered characteristic of the condition (Sass, 1992, 1994; Bovet & Parnas, 1993; Feyaerts et al., 2021).

Yet, it also seems that schizophrenia itself, perhaps also more than other psychopathological categories, often figures as the privileged object of philosophical reflection (Woods, 2011). Importantly, this philosophical fascination with schizophrenia includes but also goes beyond a mere application of philosophical concepts in order to enhance our psychopathological understanding (concepts such as self-consciousness, intentionality, voluntary action, subjectivity, etc.). It also derives from the common assumption that schizophrenia—and some of its prototypical symptoms (e.g., delusions, hallucinations, first-rank symptoms)—may be able to teach us something about the nature and meaning of these philosophical concepts themselves.

One area of current research in which this particular interplay between schizophrenia and philosophy has been expressed most clearly is in the analysis of thought insertion (henceforth: TI). In this symptom—whose presence was once regarded sufficient for the diagnosis of schizophrenia (see Schneider, 1959; Nordgaard et al., 2019)—patients typically report that their thoughts are in some puzzling sense no longer their 'own'. Determining the purported psychopathological 'essence' of this symptom, and specifically, of the sense of depersonalization it involves, has become the recurring focus of a substantial stream of philosophical literature (e.g., Billon, 2013; Bortolotti & Broome, 2009; Gallagher, 2015; Ratcliffe & Wilkinson, 2015; Henriksen, Parnas, & Zahavi, 2019—for a comprehensive overview, see López-Silva, 2018).

However, as noted here, this philosophical interest has been only partly clinically motivated. The case of TI has, in addition, often functioned as a kind of real-life thought experiment on the basis of which various philosophical intuitions regarding the nature of self-awareness, subjectivity or (mental) agency are presumed to be possibly vindicated.[1] The central assumption here is that TI, and schizophrenia more generally, offers philosophers an empirical contrastive condition that can help to shed light on implicit aspects of normal self-experience that normally remain hidden—but whose existence (in normal conditions) is revealed precisely by the fact of their absence in certain abnormal conditions.[2] Freud viewed dreams as offering the royal road to the unconscious; in somewhat analogous fashion, TI is thought to reveal the nature of our self-experience in its elusive dimension of lived immediacy.[3]

This chapter has two main aims. In the first part, we will critically discuss one prominent philosophical account that attempts to explain TI as involving a loss of a 'sense of agency' that is presumed to characterize ordinary thinking (cf. Gallagher 2015). After providing a brief overview of the discussion

---

[1] Incidentally, this specific philosophical use of psychopathology is perhaps one of the main reasons why most authors within this literature are content on analysing only a handful of clinical examples, which, furthermore, are artificially abstracted from the wider clinical Gestalt in which they occur. For an elaboration of this critique and its ramifications, see Henriksen, Parnas, and Zahavi (2019). We will return to this point at the end of our chapter.

[2] For various formulations of this same central assumption, see, e.g., Ratcliffe (2008, p. 483): 'It is not just a matter of applying phenomenological discoveries in the context of psychopathology. We can also study the structure of experience by engaging with the ways in which it can be altered. Ordinarily overlooked aspects of experience become salient when we are presented with their loss, exaggeration or distortion'; Parnas and Zahavi (2000, p. 11): 'The normal is often so familiar to us that it remains practically unnoticed; it is so pervasive that it becomes elusive. [...] However, exactly because psychopathological disorders involve such profound deviations from normal human experience, they can bring forth usually taken-for granted, unnoticed conditions of normal daily experience.'

[3] In line with this idea, some have drawn a close parallel between Husserlian phenomenology, and particularly its 'unnatural' methodological tool of epochè, and schizophrenia. Both are considered to involve a kind of revelatory detachment from one's experiences which are henceforth no longer simply lived through, but instead become open to reflection and analytic scrutiny—the former, however, by methodological fiat, the latter, qua existential predicament (see Depraz, 2003; Stanghellini, 2004).

surrounding this phenomenological description, we will use Wittgenstein's expressivist understanding of the first-person to resist the idea that TI, and concepts like thinking, agency, and selfhood more generally, can be relevantly clarified in terms of a phenomenological focus on 'experience'.

In the second part, we make use of this sense-of-agency account as a paradigmatic example that can allow us to critically reconsider the more general idea that TI offers a kind of pathological '*via negativa*' into evidences and experiences that would normally permeate ordinary life. Instead, drawing on Sass (1992/2017) and Kusters (2020), we will develop the idea that both philosophy and schizophrenia *share* a basic kind of attitude towards ordinary life, which in the case of TI is exemplified by a preoccupation with, and reflection on, the very question of the ownership and origin of thoughts and experiences. We argue that such a preoccupation engenders a paradoxical state of mind, and that reports of TI, rather than in terms of a loss of an experiential sense of mineness, should be understood as expressing but one side of this overarching reflexive paradox. In conclusion, we detail some of the implications of our discussion for current accounts of TI and related phenomena.

6.2. Thought Insertion and the Phenomenological Grounds of Self-Experience

Early discussions of TI invoked the phenomenon of thought insertion as an alleged counter-example to longstanding Cartesian intuitions regarding the infallibility of certain forms of self-consciousness (Campbell, 1999; Gallagher, 2000; Coliva, 2002). TI was viewed as possibly challenging the seemingly self-evident fact that, whenever we are conscious of our thoughts, we are (supposedly) also immediately conscious of these thoughts as *our* thoughts. Sometimes this latter is held to be a necessary or logical truth; sometimes more as a universal empirical finding. Philosophically, this principle is often discussed in terms of the technical notion of 'immunity to error through misidentification' (Schoemaker, 1968)—which means, less technically, that in first-person ascriptions of thought, we simply cannot be mistaken about *who* is thinking, since to do so would be empathically unintelligible or perhaps even logically inconceivable (cf. Jaspers, 1963; Roessler, 2013). Examples of TI would seem, however, to contradict even this last vestige of Cartesian certainty. One of Jaspers' patients describes such an experience:

I have never read nor heard them [such thoughts]; they come unasked; I do not dare to think I am the source but I am happy to know of them without thinking them. They come at any moment like a gift and I do not dare impart them as if they were my own (Jaspers, 1963, p. 123).

Since such reports seem to deny what is widely considered a necessary feature of our conscious lives—i.e., what Jaspers termed 'this particular aspect of "being mine"', 'of having an I-quality'—he famously held them to be 'incomprehensible' and as 'in principle psychologically inaccessible to us'.

Yet, to deny reports of TI any form of intelligibility has become a minority position today. The currently preferred approach is to attempt to understand such reports by offering a more careful specification of the particular *aspect* of the *sense of subjectivity* that they appear to be lacking.[4] This strategy here involves distinguishing between two distinctive ways in which thoughts can subjectively be experienced as one's own: that is, in terms of a sense of 'ownership' versus one of 'agency', and then by claiming that, whereas the former is preserved in experiences of TI, the latter is absent.

The 'sense of ownership' is meant to refer, in this context, to the fact that thoughts are not only experienced, but experienced *as being experienced by me*, that is, experienced *as* occurring as part of my own stream of experience. This 'sense of ownership' is also described in terms of the 'mineness' or 'for-me-ness' that, presumably, would characterize all forms of conscious experience. This is the idea that, regardless of the type of mental episode I am currently enjoying—e.g., whether I *intend* to drink my morning coffee or *think that* drinking coffee would be an excellent thing to do—such episodes all include and share a certain qualitative or phenomenal character or feel (i.e., a what-it-is-likeness) that individuates me as the subject or experiencer of these episodes. Moreover, this subjective character is not taken to consist in some additional 'quale' or 'feature' attached somehow to the content of experience, but rather in the very way such experiences are given to me: namely, in a specifically first-personal rather than third-personal manner of appearing. As Gallagher and Zahavi (2005/2014) put it:

> As I live through these different experiences, there is something experiential that is, in some sense, the same, namely, their distinct first-personal character. All the experiences are characterized by a quality of mineness or for-me-ness, the fact that it is I who am having these experiences.

---

[4] Throughout this chapter, we will specifically focus on so-called first-order accounts of self-consciousness which take our sense of mineness to be an immediate aspect of first-order experience, in contrast to higher-order theories in which mineness is explained as the result of a second act or thought directed towards the first-order state.

The 'sense of agency', on the other hand, is meant to refer to the experience of being the active agent or author of certain thoughts. The idea here is that thinking (just like deliberating, planning, or calculating) is a form of mental activity or action, and that the phenomenology of such active thinking is normally accompanied by a pre-reflective or first-order feeling of agency that individuates me as its agent or author. This pre-reflective, agentive feeling is considered to be the phenomenological basis for second-order or self-directed attributions of actions to myself as the agent of the action in question. By contrast, in cases of reflex movement or, e.g., when some other person pushes me, I would presumably lack the underlying feeling of agency necessary to self-attribute these movements as actions that are intentionally undertaken or performed by myself.

Armed with this phenomenological distinction, it seems possible to avoid Jaspers' conclusion that reports of TI must be fundamentally 'incomprehensible' in the sense of lying beyond the pale of either rational or empathic comprehension. If we assume (i) that thinking is normally a form of voluntary (mental) action, which (ii) is accompanied by a feeling of agency, and (iii) that expressions of thought constitute linguistic reflections of this phenomenological reality, then reports of TI can be considered—qua experience claims—as structurally similar to examples of involuntary movement or reflex behaviour: namely, as instances when thoughts do occur to me, but seem just to happen rather than to be actively entertained.

It may well seem that the 'sense of ownership' is always retained in instances of TI: a patient complains, after all, that it is she who has to endure the alienating passivity of thoughts and *not* someone else. This would seem to acknowledge that she still 'owns' these autonomous thoughts as an experiencing subject, even as she denies being the active agent of thoughts that seem to occur regardless of her personal intentions or volitional activity. Such a phenomenological interpretation of TI has at least one clear advantage: what patients tell about their experiences need not be interpreted as remaining closed to meaningful understanding (e.g., Berrios & Dening, 1996). Indeed, on this interpretation, the claim of TI concerns a perfectly coherent as well as truthful avowal. Since the disruption of agency presumably does occur on the pre-reflective level of experience, reports of TI can be considered as being, at least in part, *accurate* descriptions that are grounded in this altered sense of agency, and this validates the value and cogency of the first-person perspective of the patient.

6.3. Questions and Critique

However, this sense-of-agency account of TI has not remained unchallenged. Indeed, there are a variety of critiques (for a summary of these and a response, see Gallagher 2015), including the following. It is argued:

1. that TI should in fact be described as a disturbance in our 'sense of ownership' rather than 'agency', so long as the former is conceived appropriately: i.e., not in terms of spatial metaphors according to which 'my' thoughts occur within 'my' field of consciousness, but in terms of whether someone wants or is able to endorse the corresponding thought contents (see Bortolotti & Broome, 2009);
2. that the agentive problem is not situated at the level of immediate pre-reflective experience, but on the level of reflective or narrative attribution (Campbell, 2001);
3. that the description of TI in terms of a disturbed sense of agency is insufficient to distinguish inserted thoughts from, for example, obsessive thoughts (Billon, 2013);
4. that the phenomenological description fails to take into account the specific *contents* of thoughts that are experienced as ego-dystonic (López-Silva, 2018); or finally
5. that most or all thinking is itself (as Nietzsche once emphasized) not really an activity, but instead a predominantly passive phenomenon ('a thought comes when "it" wants to and not when "I" wish'—Nietzsche, 1886, p. 17; see Strawson, 2003).

There is, however, an assumption that remains implicitly accepted throughout these various critiques; and this is the more general philosophical assumption that concepts like thinking, agency, or ownership can all be relevantly clarified in terms of a phenomenological focus on *experience*. While authors differ, for example, on whether it is the sense of agency or the sense of ownership that is the most salient feature in TI, the very idea that such experiential senses or feelings must and do play a crucial role in ordinary thought goes unquestioned. Again, while there are different views on how our normal experience of thought should best be described (e.g., as active, passive, marked by 'mineness'), the very assumption that thinking is to be understood or conceived as being, in its essence, an experiential phenomenon, a form of lived experience, is taken for granted. This experiential assumption is also evident in the proposed interpretations of TI: what is considered strange about reports of TI is not primarily their self-directed preoccupation with the experience of thought processes, but rather, the anomalous or unusual nature of that experience. A similar emphasis can be gleaned from Jaspers' description of schizophrenic self-alienation: 'The remarkable thing about this particular phenomenon is that the individual, though he exists, is no longer able to *feel* he exists. Descartes' 'cogito ergo sum' (I think therefore I am) may still be superficially cogitated but it is no longer a valid *experience*' (1963, p. 122—our emphasis).

We will argue, however, that this generalized emphasis on self-experience as defining thinking—that is, in the well-known phrase, on 'what-it-is-like' to think, to be active, to be a self, derives less from actual phenomenological findings regarding the experiential nature of these concepts, than from a questionable philosophical interpretation of the phenomenon of *first-person authority*—that is, of our seemingly effortless ability to say what we think, feel, want, or believe (see also Feyaerts & Vanheule, 2017). To clarify these issues we will, in the following section, revisit the nature of this notion of first-person privilege and will consider the contrasting philosophical interpretations it has received in the phenomenological tradition and by Wittgenstein respectively. On the basis of comparison, we will question the idea that concepts like thinking, agency or ownership need refer to, or be defined by, phenomenological experiences, and will develop some of the implications of this critique for philosophical accounts of TI.

6.3.1. How do I know what I think?

The basic intuition which is captured by notions like first-person authority or first-person privilege is that, all things being equal, I am usually the best person to ask if you want to know what I think, feel, intend, and so on. Other classical examples of such privileged mental concepts are those that are usually invoked to put an end to philosophical temptations toward scepticism. Thus, for example, while according to Descartes, I can conceivably be mistaken about whether I'm really taking a walk or writing a text, such sceptical doubts cannot meaningfully extend to whether I *believe* this is so, whether it *seems* to me that way, or whether I *judge* it to be so. These typical *cogitatio*[5] are all members of a larger class that Wittgenstein designated as 'psychological verbs'. Among these psychological verbs, we find those which indeed point towards experiences ('I see', 'I hear', 'I have a headache'), but also cognitive

---

[5] As noted by several commentators, Descartes' uses the words 'cogitation' and 'cogitare' in both an extended as well as a more restricted sense compared to our current understanding of these notions in the

activities ('I think', 'I judge'), intentions ('I'm going to', 'I propose to') and acts of the will ('I've decided to', 'I want to').

Secondly, our 'subjective privilege' with regard to these psychological verbs basically consists in being exempt from the demands of verification or evidence that are usually attached to our ordinary acts of judgement, which can be denied, contradicted, or at least questioned about their justification. This is the feature Wittgenstein had in mind when he spoke of 'asymmetry of the first and third persons in the present indicative'. That is, if, for example, I claim that 'I lost my wallet' or that 'I broke my arm', then the reasons I would cite in order to justify these claims would be the same kind of reasons as would apply if I were to say this of someone else: roughly, reasons pertaining to observation, testimony, or inference. Hence, with respect to their justification, in these cases there is no asymmetry between the first-personal statement 'I lost my wallet' and its third-personal version 'He lost his wallet'—both are justified by, for example, checking one's own or someone else's pocket.

However, when I claim that I want to eat a pizza bianco, am thinking about Freud's *Future of an Illusion*, or desire to go on a holiday, that similarity to the third-person vanishes. Clearly, there does seem to be something strained and misguided about someone asking me to justify these claims (e.g., 'so you're thinking about Freud's writings—okay, but how do you know you are?'). And if I were nonetheless tempted to cede to such queries, citing behavioural evidence or inferences-to-the-best-explanation to the effect that I really am contemplating Freud's writings, this would seem to make matters worse. As Wittgenstein points out, an important feature of the apparently incorrigible character of self-ascriptions deploying psychological verbs in the present indicative is that one cannot ask the person *how* he knows. By contrast, the third-personal claim that someone else is contemplating Freud's writings lacks such privileges and is in principle susceptible to further demands of justification.

Yet how, in fact, should we explain this remarkable capacity to talk in such an authoritative way about our present thoughts, hopes, and fears? Here it will be instructive to contrast Wittgenstein's treatment of this topic with the one we typically find in the phenomenological tradition.

To begin with the latter: phenomenological approaches typically try to explain first-person authority by invoking some special mode of first-personal *access* or *givenness* that allows the subject of these mental states to know about them. That is, phenomenology takes the problem of first-person authority

---

sense of 'thinking' or 'cognition'. Extended because they also comprise, for example, acts of imagination, sensing and willing. Restricted because Descartes retains only those acts which are immediately and infallibly 'given' in consciousness. See Descombes (2004, p. 176–189), Anscombe (1981), and Narboux (2019).

to be one specific version of the more general epistemological question of knowledge—in this case involving '*self*-knowledge'—and the problem is therefore, as befits such epistemological queries, that of determining the origin and conditions of possibility of that knowledge. The implicit reasoning behind this idea seems to be the following: In the same way as I would be unable to say of this particular object that it is a table if I did not first recognize it *as* a table, I would not be able to say, for example, that I want to watch *Better Call Saul* if I did not first recognize a mental state as one of me-wanting-to-watch that series. Therefore, in order to explain the possibility of authoritative psychological statements, it is considered necessary to invoke a phenomenon of 'experiential evidence' for, or 'givenness' of, my mental states. As Zahavi argues in the case of beliefs and intentions:

> [...] if I am to deliberate on and access my beliefs and intentions, it is not enough that I have them: I must also have been aware of them; that is, prior to reflection I cannot have been 'mind-blind'. Reflection is constrained by what is pre-reflectively lived through. It is answerable to experiential facts and is not constitutively self-fulfilling. To deny that the reflective self-ascriptions of beliefs is based on any experiential evidence whatsoever is implausible. It is to deny that such self-ascriptions amount to a cognitive achievement. (2014, p. 36)

Now what it is that provides this 'experiential evidence', the source of 'a cognitive achievement', is something about which, even in the phenomenological tradition, a variety of views exists. Here we will only focus on the approach that underlies the sense-of-agency account and that is most commonly associated with Husserl or Sartre. This approach basically consists in stating that psychological verbs like thinking, perceiving or doubting are all 'acts of consciousness'.

In keeping with Brentano's definition of mental phenomena, such acts of consciousness are said to be *intentional*, i.e., acts through which I am immediately conscious *of* something. Perception, for example, is that 'mode of consciousness' through which a perceptual object appears; imagination, that mode of consciousness through which something is given as imagined; thinking, that by which something is thought. Therefore, on this approach—and in contrast, for example, to introspective or higher-order theories—one does not say that my intention to go on a holiday is something I 'perceive' or 'represent' by way of a further act, but rather that my intention is a 'consciousness' of a future holiday in the very way of intending it. Similarly, one does not say that my desire for a Bloody Mary is something I apperceive as a disinterested spectator, but rather that this desiring involves a mode of consciousness through which a Bloody Mary appears as desirable. One has to distinguish, as Husserl (1989, pp. 303–304) put it, the *cogitatum* from its *cogito*, the *intentional object* as it is intended, specified, or determined in its nature as an object (*im Wie seiner Bestimmtheiten*) from the *intentional act through which* it is intended or given (*im Wie seiner Gegebenheitsweisen*).

In other words, it is through my transitive or 'thetic' consciousness of, say, a burning house as perceived or imagined, that I am immediately aware of the intransitive or 'non-thetic' presence of an act of perception or of imagination. Importantly, it is only *because* these intransitive acts through which I am consciously related to objects are themselves also 'experienced' (which means that there is something 'it-is-like' to perceive, believe, think, or intend), that I am subsequently able to report on these acts and their intentional objects whenever I'm asked. To use the typical phenomenological neologisms for denoting this kind of intransitivity: such pre-reflective experiences are said to be 'intrinsically self-revealing', 'self-disclosing', 'pre-reflectively self-given', or 'self-manifesting' (for these ideas, see Henry 1973)—in short: it is in their very nature to provide their own evidence. And therefore, insofar as my ability to report on them is explained by their 'self-revealing' character, all such acts of consciousness are considered to have a distinctive phenomenology about them. As Zahavi writes:

> it is the conscious states themselves [e.g., perceiving, believing, thinking, …], and not some internal observation of them, that provide part of the justification for any subsequent self-ascription of those very states. In short, the fact that the phenomenally conscious states are already like something for the subject is what makes those very states capable of playing a justificatory role vis-à-vis any higher-order belief regarding their very existence'. (2014, p. 36—content within brackets added)

To sum up: as we argued earlier, we see that the phenomenological approach tends to treat all psychological concepts as one generic class of 'experience concepts', and that this is motivated by the attempt to explain our first-person authority in terms of some form of 'intrinsic' or 'pre-reflective' experiential access. Since this first-person authority not only extends to sensing a pain in one's shoulder, but also to the fact of remembering something or thinking certain thoughts, and throughout all these examples, that it is *I* who feels, remembers, or thinks, it becomes tempting to invoke justificatory 'I-feelings', 'experiences of thought', or 'senses of agency' as the phenomenological ground for my self-attributions. For the same reason, it becomes tempting to explain reports of TI in terms of the alteration or loss of such justificatory I-feelings.

However, if we now turn to Wittgenstein's discussion of first-person authority, we find a markedly different approach, one that questions the felt necessity, and even intelligibility, of positing all kinds of experiences to explain our self-ascriptions of psychological concepts. Wittgenstein's way of addressing this problem begins with the simple suggestion that our self-ascriptions owe their status, which is so apparently authoritative, to the fact that they are not *reports* or *experiential descriptions* of our current psychological 'states', but rather count as *expressions* of the states that, in fact, they only appear to describe based on a superficial consideration of their surface grammar. In the case of sensation-language—e.g., statements about pain—Wittgenstein puts this point as follows:

> What I do is not, of course, to identify my sensation by criteria: but to repeat an expression. But this is not the *end* of the language-game: it is the beginning. But isn't the beginning the sensation—which I describe?—Perhaps this word 'describe' tricks us here. I say 'I describe my state of mind' and 'I describe my room'. You need to call to mind the differences between the language games. (2009, p. 290)

What are 'the differences between the language-games' at issue here, that is, between describing one's room and describing one's state of mind, that Wittgenstein is hinting at in this quote? An important point seems related to—if we can put it that way—the 'temporal logic' of the descriptive assertion. Wittgenstein appears to be intent on denying that in the case of, for example, saying that I am in pain, I should begin with the examination of my pain-sensation before proceeding to the self-ascription; whereas, in the case of describing my room, it is of course indispensable that I should have observed things and looked it over before engaging in my description. In the latter case, the description comes at the *end* of the language game—after I have identified, e.g., whether the room is spacious or contains a chaise longue. Moreover, this is what in fact *justifies* my descriptive assertion.

Yet if Wittgenstein denies that this is what we ordinarily do when we offer our thoughts on some issue or complain about a pain in our back, then what is it that justifies these first-personal ascriptions? And what does it mean that in this kind of language game such ascriptions come *first*, rather than at the end of some justification? To continue the analogy with the room description: one might think, for example, that to begin with the ascription would actually amount to describing one's room without looking at it first, that is to say, to simply engage in some highly speculative endeavour. And since, in fact, Wittgenstein abrogates epistemic justifiers in the case of psychological self-ascriptions, this seems to leave us with the following option: to construe such talk as being merely the result of—to use Dennett's expression—some 'impromptu theorizing' (1991, p. 67), i.e., as groundless fictional assertions about putative mental items. However, that this is not the conclusion Wittgenstein wants to draw becomes clear in the following passage:

> When I say 'I am in pain' I am at any rate justified *before myself.*—What does that mean? Does it mean: 'If someone else could know what I am calling "pain," he would admit that I was using the word correctly'?
> To use a word without a justification does not mean to use it wrongfully. (2009, p. 289)

So, according to Wittgenstein, it is not because I am not 'justified before myself' in saying that I'm in pain, that I am therefore *unjustified* when resorting to this pain-talk in the sense of making a mistake or simply talking nonsense. The opposition between being epistemically justified or unjustified is then, in fact, a *false* opposition that does not allow us to explain what is distinctive about our first-personal ascriptions of pains or beliefs. That is, to rid oneself of the idea that, in order to avoid sceptical worries about our ordinary 'folk-psychological' practices, authoritative psychological self-ascriptions of thoughts, beliefs, and sensations *must* be grounded in experiential evidence, we have to question the assumption that first-person avowals function as *judgements* and *reports* about psychological facts the speaker has previously learned or ascertained. This is the guiding thought behind Wittgenstein's following remarks:

> The paradox disappears only if we make a radical break with the idea that language always functions in one way, always serves the same purpose: to convey thoughts— which may be about houses, pains, good and evil, or whatever. (2009, p. 304)

> When someone says 'I hope he'll come', is this a *report* [Bericht] about his state of mind, or a *manifestation* [Äusserung] of his hope?—I may, for example, say it to myself. And surely I am not giving myself a report. (2009, p. 585)

Here we retrieve the earlier suggestion that psychological utterances are primarily *manifestations* or *expressions* of the very states or activities they self-ascribe, rather than secondary thoughts or beliefs about these states or activities uttered to inform the listener about their presence. Therefore, utterances like 'I am in pain' or 'that really hurts!' are not pain reports on a par with weather-reports, but rather, like my moans and cries, manifestations of my pain; similarly, the utterance 'I want to go out' does not inform someone about some planning experience, but voices, depending on the context in which it is said, my desire to go out or my agreement to your proposal; in the same way, ardent exclamations like 'I love you' or 'I really hate your guts' do not communicate subjective facts to which you may or may not agree or proceed to inquire some further information, but should be more properly understood as verbal equivalents of bringing flowers and throwing plates in your direction.

6.3.2. Implications

What is the philosophical import of Wittgenstein's expressivist understanding of first-person authority and how precisely does it differ from the phenomenological approach we discussed? Furthermore, what are the implications of this discussion for the sense-of-agency account of TI, and more generally, for the ways in which we try to make sense of reports of TI?

First, we noted that the phenomenological temptation to posit all sorts of experiences (e.g., a feeling of mineness, a sense of agency) to explain our first-person authority results from conceiving I-statements of thoughts, actions, or intentions as descriptive or self-referential reports *about* our thoughts, feelings, and intentions. Wittgenstein's expressivist treatment of first-person authority, by contrast, offers us reasons to resist this temptation. On Wittgenstein's approach, what explains our authority in saying what we think or believe is not that we ordinarily dispose of pre-reflective evidence for our thoughts and beliefs, but rather that our psychological statements ordinarily count as *manifestations* of those thoughts and beliefs. This means that, contrary to the phenomenological effort to supply various experiential grounds to justify our psychological utterances, there is *no* epistemic question to be answered about how I am able to offer my thoughts or communicate my intentions, because such utterances do not involve subjective *judgements* about the presence of such thoughts or intentions in the first place. What, instead, might justify a thought like 'I think I have a flat tyre' or my intention 'to change it' would, on occasion, have nothing to do with me (e.g., my experience of thinking or intention), but rather with something occurring in the world (e.g., a warning signal in my car). In short, expressive psychological statements are not statements *about* the psychology of the speaker, and neither are they justified *by* the psychology of the speaker.

Secondly, however, this obviously does not amount to denying that we have experiences, or that our psychological concepts can't be grouped under a specific shared characteristic. As we have seen, it is indeed a shared feature of these concepts that they manifest an asymmetry between the first and third persons with respect to their justification. Yet, contrary to the phenomenological assumption, the fact that all these concepts display this asymmetry does not mean that they are all, *for that very reason*, concepts of experience—like, for example, 'seeing a colour' or 'feeling a pain' are. In the latter cases, I am indeed living through experiences and I am consequently able to describe their experiential content or phenomenal features ('a blueish yellow', 'a throbbing pain'). By contrast, someone who has the intention to go on a holiday may experience all sorts of feelings (excitement, restlessness), but nothing of what he experiences actually constitutes his intention. While we feel or experience emotions, we do not speak about 'experiencing' intentions. Neither expressions of belief or knowledge, nor expressions of intentions are accompanied by any particular 'what-it's-like-ness' or sensation—nor, for that matter, do they have to be in order to be authoritatively expressed:

> 'I intend' is not an expression of an experience. There is no cry of intention, any more than there is one of knowledge or belief. (Wittgenstein, 1980, p. 179)

> Intent, intention, is neither an emotion, a mood, nor yet a sensation or image. It is not a state of consciousness. It does not have genuine duration. (Wittgenstein, 1980, p. 178)

Similar observations hold with respect to the concepts of 'agency' and 'ownership' whose respective 'senses' are proposed to be disturbed or retained in experiences of TI. On the one hand, to speak about my cognitive deliberations or thinking activities as things that I actively perform—leaving aside all various instances in which thought is obviously not an activity to begin with, but something that simply occurs, or something that may suddenly strike me (for all these multifarious meanings of 'thought', see Anscombe, 1981)—is not a matter of describing 'experiences of voluntariness' or of testifying about a subjective 'sense of agency'. To do something voluntarily rather means, for example, that I acted in the way I wanted to act, that I didn't feel obliged to act by someone else or because of some situation, that I can perform the action whenever I'm asked, or that it doesn't arise when I explicitly try to avoid it, etc. (see also Scott 1996). Experiences, by contrast, even in case of an 'agentive experience', are per definition not actively performed or done by me, but passively endured or enjoyed. While I might nonetheless actively try to bring them about—say, e.g., arousing a feeling of sublime anxiety by intentionally watching a horror movie—they do not constitute my voluntary action of watching the movie, nor do I need to rely on them to know that I am acting voluntarily. A person's 'authority' with respect to his actions consists in his practical capacity to determine his course of action as an intentional *agent*, not in his knowledge about some volitional state of mind as an experiencing *subject* (see also Taylor, 2010).

The same goes, on the other hand, for the fact of 'owning' thoughts or beliefs whose 'sense' is proposed to be necessary to ascribe thoughts and beliefs to myself. In order to speak about 'my' thoughts and beliefs, I do not have to consider how they are subjectively 'given' to me, I rather have to attend to the objective grounds or reasons for having them. To determine, for example, whether I think it will rain, I need to consult empirical facts about the weather, rather than experiential facts about my thinking experience. To claim that 'I think it will rain' is not a descriptive statement about my sense of owning a meteorological thinking state, but again an expressive statement about the possible prospect of raining. Yet, not only is a 'sense of ownership' unnecessary to speak of my thoughts and beliefs, it would in fact also make it *impossible* to do so—and this for two related reasons. On the one hand, in case offering my thoughts would amount to a descriptive statement in which I refer to myself as the experiential owner of these thoughts, I would be condemned to being able to speak *only* about myself—i.e., about *my* thoughts, *my* beliefs—and never about the objective condition of the weather. In this sense, all speakers would share a similar subjective or solipsistic predicament, and would consequently never be able to contradict or to agree with each other. On the other hand, if speaking about my thoughts were to consist in attributing thoughts to myself on the basis of my phenomenological experience, then *who* exactly would I be talking about? We may ask, regarding the subject who, in turning his attention to his thinking experience, *knows* that he thinks it will rain: does he also *think* it will rain? It would seem that such a subject would always occupy a spectral position of perpetual self-commentary with regard to his experiential self, hence always existing apart from his existence as an experiencer—as was indeed the paradoxical conclusion drawn by Sartre: 'Thus the consciousness that says "I think" is precisely not the consciousness which thinks. Or, rather, it is not its own thought which it posits by this thetic act' (2004, p. 6).

In summary, Wittgenstein's treatment of the authority of the first-person shows how the phenomenological emphasis on various forms of self-experience results from a misunderstanding of the expressive nature of this authority. In order to think and to speak my mind, I do not have to have an experience *of* my thoughts as 'self-generated' or as subjectively 'owned'—in fact, such an experience would actually undermine itself. Yet, if *ordinary* thinking is not a matter of having a sense of one's thoughts as one's own, then it is clear that reports of TI cannot be rendered intelligible by referring to the *absence* of such senses. In the following section, we will develop some general ideas on how experiences of TI could alternatively be understood without these phenomenological assumptions.

6.4. Philosophy, Schizophrenia, and the Paradoxes of Subjectivity

In the preceding sections, we have been critically considering one particular philosophical attempt to render reports of TI more comprehensible by appealing to different sorts of self-experiences that are said to be disturbed in schizophrenia. In our introduction, we furthermore pointed out how this account exemplifies a more general tendency to view schizophrenia as substantiating, though in a negative or pathological way, certain philosophical assumptions regarding the essential nature of subjectivity and selfhood. Such a view is particularly evident in the phenomenological tradition, where schizophrenia has sometimes been likened to a form of unintentional or forced 'epochè' (see, e.g., Blankenburg, 1971; Stanghellini, 2004), hence as laying bare the implicit structures of subjectivity that are normally assumed in everyday life. Whereas the phenomenological philosopher has to exert effort in order to penetrate to these foundational layers of self-experience, the schizophrenic individual is thought to be spontaneously confronted with them through their imminent disintegration or erasure. In this sense, one could say that both the philosopher and schizophrenic individual are concerned with the same foundational inquiry of what it means to be a 'self', although for different reasons and from opposite directions: whereas the philosopher attempts to get a clear theoretical view on what he already possesses, the schizophrenic individual seeks to existentially regain what he is acutely aware of as having lost.

While, in the preceding, we argued against the existence and need for such a foundational self-experience, there is, however, another way to exploit this analogy between philosophy and schizophrenia, one that may also get us further in understanding reports of TI. This alternative way of framing the analogy focuses less on the 'self', and its various putative qualities, as the shared *object* of schizophrenic and philosophical preoccupations, and rather on the contradictions and paradoxes that unavoidably arise as a *result* of such preoccupations. Sass (1992/2017, 1994) and Kusters (2020),[6]π in particular, have drawn attention to the fact that a similar self-generated paradox seems to

---

[6] See especially the concluding chapter 'Paradoxes of the Reflexive' in Sass (1992) and chapter 13, 'Paradoxes: Philosophy and Madness Tied Up in Knots' in Kusters (2020).

underlie both the schizophrenic mindset and traditional philosophical reflections on the nature of subjectivity. In both cases, the paradox at issue arises from an intense and self-directed preoccupation with the phenomenon of our own consciousness and our own thinking, a scrutinizing obsession that may befall both the schizophrenic individual, who may be fascinated and captivated by the nature of his or her own experience, and the philosopher of self-consciousness, who may be driven to reflect on the ever-elusive grounds of his or her own reflection.

With respect to schizophrenic experience, Sass (1992/2017) notes the peculiar tendency of such individuals to shift between two seemingly opposite or contradictory claims: on the one hand, they may display a grandiose and quasi-solipsistic sense of being the all-constituting and omniscient centres of reality; the exclusive owners of a strangely subjectivized world in which all alterities have been reduced to mere appearances for their own totalizing gaze. Yet, on the other hand, such solipsistic tendencies may just as easily turn into their exact opposites: instead of omnipotence, patients may claim a position of extreme passivity, of being under the spell of mysterious machines or transcendent mechanisms that have taken over control of their actions, will, and indeed (as in reports of TI) their own thoughts. Yet, it is not merely that schizophrenic individuals may waver between these two opposite tendencies; they may even maintain both positions at the very same moment, as seemingly constituting but two incommensurate expressions of what is in essence one and the same insoluble experiential paradox. As Sass puts it: 'While a schizophrenia patient is as likely to identify with God as with a machine, perhaps the most emblematic delusion of this illness is of being a sort of God machine, an all-seeing, all-constituting eye camera' (1992/2017, p. 270). In a more or less similar way, Kusters defines the 'mystical-mad experience' in schizophrenia as essentially involved with 'grasping and expressing the *coincidentia oppositorum*' (2020, p. 311), or again, as 'the longing for the convergence and transcendence of paradoxical opposites' (2020, p. 544).

The initial relevance of these observations for our current discussion of TI should be readily apparent: not only are phenomenological concepts like a 'sense of mineness' or a 'feeling of agency', as we have previously argued, suspect on strictly philosophical grounds, they also seem unsuited to adequately grasp the nature of TI on more straightforward clinical grounds; that is, when the phenomenon of TI is brought back in this way to its proper paradoxical context. This is a context whereby, as Vygotsky put it, every symptom seems to be matched by a 'countersymptom, its negative double, its opposite' (1987, p. 75)—or, in present terms, whereby the apparent *loss* of 'mineness' in TI and related passivity delusions is but the obverse of a coexisting 'sense of mineness' that is *inflated*, as in moments of unbridled omnipotence and solipsistic grandeur.

Here it may seem that Jaspers' verdict regarding the essential incomprehensibility of schizophrenic experience has reached its full climax. How, indeed, are we to empathically understand a state of mind that no longer seems governed by the principle of non-contradiction, or in which the 'owning' and 'disowning' of mental contents may apparently co-exist unperturbed? Must we simply give up on the project of understanding schizophrenic experience, and fall back on non-empathic forms of reductive explanation?

As a way out of this difficulty, Sass explores a revealing analogy with a similar aporetic antinomy prevalent in modern philosophical reflections on subjectivity. This typically modern turn towards subjectivity attempts to secure or understand the possibility and validity of knowledge, as in Descartes, Kant, or Husserl, or else to foreground the possibility of autonomy and freedom, as in Fichte, Schelling, or Sartre (for overviews, see Gasché, 1986; Carr, 1999; Seigel, 2005). The common feature is a similar co-existence of two opposing developments. On the one hand, the subject emerges as the sovereign and constituting centre of consciousness, the transcendental and self-determining ground on whose existence all else depends. The philosophical valuation of this form of subjectivity may resemble the solipsistic exhilaration that can accompany the schizophrenic appreciation of this side of the duality—as when Husserl, for example, speaks of the 'discovery' of a 'region of pure consciousness', 'a primal region' to which all other regions of being 'are relative and on which they all essentially depend' (1989, p. 171). Yet, on the other hand, this same subject also appears as itself a mere fact within this constituted universe, a spatiotemporal object determined and constrained by the same laws of nature that ordinarily subsume all other empirical entities. 'Man', Kant writes, 'is one of the appearances of the sensible world, and in so far one of the natural causes the causality of which must stand under empirical laws' (1971, A546f). Therefore, being a subject, in the modern philosophical tradition, means being confronted with the same incompatible duality that may bewilder schizophrenic individuals: i.e., that of simultaneously existing as a subject *for* the world, as the condition of its possibility, but also as a mere object *in* this world, a contingent and determined entity within this field of appearance.

Yet, a further important aspect of this analysis is that, similar to the schizophrenic combination of these two incompatible positions, this philosophical duality does not merely entail two opposing yet independent views on the same phenomenon. Instead of being merely externally opposed, it was also recognized that the subjective and objective poles of the duality are in fact two dialectical moments of the same reflexive turn, in the sense that the very effort to assert and to promote the subject as the transcendental 'owner' of the world's experience ultimately engenders this subject's own objectification and alienation. The neo-Kantian Natorp, for example, emphasized how every reflexive attempt to attain and to capture the transcendental first-person perspective has the effect of 'killing' or 'mortifying' this pristine form of subjectivity, of reducing it to yet another objectified representation within the field of awareness: 'one apparently never grasps the subjective, as such, in itself. On the contrary, in order to grasp it scientifically, one is forced to strip it of its subjective character. One kills subjectivity in order to dissect it, and believes the life of the soul is on display in the result of the dissection! (Natorp, 1912, pp. 102–103). Hence, similar to the paradoxical combination of the quasi-solipsistic and passivized positions in schizophrenia, we encounter a same impossible fusion of opposites in the philosophy of the subject: the very effort to subjectivize the experience of the world, and to reflexively attend to this first-person perspective, has the effect of objectifying this subjective dimension as something that appears alienated and different from the subject. To conclude, what are the implications of this analysis of the reflexive paradoxes of schizophrenia and philosophy for our present discussion on how to understand reports of TI?

First, if the analogy is more than a fortuitous coincidence, than this means that certain key symptoms or experiences of schizophrenia are better understood as different dialectical moments in a more general and overarching paradox. Viewed from this perspective, the fact that the philosophical literature has nearly exclusively focused on the analysis of TI as one of these symptoms should be seen as something that is not merely artificial, but also as significantly distorting the phenomenon that is to be explained, and by implication, the form such an explanation might take. Secondly, with respect to this explanation, we argued that, rather than in terms of the presence or absence of various self-experiences which would normally be enjoyed in our ordinary conscious lives, reports of TI can be better understood as giving voice to one side of the paradox that arises when consciousness attempts to turn back at itself in order to be present, as it were, at its own engendering and creation. The reflexive attempt to capture or seize upon one's own epistemological centrality, to step outside one's first-person perspective in order to see it *as* a first-person perspective, is but the immediate obverse of the objectification or reification of the mind. TI is then, rather than a mute or passively endured experiential loss, the epitome of a hyper-conscious mind captivated by the paradoxes of its own making.

References

Anscombe, E. (1981). *Metaphysics and the Philosophy of Mind. Collected Papers, Volume 3*. Minneapolis, MN: University of Minnesota Press.

Berrios, G. E., & Dening, T. R. (1996). The enigma of pseudohallucinations: Current meanings and usage. *Psychopathology, 29*, 17–34.

Billon, A. (2013). Does consciousness entail subjectivity? The puzzle of thought insertion. *Philosophical Psychology, 26*(2), 291–314.

Blankenburg, W. (1971). *Der Verlust der natürlichen Selbstverständlichkeit*. Stuttgart: Enke.

Bortolotti, L., & Broome, M. R. (2009). A role for ownership and authorship in the analysis of thought insertion. *Phenomenology & the Cognitive Sciences, 8*(2), 205–224.

Bovet, P., & Parnas, J. (1993). Schizophrenic delusions: A phenomenological approach. *Schizophrenia Bulletin, 19*(3), 579–597.

Campbell, J. (1999). Schizophrenia, the space of reasons, and thinking as a motor process. *The Monist, 82*, 609–625.

Campbell, J. (2001). Rationality, meaning, and the analysis of delusion. *Philosophy, Psychiatry, and Psychology, 8*, 89–100.

Carr, D. (1999). *The Paradox of Subjectivity: The Self in the Transcendental Tradition*. Oxford: Oxford University Press.

Coliva, A. (2002). Thought insertion and immunity to error through misidentification. *Philosophy, Psychiatry, and Psychology, 9*(1), 27–34.

Dennett, D. (1991). *Consciousness Explained*. New York, NY: Back Bay Books/Little, Brown and Company.

Depraz, N. (2003). Putting the epoché into practice: schizophrenic experience as illustrating the phenomenological exploration of consciousness. In K. W. M. Fulford, K. Morris, J. Sadler, & G. Stanghellini (Eds.), *Nature and Narrative: An Introduction to the New Philosophy of Psychiatry* (pp. 187–198). Oxford: Oxford University Press.

Descombes, V. (2004). *Le complément de sujet. Enquête sur le fait d'agir de soi-même*. Paris: Gallimard.

Feyaerts, J., & Vanheule, S. (2017). Hij of het (ding) denkt, niet ik: Frith over verbale hallucinaties. *Tijdschrift Fil, 79*(2), 313–342.

Feyaerts, J., Kusters, W., Van Duppen, Z., Vanheule, S., Myin-Germeys, I., & Sass, L. (2021). Uncovering the realities of delusional experience: a qualitative phenomenology study in Belgium. *Lancet Psychiatry, 8*(9), 784–796.

Gallagher, S. (2000). Self-reference and schizophrenia. In D. Zahavi (Ed.), *Exploring the Self: Philosophical and Psychopathological Perspectives on Self-experience* (pp. 203–239). Amsterdam, the Netherlands: John Benjamins Publishing Company.

Gallagher, S. (2015). Relations between agency and ownership in the case of schizophrenic thought insertion and delusions of control. *Review of Philosophy and Psychology, 6*, 865–879.

Gallagher, S., & Zahavi, D. (2005/2014). Phenomenological approaches to self-consciousness. *The Stanford Encyclopedia of Philosophy*. http://plato.stanford.edu/entries/self-consciousness-phenomenological/.

Gasché, R. (1986). *The Tain of the Mirror. Derrida and the Philosophy of Reflection*. Cambridge, MA: Harvard University Press.

Henriksen, M., Parnas, J., & Zahavi, D. (2019). Thought insertion and disturbed for-me-ness (minimal selfhood) in schizophrenia. *Consciousness and Cognition, 74*, 102770.
Henry, M. (1973). *The Essence of Manifestation.* The Hague: Martinus Nijhoff.
Humpston, C., & Broome, M. R. (2016). Perplexity. In G. Stanghellini, & M. Aragona (Eds.), *An Experiential Approach to Psychopathology: What is It Like to Suffer From Mental Disorders?* (pp. 245–264). Berlin: Springer. *Psychiatric* Q; 89(4): 957–968.
Husserl, E. (1989). *Ideas Pertaining to a Pure Phenomenology and to a Phenomenological Philosophy. Second Book: Studies in the Phenomenology of Constitution.* Dordrecht: Kluwer Academic Publishers.
Jaspers, K. (1963). *General Psychopathology.* Manchester: Manchester University Press.
Kant, I. (1971). *Kritik der reinen Vernunft.* Frankfurt am Main: Felix Meiner.
Kusters, W. (2020). *A Philosophy of Madness. The Experience of Psychotic Thinking.* Oxford: MIT Press.
López-Silva P (2018). Mapping the psychotic mind: a review on the subjective structure of thought insertion.
Narboux, J. P. (2019). Pensées en première personne et cogitationes cartésiennes. In K. S. Ong-Van-Cung (Ed.), *Les formes historiques du Cogito* (pp. 311–350). Paris: Classiques Garnier.
Natorp, P. (1912). *Allgemeine Psychologie nach kritischer Methode.* Tübingen: J.C.B. Mohr.
Nietzsche, F. (1886). *Beyond Good and Evil (Jenseits vond Gut und Böse).* Leipzig: Naumann.
Nordgaard, J., Henriksen, M. G., Berge, J., & Nilsson, L. S. (2019). First-rank symptoms and self- disorders in schizophrenia. *Schizophrenia Research, 210*, 306–307.
Parnas, J., & Zahavi, D. (2000). The link: Philosophy-psychopathology-phenomenology. In D. Zahavi (Ed.), *Exploring the Self. Philosophical and Psychopathological Perspectives on Self-experience* (pp. 1–18). Amsterdam: John Benjamins Publishing Company.
Ratcliffe, M. (2008). *Feelings of Being: Phenomenology, Psychiatry and the Sense of Reality.* Oxford: Oxford University Press.
Ratcliffe, M., & Wilkinson, S. (2015). Thought insertion clarified. *Journal of Consciousness Studies, 22*(11–12), 246–269.
Roessler, J. (2013). Thought insertion, self-awareness, and rationality. In K. W. M. Fulford, M. Davies, R. G. T. Gipps, G. Graham, J. Sadler, G. Stanghellini, & T. Thornton (Eds.), *The Oxford Handbook of Philosophy and Psychiatry* (pp. 658–672). Oxford: Oxford University Press.
Sartre, J. P. (2004). *The Transcendence of the Ego: A Sketch for a Phenomenological Description.* London, New York, NY: Routledge.
Sass, L. (1992/2017). *Madness and Modernism. Insanity in the Light of Modern Art, Literature, and Thought (revised edition).* Oxford: Oxford University Press.
Sass, L. (1994). *The Paradoxes of Delusion. Wittgenstein, Schreber, and the Schizophrenic Mind.* New York: Cornell University Press.
Schneider K (1959). *Clinical Psychopathology.* New York: Grune & Stratton.
Schoemaker, S. (1968). Self-reference and self-awareness. *Journal of Philosophy, 65*, 556–579.
Scott, M. (1996). Wittgenstein's philosophy of action. *The Philosophical Quarterly, 46*(184), 347–363.
Seigel, J. (2005). *The Idea of the Self. Thought and Experience in Western Europe since the Seventeenth Century.* Cambridge: Cambridge University Press.
Stanghellini, G. (2004). *Disembodied Spirits and Deanimated Bodies: The Psychopathology of Common Sense.* Oxford: Oxford University Press.
Strassberg, D. (2014). *Der Wahnsinn der Philosophie. Verrückte Vernunft von Platon bis Deleuze.* Zürich, Switzerland: Chronos Verlag.
Strawson, G. (2003). Mental ballistics or the involuntariness of spontaneity. *Proceedings of the Aristotelian Society, 103*(3), 227–257.

Taylor, C. (2010). Hegel and the philosophy of action. In A. Laitin, & C. Sandis (Eds.), *Hegel on Action* (pp. 22–41). Basingstoke: Palgrave-Macmillan.

Wittgenstein, L. (1980). *Remarks on the Philosophy of Psychology. Volume 2*. Oxford: Blackwell.

Wittgenstein, L. (2009). *Philosophical Investigations* (4th ed). Wiley-Blackwell.

Woods, A. (2011). *The Sublime Object of Psychiatry. Schizophrenia in Clinical and Cultural Theory*. Oxford: Oxford University Press.

Zahavi, D. (2014). *Self and Other. Exploring Subjectivity, Empathy, and Shame*. Oxford: Oxford University Press.

SECTION 2
EXPLAINING THE INTRUDED MIND

The Aetiological Problem

7
Thought Insertion and Auditory Hallucinations

Phenomenological and Mechanistic Commonalities

Catherine Cazimir and Albert R. Powers

7.1. Introduction

Imagine you are reading a book. Whether aloud or silently, as you engage with the pages, you can recognize yourself—or, rather, your voice—to be the one currently reading. You are also able to simultaneously acknowledge that the voice embedded in the story is not your own but that of the author. You may identify with their characters and agree with their themes and ideals; yet, somehow, you are still able to maintain a hard line between what thoughts originate within your mind and those that come from the author. This hard line defines the distinct processes of thinking and perceiving. A blurring of this line could describe both thought insertion (TI) and auditory verbal hallucinations (AVH), which both involve the perception of a mental event as arising outside of oneself (Ratcliffe & Wilkinson, 2015). Typically, TI and AVH are distinct experiences, defined respectively as thoughts present in one's mind that appear to emanate from elsewhere and a percept-like experience in the absence of appropriate external stimuli (Ratcliffe & Wilkinson, 2015). Although distinctly defined, these phenomena may not be as separate as often portrayed: TI details an experience of thoughts originating from outside oneself and can also carry perceptual information; likewise, AVH, a perceptual event in the absence of an external stimulus, is often described as more thoughtlike than voicelike (Ratcliffe & Wilkinson, 2015; Waters & Fernyhough 2017). A careful account of the clinical, cognitive, and perceptual characteristics of individuals experiencing both phenomena is warranted in considering to what degree they truly overlap (Henriksen et al., 2019; Ratcliffe & Wilkinson, 2015). However, phenomenological overlap may imply a potential overlap in the cognitive and neurological underpinnings of both phenomena.

Understanding the degree to which they do overlap across levels of analysis could lead to a better understanding of common and distinct mechanisms giving rise to both phenomena, which could inform novel interventions based upon that knowledge (Badcock, 2016).

In this chapter, we outline points of commonality and difference in the phenomenological, perceptual, and neural aspects of TI and AVH in the hope that this analysis may lead to future work meant to elucidate how these potentially distressing features of psychotic illness may be better understood and treated.

7.2. Phenomenology

Unsurprisingly, the defining phenomenological feature of TI is the perceived foreignness of the thoughts in question: in early firsthand reports, TI subjects adamantly describe 'just knowing' thoughts are being placed into their minds, even when the content is similar to their own (López-Silva, 2018; Mullins & Spence, 2003). AVH subjects, on the other hand, describe hearing voices and noises in the absence of people and things (Badcock, 2016; Mullins & Spence, 2003). While TI reports highlight a sensory component in which patients describe physically feeling placement of these alien thoughts into their heads, AVH episodes lack the sensation described by these patients (López-Silva, 2018; Mellor, 1970; Mullins & Spence, 2003; Sterzer et al., 2016). Instead, AVH, both verbal and nonverbal, are classically characterized by tone, clarity, and loudness that would be typically described as part of everyday speech perception (McCarthy-Jones et al., 2014). For instance, patients may express that their hallucinations feel very real because the auditory experiences address them directly, have a clarity akin to external speech, and occur at a volume typical of normal conversation (McCarthy-Jones et al., 2014). Clinically, despite the variability in these accounts, TI and AVH have been independently characterized as either a delusion of inserted thought or a hallucination of auditory experience (Badcock, 2016). Perhaps because of this, many of the overlapping aspects of TI and auditory verbal hallucination phenomenology have yet to be entirely understood.

Individually, TI phenomenology is best understood by six main features—selectivity, lack of causal coherence, specificity, permeability, negative phenomenal features, and positive phenomenal features (López-Silva, 2018). In selectivity, regardless of whether or not the sensory component is perceived, subjects are aware of foreign states of emotion, thoughts, and impulses through a sense of realization that they experience (López-Silva, 2018; Mellor, 1970). As these alien thoughts, states of emotion, or impulses enter the mind uninhibited, they are perceived as incoherent and without context, describing the loss of causal coherence associated with normal thinking and the second main feature of TI phenomenology (López-Silva, 2018; Sterzer et al., 2016). Specificity is observed when patients recognize inserted content that appears thematically relevant to their current lives as independent of their own thinking (due to placement by another) (López-Silva, 2018). This demarcation between self and not self, as ego boundaries are blurred, describes permeability, which, along with disavowal of thought content, may compel subjects to attribute their insertions to foreign agents like famous poets, family, and even objects (López-Silva, 2018). This attribution to another and further separation of thought from self leads to a lack of ownership as the act of thinking is said to be absent, thus producing the positive and negative phenomenal aspects of TI, respectively (López-Silva, 2018).

In comparison, AVH phenomenology is characterized by a myriad of features that necessarily describe an auditory perceptual event, including content, clarity, tone, form of address, duration, and location (McCarthy-Jones et al., 2014; Nayani & David, 1996). Because AVH also connotes the presence (and maybe proximity) of another agent, relationships with AVH are capable of evolution over time and may play a central role in functioning (Chadwick et al., 2000). Voice-hearers may express changes in the relationship with their voices based on tone, receive commands from voices, and describe how the voices have become a part of their decision-making process by replacing their conscience (McCarthy-Jones et al., 2014; Nayani & David, 1996; Stephane et al., 2003). Because of its multidimensional nature, AVH phenomenology may be examined in hierarchical and multidimensional clusters that may include attribution to self vs. other, degree of control, location in space, subtypes, ability to cope, and linguistic complexity, all of which may differentially contribute to voice-hearers' ability to function (Stephane et al., 2003). Stephane and colleagues (2003) take such an approach, and note an association between attribution to self and degree of control, where patients who attribute the voices to self are more inclined to try to exert voluntary control over them, which itself predicts higher degrees of functioning (Stephane et al., 2003; Mourgues et al., 2020). Similarly, Nayani and colleagues (1996) also highlight an association between perceived internal location in space and ability to cope with AVH.

Both TI and AVH have been described as unwanted interruptions or intrusions in thought perceived to originate externally and taking the form of voices, thoughts, or noises with foreign origins (Badcock, 2016; Jaspers, 1997). Further distinguished from normal thought by a decreased sense of control, the experiential similarities between TI and AVH suggest a degree of phenomenological overlap. Most notably, this overlap lies in perception and audibility where descriptions of internally projected TI's and inaudible AVH's call into question the proposed perceptual distinctions traditionally separating the phenomena (Humpston & Broome, 2016).

Interestingly, reality monitoring abilities appear to have little to do with AVH or TI. Nayani and colleagues (1996) demonstrated that AVH subjects who believed in the reality of their hallucinations, verbal and nonverbal, were just as likely to have TI episodes when compared to AVH counterparts who doubt their hallucinations. In fact, TI descriptions in these subjects appeared to vary solely based on whether they perceived their AVH's as internal or external (Humpston & Broome, 2016). In other words, subjects with external AVH experiences went on to characterize their TI episodes as internal voices, whereas subjects with internal AVH experiences proceeded to label their TI episodes as merely bad impulses (Nayani & David, 1996). Humpston & Broome (2016) speculate that subjective differentiations lend to the idea of TI and AVH phenomenology as both lying on a perceptual spectrum where AVH internality predicts internality of TI and vice versa. Whether these phenomena fall on a spectrum or not, identification of these similarities sheds light on a degree of phenomenological overlap that also implies an overlap in the perceptual and cognitive underpinnings of both.

7.3. Perceptual and Cognitive

There is a significant overlap in theoretical accounts of how TI and AVH might arise from disruptions in self, a topic explored in depth in a rich philosophical tradition (Maiese, 2018; Young, 2006). Most prominently, these conceptualizations surround inference of self-action (Young, 2006). Instinctually, experiences where thoughts and voices are perceived as arising directly within the mind have widely been understood as follows: in order to acknowledge that the experience that has occurred in my mind is mine, then I must simultaneously acknowledge that I, even if unconsciously, initiated this experience somewhere in my mind (Maiese, 2018; Young, 2006). In other words, the ability to acknowledge that I am the one who has initiated thought implies acceptance of self as the author (or agent) of that thought (Maiese, 2018; Young, 2006). This leads naturally to the question: how is it that subjects can accept that an experience has occurred in their minds, yet deny ownership or authorship over the experience?

In fact, when considering typically occurring thought or auditory experiences in the mind, authorship is usually not distinguished from ownership

(Young, 2006). Some have maintained that authorship can only be distinguished from ownership when it is perceived as missing, such as in TI and/or AVH (Young, 2006). Thus, many theorists endorse exploring these two phenomena as they relate to a 'sense' of ownership and a 'sense' of authorship in order to ascertain whether or not TI and AVH are etiologically distinct (Maiese, 2018; Young, 2006). By proposing this clarification, Spence and colleagues (2001) suggest that the subjective experience of thoughts (or voices) being perceived as inserted or coming from another may both be due to subjects disengaging from thought itself, also explaining the restoration of the typical perception of other thoughts (or voices) as being self-generated when the subject is re-engaged.

This clarification allows us to further appreciate philosophically how one can acknowledge experiencing an (inserted) thought and yet adamantly contest being the author of the thought. This may be done by exploring the Kantian approach (Kant, 2002; Kendler & Campbell, 2014; Young, 2006). In this approach, authors have proposed first understanding how ownership of thought is maintained by Kant's proposition of 'I think' in *The Critique of Pure Reason* (Kant, 2002; Young, 2006). Here, Kant (2002) highlights the importance of the possibility of an 'I think' associated with all forms of self-representation. This 'I think', labelled as the source of production for our experience with thought, allows the experience to be ascribed to self and leads to recognition of self by self (Kant, 2002; Young, 2006). Therefore, in the absence of an 'I think' possibility, Young (2006) maintains that the possibility of what is being represented (i.e., thoughts) to be mine is also relinquished (Kant, 2002; Young, 2006). Plainly put, in this formulation, ownership is maintained in episodes of TI simply on the basis of, 'for a thought to be mine, it must be possible for me to be aware of it as mine' (Kant, 2002). As a result, the experience of an inserted thought is owned by me only if there is a possibility of me being aware of myself as the owner of the experience (i.e., 'I think') (Kant, 2002; Young, 2006). This general possibility of acknowledgement makes way for self-consciousness. Young (2006) highlights that this form of self-consciousness, which may be substantial enough to support a sense of ownership, is too minimal to allow for self to be ascribed as the author of the inserted thought.

Interestingly, although consciousness is said to be diminished, the Kantian approach does not consider the possibility of a disruption in consciousness during TI. In fact, Young (2006) states that with the placement of appropriate weight on Kant's use of 'possibility' when referring to an 'I think', one can speculate that although thoughts cannot be ascribed to a self-representation, the mere perception of an alien thought allows for the assumption that some form of unknown representation is present. This highlights a unity in consciousness simply due to the fact that subjects are able to compare alien thought to thoughts they perceive as their own (Young, 2006). In order to tackle the 'sense' of authorship, or lack thereof in TI, many question whether the recognition of active thinking is involved in being able to attribute thinking to self (Young, 2006).

While applying the Kantian approach, the activity of thinking is said to arise after the application of the following twelve categories: unity, plurality, totality, reality, negotiation, limitation, inherence-subsistence, cause and effect, community, possibility-impossibility, existence-nonexistence, and necessity (Kindler et al., 2013; Li et al., 2017; Young, 2006). These twelve categories are said to shape understanding in terms of quantity, quality, modality, and relation and only after their application can adequate judgement be applied to assess and acknowledge the activity of thought (Jaspers, 1997; Kant, 2002; Young, 2006). Thus, in TI, one may posit that all thought processes lacking this initial judgement is by default only a receptive-like perceptual experience or, more specifically, an experience in which the thought cannot be ascribed to myself as no apperception has occurred (Young, 2006). To be clear, with regard to the Kantian approach, the lack of judgement is not due to the absence of judgement nor the absence in application of the categories but instead due to the absence of self-awareness during episodes of TI (Young, 2006). So, what ultimately leads to a lack of 'sense' of authorship and self-awareness? Young (2006) proposes that the answers lie in spontaneity. An individual is truly self-aware only if they are able to acknowledge their spontaneity (Young, 2006). Therefore, spontaneous disruptions that occur just before the application of judgement onto categories leads to a discontinuity in awareness of thinking and the inability to acknowledge that thought is actually initiated by self (Jaspers, 1997; Young, 2006).

Comparatively, AVH episodes are perceptually characterized by a diminished 'sense' of ownership, a decreased sense of authorship, loss of control over inner speech, and disruption in consciousness (Maiese, 2018; Young, 2006). As subjects clearly attest to hearing noises or voices that do not belong to them, Maiese (2018) asserts that the primary cause of an AVH experience lies in understanding the lack of 'sense' of ownership ascribed to the phenomenon (Kendler & Campbell, 2014; Maiese, 2018). In other words, understanding where the 'mine-ness' goes when the hallucinatory experience begins (Maiese, 2018). While taking into account the perceived hallucinatory state of these subjects, one may argue that a lack of 'sense' in ownership may be ascribed to disruptions of selective attention where cohesive perception of auditory experiences are hindered in the subjects' mind (Maiese, 2018; Saks, 2007; Young, 2006).

Deficits in one's ability to process linguistic stimuli and employ executive control may inhibit one's ability to filter between relevant and irrelevant auditory information (Maiese, 2018; Saks, 2007). This conceptualization also dovetails with current accounts of AVH as arising from disruptions in Bayesian inference, where expectations predominate over incoming noisy sensory information (Corlett et al., 2019; Powers et al., 2016; Powers et al., 2017). Interestingly, it also extends this framework, implying that a failure to inhibit irrelevant information leads to an altered perception that hinders integration of contextual information and diminishes the sense of ownership typically attributed to auditory experiences (Maiese, 2018). This loss in perceptual organization justifies how sounds, thoughts, and voices are perceived as disconnected from self (Maiese, 2018). Thus, it can be speculated that this loss in sense of ownership leads subjects to naturally ascribe their auditory experiences to another, deny their initiation, and feel incapable of controlling them.

7.4. Neural

Voice perception involves the processing of information containing elements of speech, language, identity, and location of the speaker, among other things (Belin et al., 2011). These varying forms of vocal input are said to be processed in regions of the auditory cortex and organized into ventral and dorsal auditory pathways (Badcock, 2016). Typically, these auditory pathways, also known as processing streams, work together to allow for the integration of input and add to the complete formation of perception (Badcock, 2016). Additionally, it should be noted that as individual auditory pathways, each aforementioned vocal input can lead to intertwined and independent patterns of dysfunction, such as those seen in TI and AVH (Badcock, 2016).

The ventral processing stream is primarily involved in processing vocal identity whereas the dorsal processing stream involves the spatial features of sound (Badcock, 2016). Thus structural or functional changes in the ventral and/or dorsal auditory processing streams may contribute to the misattribution of voices and thought as well as where these voices and thoughts are said to come from (Badcock, 2016). In other words, even if only partially overlapped, the phenomenological similarities and differences of TI and AVH may simply be explained by processing stream dysfunctions.

Beginning with misattribution, one of the overlapping characteristics of TI and AVH phenomenology, studies propose that foreign thoughts and voices regardless of whether they are inserted or hallucinated arise through abnormal activation in the ventral auditory pathway (Badcock, 2016). Generally, identification of vocal input occurs as a result of a series of hierarchical processing stages when this pathway is activated. The acoustic processing stage, for example, uses familiar and unfamiliar acoustics in order to identify self-versus another (Belin et al., 2011). During episodes of TI and AVH, abnormal activation in this stage of the ventral processing stream is said to lead to errors in basic acoustic coding that spreads to the subsequent hierarchical stages (Badcock, 2016). Once propagated, this may lead to dysfunction in perceptions of thought and its recognition as either familiar or foreign (Badcock, 2016).

Another overlapping but nonetheless distinct phenomenological feature to take into account is the spatial perception of voices in TI and AVH (Badcock, 2016; Walsh et al., 2015). Potential changes in the dorsal auditory pathways function and structure may distinguish whether AVH's are perceived as external or internal experiences (Knappik et al., 2021; Looijestijn et al., 2013). Neuroimaging studies of subjects who perceive their AVH as external are observed to have increased neural responses and structural changes in dorsal processing stream structures like the middle frontal gyrus and the temporoparietal junction, respectively (Badcock, 2016; Plaze et al., 2011). However, these increased functional responses are not noted in subjects who perceive their AVH episodes as internal (Looijestijn et al., 2013). Comparatively, in episodes of TI, functional changes were identified in the dorsal pathway including abnormal activations of the angular and left supramarginal gyrus (Badcock, 2016; Gao et al., 2020; Kühn & Gallinat, 2012).

In an attempt to understand the complexities of TI phenomenology independently, models like the forward model and executive control model have been explored. Although research is limited, these explorations have helped in identifying hypoactivity and abnormal connectivity in varying locations in the brains of TI subjects (Walsh et al., 2015). For example, decreased activity has been observed in self recognition, self-monitoring, language producing, and sentence generating regions (Walsh et al., 2015). Most prominently, portions of the brain typically associated with recognition of self, like the precuneus, were identified to be bilaterally underactive. Additionally, areas that typically assist in sentence generation, sense of agency, and linguistics process information, like the thalamus, parietal, and temporal regions of the brain, were also noted to be underactive (Desmurget et al., 2009; Walsh et al., 2015). Ultimately, decreased activity leads to dysfunction in neural connectivity localized to the supplementary motor area (SMA) and primary motor cortex (M1) (Walsh et al., 2015).

Other authors emphasize the contributions of the SMA and M1 to thought ownership and control, identifying reduced connectivity between the left mid-cingulum and the SMA to TI (Walsh et al., 2015). Other changes that have been identified as TI episodes persist include connections between the left cerebellum and right superior temporal pole and disruptions in prefrontal inhibitory systems where lack of sensory suppression in SMA is associated with involuntary initiations of thought and movement (Walsh et al., 2015). AVH, on the other hand, has been widely explored in terms of brain structure, complex functional connectivity, and activation. For instance, brain regions associated with audition, language, verbal function, and sensory gating have been explored and determined to be abnormal in AVH subjects (Huang et al., 2019; Li et al., 2017). Most notably, atypical connectivity in the auditory cortex, hyperactivity in the thalamus and thalamic nuclei, and disruptions in the prefrontal cortex have been correlated to AVH episodes (Huang et al., 2019). Other anomalies commonly found in AVH subjects include decreased connectivity between the insular cortex and anterior cingulate cortex, decreased connectivity between the amygdala and the medial prefrontal cortex, and elevated glutamate levels in the prefrontal cortex (Alonso-Solís et al., 2017; Catani et al., 2011; Huang et al., 2019; Hubl et al., 2010; Knappik et al., 2021; Li et al., 2017; Plaze et al., 2011).

Neuroimaging of AVH subjects also shows decreased cortical and grey matter thickness in the right Heschi gyrus and language associated regions, respectively (Huang et al., 2019; Hubl et al., 2010; van Swam et al., 2012). In regards to connectivity, Kindler et al. (2013) demonstrates this in a study in which attenuation of the auditory cortex led to minimization or shortening of AVH episodes (Huang et al., 2019). Moreover, Li et al (2017) argues that previous associations identified between audition and the thalamic nuclei as well as fluctuations seen in thalamic potentiation of AVH subjects explains how sound could be perceived in the absence of external stimulation (Horga et al., 2014; Huang et al., 2019; Hubl et al., 2010; Li et al., 2017). In fact, when thalamic overstimulation occurs, a disruption to the inhibitory gating system is noted (Li et al., 2017). As a result, this disruption no longer allows incoming acoustic stimuli to be separated and refined (Horga et al., 2014; Huang et al., 2019; Li et al., 2017).

7.5. Conclusion and Future Directions

The evidence presented here suggests that TI and AVH are connected phenomenologically, conceptually, and mechanistically. The perceptual complexities found within a 'sense' of ownership and a 'sense' of authorship continues to raise the question of whether TI and AVH are simply varying degrees of the same one phenomenon. Nevertheless, it is clear that neither phenomenon is sufficiently understood to conclude this with certainty: it remains unclear whether their differences simply lie in the perceptual processes that subjects undergo when transitioning from lack of sense of ownership (or authorship) to alien ascription, or whether the description of these experiences vary or overlap based on other cognitive abilities. Further research is needed to compare non-clinical TI to clinical TI subjects and their AVH-experiencing counterparts. There is a notable gap in knowledge in this area spanning across all perspectives, as most comparisons are made between clinical vs. nonclinical AVH subjects and clinical TI vs. clinical AVH subjects. As it is understood right now, TI/AVH co-occurrence may be integral to the emergence of psychosis (Catani et al., 2011; Smeets et al., 2012). Study of non-clinical TI subjects could be key to conclusively understanding whether the phenomena are different while simultaneously answering a cascade of other questions, beginning most notably with—why do certain individuals develop psychosis while others do not?

References

Alonso-Solís, A., Vives-Gilabert, Y., Portella, M. J., Rabella, M., Grasa, E. M., Roldán, A., et al. (2017). Altered amplitude of low frequency fluctuations in schizophrenia patients with persistent auditory verbal hallucinations. *Schizophrenia Research, 189*, 97–103.

Badcock, J. C. (2016). A neuropsychological approach to auditory verbal hallucinations and thought insertion—grounded in normal voice perception. *Review of Philosophy and Psychology, 7*(3), 631–652.

Belin, P., Bestelmeyer, P. E. G., Latinus, M., & Watson, R. (2011). Understanding voice perception. *British Journal of Psychology, 102*(4), 711–725.

Catani, M., Craig, M. C., Forkel, S. J., Kanaan, R., Picchioni, M., Toulopoulou, T., et al. (2011). Altered integrity of Perisylvian language pathways in schizophrenia: Relationship to auditory hallucinations. *Biological Psychiatry, 70*(12), 1143–1150.

Chadwick, P., Sambrooke, S., Rasch, S., & Davies, E. (2000). Challenging the omnipotence of voices: Group cognitive behavior therapy for voices. *Behaviour Research and Therapy, 38*(10), 993–1003.

Corlett, P. R., Horga, G., Fletcher, P. C., Alderson-Day, B., Schmack, K., & Powers, A. R. (2019). Hallucinations and strong priors. *Trends in Cognitive Sciences, 23*(2), 114–127.

Desmurget, M., Reilly, K. T., Richard, N., Szathmari, A., Mottolese, C., & Sirigu, A. (2009). Movement intention after parietal cortex stimulation in humans. *Science, 324*(5928), 811–813.

Gao, J., Zhang, D., Wang, L., Wang, W., Fan, Y., Tang, M., et al. (2020). Altered effective connectivity in schizophrenic patients with auditory verbal hallucinations: A resting-state fMRI study with granger causality analysis. *Frontiers in Psychiatry, 11.* https://doi.org/10.3389/fpsyt.2020.00575

Henriksen, M. G., Parnas, J., & Zahavi, D. (2019). Thought insertion and disturbed for-me-ness (minimal selfhood) in schizophrenia. *Consciousness and Cognition, 74*, 102770.

Horga, G., Fernández-Egea, E., Mané, A., Font, M., Schatz, K. C., Falcon, C., et al. (2014). Brain metabolism during hallucination-like auditory stimulation in schizophrenia. *PLoS ONE, 9*(1), e84987.

Huang, J., Zhuo, C., Xu, Y., & Lin, X. (2019). Auditory verbal hallucination and the auditory network: From molecules to connectivity. *Neuroscience, 410*, 59–67.

Hubl, D., Dougoud-Chauvin, V., Zeller, M., Federspiel, A., Boesch, C., Strik, W., et al. (2010). Structural analysis of Heschl's gyrus in schizophrenia patients with auditory hallucinations. *Neuropsychobiology, 61*(1), 1–9.

Humpston, C.S., & Broome, M.R. (2016). The spectra of soundless voices and audible thoughts: Towards an integrative model of auditory verbal hallucinations and thought insertion. *Review of Philosophy and Psychology, 7*(3), 611–629.

Jaspers, K. (1997). *General Psychopathology* (Vol. 2). Baltimore, MD: JHU Press.

Kant, I. (2002). *Three Critiques, 3-Volume Set: Vol. 1: Critique of Pure Reason; Vol. 2: Critique of Practical Reason; Vol. 3: Critique of Judgment.* Indianapolis, IN: Hackett Publishing Company, Incorporated.

Kendler, K. S., & Campbell, J. (2014). Expanding the domain of the understandable in psychiatric illness: an updating of the Jasperian framework of explanation and understanding. *Psychological Medicine, 44*(1), 1–7.

Kindler, J., Homan, P., Jann, K., Federspiel, A., Flury, R., Hauf, M., et al. (2013). Reduced neuronal activity in language-related regions after transcranial magnetic stimulation therapy for auditory verbal hallucinations. *Biological Psychiatry, 73*(6), 518–524.

Knappik, F., Bless, J. J., & Larøi, F. (2021). Confusions about 'inner' and 'outer' voices: Conceptual problems in the study of auditory verbal hallucinations. *Review of Philosophy and Psychology, 13*, 215–236.

Kühn, S., & Gallinat, J. (2012). Quantitative meta-analysis on state and trait aspects of auditory verbal hallucinations in schizophrenia. *Schizophrenia Bulletin, 38*(4), 779–786.

Li, B., Cui, L.-B., Xi, Y.-B., Friston, K. J., Guo, F., Wang, H.-N., et al. (2017). Abnormal effective connectivity in the brain is involved in auditory verbal hallucinations in schizophrenia. *Neuroscience Bulletin, 33*(3), 281–291.

Looijestijn, J., Diederen, K. M. J., Goekoop, R., Sommer, I. E. C., Daalman, K., Kahn, R. S., et al. (2013). The auditory dorsal stream plays a crucial role in projecting hallucinated voices into external space. *Schizophrenia Research, 146*(1–3), 314–319.

López-Silva, P. (2018). Mapping the psychotic mind: A review on the subjective structure of thought insertion. *Psychiatric Quarterly, 89*(4), 957–968.

Maiese, M. (2018). Auditory verbal hallucination and the sense of ownership. *Philosophy, Psychiatry, & Psychology, 25*(3), 183–196.

McCarthy-Jones, S., Trauer, T., Mackinnon, A., Sims, E., Thomas, N., & Copolov, D. L. (2014). A new phenomenological survey of auditory hallucinations: evidence for subtypes and implications for theory and practice. *Schizophrenia Bulletin, 40*(1), 231–235.

Mellor, C. S. (1970). First rank symptoms of schizophrenia: I. The frequency in schizophrenics on admission to hospital II. Differences between individual first rank symptoms. *British Journal of Psychiatry, 117*(536), 15–23.

Mourgues, C., Negreira, A. M., Quagan, B., Mercan, N. E., Niles, H., Kafadar, E., et al. (2020). Development of voluntary control over voice-hearing experiences: Evidence from treatment-seeking and non-treatment-seeking voice-hearers. *Schizophrenia Bulletin Open, 1*(1), sgaa052.

Mullins, S., & Spence, S. A. (2003). Re-examining thought insertion. Semi-structured literature review and conceptual analysis. *British Journal of Psychiatry, 182*, 293–298.

Nayani, T. H., & David, A. S. (1996). The auditory hallucination: a phenomenological survey. *Psychological Medicine, 26*(1), 177–189.

Plaze, M., Paillère-Martinot, M. L., Penttilä, J., Januel, D., de Beaurepaire, R., Bellivier, F., et al. (2011). 'Where do auditory hallucinations come from?'—a brain morphometry study of schizophrenia patients with inner or outer space hallucinations. *Schizophrenia Bulletin, 37*(1), 212–221.

Powers, A. R., III, Kelley, M., & Corlett, P. R. (2016). Hallucinations as top-down effects on perception. Biological Psychiatry. *Cognitive Neuroscience and Neuroimaging, 1*(5), 393–400.

Powers, A. R., Mathys, C., & Corlett, P. R. (2017). Pavlovian conditioning-induced hallucinations result from overweighting of perceptual priors. *Science (New York, N.Y.), 357*(6351), 596–600.

Ratcliffe, M., & Wilkinson, S. (2015). Thought insertion clarified. *Journal of Consciousness Studies: Controversies in Science & the Humanities, 22*(11–12), 246–269.

Saks, E. R. (2007). *The Center Cannot Hold: My Journey Through Madness*. London: Hachette UK.

Smeets, F., Lataster, T., Dominguez, M. D., Hommes, J., Lieb, R., Wittchen, H. U., & van Os, J. (2012). Evidence that onset of psychosis in the population reflects early hallucinatory experiences that through environmental risks and affective dysregulation become complicated by delusions. *Schizophrenia Bulletin, 38*(3), 531–542.

Spence, S. (2001). Alien control: From phenomenology to cognitive neurobiology. *Philosophy, Psychiatry, & Psychology, 8*(2), 163–172.

Stephane, M., Thuras, P., Nasrallah, H., & Georgopoulos, A. P. (2003). The internal structure of the phenomenology of auditory verbal hallucinations. *Schizophrenia Research, 61*(2–3), 185–193.

Sterzer, P., Mishara, A. L., Voss, M., & Heinz, A. (2016). Thought insertion as a self-disturbance: An integration of predictive coding and phenomenological approaches. *Frontiers in Human Neuroscience, 10*, 502.

van Swam, C., Federspiel, A., Hubl, D., Wiest, R., Boesch, C., Vermathen, P., et al. (2012). Possible dysregulation of cortical plasticity in auditory verbal hallucinations—a cortical thickness study in schizophrenia. *Journal of Psychiatric Research, 46*(8), 1015–1023.

Walsh, E., Oakley, D. A., Halligan, P. W., Mehta, M. A., & Deeley, Q. (2015). The functional anatomy and connectivity of thought insertion and alien control of movement. *Cortex, 64*, 380–393.

Waters, F., & Fernyhough, C. (2017). Hallucinations: A systematic review of points of similarity and difference across diagnostic classes. *Schizophrenia Bulletin, 43*(1), 32–43.

Young, G. (2006). Kant and the phenomenon of inserted thoughts. *Philosophical Psychology, 19*, 823–837.

8
Schizophrenia and the Error-Prediction Model of Thought Insertion

Pablo López-Silva and Álvaro Cavieres

8.1. The Aetiological Problem of Thought Insertion

Thought insertion—TI *henceforth—is* regarded as one of the most severe symptoms of psychiatric alterations (Schneider, 1959; Mullins & Spence, 2003; López-Silva, 2018). Most common in schizophrenia, patients suffering from TI report entities of different nature introducing thoughts/ideas into their minds/skulls (Jaspers, 1963; Mellor, 1970; López-Silva, 2018). In a highly discussed case, a patient reports that in TI: 'thoughts are put into my mind like "Kill God", it's just like my mind working, but it isn't. They come from this chap, Chris. They are his thoughts' (Frith, 1992, p. 66). It is important to note that TI is usually reported as preceded and accompanied by a generally rarefied experience of the subjective, intersubjective, and physical world (Mayer-Gross, 1932; Conrad, 1958; Fuchs, 2005; Payne, 2013; López-Silva et al. 2022). In the phenomenological tradition, the period—that can last from days to months—preceding the emergence of full-blown cases of TI and other positive psychotic symptoms has been referred to as 'delusional atmosphere' (*Wahnstimmung*; Conrad, 1958). As patient BS indicates, during the months preceding her own episode of TI, she experienced a generalized sense of unreality, a general transformation of the social and subjective world: 'I had short periods of time in which I felt like I didn't exist. I had other experiences in which I had to, for instance, touch a coffee table in front of me to make sure it was real' (BS in López-Silva, 2018). In light of its unique features, both psychiatrists and philosophers have found in TI a formidable challenge for the way in which consciousness, self-awareness, agency, the nature of beliefs, and a number of other critical concepts have been characterized (Gibbs, 2000; Stephens & Graham, 2000; Billon & Kriegel, 2015; López-Silva, 2016, 2019, 2020; Guillot, 2017; Gennaro, 2021; Humpston, 2022; Billon, 2023).

A unique challenge arises when we try to offer a story about how TI is produced. We call this the *aetiological problem*. Every alternative available to this problem should be consistent with the patients' phenomenological reports and the empirical evidence. While the former element will establish clear *explananda* for the proposed theory, the latter will provide independent support for it. Over the years, a number of functional alterations have been regarded as responsible for the aetiology of positive symptoms, such as auditory-verbal hallucinations and delusion. Nelson et al. (2014) report that people with schizophrenia have problems distinguishing the consequences of their own actions from those of others and tend to confuse their own thoughts with other types of mental states. Along with other cognitive problems such as source monitoring abnormalities, these alterations would make subjects prone to offering bizarre explanations for the occurrence of bizarre experiences. Finally, this would lead up to the emergence of delusions such as TI (Nelson et al., 2014). Phenomenologically informed views have claimed that TI patients fail to attribute agency to certain actions and thoughts, thus producing the externalization of those states (Gallagher, 2004, 2014). Of course, such claims are not far from controversy. For example, Proust (2009) and López-Silva (2020) claim that the popular lack-of-agency views of TI arise from a problematic parallelism between thoughts and motor actions, making it unclear whether we can really conceptualize thinking in psychosis as akin to motor action without reproducing a number of problems.[1] In addition to this, the scarcity and specificity of first-person phenomenological account of TI along with the difficulties for gathering specific empirical evidence make the task of offering plausible answers for the aetiological problem highly complex. So, although progress has been made over the last few years (Kusters, 2014; López-Silva, 2018; Feyaerts et al., 2021), the aetiological problem of TI is still open.

In recent years, the so-called *error-prediction model* of delusions has been gaining explanatory traction due to its capacity to link empirical evidence and computational psychiatry with phenomenological descriptions of psychotic experiences (Fletcher & Frith, 2009; Sterzer et al. 2018; Corlett et al. 2019; Corlett & Fletcher, 2021; Adams et al. 2022). The prediction-error model derives from a general theory—predictive processing—about the way in which the brain produces our conscious experience of reality and claims that, in doing so, the brain uses prior learned predictions to infer the causes of incoming sensory data. On this view, the brain is an organ of predictive

---

[1] For another appraisal on the agency-based view of TI, see: López-Silva (2020) and Mishara, López-Silva, Rosen, and Heinz (this compilation).

inference (Friston, 2010, 2012a, 2012b; Friston et al., 2016; Clark, 2016, 2019). For the advocates of this view, the brain's inferential processing can be formalized as a type of Bayesian inference where a probabilistic prediction is combined with observed sensory data (*likehood*) to compute (see Friston, 2012a; Lee & Mumford, 2003). After clarifying some cognitive and phenomenological aspects often linked to the aetiology of TI in the literature, this paper examines the error-prediction model of delusions and discusses some of the main challenges faced by its application to the aetiology of TI. After that, in order to motivate further research in the field, the final section discusses an issue that seems to remain open within our target debate.

8.2. Elements for a Neuropsychiatric Approach to TI

Contrasting with psychoanalytic and purely phenomenological traditions, neuropsychiatric models of psychopathological phenomena focus on providing empirically based explanatory theories appealing to different types of sensorial and cognitive deficits. For this reason, they have also been called *deficit accounts* (McKay, Langdon, & Colheart, 2009; McKay & Dennett, 2009).[2] From a conceptual point of view, most neuropsychiatric approaches explicitly endorse a doxastic concept of delusions, i.e., the idea that states labelled as 'delusions' are abnormal beliefs (Bayne & Pacherie, 2005; Bayne, 2010; McKay & Dennett, 2009; López-Silva, 2016; Miyazono & McKay, 2019; Corlett et al., 2019, Corlett & Fletcher, 2021).[3] Lately, some authors within the phenomenological traditions have suggested that delusions cannot be merely characterized as beliefs because they involve an entire transformation of the structure of consciousness (see for example, Pienkos, Silverstein, & Sass, 2017; Sass &

---

[2] Opposing the *deficit* approach, some have suggested the existence of a subtype of delusions named as 'motivated delusions'. These delusional states would arise as a way of dealing with psychologically threatening stimuli without underlying specific neuro-functional *deficit* (see for example, Bell, 2003). Deeply grounded in the psychoanalytic tradition, we think this view is difficult to defend. It might be the case that clear deficits are not identified in certain cases, but (i) this is not reason to rule out the potential identification of certain deficits in the future (after all, that is how scientific progress works); (ii) the pathological nature of the type of response that a delusion is offers *prima face* reason to claim that some kind of deficit must be at the origin of the production of such an state, even if this deficit is 'purely' psychological (if that even exists, given how hard it is to conceive a psychological deficit without an underlying neuro-cognitive alteration). A potential reply to our comment is that the type of psychological mechanism underlying motivated delusions is designed to act in that exact way under specially stressing circumstances (acting as a way of coping with the circumstances). However, this can also mean that psychologically defensive mechanisms are activated as a way of dealing with deficits in other dimensions.

[3] It is important to note that the doxastic approach does not necessarily entail that delusional beliefs are 'irrational'. In addition, the claim that delusions are an abnormal type of belief seems to apply to the mental states finally reported by patients in clinical settings. The doxastic model as such is flexible when trying to provide an explanation for the type of experience underlying the formation of such abnormal beliefs (see, Davies et al., 2001; Bayne & Pacherie, 2005; Sollberger, 2014).

Pienkos, 2013; Feyaerts et al. 2021). As suggested by the Early Heidelberg School of authors such as Beringer, Grule, and Mayer-Gross (see Kendler & Mishara, 2019), clinically relevant delusions arise from multimodal perceptual alterations in the general structure of consciousness where different sensory modalities tend to merge creating a phenomenologically bizarre experience of the body, reality, and the self. However, as we have suggested elsewhere, claiming that psychotic delusions involve alterations in the structure of phenomenal experience is not incompatible with claiming that delusions are beliefs, taken as endorsements (Bayne & Pacherie, 2005; López-Silva, 2020; López-Silva et al., 2022) or explanations (Sterzer et al. 2016, 2018; Corlett et al 2011; Corlett, 2018; Corlett & Fletcher, 2021) for such experiences. Before examining a potential application of the error-prediction model to TI, in this section we offer a description of some of the main experiential and cognitive alterations that have been associated with the aetiology of delusions in schizophrenia. After this, we explore how these aspects could inform the error-prediction approach to TI.

8.2.1. The experiential context of schizophrenia

Descriptions in the neuropsychiatric literature of TI do not usually consider the context in which they emerge (Mishara & Zaytseva, 2019). Furthermore, clear description of the symptom and its phenomenological context of emergence are very difficult to find (Sterzer et al., 2016; López-Silva, 2018; López-Silva et al., 2022). Some of them may refer to the content of the delusion (Frith, 1992), while some others to the process of thinking in psychosis (Sollberger, 2014; Kusters, 2021). Other descriptions might even describe TI in terms of a physical experience of insertion. For example, Cahill and Frith (1996) report that, apart from feeling certain thoughts as not being their own, some TI patients refer to a physical experience of insertion, one of their patients even showing with his finger the point of entry of the specific inserted thought (p. 278). It is crucial for a neuropsychiatric approach to TI to take seriously the idea that delusional reports might be based on a generalized altered awareness of thoughts and bodily experiences; and more importantly, on complex multimodal experiences that combine phenomenal features of both (see Mayer-Gross, 1932; Kaminsky, Sterzer & Mishara, 2019; see also Mishara et al. in this compilation).

During the period preceding the emergence of TI, thoughts might acquire non-paradigmatic sensory-like features as a part of a general transformation of the conscious experience of the world and the self. This seems to be a fundamental feature of the strangeness of delusional atmospheres prior to production of delusions in schizophrenia (see for example, Payne 2013). Consequently, and contrasting with a dominant view in current literature, TI should not be characterized as purely appealing to certain thoughts lacking a sense of agency. Such a common over-intellectualization in the analysis of TI neglects the fact that the type of experience leading up to TI might lack the paradigmatic phenomenal features of common thinking, but more importantly, it overlooks the fact that such thoughts would represent a completely novel class of experience of multimodal nature; experience that only can be understood in the context of delusional atmospheres (see for example, Mayer-Gross, 1932; Mishara et al. this compilation). Reporting his own psychotic experiences, Kusters (2014, p, 105) claims that during the period preceding TI: 'you can even feel them [the thoughts] stream away through your hands or your head', adding that 'in madness, they become more sense-like and may, for example, have shape and colour'. The same is reported by Payne (2013). With some exceptions, dominant neuropsychiatric approaches to TI seem to have neglected this fundamental phenomenological remark.

One way of understanding how thoughts may acquire sensorial properties found in the literature appeals to the relation between thoughts and language (Vygotsky, 1962). Vygotsky (1997) claims that mental functions appear twice in development. First, as an interpsychological activity taking place between more than one individual, and second, intrapsychologically, that is, as the result of an internalization process (Rieber, 1987). In this context, thoughts are the transformation of external into internal dialogue, which, by definition, enjoys sensory features. According to Vygotsky, the original external speech undergoes important syntactic and semantic changes losing most of its acoustic and structural qualities becoming finally 'thinking in pure meanings' (Rieber, 1987). Expanding this idea, Fernyhough (2004) proposes a four-level developmental scheme allowing also for a reverse movement between the levels at any given point in development or, relevant for our discussion, within unusually demanding cognitive conditions. This means that, under special circumstances, our normal inner speech could be experienced as an expanded dialogue with the qualities of normal conversation. From this point of view, silent expression of thoughts in a coherent linguistic form is referred to as *inner speech* (Vygotsky, 1962). It has also been described as the silent production of words in one's mind, or the activity of talking to oneself in silence (Zivin, 1979). The problem with this suggestion is that it does not seem to be able to explain how thoughts would acquire features such as colour and shape, so more complete account of the multimodality of thoughts in psychosis is needed (for a proposal, see Sterzer et al. 2016).

Inner speech has been regarded as crucial to consciousness, self-awareness, self-regulation (Morin & Michaud, 2007; Morin, 2009, 2012), and a number of other cognitive functions. However, there is an ongoing debate on whether inner speech is processed in a similar way to overt speaking. Some suggest that inner speech only lacks the production of sound (Oppenheim & Dell, 2008); others, that it is processed without articulatory information (Abramson & Goldinger, 1997) by the same or different neural mechanisms (Stephan, Saalbach, & Rossi, 2020). Within this debate, it has been argued that inner speech could become perceptible to the subject due to failures in inhibitory mechanisms (Cho & Wu, 2014). For some authors, this seems to be the foundation of the hypotheses concerning the perception of internal thought, as the origin of auditory-verbal hallucinations (Cho & Wu, 2014). But, for others, it is also reminiscent of the view that inserted thoughts may belong in a group with other similar phenomena such as loud thoughts and verbal hallucinations (Langland-Hassan, 2008). About this, Schröder (1915) proposed a sequence progressing from thought insertion to loud thoughts and finally verbal hallucinations. What unifies all these symptoms would be a *feeling of foreignness*, namely, a primary non-analysable property of this set of phonemes. Mayer-Gross (1932) would later contend Schröder's proposition and argue that, in TI, the underlying anomaly is perceptual in nature, namely, 'the experience of individual thoughts becoming sensory' in the context of a radical alteration of previous perceptions. Schröder's view is certainly problematic in a number of respects. For example, if hallucinations and delusions are part of the very same group of symptoms, why is the former so common in the general population, while the latter seems to appear only in severe cases of psychiatric alterations? If hallucinations and delusions are part of the very same group of symptoms, why do patients tend to be able to distinguish between them? If hallucinations and delusions are part of the very same group of symptoms, what elements account for their phenomenological differences? Do we have empirical data supporting common neurological paths underlying the production of such different phenomena? Certainly, some of these observations are consistent with the findings of López-Silva et al. (2022). Examining 20 years' data of psychiatric patients, they conclude that episodes of TI are rarely experienced without other accompanying symptoms such as other delusions and auditory-verbal hallucinations. Now, even if this is the case, theories still need to account for the ways in which such different symptoms arise from the general multimodality of the psychotic experience.

8.2.2. Cognitive abnormalities and delusion formation

A neuropsychiatric approach to TI needs to identify the elements that would explain why such bizarre experientially based doxastic hypotheses are finally crystalized in the form of a delusional belief and maintained over time against counterevidence, a characteristic feature of delusions (Jaspers, 1963; López-Silva, 2016). This feature has been commonly associated with the role of certain cognitive impairments in the psychotic population. It has been suggested that people with schizophrenia develop different forms of reasoning anomalies or cognitive biases such as (a) abnormal data gathering or jumping-to-conclusions bias which lead subjects to arrive at conclusions despite insufficient evidence for it (Merrin, Kinderman, & Bentall, 2007; Evans, Averbeck, & Furl, 2015), (b) bias against disconfirmatory evidence or not being able to change beliefs in the presence of new contradictory information (Moritz & Woodward, 2005; Moritz et al. 2020) and/or (c) attributional biases that lead patients to explain their negative experiences as caused by others rather than by themselves, or caused by few rather than by many factors (Moritz et al., 2016, 2020; Coltheart & Caramazza, 2006). Some have claimed that the existence of such cognitive alterations in psychotic patients might account for the maintenance and resistance to counterevidence observed in delusional phenomena. For example, Coltheart (2015) claims that the presence of these cognitive problems is fundamental to distinguish between people who only undergo aberrant experiences from those who have abnormal experiences and end up developing delusional beliefs.

However, López-Silva and Cavieres (2021) have recently suggested that there is no clear consensus on the specific role that these cognitive impairments play in certain accounts of delusions (mostly, two-factor accounts). The point made is not whether or not these phenomena are present, rather, that their presence and importance are highly variable, seeming to depend on the influence and interactions with other factors. This makes it very difficult to define a precise role of these cognitive alterations in delusion formation. For example, the most replicated and cited evidence for the existence of cognitive biases in people with schizophrenia is *jumping to conclusions*, namely, the tendency to make hasty decisions with insufficient evidence (Dudley et al., 2016; Evans, Averbeck, & Furl, 2015). However, there is no general agreement regarding the occurrence of jumping to conclusions in schizophrenia in current literature (Ross et al., 2015; Dudley et al., 2016; Strube et al., 2022). In fact, the same results presented as supporting the presence of this cognitive bias have also been interpreted as evidence for the presence of *hypersalience*, a phenomenon that cannot even be classified as a reasoning bias (Speechley et al., 2012). Some authors have even suggested that, in psychosis, reasoning processes may be unaltered, and their performance would be poor for the limited amount of information available (Speechley et al., 2012); others claim that the cognitive errors seem independent from the information gathered (Garety et al., 2015).

Another problem is that not all studies find a specific association between jumping to conclusions and delusions in schizophrenia (see López-Silva and Cavieres, 2021). This cognitive bias has been described in both deluded and non-deluded subjects (Moritz et al., 2016); and antipsychotic treatment does not seem to affect it (Menon, Mizhari, & Kapur, 2008), so it could be a general feature of schizophrenia (Menon et al., 2006), a feature of many other psychiatric disorders (Wittorf et al., 2013), or even a cognitive trait present in a significant proportion of the general population (Freeman, Pugh, & Garety 2008). As for the existence of a cognitive bias against disconfirmatory evidence—BADE henceforth—although much less investigated, there is evidence of its presence in healthy controls with subclinical features of schizotypy, patients at risk of psychosis, subjects in their first episode of psychosis and subjects with chronic schizophrenia (Eisenacher & Zink, 2017). In addition, BADE has been specifically related to patients with psychotic symptoms (Speechley et al., 2012). Balzan et al. (2012) hypothesize that the most fundamental cognitive alteration underlying the neglect of contradictory new evidence is the hypersalience of previous evidence-hypothesis matches, thus reducing the flexibility of the integration of new information. Although not all studies find an association between BADE and delusions (Moritz et al., 2016) this cognitive bias could be especially important in the maintenance of already formed (pathological) beliefs, potentially reinforcing delusional conviction when they have already developed.

8.3. A Prediction-Error Approach to Thought Insertion

Prediction-error models derive from a general theory about the way in which the brain works and build up our conscious experience of reality and the self. Strongly informed by computational neuroscience, this model involves the application of predictive coding and Bayesian inference to the understanding of the mind (Sterzer et al., 2018; Corlett, 2018; Corlett et al., 2019; Corlett & Fletcher, 2021). Based on Von Helmholtz's idea of unconscious inference, this approach claims that our brain uses prior learned predictions (so-called *priors*) to infer the causes of inherently impoverished incoming sensory data, and that this process can be formalized as a type of Bayesian inference where a probabilistic prediction is combined with observed sensory data (*likehood*) to compute (*posteriors*) (see Friston, 2010; Lee & Mumford, 2003). Inferences regarding the current state of the world are made by combining prior beliefs about the way the world is supposed to be with incoming sensory signals (Fletcher & Frith, 2009). Important for our target discussion, 'these predictions can be based in principle on any source of information other than the actual sensory stimulus that is subject to inference, that is, the stimulus whose cause is to be inferred' (Sterzer et al., 2016, p. 2). The predictive coding framework conceives of the brain as a hierarchy aiming at maximizing the evidence for its model of the world comparing prior beliefs with incoming sensory data. When predictions match sensory data, the brain's model of the world is reinforced, this improving our general understanding of reality. However, when incoming signals do not match our predictions, the brain uses those prediction errors to update the model, allowing new learning. Here, prediction errors are weighted by the precision of the prior belief and the sensory data. As Sterzer et al. (2016) suggest, 'if the precision […] of the sensory data is high relative to the precision of the prior belief, the precision-weighted prediction error will be greater and vice versa' (p. 2).

In the context of psychosis, it is suggested that decreasing precision in the encoding of prior beliefs about sensory data would lead to maladaptive inferences. Decreased precision in the representation of prior beliefs relative to an increased precision in the encoding of the sensory data would result in an abnormally strong weighting of precision error (Adams et al., 2022). The idea is that imbalance in precisions shifts the posteriors toward the sensory data and away from priors, and inference is thus driven more strongly by the sensory data (Sterzer et al., 2018). Here we note an idea that might lead to some worries and that we will discuss later. On this view, it is suggested that prediction problems result on the attribution of salience to otherwise irrelevant, leading to delusional mood (Sterzer et al., 2016), and leading to the production of positive symptoms of schizophrenia such as delusions and auditory-verbal hallucinations (Notredame et al., 2014; Sterzer et al., 2018). The notion of 'attribution of salience' is pivotal for the application of predictive processing to psychosis. According to Kapur (2003), this is 'the process whereby events and thought come to grab attention, drive action, and influence goal-directed behaviour because their association with reward or punishment' (p. 14). On this model, abnormal attribution of salience is the product of aberrant prediction-error signals. According to Corlett et al. (2009), in psychosis, events that are insignificant and merely coincident demand attention, relating to each other in new meaningful and non-paradigmatic ways. Under the influence of abnormal prediction-error signals, delusions would arise as a way of explaining these experiences. So, according to Kapur (2003), delusions are '"top-down" cognitive explanations that the individual imposes on these experiences of aberrant salience in an effort to make sense of them' (p. 15). There is strong evidence supporting the existence of abnormalities in dopamine transmission in schizophrenia leading to an inappropriate attribution of salience. To prediction-error model advocates, in schizophrenia these prediction errors are produced in the absence of real mismatch between prediction and actual sensory inputs due to this dopaminergic alteration. Over the last 5 years, the prediction-error model has gained explanatory traction due to its empirical support and experimental applicability (see Sterzer et al., 2018).

In the case of TI, Sterzer et al. (2016) claim that the symptom is produced by a failure of hierarchical Bayeseian inference to contextualize or predict the narrative of interconnectedness of thoughts. In TI, there would exist an imprecise representation of context that leads to a failure to provide top-down predictions of the neural representations of thoughts. Then, these representations would be experienced as being caused by external agents, in the manner that percepts are experienced as being caused by sensory input (For the authors, it is the experience of *thoughts as sensations* that characterizes TI). This would explain why TI are experienced as coming from nowhere (see also Martin & Pacherie, 2013). So, in analogy with the salience of external events, internal events such as thoughts can also be experienced as overly salient and, in consequence, unusual and surprising. As Sterzer et al. (2016) claim, 'the individual's attempt to explain the aberrant salience and unusual character of thoughts (what Mayer-Gross 1932 identifies as "how" they are given) results in their interpretation as being caused by an alien agent' (p. 6). More specifically, 'the resulting thoughts may be experienced as coming from nowhere, since the trigger cannot be traced back anymore, even implicitly, as non-conscious context. In order to explain the unusual experience, the individual may form a delusional explanation for the occurrence of the untraceable thought (p. 7).

8.4. Examining the Error-Prediction Approach to TI

The prediction-error model seems well-equipped to explain most aspects of the experiential dimension of TI formation (see for example Corlett et al., 2009; Sterzer et al., 2016; Mishara et al., this compilation). However, a number of difficulties can be identified when error-predictions models are applied to TI. First of all, the claim that aberrant salient is sufficient for explaining the phenomenon—the error-prediction claim henceforth—seems too general to explain the complexity of the multimodal experiences leading up to delusions of TI. The model does not explain how aberrant salience is able to diminish the phenomenal limits of the different sensory modalities that merge together in pre-psychotic periods. The model could be able to explain why sensory modalities collide but not why and how they *merge*. TI cases are characterized for experiences of thoughts becoming sensory and acquiring strange quasi-perceptual features (Mayer-Gross, 1932; Payne, 2013; Kusters, 2021). So, it is not clear if these transformations lead up to aberrant salience, or if aberrant salience produces this type of experience. In both cases, applications of the model would need to specify the nature of the relationship between aberrant salience and the type of experience that seems to lead to TI experiences described in the phenomenological literature of early delusion formation (see Fusar-Poli et al., 2022). At the same time, the model would benefit from the clarification of a theory of perception that allow it to make sense of multimodal experiences. It is important to note that predictive processing is a model predominantly focused on the relationship between perception and action (Hohwy, 2013; Clark, 2016). Taking this into consideration, it becomes very challenging to picture the priors related to *thinking*. If TI is somehow related to abnormal thinking in psychosis, it is not clear to define what the priors of a thought would look like as it is not clear what is to be predicted when we have a specific thought. It is extremely problematic to characterize thinking in terms of expectations, for we do not expect to think a certain way in light of certain incoming stimulus. In the same way, contextual information might help to make retrospective sense of our thoughts but predicting is different from integration of contextual information. Now, it is true that thoughts can be experienced as overly salient (the case of *obsessive thoughts* is a good example of this); however, this would only explain why certain thoughts are experienced as unusual and surprising; it cannot explain either the externalization of such thoughts or the nature of the agents identified by patients. We will come back to this in the last section.

A second relevant issue in the application of the error-prediction model to TI is that it appeals to the same claim—i.e., that aberrant prediction-error signals are sufficient for the development of positive symptoms of delusions—to account for different sets of symptoms such as auditory-verbal hallucinations, visual hallucinations, delusions about the relationship between the body and the self, and delusions about the experience of thinking. The problem is that, although some of their phenomenal features might be similar, these phenomena can actually be distinguished by patients in clinical interviews. This lack of specificity in explaining the phenomenological differences between positive symptoms is evident in most proposals within the error-prediction framework, where all these phenomena are often treated as explanations for aberrant experiences indistinctively. The question here is not whether different sensory modalities can be grasped in a Bayesian predictive manner (in fact, that idea seems quite plausible); rather, the question here is about how to account for the phenomenological and representational differences between the many different symptoms arising if all of them are produced by aberrant salience attribution in schizophrenia. In other words, the question is how to account for the diversity of symptoms by using just one claim, namely, the error-prediction claim. Certainly, this issue seems to remain open for the error-prediction model of TI, and psychotic symptoms in general. Lately, it has been suggested that phenomenological differences between co-ocurrent symptoms could be explained by a differential weighting of specific hierarchical levels in different psychotic symptoms (Kwisthout, Bekkering, & van Rooij, 2017; Sterzer et al., 2018). More specifically, while hallucination proneness might be correlated with stronger employment of global (gist) and local (detail) priors, delusion proneness would be associated with less reliance on local priors. This alternative certainly requires the clarification of such levels and the reasons why those levels act in such a way. As, it has been proposed by Sterzer et al. (2018): 'Where to draw the line between perceptual and conceptual processing remains a challenge, and indeed, whether and how high-level prior beliefs modulate perceptual processes is controversial' (p. 4).

A third associated difficulty for error-prediction models of TI and related symptoms has to do with the dissociability problem (Miyazono et al., 2015). The error-prediction claim seems to assume that every episode of delusional atmosphere ends up in the development of delusions; in most proposal it is suggested that aberrant salience leads to delusional moods that, in turn, lead to positive symptoms (see Sterzer et al., 2016, 2018). At least *prima facie*, this is not necessarily the case. It might be that every case of TI is preceded by a delusional mood, but the reverse case is not guaranteed. On this model, delusions of TI are produced as explanations for the abnormal experiences arising during the delusional mood (Sterzer et al., 2016). Many phenomenological features of delusional moods resemble phenomenal features of other altered states of consciousness, so it is, at least in principle, possible to think about cases of delusional mood-type of experience not leading up to delusions, and therefore, that aberrant prediction-error signals would not be sufficient for the development of delusions. As suggested by Miyazono et al. (2015), a potential response to this problem is to say that prediction errors in people with delusional mood-type of experience not leading up to delusions are not as serious as prediction errors in people with schizophrenia, because 'the salience of the data in question has simply not passed a certain threshold' (2012, p. 348). However, even if this is the case, a plausible theory needs to specify the criteria and nature of this threshold, and what abnormalities play a significant role in the trespassing of that threshold in especially schizophrenia. Perhaps, advocates of the model could appeal to the role played by the type of top-down cognitive alterations described earlier. In this way, the presence of aberrant prediction-error signals would interact with cognitive biases and other abnormalities in cognitive performance in other hierarchical levels leading up to the crystallization of implausible doxastic hypothesis into delusional beliefs (for a discussion of this idea, see Corlett & Fletcher, 2021). The presence and interaction of these different types of abnormalities could inform an error-prediction approach to TI. A final suggestion might be to appeal to specific neurobiological alterations absent in non-psychotic populations to account for the ways in which prediction errors and cognitive impairments lead up to the formation of positive symptoms such as TI as the result of anomalies in multiple levels in the brain's hierarchy. Certainly, more research is needed in order to clarify this issue.

A final issue for error-prediction models has to do with how to explain the maintenance of delusions. After their initial adoption, delusions such as TI are maintained despite overwhelming evidence. In fact, this is one of the most critical issues when thinking about psychotherapeutic approaches to delusions (Moritz et al., 2023; Kumar, 2020). Recognizing this issue, advocates of the model initially claimed that 'this mode accounts for why delusions emerge but not for why they persist' (Corlett et al., 2013, p. 2). However, the perseverance of delusions is a fundamental aspect for the description of the phenomenon (APA, 2013). In dealing with this challenge, Corlett et al. (2009) suggest that aberrant prediction errors in schizophrenia re-evoke the representation of the delusion without disconfirming it completely. This drives preferential reconsolidation over and above any new extinction learning so that 'the net effect would be a strengthening of the delusion through reconsolidation rather than a weakening by extinction' (p. 9). Resistance against counterevidence seems to suggest an excessively high influence of delusional beliefs on the perception of new incoming information, 'which would entail an increased precision of delusion-related priors' (Sterzer et al., 2018, p. 5). However, it is suggested that the emergence of delusions might result from decreased precision of priors (Corlett et al., 2009; Fletcher & Frith, 2009; Adams et al., 2022). Evidence from experiments using the NMDAR antagonist ketamine, which has been previously shown to induce aberrant PEs, suggests a link between PE signalling and memory reconsolidation, which could strengthen delusional beliefs and foster their persistence (Sterzer et al., 2018). Lately, Corlett and Fletcher

(2021) have claimed that delusions should be characterized as an evolving uncertainty-driven negotiation between beliefs and evidence. The idea is that the initial formation of a delusion is fuelled by unexpected uncertainty—an observation that is consistent with the phenomenology of schizophrenia. After this, the delusion would engender new expectations about uncertainty that tune down updating but, at the same time, facilitate the elastic assimilation of contradictory evidence. Although these suggestions add interesting elements to the discussion, a number of specifications are needed in order to provide a clear-cut account for how and why delusions such as TI persist. It is important for the error-prediction model to specify the conditions for a delusion to become such an important part of the subject's internal model of the world so that it becomes so resistant to counterevidence.

8.5. Concluding Remarks: Externalization of Thoughts as an Open Challenge

TI is certainly one of the most complex symptoms of psychosis. In this chapter, we have examined the application of a promising framework to the aetiology problem of TI, the error-prediction model. Over the last years, this framework has been gaining explanatory traction due to its congruency with the phenomenology of psychosis, computational psychiatry, and current neuropsychiatry. The model seems to be well-equipped for explaining a number of key elements in the process of formation of TI that other alternatives do not seem to integrate. For example, the two-factor view does not seem to be able—in its current form—to integrate the process of delusional mood into the formation of TI. However, an important issue seems to remain an open challenge with the error-prediction model of TI.

A general challenge for any attempt to solve the aetiology problem of TI concerns how to explain the nature of the external attribution identified as a fundamental part of the structure of the symptom, namely, the 'positive aspect of TI' (López-Silva, 2018). Inserted thoughts are not only 'inserted' or 'foreign', they are reported as inserted by agents of different nature (Jaspers, 1963; Mellor, 1970; Mullins & Spence, 2003; López-Silva, 2018). The error-prediction model of TI suggests that 'aberrant salience is sufficient to explain why patients experience such thoughts as inserted by an alien agent' (Sterzer et al., 2016, p. 9). Contrasting with approaches that focused on the idea that the absence of certain features commonly associated with thinking (sense of agency and sense of mineness), error-prediction advocates suggest that it is not the case that something missing in those thoughts leads to their externalization; rather, it is 'something added or different about the experience of thinking' (Sterzer et al., 2016, p. 9).

As mentioned earlier, the error-prediction model of TI suggests that the description of thoughts becoming sensory in the interruption of context and interconnectedness of experience does not point towards the absence of certain features, but to additional elements in the experience of thinking. The idea is that everyday thoughts commonly experienced as one's own are the result of the prediction of contextual information about that thought matching prior beliefs. This online prediction of the inner continuity and connectedness of one's own thoughts would be the everyday default mode of thinking. However, 'if the precision of prior beliefs is abnormally low [as in the case of psychosis], and the posterior belief is biased towards the precision of sensory evidence (as the mode of givenness of the thoughts), however, the thoughts may be associated with aberrant salience' (p. 9). This unusual salience seems to require some explanation, and the misattribution of thoughts to alien agents serves as that explanation (Vosgerau & Newen, 2007; Sterzer et al., 2018).

It is not clear if this idea really works. First, aberrant salience leading to the breakdown in the experience of interconnectedness of thoughts would only explain why those thoughts are experienced, exactly, as *disconnected* or *surprising* (which is the case in TI). Similarly, the resulting interruption of context would explain why inserted thoughts are experienced, exactly, as *decontextualized* (which is also the case in TI). All of this would explain the phenomenology of discontinuity that characterizes TI (Jaspers, 1963). Martin and Pacherie (2013) suggest that external attribution is an attempt to re-contextualize these thoughts. However, as well as the error-prediction model of TI, this cannot account for the bizarre nature of such an explanation, and why the mind's attempt to re-contextualize thoughts takes this form. It is one thing to claim that thoughts are decontextualized, but quite another to say that decontextualization is why thoughts are ultimately attributed to external agents. Appeals to decontextualization need to explain the content of the delusions, namely, the external agent that is identified by the patients. It is not clear how this mechanism works because these agents can be, among other things, surrounding elements (houses, threes, etc.), abstract entities (deities and the like), or deceased relatives. Consequently, there seems to be a missing link between the phenomenological features explained by aberrant salience in psychosis, and the externalization of those thoughts in TI. Arguably, such an explanation might need to appeal to biographical (personal), environmental (material), and ecological (social) elements in order to make sense of the content of the delusion. As it stands, the explanation for how and why decontextualized thoughts end up being externalized in the error-prediction model seems to remain an open challenge. This is not to say that the model does not have the resources to answer this challenge, but rather, that further development is needed in order to explain it. We hope to have motivated the community to pursue this further task.

Acknowledgements

This work was supported by the project FONDECYT regular n° 1221058, 'The architecture of delusions' granted by the Chilean National Agency for Research and Development (ANID) of the Government of Chile and the Project FACSO 2/2021 granted by the Universidad de Valparaíso Faculty of Social Sciences, Chile.

References

Abramson, M., & Goldinger, S. D. (1997). What the reader's eye tells the mind's ear: Silent reading activates inner speech. *Perception and Psychophysics, 59*(7), 1059–1068.

Adams, R., Vincent, P., Benrimoh, D., Friston K. J., & Parr, T. (2022). Everything is connected: Inference and attractors in delusions. *Schizophrenia Research, 245*, 5–22.

American Psychiatric Association (APA) (2013). *Diagnostic and Statistical Manual of Mental Disorders* (DSM-V) (5th ed.). Washington, DC: American Psychiatric Association.

Balzan, R., Delfabbro, P., Galletly, C., & Woodward, T. (2012). Reasoning heuristics across the psychosis continuum: The contribution of hypersalient evidence hypothesis matches. *Cognition Neuropsychiatry, 17*(5), 431e450.

Bayne, T. (2010). Delusions as doxastic states: contexts, compartments and commitments. *Philosophy, Psychiatry and Psychology, 17*(4), 329–336.

Bayne, T., & Pacherie, E. (2005). In defence of the doxastic conception of delusion. *Mind and Language, 20*(2), 163–188.

Bell, D. (2003). *Paranoia*. Cambridge, UK: Icon.

Billon, A. (2023). What is it like to lack mineness? In M. García-Carpintero & M. Guillot (Eds.), *Self-Experience: Essays on Inner Awareness* (pp. 314–340). Oxford: Oxford University Press.

Billon, A., & Kriegel, U. (2015). Jaspers' dilemma: The psychopathological challenge to subjectivities theories of consciousness. In R. Gennaro (Ed.), *Disturbed Consciousness* (pp. 29–54). Cambridge, MA: MIT Press.

Cahill, C., & Frith, C. D. (1996). A cognitive basis for the signs and symptoms of schizophrenia. In C. Pantelis, H. E. Nelson, & T. Barnes (Eds.), *Schizophrenia: A Neuropsychological Perspective* (pp. 373–395). New York, NY: John Wiley and Sons.

Cho, R., & Wu, W. (2014). Is inner speech the basis of auditory verbal hallucination in schizophrenia? *Frontiers in Psychiatry, 5*, 1–3.

Clark, A. (2016). *Surfing Uncertainty: Prediction, Action, and the Embodied Mind*. New York: Oxford University Press.

Clark, A. (2019). Consciousness as generative entanglement. *The Journal of Philosophy* 116 (12): 645–662.

Coltheart, M. (2015). Delusions. In R. Scott & S. Kosslyn (Eds.), *Emerging Trends in the Social and Behavioral Sciences* (pp. 1-12). Hoboken, NJ: John Wiley and Sons.

Coltheart, M., & Caramazza, A. (Eds.). (2006). *Cognitive Neuropsychology Twenty Years On*. Hove, UK: Psychology Press.

Conrad, K. (1958). *Die beginnende Schizophrenie*. Stuttgart, Germany: Thieme Verlag.

Corlett, P. (2018). Delusions and prediction error. In L. Bortolotti (Ed.), *Delusions in Context* (pp. 35-66). Amsterdam: Springer International Publishing.

Corlett, P. R., Cambridge, V., Gardner, J. M., Piggot, J. S., Turner, D. C., Everitt, J. C., et al. (2013). Ketamine effects on memory reconsolidation favor a learning model of delusions. *PloS One, 8*, e65088.

Corlett, P. R., & Fletcher, P. C. (2021). Modelling delusions as temporally-evolving beliefs. *Cognitive Neuropsychiatry, 26*(4), 231-241.

Corlett, P. R, Honey, G. D., Krystal, J. H., & Fletcher, P. C. (2011): Glutamatergic model psychoses: Prediction error, learning, and inference. *Neuro- psychopharmacology, 36*, 294-315.

Corlett, P. R., Horga, G., Fletcher, P. C., Alderson-Day, B., Schmack, K., & Powers III, A. R. (2019). Hallucinations and strong priors. *Trends in Cognitive Science, 23*(2), 114-127.

Corlett, P. R., Krystal, J. H., Taylor. J. R., & Fletcher, P. C. (2009). Why do delusions persist? *Frontiers in Human Neuroscience, 3*, 12.

Davies, M., Coltheart, M., Langdon, R., & Breen, N. (2001). Monothematic delusions: towards a two-factor account. *Philosophy, Psychiatry, & Psychology, 8*, 133-158.

Dudley, R., Taylor, P., Wickham, S., & Hutton, P. (2016). Psychosis delusions and the 'jumping to conclusions' reasoning bias: A systematic review and meta-analysis. *Schizophrenia Bulletin, 42*, 652-665.

Eisenacher, S., & Zink, M. (2017). Holding on to false beliefs: The bias against disconfirmatory evidence over the course of psychosis. *Journal of Behavior Therapy and Experimental Psychiatry, 56*, 79-89.

Evans, S., Averbeck, B., & Furl, N. (2015). Jumping to conclusions in schizophrenia. *Neuropsychiatric Disease and Treatment, 11*, 1615-1624.

Fernyhough, C. (2004). Alien voices and inner dialogue: Towards a developmental account of auditory verbal hallucinations. *New Ideas in Psychology, 22*(1), 49-68.

Feyaerts, J., Henriksen, M. G., Vanheule, S., Myin-Germeys, I., & Sass, L. A. (2021). Delusions beyond beliefs: A critical overview of diagnostic, aetiological, and therapeutic schizophrenia research from a clinical-phenomenological perspective. *The Lancet Psychiatry, 8*(3), 237-249.

Fletcher, P. C., & Frith, C. D. (2009). Perceiving is believing: A Bayesian approach to explaining the positive symptoms of schizophrenia. *Nature Reviews Neuroscience, 10*(1), 48-58.

Freeman, D., Pugh, K., & Garety, P. (2008). Jumping to conclusions and paranoid ideation in the general population. *Schizophrenia Research, 102*, 254-60.

Friston, K. J. (2010). The free-energy principle: A unified brain theory? *Nature Reviews Neuroscience, 11*(2), 127-138.

Friston, K. J. (2012a). A free energy principle for biological systems. *Entropy, 14*(11), 2100-2121.

Friston, K. (2012b). Prediction, perception and agency. *International Journal of Psychophysiology, 83*(2), 248-252.

Friston, K., FitzGerald, T., Rigoli, F., Schwartenbeck, P., & O' Doherty, J. (2016). Active inference and learning. *Neuroscience & Biobehavioral Reviews, 68*, 862-879.

Frith, C. (1992). *The Cognitive Neuropsychology of Schizophrenia*. Hove, UK: Erlbaum.

Fuchs, T. (2005). Delusional mood and delusional perception. A phenomenological analysis. *Psychopathology, 38*, 133-139.

Fusar-Poli, P., Estradé, A., Stanghellini, G., Venables, J., Onwumere, J., Messas, G., et al. (2022). The lived experience of psychosis: a bottom-up review co-written by experts by experience and academics. *World Psychiatry*, 21(2), 168–188.

Gallagher, S. (2004). Neurocognitive models of schizophrenia. A neurophenomenological critique. *Psychopathology*, 37, 8–19.

Gallagher, S. (2014). Relations between agency and ownership in the case of schizophrenic thought insertion and delusions of control. *The Review of Philosophy and Psychology*, 6, 865–879.

Garety, P., Waller, H., Emsley, R., Jolley, S., Kuipers, E., Bebbington, P., Dunn, G., Fowler, D., Hardy, A., & Freeman, D. (2015). Cognitive mechanisms of change in delusions: An experimental investigation targeting reasoning to effect change in paranoia. *Schizophrenia Bulletin*, 41(2), 400–410.

Gennaro, R. (2021). Inserted thoughts and the higher-order thought theory of consciousness. In P. A. Gargiulo, & H. L. Mesones- Arroyo (Eds.), *Psychiatry and Neurosciences Update*: Vol 4 (pp. 61–71). Dordrecht: Springer.

Gibbs, P. (2000). Thought insertion and the inseparability thesis. *Philosophy, Psychiatry, & Psychology*, 7(3), 195–202.

Guillot, M. (2017). I me mine: on a confusion concerning the subjective character of experience. *Review of Philosophy and Psychology*, 8, 23–53.

Hohwy, J. (2013). *The Predictive Mind*. Oxford: Oxford University Press.

Humpston, C. S. (2022). Isolated by oneself: Ontologically impossible experiences in schizophrenia. *Philosophy, Psychiatry, & Psychology*, 29(1), 5–15.

Jaspers, K. (1963). *General Psychopathology* (7th ed.). Manchester: Manchester University Press.

Kaminsky, J. A., Sterzer, P., & Mishara, A. (2019). 'Seeing rain': Integrating phenomenological and Bayesian predictive coding approaches to visual hallucinations and self- disturbances (Ichstörungen) in schizophrenia. *Consciousness and Cognition*, 73, 1–15.

Kapur, S. (2003). Psychosis as a state of aberrant salience: A framework linking biology, phenomenology, and pharmacology in schizophrenia. *American Journal of Psychiatry*, 160, 13–23.

Kendler, K. S., & Mishara, A. (2019). The prehistory of Schneider's first rank symptoms: texts from 1810 to 1932. *Schizophrenia Bulletin*, 45, 971–990.

Kumar, D. (2020). Promoting insight into delusions: Issues and challenges in therapy. *International Journal of Psychiatry in Clinical Practice*, 24(2), 208–213.

Kusters, W. (2014). *Filosofie van de waanzin*. Holland: Lemniscaat.

Kusters, W. (2021). *A Philosophy of Madness*. Cambridge, MA: MIT Press.

Kwisthout, J., Bekkering, H., & van Rooij, I. (2017). To be precise, the de- tails don't matter: On predictive processing, precision, and level of detail of predictions. *Brain and Cognition*, 112, 84–91.

Langland-Hassan, P. (2008). Fractured phenomenologies: Thought insertion, inner speech, and the puzzle of extraneity. *Mind and Language*, 23(4), 369–401.

Lee, T. S., & Mumford, D. (2003). Hierarchical Bayesian inference in the visual cortex. *Journal of the Optical Society of America*, 20, 1434–1448.

López-Silva, P. (2016). The typology problem and the doxastic approach to delusions. *Filosofía Unisinos*, 17(2), 202–211.

López-Silva, P. (2018). Mapping the psychotic mind: A review on thought insertion. *Psychiatric Quarterly*, 89(1), 957–968.

López-Silva, P. (2019). Me and I are not friends, just acquaintances: On thought insertion and self-awareness. *The Review of Philosophy & Psychology*, 10, 319–335.

López-Silva, P. (2020). Atribuciones de Agencia Mental y el Desafío desde la Psicopatología. *Kriterion*, 61(147), 1–19.

López-Silva, P., & Cavieres, A. (2021). Salto a Conclusiones y Formación de Delirios en Psicosis: Un Análisis Crítico. *Psiquiatría Biológica, 28*(1), 9–13.

López-Silva, P., Harrow, M., Jobe, T. H., Tufano, M., Harrow, H., & Rosen, C. (2022). 'Are these my thoughts?': A 20-year prospective study of thought insertion, thought withdrawal and thought broadcasting and their relationship to auditory verbal hallucinations. *Schizophrenia Research*. doi.org/10.1016/j.schres.2022.07.005.

López-Silva, P., Núñez de Prado, M., & Fernández, V. (2022). Sobre Doxasticismos y Anti-Doxasticismos: Hacia un Mapeo del Problema Tipológico de los Delirios. *Resistances: Journal of Philosophy of History*. doi.org/10.46652/resistances.v3i6.95.

Martin, J. M., & Pacherie, E. (2013). Out of nowhere: Thought insertion, ownership and context-integration. *Consciousness and Cognition, 22*(1), 111–122.

Mayer-Gross, W. (1932). Psychopathologie und Klinik der Trugwahrnehmungen. In O. Bumke (Ed.). *Handbuch der Geisteskrankheiten. Band I. Allgemeiner Teil I* (pp. 293–578). Berlin, Germany: Verlag von Julius Springer.

McKay, R., & Dennett, D. (2009). The evolution of misbelief. *Behavioural and Brain Sciences, 32*(6), 493–561.

McKay, R., Langdon, R., & Colheart, M. (2009). Sleights of mind: Delusions, and self deception. In T. Bayne and J. Fernàndez (Eds.), *Delusion and Self-deception: Affective and Motivational Influences on Belief Formation* (pp. 165–186). Hove: Psychology Press.

Mellor, C. S. (1970). First rank symptoms of schizophrenia. *The British Journal of Psychiatry, 117,* 15–23.

Menon, M., Mizrahi, R., & Kapur, S. (2008). Jumping to conclusions and delusions in psychosis: Relationship and response to treatment. *Schizophrenia Research, 98,* 225–231.

Menon, M., Pomarol-Clotet, E., McKenna, P. J., & McCarthy, R. A. (2006). Probabilistic reasoning in schizophrenia: A comparison of the performance of deluded and non-deluded schizophrenic patients and exploration of possible cognitive underpinnings. *Neuropsychiatry, 11,* 521–536.

Merrin, J., Kinderman, P., & Bentall, RP. (2007). Jumping to conclusions and attributional style in persecutory delusions. *Cognitive Therapy and Research, 31,* 741–758.

Mishara, A. L., & Zaytseva, Y. (2019). Hallucinations and phenomenal consciousness. In G. Stanghellini, A. Raballo, M. R. Broome, A. V. Fernandez, P. Fusar-Poli, & R. Rosfort (Eds.), *Oxford Handbook of Phenomenological Psychopathology* (pp. 484–508). Oxford: Oxford University Press.

Miyazono, K., Bortolotti, L., & Broome, M. (2015). Prediction error and two factors theories of delusion formation. In G. Galbraith (Ed.), *Aberrant Beliefs and Reasoning* (pp. 43–44). New York: Psychology Press

Miyazono, K., & McKay, R. (2019). Explaining delusional beliefs: A hybrid model. *Cognitive Neuropsychiatry, 24*(5), 335–346.

Morin, A. (2009). Self-awareness deficits following loss of inner speech: Dr. Jill Bolte Taylor's case study. *Consciousness and Cognition, 18*(2), 524–529.

Morin, A. (2012). Inner speech. In V. S. Ramachandran (Ed.), *Encyclopedia of Human Behavior* (2nd ed.) (pp. 436–443). London: Elsevier Inc.

Morin, A., & Michaud, J. (2007). Self-awareness and the left inferior frontal gyrus: Inner speech use during self-related processing. *Brain Research Bulletin, 74*(6), 387–396.

Moritz, S., Menon, M., Balzan, R., & Woodward, T. (2023). Metacognitive training for psychosis (MCT): past, present, and future. *European Archives of Psychiatry and Clinical Neuroscience, 273*(4), 811–817.

Moritz, S., Scheu, F., Andreou, C., Pfueller, U., Weisbrod, M., & Roesch-Ely, D. (2016). Reasoning in psychosis: Risky but not necessarily hasty. *Cognitive Neuropsychiatry, 21,* 91–106.

Moritz, S., Scheunemann, J., Lüdtke, T., Westermann, S., Pfuhl, G., Balzan, R. P., & Andreou, C. (2020). Prolonged rather than hasty decision-making in schizophrenia using the box task. Must we rethink the jumping to conclusions account of paranoia? *Schizophrenia Research*, *222*, 202–208.

Moritz, S., & Woodward, T. S. (2005). Jumping to conclusions in delusional and non-delusional schizophrenic patients. *British Journal of Clinical Psychology*, *44*, 193–207.

Mullins, S., & Spence, S. (2003). Re-examining thought insertion. *British Journal of Psychiatry*, *182*, 293–298.

Nelson, B., Whitford, T. J., Lavoie, S., & Sass, L. A. (2014). What are the neurocognitive correlates of basic self-disturbance in schizophrenia?: Integrating phenomenology and neurocognition. Part 1 (Source monitoring deficits). *Schizophrenia Research*, *152*(1), 12–19.

Notredame, C. E, Pins, D., Deneve, S., & Jardri, R. (2014). What visual illusions teach us about schizophrenia. *Frontiers in Integrative Neuroscience*, *8*, 63.

Oppenheim, G. M., & Dell, G. S. (2008). Inner speech slips exhibit lexical bias, but not the phonemic similarity effect. *Cognition*, *106*(1), 528–537.

Payne, E. (2013). *Speaking to my Madness*. Scotts Valley, CA: CreateSpace.

Pienkos, E., Silverstein, S., & Sass, L. (2017). The phenomenology of anomalous world experience in schizophrenia: a qualitative study. *Journal of Phenomenological Psychology*, *48*(2), 188–213.

Proust, J. (2009). Is there a sense of agency for thoughts? In L. O'Brien, & M. Soteriou (Eds.), *Mental Actions* (pp. 207–226). Oxford: Oxford University Press.

Rieber, R. W., & Carton, A. S. (1987). The genetic roots of thinking and speech. In R. W. Rieber, & A. S. Carton (Eds.), *The Collected Works of L. S. Vygotsky* (pp. 101–120). New York: Springer.

Ross, R. M., McKay, R., Coltheart, M., & Langdon, R. (2015). Jumping to conclusions about the beads task? A meta-analysis of delusional ideation and data-gathering. *Schizophrenia Bulletin*, *41*, 1183–1191.

Sass, L. A., & Pienkos, E. (2013). Delusion: the phenomenological approach. In K. W. M. Fulford, M. Davies, R. G. T. Gipps, G. Graham, J. Z. Sadler, G. Stanghellini, & T. Thornton (Eds.), *The Oxford Handbook of Philosophy and Psychiatry* (pp. 632–657). Oxford: Oxford University Press.

Schneider, K. (1959). *Clinical Psychopathology* (trans. By M.W. Hamilton). New York: Grune & Stratton

Schröder, P. (1915). Von den halluzinationen. *European Journal of Neurology*, *37*, 1–11.

Sollberger, M. (2014). Making sense of an endorsement model of thought insertion. *Mind and Language*, *29*(5), 590–612.

Speechley, W. J., Ngan, E. T.-C., Moritz, S., & Woodward, T. S. (2012). Impaired evidence integration and delusions in schizophrenia. *Journal of Experimental Psychopathology*, *3*(4), 688–701.

Stephan, F., Saalbach, H., & Rossi, S. (2020). The brain differentially prepares inner and overt speech production: Electrophysiological and vascular evidence. *Brain Sciences*, *10*(3), 148.

Stephens, G. L., & Graham, G. (2000). *When Self-Consciousness Breaks: Alien Voices and Inserted Thoughts*. Cambridge MA: MIT Press.

Sterzer, P., Adams, R. A., Fletcher, P., Frith, C., Lawrie, S. M., Muckli, L., Petrovic, P., Uhlhaas, P., Voss, M., Corlett, P. R. (2018). The predictive coding account of psychosis. *Biological Psychiatry*, *84*(9), 634–643.

Sterzer, P., Mishara, A. L., Voss, M., & Heinz, A. (2016). Thought insertion as a self-disturbance: An integration of predictive coding and phenomenological approaches. *Frontiers in Human Neuroscience*, *10*, 502.

Strube, W., Cimpianu, C. L., Ulbrich, M., Öztürk, Ö. F., Schneider-Axmann, T., Falkai, P., et al. (2022). Unstable belief formation and slowed decision-making: Evidence that the jumping-to-conclusions bias in schizophrenia is not linked to impulsive decision-making. Schizophrenia *Bulletin*, 48(2), 347–358.

Von Helmholtz, H. (1867). *Handbuch der physiologischen Optik*. Leipzig, Germany: Leopold Voss.

Vosgerau, G., & Newen, A. (2007). Thoughts, motor actions and the self. *Mind & Language*, 22, 22–43.

Vygotsky, L. S. (1962). *Thought and Language*. Cambridge, MA: MIT Press.

Vygotsky, L. S. (1997). Genesis of higher mental functions. In Rieber, R. W. (Ed.), *The Collected Works of L. S. Vygotsky*, Vol 4 (pp. 97–119). New York: Plenum Press

Wittorf, A., Giel, K. E., Hautzinger, M., Rapp, A., Schönenberg, M., Wolkenstein, L., et al. (2013). Specificity of jumping to conclusions and attributional biases: A comparison between patients with schizophrenia, depression, and anorexia nervosa. *Cognitive Neuropsychiatry*, 17, 262–286.

Zivin, G. (1979). *The Development of Self-regulation Through Private Speech*. New York: Wiley.

9
A Hybrid Account of Thought Insertion

Kengo Miyazono

9.1. Introduction

There are two influential theories of delusions in the recent literature: the two-factor ('TF') theory and the prediction error ('PE') theory. According to the TF theory, delusions are explained by two distinct neurocognitive factors that play different explanatory roles. According to the PE theory, delusions are explained by the disrupted processing of prediction errors (i.e., mismatches between expectations and actual inputs). While the TF theory and the PE theory are often construed as rival accounts, I have previously argued that the two theories might not be irreconcilable alternatives (Miyazono, 2019; Miyazono, Bortolotti, & Broome, 2014) and proposed a hybrid theory that combines the central insights of the two theories (Miyazono & McKay, 2019). The core idea of the hybrid theory is that delusions are explained by erroneous data[1] due to some misleading PEs (Coltheart, 2010; Corlett, Honey, & Fletcher, 2016) that are prioritized over prior beliefs (McKay, 2012; Stone & Young, 1997) due to overestimating the precision of the misleading PEs (Adams et al., 2013; Fletcher & Frith, 2009; Frith & Friston, 2012).

In this chapter, I will apply this hybrid theory to thought insertion ('TI') and show that many important features of TI can be explained by the theory. I begin by describing the central ideas of the hybrid theory (Section 9.2) and then apply them to TI (Section 9.3). The hybrid account explains TI in terms of erroneous data occurring due to some 'imagistic PEs', which are prioritized over prior beliefs due to overestimating the precision of the imagistic PEs. After, I will discuss notable features and implications of the hybrid account of TI (Section 9.4). In particular, I will compare the hybrid account with the

---

[1] I use the term 'data' rather than 'experience' because the former is more neutral as to whether the data are consciously accessible or not (Coltheart, Menzies, & Sutton, 2010). Conscious or not, 'data' is a psychological notion that belongs to the psychological (rather than neurophysiological) level of explanation. I use the term 'erroneous' rather than 'abnormal' because I remain neutral on whether the data are normal or not; see footnote 2. Normal or not, the data are expected to be erroneous in the sense that they support a false representation of the world.

self-monitoring account (Section 9.4.1), clarify the role of inner speech in TI (Section 9.4.2), and discuss the commonalities and differences between TI and auditory verbal hallucination ('AVH') (Section 9.4.3).

9.2. Hybrid Theory

According to the TF theory (Coltheart 2007; Coltheart, Langdon, & McKay 2011; Davies et al., 2001), delusions (especially monothematic delusions) can be explained by two distinct causal factors: 'the first factor' and 'the second factor'.[2] For example, the Capgras delusion is a response to an erroneous psychological datum that is caused by a reduced autonomic response to familiar faces (Ellis & Young, 1990; Ellis et al., 1997); this is the first factor. The second factor might be a 'bias towards observational adequacy' (i.e., the biased tendency to prioritize observational data over prior beliefs) (Stone & Young, 1997; McKay, 2012; for another account of the second factor, see Coltheart, Menzies, & Sutton, 2010).

According to the PE theory (Adams et al., 2013; Corlett et al., 2010; Fletcher & Frith, 2009; Sterzer et al., 2018), delusions (particularly those in schizophrenia) can be explained by abnormalities in processing PEs. For example, due to the abnormal processing of PEs (Corlett et al., 2007), people with schizophrenia might find some events and objects around them (which are completely normal and expected for other people) abnormally salient and surprising (Kapur, 2003). The abnormally salient events and objects attract attention and drive learning. The delusion of reference, which is common in the context of schizophrenia, is an explanation of the salient events and objects.

While the TF theory and the PE theory are often construed as rival accounts, I have previously argued that the two theories might not be irreconcilable alternatives (Miyazono, 2019; Miyazono et al., 2014), and I have proposed a hybrid theory that combines the central insights of the two theories (Miyazono & McKay, 2019). The TF theory and the PE theory are not formulated at the same level of explanation. The former primarily belongs to the psychological level of explanation and the latter to the neurophysiological

---

[2] It is sometimes assumed that the first factor and the second factor are *abnormal* factors. But this assumption is not widely shared in the two-factor theory literature. This assumption is coherent with the two-deficit theory rather than the two-factor theory (Coltheart, 2007). Coltheart, Langdon, and McKay (2011) explicitly deny this assumption when they consider the disposition to accept 'New Age' beliefs as the possible second factor of the alien abduction delusion. See Miyazono (2019) for a discussion of the two-factor theory and its central commitments.

level of explanation. Providing a 'hybrid' theory requires linking these two levels of explanations. The hybrid theory explains how the (TF theoretic) factors at the psychological level are physically grounded in the (PE theoretic) factors at the neurophysiological level. I propose that the first factor (at the psychological level) is physically grounded in a misleading PE (at the neurophysiological level), and the second factor (at the psychological level) is physically grounded in overestimating the precision of this misleading PE (at the neurophysiological level).

Consider a person with the Capgras delusion who believes that her husband has been replaced by an impostor. She encounters erroneous data concerning the face of her husband (the first factor), which are physically grounded in autonomic PEs (i.e., mismatches between the expected and the actual autonomic responses) (Coltheart, 2010; Corlett et al., 2010). She finds herself in a situation where her prior beliefs support the hypothesis that the person is her husband), but where the erroneous data support the alternative hypothesis that the person is an impostor. She ends up adopting the impostor hypothesis because of her bias towards observational adequacy (the second factor) (McKay, 2012; Stone & Young, 1997), which is physically grounded in overestimating the precision of the autonomic PEs (Adams et al., 2013; Fletcher & Frith, 2009; Frith & Friston, 2012).

9.3. Explaining Thought Insertion

In its general form, the hybrid theory explains delusions in terms of the erroneous data that are physically grounded in some misleading PEs as well as the bias towards observational adequacy that is physically grounded in overestimating the precision of the PEs. This account can easily be generalized to many other monothematic delusions, such as the delusion of mirrored self-misidentification and the delusion of control, and to common delusions in schizophrenia, such as the delusion of reference (see Miyazono, 2019; Miyazono & McKay, 2019).[3] This section applied the hybrid theory to TI.

My account of TI inherits central ideas from the self-monitoring account (Campbell, 1999; Feinberg, 1978; Frith, 1992), but there are important differences between the two, which I discuss in Section 9.4.1. According to the

---

[3] Note that 'monothematic delusions' and 'delusions schizophrenia' are not exclusive categories. TI is often treated as a monothematic delusion (Davies et al., 2001), while TI often occurs in the context of schizophrenia (where delusions tend to be polythematic). See Coltheart (2013) and Coltheart, Langdon, and McKay (2007) for the discussion of monothematic delusions, polythematic delusions, and schizophrenic delusions.

hybrid account, TI is explained in terms of the erroneous data that are physically grounded in some 'imagistic PEs' as well as the bias towards observational adequacy that is physically grounded in overestimating the precision of the imagistic PEs.

Let us think about the classic report of TI: 'Thoughts come into my head like "Kill God". It's just like my mind working, but it isn't. They come from this chap, Chris. They're his thoughts' (Frith, 1992, p. 66). According to my proposal, the auditory imagery 'Kill God' creates an imagistic PE (where the person has the top-down expectation of the auditory input 'Kill God', which does not match the actual bottom-up inputs), which constitutes an erroneous datum. This is analogous to the Capgras delusion in which an autonomic PE (where the person expects an autonomic response that does not match actual autonomic response) constitutes an erroneous datum. The imagistic PE is expected to be highly precise, which results in a bias towards observational adequacy (whereby the erroneous datum is prioritized over prior beliefs) and thereby drives the belief-revision processes. This is also analogous to the Capgras delusion in which the autonomic PE is expected to be highly precise, which results in a bias towards observational adequacy.

The key to this proposal is the idea of 'imagistic PEs', which I will now explain. The PE account of delusion is based on the predictive coding ('PC') theory of the brain and its function (Clark, 2013; Friston, 2010; Hohwy, 2013). A fundamental idea of the PC account of perception is that what we perceive is determined by the interactions between top-down expectations as well as bottom-up sensory inputs. In this framework, any agents with perception have the capacity for top-down expecting, which entails a capacity for imagining. As Clark notes, there is a 'deep duality of between online perception (as enabled by the predictive processing architecture) and capacities for the endogenerous generation of quasi-sensori states' (Clark, 2016, p. 94) because any agents 'simply as part and parcel of learning to perceive, develop the ability to self-generate perception-like states from the top down, by driving the lower populations into the predicted patterns' (Clark, 2013, p. 198).

According to the PC theory, top-down imaginative processing is a basic building block of any experience; every experience is partly determined by top-down imaginative expectations. As Jones and Wilkinson (2020) pointed out, however, this conception of imagination can be (terminologically) confusing; it does not distinguish the broad sense of 'imagination' as a basic building block of experience from the narrow sense of 'imagination', or imagination proper, as an offline or simulative state. Imagination in the broad sense is an ingredient of any kind of experience, including perceptual experience (e.g., perceiving the face of your mother who is in front of you right now), while imagination in the narrow sense is a kind of experience that is contrasted with perceptual experience (e.g., imagining the face of your mother who is not in front of you right now). Imagination in the narrow sense can be understood as a form of experience in which the imagination in the broad sense plays an overwhelmingly strong role. Hereafter, the term 'imagination' means the imagination in the narrow sense.

In a nutshell, the PC theory explains imagination in terms of top-down expectation, as a form of experience in which top-down expectations are dominant.[4] Within the PC framework, imagination has a peculiar feature; 'the purpose of imagination is, in most cases, to envisage a departure from reality' (Jones & Wilkinson, 2020, p. 100). For instance, when you imagine the face of your mother, you top-down expect her face—yet your mother is not physically within sight at that moment. This is another way of saying that an imaginer knowingly generates a PE (e.g., knowingly creates a false prediction of the face of your mother in front of you). I call those PEs that are created by top-down imagination 'imagistic PEs'.

The idea of imagistic PEs raises a theoretical puzzle. There seems to be a tension between the idea that, in imagining something, we knowingly create a PE and the fundamental idea of the PC framework that the ultimate goal of the brain is to minimize PEs. But there are some possible solutions to this puzzle. One might argue, for instance, that the imagistic capacity for knowingly creating a PE is epistemically useful for simulating, counterfactual thinking, etc., which contributes to minimizing PEs in the long run.

It is important for the brain to have the reality-monitoring capacity, i.e., the capacity for distinguishing imagistic PEs from perceptual PEs and treating them differently. In particular, the brain is supposed to update prior beliefs in response to perceptual PEs, but it is not supposed to do so in response to imagistic PEs. For example, if you unexpectedly see an apple on the table when you have a prior belief that there is not an apple on the table (a perceptual PE), then you are supposed to revise the prior belief and come to believe that there is an apple on the table. In contrast, if you imagine an apple on the table when you have a prior belief that there is not an apple on the table, then you are not supposed to revise the prior belief. How is such a reality-monitoring capacity realized in the brain? How does the brain distinguish imagistic PEs from non-imagistic ones?

---

[4] This account of imagination is still too crude and it might not explain all the features of imagination. For example, how does it explain the fact that imagination is typically under voluntary control? Can top-down expectations be under voluntary control? Obviously, more work needs to be done on the PC account of imagination, but it goes beyond the scope of this chapter (see Clark, 2016; Jones & Wilkinson, 2020; Kirchhoff, 2018).

This is an empirical question to which I do not have a full answer, but the PC framework offers the following hypothesis: the reality-monitoring capacity is realized by the expected precision of PEs. Both the perceived apple on the table and the imagined apple on the table involve a PE. The brain distinguishes the former from the latter by assigning different degrees of precision to them. Perceptual PEs (which contain rich information about reality) are expected to be highly precise, while imagistic PEs (which do not contain much information about reality) are not.[5] The brain can achieve this by keeping track of the relative strength of top-down and bottom-up influence on PEs. When bottom-up influence on a PE is dominant, the PE is expected to be perceptual and precise. In contrast, when top-down influence on a PE is dominant, the PE is expected to be imagistic and imprecise.

I hypothesize that TI involves overestimating the precision of imagistic PEs, which causes the imagistic PEs to be confused with perceptual PEs and thereby drives the belief-revision processes.[6] This hypothesis about TI is analogous to my hypothesis about the Capgras delusion: the Capgras delusion involves overestimating the precision of autonomic PEs, which causes autonomic PEs to drive the belief-revision processes.

At the core of this hypothesis is the idea that TI is a disorder of imagination in which top-down imaginative processes play a crucial role. The relevance of top-down processes is consistent with a recent study by Powers, Mathys, and Corlett (2017) of auditory hallucination induced by Pavlovian conditioning (see also Corlett et al., 2019). Exposure to the association between an auditory stimulus and a visual stimulus establishes a prior, top-down expectation of their co-occurrence. In this study, after learning the auditory-visual association, the participants were presented with the visual stimulus without the auditory stimulus, which caused some participants to report the hallucinatory auditory stimulus. Powers and colleagues (2017) found that those with a daily experience of AVH were more susceptible to this top-down effect than those without a daily experience of AVH. Although this study focused on auditory hallucination rather than TI, it is reasonable to assume that they are closely

---

[5] This means that we have an answer to Langland-Hassan's (2016, 2018) objection to the inner speech/comparator model: the inner speech/comparator account implies that inner speech always involves some prediction errors, but then 'we cannot explain the sense in which [AVH and TI] seem alien by saying that they occur in the absence of any adequately fulfilled prediction' because 'ordinary inner speech does as well' (Langland-Hassan, 2016, p. 684). In response, we can argue that although both ordinary inner speech and AVH/TI involve some PEs, they might be different in their expected precision; the former is expected to be rather imprecise, while the latter is expected to be highly precise.

[6] This hypothesis is similar to what Swiney calls the 'reality monitoring approach' to explaining AVH in the PC framework, according to which 'it is a complete loss of bottom-up sensory signals and resultant over-reliance on top-down expectation or prediction that leads to hallucinatory episodes of inner speech' (Swiney, 2018, p. 319).

related phenomena. I will come back to the relationship between auditory hallucination and TI in Section 9.4.3.

This section has presented a rough sketch of the hybrid account of TI, which subsumes TI in the general hybrid framework that I presented before (Miyazono, 2019; Miyazono & McKay, 2019). The next section examines the details of this account, compares it with other accounts of TI, and clarifies its implications and advantages.

9.4. Implications

9.4.1. Self-monitoring

The self-monitoring account (Blakemore, Wolpert, & Frith 2002; Frith, Blakemore, & Wolpert, 2000) posits a mechanism (often known as a 'comparator') which distinguishes self-generated bodily movements from externally generated bodily movements by comparing expected bodily changes (which are estimated based on the motor commands, or their 'efference copies') with actual bodily changes. Recently, this model has been subsumed into the PC framework (Fletcher & Frith, 2009; Frith, 2012). The comparator's function is to compare the expected and actual bodily movements, which can be seen as an instance of the more general function of the brain to compare expectations with actual inputs. In other words, '[t]he comparator model would be seen as a special case within this [PC] framework' (Frith, 2012, p. 53). The self-monitoring account offers a plausible explanation of the delusion of control. The delusion of control is explained by some abnormalities in the comparative process, which cause self-generated bodily movements to be mistakenly classified as externally generated. The self-monitoring account extends this framework from bodily actions to thoughts (Campbell, 1999; Feinberg, 1978; Frith, 1992), assuming the 'view of thinking as a motor process' (Campbell, 1999, p. 615). TI is explained by some abnormalities in the comparative process in which expected thoughts and actual thoughts are compared, which causes some self-generated thoughts to be mistakenly classified as externally generated.

However, the self-monitoring account of TI and its reliance on the action/thought analogy invites several objections (Gallagher, 2004; Stephens & Graham, 2000; Vosgerau & Newen, 2007): for example, the account invites an infinite regress, it fails to distinguish TI from obsessive or intrusive thoughts, etc. It has also been suggested that the self-monitoring capacity for thought is simply redundant. What is the purpose of having a mechanism for monitoring whether a thought is internally generated or externally generated? Such a monitoring mechanism seems redundant since all thoughts are internally generated. Because of these problems, Frith (2012) is sceptical about the PC/self-monitoring account of TI: 'even a general, Bayesian approach does not provide a plausible account for the most striking of all first-rank symptoms, *thought insertion*' (Frith, 2012, p. 53). But other researchers are not as pessimistic as Frith. A possible solution to the problem of the action/thought analogy is to regard TI as misidentifying inner speech. Producing inner speech can be thought of as an (imaginary) action and thus the PC/self-mentoring account can easily apply to inner speech (Gerrans, 2014, 2015; Seal, Aleman, & McGuire, 2004). I will say more about inner speech in Section 4.2.

Sterzer and colleagues (2016) explore another possible solution to the problem of the action/thought analogy. They argue that the PC framework frees us from the problematic action/thought analogy and opens up the possibility of a more plausible account of TI. Sterzer and colleagues (2016) posit the process of monitoring the narrative interconnectedness of thoughts. TI is explained by some failures in the monitoring process where some thoughts are mistakenly 'perceived as especially surprising and hence not in continuity with previous thoughts' and thus 'are experienced as coming from 'nowhere' and interpreted as being inserted by somebody else' (Sterzer et al., 2016, p. 6).

I am sympathetic to Sterzer and colleagues' proposal; my proposal follows their departure from the action/thought analogy. Nonetheless, Sterzer and colleagues' proposal might not solve all the problems of the traditional self-monitoring account, including the problem of redundancy. Their proposal posits a process of distinguishing internally generated thoughts from externally generated ones by monitoring the narrative interconnectedness between thoughts: 'thoughts are normally experienced as our own thoughts because they are embedded in a context' (Sterzer et al., 2016, p. 7). Such a monitoring process seems to be redundant; your thoughts are your own and you do not need to examine whether a thought is internally generated or externally generated. Moreover, it is not obvious that the alleged inserted thoughts are always narratively disconnected from other thoughts. For example, a person with TI can endorse the alleged inserted thoughts; e.g., she might admit that 'own thoughts might say the same thing' but insist that 'the feeling isn't the same' (Allison-Bolger 1999, p. 89).

My own proposal is free from the problems just described. Unlike the self-monitoring account and the narrative interconnectedness account, my account does not argue for anything more than the processes that are already posited in the basic PC framework, such as the top-down process of imagination. Having a monitoring mechanism for distinguishing internally generated thoughts from externally generated thoughts is redundant; all thoughts are internally generated. In contrast, it is crucial, not redundant, to have a reality-monitoring mechanism for distinguishing imaginative PEs from perceptual PEs.

9.4.2. Inner speech

According to a hypothesis, TI involves misidentified inner speech (Gerrans, 2014, 2015; Langland-Hassan, 2008). For example, a person may have the inner speech 'Kill God', but for some reason fails to identify it as self-generated inner speech; he instead misidentifies it as a thought that is inserted from outside. My account is (at least partially) compatible with the inner speech account of TI in so far as inner speech involves auditory imagery (for inner speech and auditory imagery, see Langland-Hassan, 2018; Wilkinson & Fernyhough, 2018). But my account has a broader scope of application and has some theoretical advantages. The main theoretical advantage is that the heterogeneity of TI can be explained by the heterogeneity of imagery.

Imagery is heterogeneous in the sense that there are different kinds of imagery other than an auditory one. This heterogeneity nicely explains some features of TI. It is not obvious that every case of TI can be explained as misidentified auditory imagery. For example, the classic case of TI below seems to involve visual, rather than auditory, inserted thoughts:

> I look out of the window and I think the garden looks nice and the grass looks cool, but the thoughts of Eamonn Andrews come into my mind. There are no other thoughts there, only his... He treats my mind like a screen and flashes his thoughts on to it like you flash a picture. (Mellor, 1970, p. 17)

The expressions 'screen' and 'picture' seem to suggest that the thoughts that are allegedly inserted by Eamonn Andrews are visual in nature. My account can easily be applied to cases of this kind because it straightforwardly accommodates the possibility of misidentified visual imagery. Imagery is heterogeneous in another sense: you can easily imagine the voices of different people, such as the voice of your father, your mother, John Lennon, Édith Piaf, Donald Trump, Jacinda Ardern, etc. This kind of heterogeneity constitutes another explanatory advantage. For example, Cho and Wu (2013) challenge the inner speech account of AVH by arguing that it does not explain why the voice is attributed to some particular person; after all, 'inner speech is generally in one's own voice, is in the first-person point of view ('I'), and often lacks acoustical phenomenology' (Cho & Wu, 2013, p. 2). This objection might apply to the inner speech account of TI as well; the inner speech account does not explain the fact that the inserted thought is attributed to some particular person, such as Eamonn Andrews.

My account allows for the possibility of misidentified imagery of somebody else's voice. Perhaps part of the reason why an alleged inserted thought is attributed to a particular person, such as Eamonn Andrews, is because the inserted thought is misidentified imagery of that particular person's voice.[7] (However, this raises a puzzle: misidentified auditory imagery of Eamonn Andrews' voice explains the auditory hallucination of Andrews' voice, rather than the inserted thought by Andrews. I will come back to this issue in the discussion of TI and AVH in Section 9.4.3.)

There is another sense in which imagery is heterogeneous: imagery can vary with regard to the amount of sensory detail. It is well-known that one can imagine an object without sensory detail; for example, you can imagine a tiger without specifying how many stripes it has (Dennett, 2010). But this does not mean that these details are never imagined; for example, you can easily imagine a tiger with a specific number of stripes, say five, if you want. This kind of heterogeneity might constitute another explanatory advantage. For example, some might challenge the inner speech account of TI by claiming that TI is often less sensory than typical inner speech (Stephens & Graham, 2000). But this might not pose a serious threat to my proposal. Imagery has rich sensory detail in some cases (e.g., imagining a tiger without a specific number of stripes), but not in other cases (e.g., imagining a tiger with five stripes). Perhaps the less sensory cases of TI might be explained by misidentified imagery with less sensory detail.

9.4.3. Thought insertion and auditory verbal hallucination

One possible challenge to the inner speech account of TI is to distinguish TI from AVH. It is a popular view that AVH (or, at least one of its subsets; Jones

---

[7] This is coherent with Cho and Wu's suggestion about the self-monitoring account of AVH: 'self-monitoring accounts should endorse auditory imagination of another person's voice as the substrate of AVH. [...] Auditory imagination is characterized by acoustical phenomenology that is in many respects like hearing a voice: it represents another's voice with its characteristic acoustical properties. Thus, our patient may auditorily imagine the neighbour's voice saying certain negative things, and this leads to a hallucination when the subject loses track of this episode as self-generated' (Cho & Wu, 2013, p. 2).

2010) involves (misidentified) inner speech (Jones & Fernyhough, 2007; Seal et al., 2004). But if both TI and AVH involve misidentified inner speech, then how do we explain the difference between them? We face a *prima facie* problem to explain why in some cases misidentified inner speech is reported as an (inserted) thought, but in other cases reported as an (hallucinatory) auditory experience. A possible solution to this puzzle is to deny the inner speech account of AVH. Some researchers are sceptical about the inner speech account of AVH. One challenge is to explain the auditory quality of AVH (the 'auditory phenomenology challenge'; Wilkinson, 2014). Cho and Wu (2013) argue that 'the experience of the subject's own inner voice, in the first person and often lacking acoustical properties such as pitch, timbre, and intensity' does not explain 'the experience of someone else's voice, in the second- or third-person, with acoustical properties' (Cho & Wu, 2013, p. 2).

Another possible solution is to deny the inner speech account of TI. The inner speech account of TI can be, and has been, challenged. For example, Vosgerau and Newen (2007) distinguish the cases of misidentified inner speech from the cases of TI proper. They admit that misidentified inner speech can be reported as TI, but still insist that 'the mechanisms involved in such cases are different from the mechanisms involved in proper thought insertion, and hence these cases should be classified as a different phenomenon (e.g., verbal hallucination)' (Vosgerau & Newen, 2007, p. 38).

The third solution to the puzzle is to deny the categorical distinction between TI and AVH. Perhaps they are the same phenomenon (or similar phenomena) in two different descriptions (Langland-Hassan, 2008, 2016; Ratcliffe & Wilkinson, 2015). For example, Langland-Hassan (2018) argues that, to the extent that TI and AVH are felt to occur in a natural language, they share the same auditory-phonological component and, possibly, are explained by a unified account. I am sympathetic to this option, but a question remains: if both TI and AVH involve the same phenomenon, what makes it the case that the phenomenon is described in different ways in different cases? Why is the same phenomenon described as an (hallucinatory) auditory experience in some cases and as an (inserted) thought in other cases? The full answer to this question might be complex. The attribution style might be a factor. People with TI and people with AVH share the same phenomenon, but they have different attribution styles.[8]

---

[8] See Young, Leafhead, and Szulecka (1994) for a similar suggestion that the Capgras delusion and the Cotard delusions are similar phenomena that are described in different ways due to different attribution styles.

My account of TI opens up some other possibilities. Both AVH and TI involve misidentified imagery, while there are some slight differences between the imagery in the case of AVH and the imagery in the case of TI, which explains the fact that the former is described as an (hallucinatory) auditory experience and the latter is described as an (inserted) thought. The imagery in TI and the imagery in AVH might be located on a continuum (which is consistent with Humpston and Broome's (2016) view that TI and AVH are on a continuum). As I have already noted, imagery has rich sensory detail in some cases (e.g., imagining a tiger with a specific number of stripes) but not in other cases (e.g., imagining a tiger without a specific number of stripes). We can think of a spectrum of cases from the imagery with maximal sensory detail at one end to the imagery, with minimal sensory detail at the other end. TI might involve misidentified imagery with relatively sparse sensory detail, while AVH might involve misidentified imagery with relatively rich sensory detail.

In the PC framework, there can be another kind of continuity between TI and AVH; TI and AVH are located at different levels of the same predictive hierarchy. The PC framework denies the categorical distinction between perceptual processes and cognitive processes, at least at the neurophysiological level; the framework 'makes the lines between perception and cognition fuzzy, and perhaps vanishing' (Clark, 2013, p. 190). 'Perceptual processes' refer to some lower-level processes in the hierarchy that are relatively close to sensory inputs, while 'cognitive processes' refer to some higher-level processes that are relatively distant from sensory inputs.[9] In the PC framework, then, (perceptual) experience and (cognitive) thought need not be categorically distinct; they belong to different levels of the same predictive hierarchy. This idea opens up the possibility that TI and AVH involve imagistic PEs in different levels of the hierarchy. An imagistic PE in a lower level tends to be described as an (hallucinatory) experience, while an imagistic PE in a higher level tends to be described as a (inserted) thought.

9.5. Conclusion

In this chapter, I have applied the hybrid theory of delusion formation (Miyazono, 2019; Miyazono & McKay, 2019) to TI and have argued that many important features of TI can be explained in the hybrid theoretical

---

[9] This is similar to Humpston and Broome's (2016) continuum model of TI and AVH according to which TI and AVH are located towards the 'silent' end and the 'audible' end of the spectrum, respectively, with soundless voices located in-between.

framework. The core idea of the hybrid account is that TI is a disorder of imagination, in which top-down imaginative processes play a crucial role. The hybrid account explains TI in terms of the erroneous datum that is physically grounded in some 'imagistic PEs' as well as the bias towards observational adequacy that is physically grounded in overestimating the precision of the imagistic PEs. Although the hybrid account provides us with an explanation of TI, there are many issues to be examined and discussed in future research. An empirical issue is to test the hybrid account and to see whether empirical data support it. A theoretical issue is to explain some puzzling facts about TI, such as the fact that people with TI regard some of their thoughts but not others as being inserted. Another theoretical issue is to explain not only TI but also related phenomena, such as thought withdrawal and thought broadcasting. An open question is whether there can be a unified account of thought insertion, thought withdrawal, and thought broadcasting in terms of the disorders of top-down imaginative processing.

Acknowledgements

I thank the audience at Hokkaido Mind Group work-in-progress seminar (10 March 2021) for helpful and insightful feedback. I acknowledge the support of JSPS KAKENHI (grant number 20H00001, 21H00464).

References

Adams, R. A., Stephan, K. E., Brown, H. R., Frith, C. D., & Friston, K. J. (2013). The computational anatomy of psychosis. *Frontiers in Psychiatry*, 4(47). doi.org/10.3389/fpsyt.2013.00047.
Allison-Bolger, V. Y. (1999). Collection of case histories. unpublished manuscript.
Blakemore, S. J., Wolpert, D. M., & Frith, C. D. (2002). Abnormalities in the awareness of action. *Trends in Cognitive Sciences*, 6(6), 237–242.
Campbell, J. (1999). Schizophrenia, the space of reasons, and thinking as a motor process. *The Monist*, 82(4), 609–625.
Cho, R., & Wu, W. (2013). Mechanisms of auditory verbal hallucination in schizophrenia. *Frontiers in Psychiatry*, 4, 155.
Clark, A. (2013). Whatever next?: Predictive brains, situated agents, and the future of cognitive science. *Behavioral and Brain Sciences*, 36, 181–204.
Clark, A. (2016). *Surfing Uncertainty: Prediction, Action, and the Embodied Mind*. Oxford: Oxford University Press.
Coltheart, M. (2007). Cognitive neuropsychiatry and delusional belief: The 33rd Sir Frederick Bartlett lecture. *The Quarterly Journal of Experimental Psychology*, 60, 1041–1062.
Coltheart, M. (2010). The neuropsychology of delusions. *Annals of the New York Academy of Sciences*, 1191, 16–26.

Coltheart, M. (2013). On the distinction between monothematic and polythematic delusions. *Mind & Language, 28*(1), 103–112.
Coltheart, M., Langdon, R., & McKay, R. (2007). Schizophrenia and monothematic delusions. *Schizophrenia Bulletin, 33*(3), 642–647.
Coltheart, M., Langdon, R., & McKay, R. (2011). Delusional belief. *Annual Review of Psychology, 62*, 271–298.
Coltheart, M., Menzies, P., & Sutton, J. (2010). Abductive inference and delusional belief. *Cognitive Neuropsychiatry, 15*, 261–287.
Corlett, P. R., Honey, G. D., & Fletcher, P. C. (2016). Prediction error, ketamine and psychosis: An updated model. *Journal of Psychopharmacology, 30*, 1145–1155.
Corlett, P. R., Horga, G., Fletcher, P. C., Alderson-Day, B., Schmack, K., & Powers III, A. R. (2019). Hallucinations and strong priors. *Trends in Cognitive Sciences, 23*(2), 114–127.
Corlett, P. R., Murray, G. K., Honey, G. D., Aitken, M. R., Shanks, D. R., Robbins, T., et al. (2007). Disrupted prediction-error signal in psychosis: Evidence for an associative account of delusions. *Brain, 130*, 2387–2400.
Corlett, P. R., Taylor, J. R., Wang, X. -J., Fletcher, P. C., & Krystal, J. H. (2010). Toward a neurobiology of delusions. *Progress in Neurobiology, 92*, 345–369.
Davies, M., Coltheart, M., Langdon, R., & Breen, N. (2001). Monothematic delusions: Towards a two-factor account. *Philosophy, Psychiatry, & Psychology, 8*, 133–158.
Dennett, D. C. (2010). *Content and Consciousness*. Oxford: Routledge.
Ellis, H. D., & Young, A. W. (1990). Accounting for delusional misidentifications. *The British Journal of Psychiatry, 157*(2), 239–248.
Ellis, H. D., Young, A. W., Quayle, A. H., & De Pauw, K. W. (1997). Reduced autonomic responses to faces in Capgras delusion. *Proceedings of the Royal Society of London. Series B: Biological Sciences, 264*, 1085–1092.
Feinberg, I. (1978). Efference copy and corollary discharge: Implications for thinking and its disorders. *Schizophrenia Bulletin, 4*(4), 636–640.
Fletcher, P. C., & Frith, C. D. (2009). Perceiving is believing: A Bayesian approach to explaining the positive symptoms of schizophrenia. *Nature Reviews Neuroscience, 10*, 48–58.
Friston, K. (2010). The free-energy principle: A unified brain theory?. *Nature Reviews Neuroscience, 11*, 127–138.
Frith, C. D. (1992). *The Cognitive Neuropsychology of Schizophrenia*. London: Psychology Press.
Frith, C. (2012). Explaining delusions of control: The comparator model 20 years on. *Consciousness and Cognition, 21*(1), 52–54.
Frith, C. D., Blakemore, S. J., & Wolpert, D. M. (2000). Abnormalities in the awareness and control of action. *Philosophical Transactions of the Royal Society of London. Series B: Biological Sciences, 355*(1404), 1771–1788.
Frith, C. D., & Friston, K. J. (2012). False perceptions and false beliefs: Understanding schizophrenia. In A. M. Battro, S. Dehaene, M. S. Sorondo, & W. J. Singer (Eds.), *The Proceedings of the Working Group on Neurosciences and the Human Person: New Perspectives on Human Activities* (pp. 134–148). Rome: The Pontifical Academy of Sciences.
Gallagher, S. (2004). Neurocognitive models of schizophrenia: A neurophenomenological critique. *Psychopathology, 37*(1), 8–19.
Gerrans, P. (2014). *The Measure of Madness: Philosophy of Mind, Cognitive Neuroscience, and Delusional Thought*. Cambridge, MA: MIT Press.
Gerrans, P. (2015). The feeling of thinking: Sense of agency in delusions of thought insertion. *Psychology of Consciousness: Theory, Research, and Practice, 2*(3), 291–300.
Hohwy, J. (2013). *The Predictive Mind*. Oxford: Oxford University Press.

Humpston, C. S., & Broome, M. R. (2016). The spectra of soundless voices and audible thoughts: Towards an integrative model of auditory verbal hallucinations and thought insertion. *Review of Philosophy and Psychology, 7*(3), 611–629.

Jones, S. R. (2010). Do we need multiple models of auditory verbal hallucinations? Examining the phenomenological fit of cognitive and neurological models. *Schizophrenia Bulletin, 36*(3), 566–575.

Jones, S. R., & Fernyhough, C. (2007). Thought as action: Inner speech, self-monitoring, and auditory verbal hallucinations. *Consciousness and Cognition, 16*(2), 391–399.

Jones, M., & Wilkinson, S. (2020). From prediction to imagination. In A. Abraham (Ed.) *The Cambridge Handbook of the Imagination* (pp. 94–110). Cambridge: Cambridge University Press.

Kapur, S. (2003). Psychosis as a state of aberrant salience: A framework linking biology, phenomenology, and pharmacology in schizophrenia. *American Journal of Psychiatry, 160*, 13–23.

Kirchhoff, M. D. (2018). Predictive processing, perceiving and imagining: Is to perceive to imagine, or something close to it?. *Philosophical Studies, 175*(3), 751–767.

Langland-Hassan, P. (2008). Fractured phenomenologies: Thought insertion, inner speech, and the puzzle of extraneity. *Mind & Language, 23*(4), 369–401.

Langland-Hassan, P. (2016). Hearing a voice as one's own: two views of inner speech self-monitoring deficits in schizophrenia. *Review of Philosophy and Psychology, 7*(3), 675–699.

Langland-Hassan, P. (2018). From introspection to essence: The auditory nature of inner speech. In P. Langland-Hassan (Ed.) *Inner Speech: New Voices* (pp. 78–104). Oxford: Oxford University Press.

McKay, R. (2012). Delusional inference. *Mind & Language, 27*, 330–355.

Mellor, C. S. (1970). First rank symptoms of schizophrenia: I. the frequency in schizophrenics on admission to hospital II. Differences between individual first rank symptoms. *The British Journal of Psychiatry, 117*(536), 15–23.

Miyazono, K. (2019). *Delusions and Beliefs: A Philosophical Inquiry*. London: Routledge.

Miyazono, K., Bortolotti, L., & Broome, M. R. (2014). Prediction-error and two-factor theories of delusion formation. In N. Galbraith (Ed.) *Aberrant Beliefs and Reasoning*. Psychology Press (pp. 34–54). London: Routledge.

Miyazono, K., & McKay, R. (2019). Explaining delusional beliefs: A hybrid model. *Cognitive Neuropsychiatry, 24*(5), 335–346.

Powers, A. R., Mathys, C., & Corlett, P. R. (2017). Pavlovian conditioning–induced hallucinations result from overweighting of perceptual priors. *Science, 357*(6351), 596–600.

Ratcliffe, M., & Wilkinson, S. (2015). Thought insertion clarified. *Journal of Consciousness Studies, 22*(11–12), 246–269.

Seal, M., Aleman, A., & McGuire, P. (2004). Compelling imagery, unanticipated speech and deceptive memory: Neurocognitive models of auditory verbal hallucinations in schizophrenia. *Cognitive Neuropsychiatry, 9*(1–2), 43–72.

Stephens, G. L., & Graham, G. (2000). *When Self-Consciousness Breaks: Alien Voices and Inserted Thoughts*. Cambridge, MA: MIT Press.

Sterzer, P., Adams, R. A., Fletcher, P., Frith, C., Lawrie, S. M., Muckli, L., et al. (2018). The predictive coding account of psychosis. *Biological Psychiatry, 84*(9), 634–643.

Sterzer, P., Mishara, A. L., Voss, M., & Heinz, A. (2016) Thought insertion as a self-disturbance: An integration of predictive coding and phenomenological approaches. *Frontiers in human Neuroscience, 10*, 502. doi:10.3389/fnhum.2016.00502

Stone, T., & Young, A. W. (1997). Delusions and brain injury: The philosophy and psychology of belief. *Mind & Language, 12*, 327–364.

Swiney, L. (2018). Activity, agency, and inner speech pathology. In P. Langland-Hassan (Ed.) *Inner Speech: New Voices* (pp. 299–332). Oxford University Press.

Vosgerau, G., & Newen, A. (2007). Thoughts, motor actions, and the self. *Mind & Language*, 22(1), 22–43.

Wilkinson, S. (2014). Accounting for the phenomenology and varieties of auditory verbal hallucination within a predictive processing framework. *Consciousness and Cognition*, 30, 142–155.

Wilkinson, S., & Fernyhough, C. (2018). When inner speech misleads. In P. Langland-Hassan (Ed.) *Inner Speech: New Voices* (pp. 244–260). Oxford: Oxford University Press.

Young, A. W., Leafhead, K. M., & Szulecka, K. (1994). The capgras and cotard delusions. *Psychopathology*, 27(3–5), 226–231.

10

Thought Insertion Delusion

A Multifactorial Approach

Emilia Vilatta

10.1. Introduction

Thought insertion (hereinafter TI) is a delusion in which a person believes that some of her thoughts are not her own but have been implanted into her mind by an outside agency or an external force. It is considered one of the Schneiderian first-rank symptoms (FRS), that is to say, a pathognomonic sign of schizophrenia: the presence of this symptom is sufficient to reach the diagnosis (Shinn et al., 2013). Despite their prevalence, TI delusions are still not well understood and their aetiology remains unknown. This phenomenon has also elicited a growing interest among philosophers since it challenges classical assumptions, such as immunity from error through misidentification. We typically say that our own judgements have such immunity since when someone says 'I think that *p*', the person could be wrong about the thought *p* but not about who is thinking it (Campbell, 1999; Peacocke, 2014). However, patients with TI delusion claim that they are entertaining a thought, but at the same time, they claim that it is not their own and, as a consequence, usually elaborate a story about how that thought has been inserted in their mind, that is to say, they provide a *delusional explanation*.

A remarkable feature is the *selectivity* of inserted thoughts. Only a certain kind of thought-contents are experienced as alien by patients, and these are usually associated with affectively relevant topics with a negative valence (Gallagher, 2004), and the rest of the thoughts are normally experienced. As Hughlings Jackson (1958) has suggested, it is convenient to distinguish between two sides of the phenomenon in order to explain TI. On the one hand, there is a 'negative element', which is the *lack of recognition* of certain thoughts as one's own; on the other hand, there is a 'positive element', which is an *explanation* as to whom the thought belongs. Therefore, a comprehensive explanation of TI needs to include an account of (a) what the delusional experience consists of, that is, its *phenomenology*, (b) how TI delusion can arise, that is, by way of which *psychological mechanisms*, and (c) why the delusional hypothesis is accepted as plausible by the patient.

In recent literature on how to explain delusions, it is possible to distinguish between two major approaches: *deficit approaches* and *motivational approaches*, which have often been deemed as opposites. Briefly explained, deficit approaches posit that delusions are the result of a number of cognitive biases that affect the process of belief acquisition or evaluation (Coltheart, Langdon, & McKay, 2011; Davies, 2000; Ellis & Young, 1990; Maher, 2001; Stone & Young, 1997). According to these approaches, the delusional content does not seem to have any relevant causal role and the description of the deficits is carried out at a functional or subpersonal level. Current deficit approaches have tended to focus only on the epistemic failures of delusions, usually overlooking the affective components of the symptom. In this sense, it can be said that the focus of the most recent theorizing about delusion has been on 'cold' rather than 'hot' factors (Bayne & Fernandez, 2010, p. 2).

On the contrary, motivational approaches consider that the delusion-formation is caused by the psychological benefits that it would confer on the subject. According to this view, the delusional phenomenon is characterized as an active psychological response to an internal threat or an external psychological stimulus[1] (Bell, 2003; Bentall, 1994; Bortolotti, 2015, 2020). This approach is usually tied to what is called *'the content view'* (Ratcliffe & Wilkinson, 2015, p. 4), namely, a perspective that considers that a subject fails to recognize a thought as her own because of an aversion to the thought-*content*.

Approaches based on the content view have been criticized because they seem to fail to distinguish between two kinds of pathological thoughts: inserted thoughts of TI delusion and intrusive and obsessive thoughts experienced by people with obsessive-compulsive disorder (hereinafter OCD). The two disorders are compared in large part due to the fact that both have been considered in psychiatry as *content-thought disorders*. The similarity lies in the fact that patients who suffer from any of the two disorders experience intrusive and aversive thoughts that are involuntarily imposed on their consciousness and that lead to experiencing unpleasant emotions. Intrusive thoughts of OCD usually include sexual or aggressive impulses and are characterized by being uncontrollable, reoccurring, and aversive. Although in both cases some of the patient's thoughts are experienced as aversive and intrusive, OCD patients ultimately know that these thoughts belong to them. In contrast, TI

---

[1] This approach has generally been associated with psychodynamic explanations, but not all motivational explanations are psychodynamic. On the contrary, most recent approaches are cognitive ones.

patients do not recognize intrusive thoughts as their own and elaborate a delusional explanation about some external agent. Thus, an adequate approach should be able to capture the relevant clinical differences of these disorders.

The main criticism on the motivational approaches and the content view is that the fact that a content appears as aversive or strange to someone is not a sufficient reason for it to be rejected as her own and for a delusion to arise (Graham & Stephens, 1994; Stephen & Graham, 2000). I agree that a purely motivational approach that explains TI delusions only by their content does not clarify the route from aversion to external attribution and fails to explain the differences between TI and OCD. Thus, what I would like to propose here is that appealing to the content is not sufficient to explain TI delusion, even though it is still *relevant*. With this in mind, in this chapter, I will sketch a tentative theoretical multifactorial approach that offers a more complete picture of the phenomenon integrating the 'hot' factors posited by motivational approaches and the 'cold' factors accounted by deficit approaches.

First of all (Section 10.2), I will start with a characterization of the phenomenology of TI, attending to different ways in which the agency of thoughts can be experienced as altered. After that (Section 10.3), I will argue that in order to explain why mistaken self-attributions of thoughts are *selective* and not generalized, both in TI and OCD, we need to consider the thought-contents that are causing psychological disturbances to patients. That will be the main reason that I will offer in order to support *the content view*. With the purpose of prompting this idea I will consider the motivational ('hot') factors involved in delusion-formation to show that the rejected thoughts are mostly experienced as *ego-dystonic* contents by patients.

Then in Section 10.4, I will point out why, if we wish to explain how it is possible to feel some form of cognitive dissonance or alienation from our thoughts, we should assume that the mind is fragmented or compartmentalized in a Davidsonian fashion. Next, in Section 10.5, I will consider the psychological mechanism that could be present in both TI and OCD and that turns them into pathological cases. Specifically, I will suggest that these patients seem to exhibit a pattern of *experiential avoidance* that leads them to having dysfunctional relations with some disturbing thoughts. Finally, I will consider why it is not enough to experience a thought as aversive for a delusion to arise. Then, in Section 10.6, I will argue that we additionally need to take into account: on one hand, (i) the phenomenological alterations experienced by patients with TI (Section 10.6.1) and, on the other hand, the cognitive biases that affect the process of acquisition and evaluation of beliefs (Section 10.6.2). The upshot is that a multifactorial approach is needed to explain how TI comes about.

10.2. The Phenomenology of Agency in TI

The psychiatric tradition has considered TI as one of the forms of *thought alienation*, in conjunction with 'thought withdrawal' and 'thought broadcasting' delusions, since patients feel victims of some external force over which they have no control, experiencing an intrusion on their *ego* (Jaspers, 1963). In TI cases, the patient 'does not feel master of his own thoughts and in addition he feels in the power of some incomprehensible external force' (Jaspers, 1963, p. 123). Some examples of TI delusion are illustrated next:

> Thoughts are put into my mind like 'Kill God'. It's just like my mind working, but it isn't. They come from this chap, Chris. They are his thoughts. (Frith, 1992, p. 66)

> One man said that thoughts were being put into his mind and that they "felt different" from his own; another said that television and radio were responsible for different thoughts, which were 'tampered with electrically' and always felt the same way (i.e., recognizably different from his 'own') (Spence et al., 1997, p. 2010).

In recent times, different philosophers have claimed that some kind of abnormal sense of agency regarding thoughts would constitute the core phenomenology of TI. This has been considered as the *standard approach* of TI (Campbell, 2002; Carruthers, 2012; Gallagher, 2014; Gerrans, 2001; Proust, 2006; Stephens & Graham, 2000). Although several philosophers agree to characterize the phenomenon in this way, they differ in the notion of agency they use and in what element, in particular, they consider as damaged.

Different distinctions have been made around the sense in which we feel owners of our thoughts. Gallagher (2014), for example, uses the notion of *ownership*[2] as the conjunction of the condition of spatiality and introspection.[3] This experience would be different from recognizing the responsibility for producing a thought (*authorship*). For the latter, it is needed the pre-reflective experience that I am the cause of my action or thinking and have some control over it (Gallagher, 2014). Stephens & Graham (1994, 2000) have distinguished between *sense of subjectivity* and *sense of agency*. The former refers to the subject being able to recognize a mental state as belonging to their

---

[2] This notion is equivalent to 'subjectivity', 'my-ness' or mineness (Gallagher, 2014).
[3] The 'spatiality condition' refers to locating a thought in one's personal boundaries and the 'introspection condition' refers to accessing the thought-contents directly and first-personally (Bortolotti & Broome, 2008, p. 211).

psychological story and their ego boundaries. The latter refers to feeling causally active regarding some mental state, as opposed to what merely happens to me and for which I am not causally responsible. It is this second sense, that would make us consider ourselves as *authors* of our thoughts.

According to these distinctions, in TI delusion, the sense of subjectivity (or ownership) would be preserved since patients feel owners of their inserted thoughts, while the sense of agency (or authorship) would be missing.[4] The distinctions are enlightening to make sense of patients' statements insofar as they recognize two kinds of agency attributions: one that answers the question of 'who is the subject of those thoughts?' and the other that answers 'who is the agent of those thoughts?'. In this way, we can understand how the patient can claim at the same time that she has a thought and that it does not belong to her without this being a contradiction. However, these distinctions do not seem to help us to understand why the agency attribution error occurs in the first place, that is, why the subject does not feel the author of the inserted thoughts, and more specifically, why the error is selective. In the following section, I will start considering how motivational factors could be playing a role in the genesis of TI delusion and how it could explain the selectiveness of the inserted thoughts.

10.3. Motivational Factors: The 'Hot' Side

Motivational approaches understand delusions as a way for patients to deal with certain conflicting situations that are overwhelming. In a broad sense, these approaches support the *content view* and consider that delusions emerge because they help to manage strong negative emotions and incorporate negative experiences into the subject's psychological life (Bell, 2003; Bentall, 1994; Bentall, 2003; Bortolotti, 2015, 2020). This kind of motivational explanation could be aligned with a broader framework that considers the role of affective factors in the processes of acquisition and revision of beliefs. The important role of emotions in maintaining or rejecting our beliefs is well-known (Davies, 2000; Pacherie, 2009) and what we know about our belief system is that people tend to adjust their beliefs to avoid psychological discomfort or threats to one's own sense of self (Quilty-Dunn & Mandelbaum, 2018).

---

[4] This is consistent with recent empirical evidence (e.g., Lincoln et al., 2010; Moritz et al., 2007), that suggesting that some patients experience a reduced sense of self-causation for both positive and negative internal events.

This fact is the basis of what is called the *'psychological immune system'* (Gilbert, 2006). This concept is part of a tradition that goes from Freud through Festinger, Aronson, and Gilbert, which understands cognition according to the principles of cognitive economy: the beliefs that one changes—or maintains—are due to what feels easiest to do while preserving our self-image (Mandelbaum, 2019). This drives the cognitive processes of belief change in a particular way: 'one can leverage the fact that inconsistencies hurt to explain how the shape of one's web of beliefs will change' (p. 13). Thus, the notion of *self* is crucial to understanding what kinds of inconsistencies hurt the most: those that challenge the sense of self.

Paying attention to motivational factors in psychological disorders such as TI and OCD seems fundamental, since the inserted and intrusive thoughts are mostly related to *ego-dystonic* contents, that is, affectively laden thoughts that mainly go against one's self-image.[5] In the light of this, it makes sense that thoughts that are felt as intrusive are those that cause some kind of psychological and emotional conflict because of their content. This would suggest that the *content* of the rejected thoughts, both in TI and OCD, is a relevant element at the time to evaluate why just *some* thoughts, and not others, lack a sense of agency. According to the content view, the subject would make some kind of evaluation, probably unconsciously, of the thought-content that is causing her an emotional discomfort and this type of psychological dissociation would lead—at least partially—to feelings of aversion towards that thought. If a patient thinks, for example, *'I must kill my father'*, she might feel bad about it and reject it as if it does not belong to her.

Stephens and Graham (2000) have challenged the content view, arguing that the fact that a thought is not pleasant is not necessary for a TI delusion to occur. Fair enough. They argue that in some cases of auditory hallucinations (i.e., *voices*), the content is not always negative, but even sometimes comforting. However, in the clinical literature, TI is usually distinguished from auditory hallucinations. Indeed, TI is reported as a delusional *belief* while auditory hallucinations are a sort of anomalous *perception* (one without an object), which consists of people reporting *hearing* voices. So, in principle, these seem to be two different symptoms. Or at least, the evidence available could be interpreted as in favour of both Stephens and Graham's view and the content-interpretation view. Additionally, most of the TI cases and other delusions seem to involve unpleasant contents. Inserted thoughts are, most of the time,

---

[5] It should be clarified that the *ego-dystonic* must be understood in a broad sense in which a mental state is evaluated as having a negative valence insofar it can contradict some aspect of the psychological background of the subject.

associated with topics that are emotionally relevant to patients, involving feelings of shame, worthlessness, and social estrangement (Gallagher, 2004; Ratcliffe & Wilkinson, 2015). Consider the following example:

> [...] it's mocking me, I hate that one [...] I am left in a state of fear [...] They don't sound like me. They are angry most of the time. I don't like to think of mean things, I try hard not to, but the more I try not to think the more the voices get nasty. (Ratcliffe & Wilkinson, 2015, p. 14)

What I am trying to point out here is that inserted or intrusive thoughts are experienced as *alien* maybe not only but at least partially because of their unpleasant contents. My thought is that Stephen and Graham are right in claiming that the content view is not enough for explaining TI, but for different reasons than those they allege, as we will see later. In the next section, I will focus on the *ego-dystonic* experience that occurs in cases of TI and OCD. Specifically, I will propose that we need to consider some kind of compartmentalization of the mind to understand why any thought can be experienced as intrusive or alien.

10.4. The Compartmentalization of the Mind

Several philosophical accounts and empirical studies support the idea that our belief system is fragmented or compartmentalized and that this is a consequence of our limited information-processing resources (Egan, 2008; Cherniak, 1986; Davies & Egan, 2013).[6] This idea is not novel; in fact, it can be traced firstly to Donald Davidson's philosophical writings on irrationality (1982, 1985, 2004), where he provides some conceptual clues to understand irrational phenomena such as self-deception, *akrasia*, and wishful thinking. Davidson proposes a conceptual solution to the puzzle of ordinary irrationality that, in my opinion, can also enlighten certain aspects of some psychopathological phenomena such as TI delusion or OCD.

Davidson (2004) focuses on a particular kind of irrationality: one in which an agent acts or thinks 'against his *own* conception of what is reasonable' (p. 210). That is, cases where there is some kind of *internal* inconsistency. Accordingly, when we speak of irrationality, we refer to certain thoughts or behaviours that do not go along fully with the rest of the agent's attitudes,

---

[6] Here, I use the term 'mind' to refer to the subject's set of internal events (thoughts, desires, fears, etc.). I am not making any additional ontological commitments here.

which do exhibit a background of rationality. No particular mental state is irrational by itself, no matter how strange it may be to other individuals. Irrationality only appears when 'beliefs are inconsistent with other beliefs according to the principles maintained by the agent himself' (Davidson, 1985, p. 348). So, the sort of irrational phenomena that produce conceptual puzzles are not the cases in which someone can't believe or feel or do what *we* consider reasonable, but in the impossibility *within oneself* of being coherent in the structure of our beliefs, intentions, emotions, and actions. For example, acting contrary to our best judgement (*akrasia*), cases of wishful thinking, self-deception, or we can add, cases of inserted or intrusive thoughts that are experienced are alien for being incoherent with the global network of mental states.

When Davidson (2004) considers how it is possible to explain this kind of irrational phenomenon, he claims that any satisfactory approach to irrationality should encompass some of Freud's most important ideas,[7] mainly the thesis of the compartmentalization of the mind. According to this thesis, the mind can be divided into two or more quasi-independent structures (compartments). Within each of these structures, the mental events would be linked according to the principles of rationality. However, a mental state that belongs to one compartment could be just *causally* related to the mental state of another compartment *without being rationally linked* to it. The necessary feature to make this possible is that one part of the mind (the largest network of mental states) exhibits a higher degree of rationality (internal coherence and consistency) than that attributed to the whole system. This means that assuming the compartments have some degree of independence from each other, it is possible to understand how different compartments can harbour inconsistencies between them and at the same time be operating according to the modality of the non-rational causality. Therefore, we have three elements: the fragmentation of the mind, the existence of an important structure in each of the compartments, and the possibility of non-logical causal relationships, which provide the foundation for a coherent way of describing and explaining some relevant kinds of irrationality.

As we know, in instances of irrationality, logical relations are missing or distorted. For example, in cases of *wishful thinking*, a desire causes a belief. But it is also well-known that the judgement that a state of affairs would be

---

[7] Despite the fact that Davidson (2004) picks up the Freudian idea of the division of the mind, he also distances himself from Freud and does not make any substantial statement regarding the nature of such divisions, since his theory regarding the functioning of the mind as operating at a different level of abstraction than Freud's. Accordingly, my proposal is not psychodynamic either and I refer to the fragmentation of the mind in a cognitive sense aligned with the proposal of Davies and Egan (2013).

desirable is not a reason to believe that such a state of affairs is true. Likewise, in cases of patients who suffer from TI delusions or OCD, the disturbing emotions caused by some thought-content makes them reject it, although we know that the fact that a thought-content is undesirable or unpleasant is not a *reason* to stop believing it. If we accept that the actual belief system is fragmented, we can understand that, as Davies and Egan (2013) point out, individual fragments are consistent and coherent but fragments are not consistent or coherent with each other, and different fragments guide action in different contexts. Let's explore an example. A patient may have—at least—two sets of mental states. In the largest set, she holds thoughts such as '*I love my sister*' '*I don't want anything bad to happen to her*', and in another, she has the following thoughts: '*I should kill my sister*', '*she is a hindrance*'. This second set of thoughts could appear to the patient as *ego-dystonic* and emotionally disturbing due to the thought-contents, which are incoherent with the beliefs and emotions of the first set of mental states.

It is worth mentioning that the sense of agency has been considered by several philosophers as dependent on our ability to integrate mental episodes into a larger picture of ourselves (Dennett, 1987; Flanagan, 1992). We attribute thoughts to ourselves based on introspection, psychological information about ourselves, and considerations of reasons in favour of the content of thoughts, at least in a potential sense (Bortolotti & Broome, 2008; Campbell, 2002). In particular, the *top-down* theory of mental agency ascriptions (Campbell 1999; Stephens & Graham, 2000) states that such attributions emerge as a retrospective and rational explanation in response to the occurrence of certain thoughts in the stream of consciousness. According to this theory, we access the thought-content and carry out an inference from an evaluation of such content in contrast with the rest of our underlying mental states. In a nutshell, the sense of agency depends on whether we take the occurrence of this thought as coherent and explicable in terms of our psychological background (Graham & Stephens, 1994, 2000).

Patients with OCD and TI delusion experience their problematic thoughts as *ego-dystonic*, aversive, and having a negative valence. At the same time, it is well-known that they have serious difficulties integrating these thoughts with the rest of their mental states because these do not fit well or are inconsistent with their global psychological background. Thus, when a thought appears as incoherent or inconsistent, it makes sense that the first psychological reaction of the person would be to feel as if it were not their own. However, in a non-pathological case, an expected second move should be dismissing the thought or trying to solve the inconsistency in a rational way. In the next section,

I would suggest that when these patients are faced with these experiences of dissonance, instead of trying to solve the inconsistency, they try to *avoid* these thoughts. But in that precise effort to avoid them, they end up intensifying their attention to them in a pathological way.

10.5. Experiential Avoidance

One of the most important contributions from Acceptance and Commitment Therapy (hereinafter ACT)[8] is the description of the phenomenon of *experiential avoidance* as an element related to a wide range of psychological disorders (Boulanger, Hayes, & Pistorello, 2010), including psychotic disorders (Udachina et al., 2014). Experiential avoidance has been defined as a behavioural pattern of resistance to remain in contact with particular private events (e.g., thoughts, emotions, bodily sensations, etc.) and individuals' efforts to alter the form, frequency, or situational sensitivity of these experiences. According to Wilson and Luciano (2002) a person trapped in this recurring pattern of avoidance would be immersed in a vicious circle in which the presence of any aversive stimulus, such as a negative thought, will be followed by a need to mitigate it. Two common examples: someone could refuse to attend social events to avoid feelings of embarrassment, or someone might avoid taking an exam because of the anxiety and fear that it can go wrong. In short, experiential avoidance is a functional category of behaviours that is negatively reinforced by the effect of avoiding or diminishing some type of discomfort (Boulanger, Hayes, & Pistorello, 2010).

Although this behavioural pattern is apparently effective in the short term, to the extent that it manages to reduce or temporarily eliminate an experience that causes discomfort (e.g., embarrassment, fear, or anxiety). However, in the long term, this would prevent her from having valuable experiences, like attending social events or the possibility of advancing in her career. If this becomes chronic it provokes a 'boomerang effect' afterward, i.e., the discomfort is present again, sometimes even more intensely and widespread, and the relief is short-lived (Boulanger, Hayes, & Pistorello, 2010). As a consequence of the experiential avoidance patterns, and due to the boomerang effect, patients end up over-focusing on the problematic thoughts, increasing the

---

[8] ACT (Hayes, Strosahl, & Wilson, 1999) is one of the most representative therapies of the so-called third wave of behaviour therapy. It is a model of psychological intervention that is philosophically rooted in Functional Contextualism and Relational Frame Theory. ACT is conceived as the treatment of the experiential avoidance through a functional dimensional approach to Psychopathology (Wilson & Luciano, 2002).

levels of anxiety or fear, and limiting the behavioural repertoire of the subject, negatively affecting their life.

Thus, the concept of experiential avoidance could enlighten the pathological way in which patients with TI and OCD relate to some of their thoughts. According to this view, TI and OCD could be seen as two instances that imply patterns of experiential avoidance. These patients are trying to avoid recognizing some content thoughts as their own due to cognitive reasons (because they do not fit with other mental states) and motivations (because they are unpleasant, *ego-dystonic*, and affect their self-image). However, it should be noted that the psychological problems do not arise due to the content but due to the avoidance functions of the thoughts that patients consider to have been inserted. In fact, ACT treatment focuses neither on the content nor on the rationality of those thoughts, but on their pathological function.[9]

10.6. The External Attribution and the Alien Experience

So far, I have suggested that TI delusion and OCD imply some kind of experiential avoidance pattern regarding disturbing thoughts. I have also pointed out that it is necessary to assume that the mind is fragmented in order to give meaning to these intrusive experiences. However, despite the similarities between these pathological cases, there are some clinical differences between them that we should be able to apprehend. Let's take a look at the following example in which a psychiatrist distinguishes TI from obsessional thinking:

> While the obsessed patient recognizes that he is compelled to think about things against his will, he does not regard the thoughts as foreign, i.e., he recognizes that they are his own thoughts. In thought alienation, the patient has the experience that others are participating in his thinking. He feels that thoughts are being inserted into his mind and he recognizes them as foreign and coming from without (Fish, 1985, p. 43).

Hence, it can be seen that the patient with OCD can consider himself as the *author* of his thoughts, ultimately, because he accepts that these thoughts belong to him and this is precisely why he is distressed and seeking psychological care. But the delusional patient with TI denies that his thoughts belong

---

[9] The function of the pathological thoughts and their psychological treatment is a topic worth exploring in itself, but it is beyond the scope of this chapter.

to him and claims that the thought has been inserted into his mind *by an external agent*. Thus, we have a clinically relevant difference between both cases. If we look at the primary phenomenology of TI patients, they lack the sense of *authorship* insofar as they feel that the intrusive thoughts are incoherent with their mental background and do not consider themselves authors of them. However, patients with OCD, unlike delusional patients, are able to finally recognize that they are the owners and authors of these thoughts.

Then, we return to our starting point. Why is the delusional patient not able to recognize the thought as his own? It remains to be explained the passage from aversion to the thoughts into external attributions, that is to say, why the subject ends up holding a *delusional explanation*. In what follows, I will consider what other contributory factors enable the delusion-formation. First of all (Section 10.6.1), I will focus on some phenomenological alterations that patients experience, then, I will focus on the cognitive biases that they manifest (Section 10.6.2).

10.6.1. Phenomenological alterations

It has been documented that there are some phenomenological changes associated with the prodromal stages of psychotic disorders, especially schizophrenia, that weaken the boundaries between intentional states in a way that increases vulnerability to content-specific disturbances. Before the adoption of delusional beliefs, the atmosphere experienced in the initial stages of a psychotic disorder is characterized by a radical alienation from the perceived environment (Jaspers, 1963). Many patients experience several affective disturbances that affect their entire experience of the world and themselves with a commonly overwhelming and negative character (Fuchs, 2020). Moreover, patients usually report pervasive feelings of anxiety and estrangement, which would render them more vulnerable to delusions in those cases where thought-contents are especially troubling (Ratcliffe & Wilkinson, 2015).

Sass and Parnas (2003) have made some enlightening considerations regarding this topic. They state that we generally have an active *sense of involvement* in our lives. A kind of self-organizing unity between our perceptions, thoughts, emotions, and actions that make us integrate all this into a personal universe. In patients with schizophrenia, the experience of unity would break down. This is consistent with the idea that TI involves the erosion of *ego-boundaries* (Hoerl, 2001), which is evidenced by the fact that it is difficult for them to organize and integrate their thoughts, emotions, and actions. Besides, these patients suffer from a *relentless introspection* that prevents them from generating a global image of themselves. As a result, they end up evaluating each component of their mental life in a fragmented way, losing their ability to integrate and self-narrate:

> Unable to be content with a global impression of unity, the schizophrenic subject scrutinizes his mental universe, searching out the joints between its various components. Rather than sustaining a sense of self, this 'hyper-reflexive' observation may actually serve to undermine it. (Sass, 1992, p. 230)

By making strong scrutiny of their mental life, the patients find inconsistent beliefs, feelings, and actions, which generate various kinds of emotional disturbances like the feeling of strangeness. However, these patients are considered *delusional* not because they have feelings of strangeness regarding some thoughts—such a feeling also happens in OCD cases—but because of their *explanation* that these thoughts belong to *someone else*. Let's see one example:

> She said that sometimes it seemed to be her own thought 'but I don't get the feeling that it is'. She said her 'own thoughts might say the same thing', 'but the feeling isn't the same', 'the feeling is that it is somebody else's' [. . .] She was asked if she had other people's thoughts put inside her head. She said 'possibly they are but I don't think of them in that way' [. . .], 'they were being put into me into my mind', 'very similar to what I would be like normally'. (Hoerl 2001, p. 190)

How can we explain that the feeling that a thought is intrusive leads someone to insist that it belongs to someone else? I have suggested that people with some psychiatric disorders like OCD or TI would experience a certain kind of dissonance. As Festinger (1957) has pointed out, when dissonance appears in a very appreciable way, the person is automatically motivated to generate new ideas to help reduce tension until their set of ideas and attitudes fit together with greater internal coherence. There can be different ways of reducing the dissonance, which may be more or less pathological, and one of them is seeking an external explanation of private events.

In the same direction, Marwaha et al. (2014) have pointed out that feeling that emotional experiences are out of control can drive the search for explanations in terms of external influences. The phenomenological alterations experienced by patients lead them to a loss of sense of reality that makes them more susceptible to adopting bizarre explanations for their private events. In this search for meaning, the various pre-existing beliefs about oneself, about others, and the world, would influence the elaboration of the *delusional explanation* (Freeman et al., 2002; Garety et al., 2013). In turn, a high degree of personification may also be linked to delusion-formation, 'in so far as it involves an increasingly elaborate attempt to *make sense of* the experience in terms of another agent, who may have specific characteristics and intentions' (Ratcliffe & Wilkinson, 2015, p. 9). However, one may still wonder why does the subject accept such a far-fetched or atypical hypothesis.[10] For the experience of alienation to become a *full-blown* TI delusion, other factors must contribute, in addition to those aforementioned.

10.6.2. The 'cold' factors: Cognitive biases

In this section, I would like to turn to the 'cold' factors postulated by *deficit approaches* that might explain why a person can end up holding a TI delusion. Several studies have pointed out that a number of cognitive impairments and biases might have a central role in the genesis of overreactions to life experiences like delusions or hallucinations as long as they affect their processes of belief acquisition or evaluation (Bentall, 1994; Broyd et al., 2017; Gawęda et al., 2017; Goldberg et al., 2003; Menon et al., 2013; Prochwicz & Gawęda, 2015). It has been found that patients with schizophrenia perform worse than healthy subjects in *all* fields of neurocognitive assessments, with a statistically significant difference. These differences have led to the consideration of cognitive impairments as a central feature of schizophrenia that would be present before the psychotic symptoms manifest[11] (Gur & Gur, 2005).

Theoretical cognitive models (e.g., Bentall et al., 2009; Freeman, 2007) state that the formation and maintenance of delusional beliefs are considered to be mediated by content-specific information-processing and reasoning biases (Wittorf et al., 2012). Particularly, it has been postulated that *attributional biases* (biases in the sort of explanations that the subjects give of their behaviour) play an important role in the formation and maintenance of persecutory delusions and other positive symptoms of schizophrenia (Mehl et al., 2014). Some findings suggest that these patients tend to attribute blame for negative events to external causes and blame for positive events to internal causes to an abnormal degree (Fear et al., 1996; Mehl et al., 2014). The literature refers to

---

[10] I do not focus on why the patient can hold the delusion over a long time, but rather, on why, in the face of the occurrence of the delusional hypothesis, she is not able to reject it.

[11] There is a relative consensus there might be some brain alterations that correlate with these cognitive impairments, but the evidence is still inconclusive (Beck et al., 2009).

this reasoning anomaly as *externalizing* and *self-serving bias* (Kinderman & Bentall, 1996; Wittorf et al., 2012).

Additionally, it has been found that patients with persecutory delusions preferentially attend to threat-related information (Bentall & Kaney, 1989) and usually blame other people for the negative things that happen to them (Beck et al., 2009; Bentall, 2003; Randall et al., 2003). A recent study found that these delusions were predicted by a personalizing bias for negative events (Mehl et al., 2014) and another one (Berry et al., 2015) showed that patients had a higher personalizing bias for negative events compared to control participants. This bias was associated with a lower IQ, a tendency to make perseverative errors and a poorer performance on the second-order false belief tasks. Another comparative study showed that the schizophrenia group had the highest mean externalizing bias score. These patients were significantly more *externalizers* but not more *personalizers* than patients with depression, providing evidence for the specificity of an externalizing bias in paranoid schizophrenia. Additionally, the schizophrenia group exhibited a tendency towards a self-serving bias, whereas clinical controls exhibited the opposite attributional pattern (a self-blaming bias) (Wittorf et al., 2012).

Although several studies have analysed the assumption that persecutory delusions are associated with abnormal attributions (Bentall et al., 2001; Garety & Freeman, 1999), the evidence for that association is rather ambiguous and the current literature has gathered conflicting findings (Mehl et al., 2014). For that reason, some authors prefer to speak about these biases as constituting a *vulnerability* to psychosis (Langdon et al., 2013).

From other authors' point of view, more basic *reasoning biases* might also be implicated in delusions, such as selective abstraction, excessive generalization, absolute judgements, and inadequate data rejoicing (Beck et al., 2009). The main emphasis has been on the *jumping to conclusions bias* (JTC), the tendency to consider less evidence and make or accept hasty conclusions or explanations (Freeman, 2007; Garety & Freeman, 1999). Some authors have concluded that JTC is not primarily a bias of probabilistic reasoning but a data-gathering bias, since patients make decisions on the basis of little evidence (Dudley & Over, 2003).

Although the results in the probabilistic reasoning experiments with delusional subjects do not reveal a *total* inability to reason probabilistically, they do show a high bias towards hasty acceptance of hypotheses (Garety et al., 2013). While some studies have found no specific association between paranoia and JTC bias (Bentall et al., 2009), other studies have reported (Lincoln et al., 2010) that the association between anxiety and paranoia was mediated by an increase in the tendency to jump to conclusions, and a recent meta-analysis on JTC (Fine et al., 2007) has demonstrated a high effect size for the comparison between delusional patients and non-psychiatric controls. As Coltheart, Langdon, and McKay (2011) have argued, no style of reasoning seems to be as biased as that of delusional patients and, consequently, the aetiology of delusions must include some deficit in reasoning.

In summary, the evidence suggests that there could be a number of cognitive biases that affect to the processes of acquisition and revision of beliefs of delusional subjects (Davies, 2000). Despite the different findings, recent reviews (Bell et al., 2006; Freeman, 2007) agree on the fact that an excessive self-serving attributional bias and JTC might contribute to the uncritical adoption of implausible beliefs in deluded patients (Wittorf et al., 2012, p. 265). These factors could explain why the delusional hypothesis is prioritized and accepted as an explanatory candidate for an unusual experience. Nevertheless, it has remained unclear whether other biases are involved, and the evidence is still inconclusive as to which of all the biases would be specifically involved and what level of deficit is necessary for a delusion to emerge and persist.

10.7. Concluding Remarks

In this chapter, I have provided a tentative theoretical account to make sense of the puzzling phenomena of TI delusions. Since, in the face of the explanatory debate, neither the motivational approach nor the deficit approach seems able to respond to the explanatory challenges of TI delusion, my proposal here has been to consider a conjunction of factors that could be contributing to the emergence of the phenomenon.

I have proposed that the content of inserted thought plays a relevant but insufficient role in explaining TI delusion. Although the content is relevant for an explanation of the phenomenon, if we analyse both TI and OCD *only* at the content level, we will fail to distinguish them or to explain relevant clinical differences. Moreover, the recent evidence seems to prevent us from considering that delusions emerge only as a defence mechanism when faced with psychologically threatening content. For that reason, I have also suggested that other aspects should be considered: the phenomenological alterations in the sense of self in this delusion (Section 10.2), and a number of cognitive biases that patients exhibit in the processes of adoption and revision of beliefs. I consider that these two last clinical characteristics can lead us to a differential diagnosis between TI and OCD. Furthermore, I have suggested that the compartmentalization of the mind could explain why some thoughts have a strangeness or intrusiveness character (Section 10.4) and that a pattern of experiential avoidance could be the psychological mechanism that leads to TI delusion (Section 10.5). Conceiving TI as a condition that implies experiential avoidance opens up a series of possibilities for clinical treatment that, at least, are worth exploring.

I do not wish to claim that this account applies to every case of TI; such experiences could well arise in several different ways because the factors that lead to a psychotic experience appear to be multiple and complex. Rather, I have tried to offer a plausible theoretical approach for most cases of TI, which present themselves with *ego-dystonic* inserted thoughts, thus moving towards a more comprehensive explanation of the phenomenon. I do not rule out the possibility that additional factors are involved in the delusion formation. It is still necessary to explore the precise way in which all these factors are interacting to contribute to the genesis of the delusion. I hope that this attempt will serve as a first approximation in that direction.

References

Bayne, T., & Fernandez, J. (Eds.). (2010). *Delusion and Self-Deception: Affective and Motivational Influences on Belief Formation*. New York: Psychology Press.

Beck, A., Rector, N., Stolar, N. & Grant, P. (2009). *Schizophrenia. Cognitive Theory, Research, and Therapy*. New York The Guilford Press.

Bell, D. (2003). *Paranoia*. Cambridge: Icon.

Bell, V., Halligan, P., & Ellis, H. (2006). Explaining delusions: A cognitive perspective. *Trends in Cognitive Sciences*, *10*, 219–226.

Bentall, R. (1994). *The Neuropsychology of Schizophrenia*. London: Erlbaum.

Bentall, R. (2003). *Madness Explained: Psychosis and Human Nature*. London: Penguin.

Bentall, R., & Kaney, S. (1989). Content specific information processing and persecutory delusions: An investigation using the emotional Stroop test. *British Journal of Medical Psychology*, 62(4), 355–364.

Bentall, R., Corcoran, R., Howard, R., Blackwood, N., & Kinderman, P. (2001). Persecutory delusions: A review and theoretical integration. *Clinical Psychology Review*, *21*(8), 1143–1192.

Bentall, R., Rowse, G., Shryane, N., Kinderman, P., Howard, R., Blackwood, N., Moore, R., Corcoran, R. (2009). The cognitive and affective structure of paranoid delusions. *Archives of General Psychiatry*, 66, 236–247.

Berry, K., Bucci, S., Kinderman, P., Emsley, R., & Corcoran, R. (2015). An investigation of attributional style, theory of mind and executive functioning in acute paranoia and remission. *Psychiatry Research*, 226(1), 84–90.

Bortolotti, L. (2015). The epistemic innocence of motivated delusions. *Consciousness and Cognition*, 33, 490–499.

Bortolotti, L. (2020). *The Epistemic Innocence of Irrational Beliefs*. Oxford: Oxford University Press.

Bortolotti, L., & Broome, M. (2008). Delusional beliefs and reason giving. *Philosophical Psychology*, 21(3), 1–21.

Boulanger, J. L., Hayes, S. C., & Pistorello, J. (2010). Experiential avoidance as a functional contextual concept. In A. M. Kring & D. M. Sloan (Eds.), *Emotion Regulation and Psychopathology: A Transdiagnostic Approach to Etiology and Treatment* (pp. 107-136). New York: The Guilford Press.

Broyd, A., Balzan, R., Woodward, T., & Allen, P. (2017). Dopamine, cognitive biases and assessment of certainty: A neurocognitive model of delusions. *Clinical Psychology Review*, 54, 96–106.

Campbell, J. (1999). Schizophrenia, the space of reasons, and thinking as a motor process. *The Monist*, 82(4), 609–625.

Campbell, J. (2002). The ownership of thoughts. *Philosophy, Psychiatry and Psychology*, 9, 35–39.

Carruthers, G. (2012). The case for the comparator model as an explanation of the sense of agency and its breakdowns. *Consciousness and Cognition*, 21(1), 30–45.

Cherniak, C. (1986). *Minimal Rationality*. Cambridge, MA: MIT Press.

Coltheart, M., Langdon, R., & McKay, R. (2011). Delusional belief. *Annual Review of Psychology*, 62, 271–298.

Davidson, D. (1982). Two paradoxes of irrationality. In R. Wollheim & J. Hopkins (Eds.), *Philosophical Essays on Freud* (pp. 289–305). Cambridge: Cambridge University Press.

Davidson, D. (1985). Incoherence and irrationality. *Dialéctica*, 39(4), 345–354.

Davidson, D. (2004). *Problems of Rationality*. Oxford: Oxford University Press.

Davies, M. (2000). *Pathologies of Belief*. Oxford: Blackwell.

Davies, M., & Egan, A. (2013). Delusion: Cognitive approaches—Bayesian inference and compartmentalization. In K. Fulford, M. Davies, R. Gipps, G. Graham, J. Sadler, G. Stanghellini, & T. Thornton (Eds.), *The Oxford Handbook of Philosophy and Psychiatry* (pp. 689–727). London: Oxford University Press.

Dennett, D. (1987). *The Intentional Stance*. Cambridge, MA: MIT Press.

Dudley, R., & Over, D. (2003). People with delusions jump to conclusions: A theoretical account of research findings on the reasoning of people with delusions. *Clinical Psychology and Psychotherapy*, 10, 263–274.

Egan, A. (2008). Seeing and believing: Perception, belief formation and the divided mind. *Philosophical Studies*, 140(1), 47–63.

Ellis, H., & Young, A. W. (1990). Accounting for delusional misidentifications. *British Journal of Psychiatry*, 157, 239–248.

Fear, C., Sharp, H., & Healy, D. (1996). Cognitive processes in delusional disorders. *The British Journal of Psychiatry*, 168(1), 61–67.

Festinger, L. (1957). *A Theory of Cognitive Dissonance*. Stanford, CA: Stanford University Press.

Fine, C., Gardner, M., Craigie, J., & Gold, I. (2007). Hopping, skipping or jumping to conclusions? Clarifying the role of the JTC bias in delusions. *Cognitive Neuropsychiatry*, 12, 46–77.

Fish, F. (1985). *Clinical Psychopathology: Signs and Symptoms in Psychiatry*. Bristol: John Wright & Sons.

Flanagan, O. (1992). Book review: On becoming responsible. Michael S. Pritchard. *Ethics*, 102(2), 390.

Freeman, D. (2007). Suspicious minds: The psychology of persecutory delusions. *Clinical Psychology Review*, 27, 425–457.

Freeman, D., Garety, P. A., Kuipers, E., Fowler, D., & Bebbington, P. E. (2002). A cognitive model of persecutory delusions. *British Journal of Clinical Psychology*, 41(4), 331–347.

Frith, C. (1992). *The Cognitive Neuropsychology of Schizophrenia*. NY: Psychology Press.

Fuchs, T. (2020). Delusion, reality, and intersubjectivity: A phenomenological and enactive analysis. *Philosophy, Psychiatry, & Psychology*, 27(1), 61–79.

Gallagher, S. (2004). Neurocognitive models of schizophrenia: A neurophenomenological critique. *Psychopathology, 37*(1), 8–19.

Gallagher, S. (2014). Relations between agency and ownership in the case of schizophrenic thought insertion and delusions of control. *Review of Philosophy and Psychology, 6*(4), 865–879.

Garety, P., & Freeman, D. (1999). Cognitive approaches to delusions: A critical review of theories and evidence. *British Journal of Clinical Psychology, 38*, 113–154.

Garety, P. A., Gittins, M., Jolley, S., Bebbington, P., Dunn, G., Kuipers, E., & Freeman, D. (2013). Differences in cognitive and emotional processes between persecutory and grandiose delusions. *Schizophrenia Bulletin, 39*(3), 629–639.

Gawęda, Ł., Staszkiewicz, M., & Balzan, R. (2017). The relationship between cognitive biases and psychological dimensions of delusions: The importance of jumping to conclusions. *Journal of Behaviour Therapy and Experimental Psychiatry, 56*, 51–56.

Gerrans, P. (2001). Authorship and ownership of thoughts. *Philosophy, Psychiatry & Psychology, 8*, 231–237.

Gilbert, D.T. (2006) *Stumbling on Happiness*. New York: A. Knopf.

Goldberg, T., David, A., & Gold, J. (2003). Neurocognitive deficits in schizophrenia. In S. Hirsch, & D. Weinberger (Eds.) *Schizophrenia* (pp. 168–184). Oxford: Blackwell.

Graham, G., & Stephens, G. L. (2000). *When Self-consciousness Breaks*. Cambridge, MA: MIT Press.

Gur, R., & Gur, E. (2005). Neuroimaging in schizophrenia: Linking neuropsychiatric manifestations to neurobiology. In B. Sadock, & V. Sadock (Eds), *Kaplan and Sadock's Comprehensive Textbook of Psychiatry* (pp. 1396–1408). Philadelphia, PA: Williams & Wilkins.

Hayes, S. C., Strosahl, K., & Wilson, K. G. (1999). *Acceptance and Commitment Therapy: Understanding and Treating Human Suffering*. New York: Guilford Press.

Hoerl, C. (2001). Introduction: Understanding, explaining, and intersubjectivity in schizophrenia. *Philosophy, Psychiatry, & Psychology, 8*(2), 83–88.

Jackson, J. H. (1958). *Selected Writings of John Hughlings Jackson*. New York: Basic Books.

Jaspers, K. (1963). *General Psychopathology* (7th ed.). Manchester: Manchester University Press.

Kinderman, P., & Bentall, R. (1996). Self-discrepancies and persecutory delusions: Evidence for a model of paranoid ideation. *Journal of Abnormal Psychology, 105*(1), 106–113.

Langdon, R., Still, M., Connors, M., Ward, P., & Catts, S. (2013). Attributional biases, paranoia, and depression in early psychosis. *British Journal of Clinical Psychology, 52*(4), 408–423.

Lincoln, T., Lange, J., Burau, J., Exner, C., & Moritz, S. (2010). The effect of state anxiety on paranoid ideation and jumping to conclusions: An experimental investigation. *Schizophrenia Bulletin, 36*, 1140–1148.

Lincoln, T., Mehl, S., Exner, C., Lindenmeyer, J., & Rief, W. (2010). Attributional style and persecutory delusions: Evidence for an event independent and state specific external-personal attribution bias for social situations. *Cognitive Therapy and Research, 34*, 297–302.

Maher, B. A. (2001). Delusions. In P. B. Sutker & H. E. Adams (Eds.), *Comprehensive Handbook of Psychopathology* (pp. 309–341). New York: Kluwer.

Mandelbaum, E. (2019) Troubles with Bayesianism: An introduction to the psychological immune system. *Mind & Language, 34*, 141–157.

Marwaha, S., Broome, M. R., Bebbington, P. E., Kuipers, E., & Freeman, D. (2014). Mood instability and psychosis: Analyses of British national survey data. *Schizophrenia Bulletin, 40*(2), 269–277.

Mehl, S., Landsberg, M., Schmidt, A., Cabanis, M., Bechdolf, A., Herrlich, J., Loos-Jankowiak, S., Kircher, T., Kiszkenow, S., Klingberg, S., Kommescher, M., Moritz, S., Müller, B., Sartory, G., Wiedemann, G., Wittorf, A., Wölwer, W., Wagner, M. (2014). Why do bad things happen to me? Attributional style, depressed mood, and persecutory delusions in patients with schizophrenia. *Schizophrenia Bulletin, 40*(6), 1338–1346.

Menon, M., Addington, J., & Remington, G. (2013). Examining cognitive biases in patients with delusions of reference. *European Psychiatry, 28*(2), 71–73.

Moritz, S., Woodward, T., Burlon, M., Braus, D., & Andresen, B. (2007). Attributional style in schizophrenia: Evidence for a decreased sense of self-causation in currently paranoid patients. *Cognitive Therapy and Research, 31*, 371–383.

Pacherie, E. (2009). Perception, emotions, and delusions: The case of the Capgras delusion. In T. Bayne & J. Fernández. *Delusion and Self-deception: Affective and Motivational Influences on Belief Formation* (pp. 107–125). New York: Psychology Press.

Peacocke, C. (2014). *The Mirror of the World: Subjects, Consciousness, and Self-consciousness.* Oxford: Oxford University Press.

Prochwicz, K., & Gawęda, Ł. (2015). The Polish version of the Peters et al. Delusions Inventory: Factor analysis, reliability and the prevalence of delusion-like experiences in the Polish population. *Psychiatria Polska, 49*(6), 1203–1222.

Proust, J. (2006). Agency in schizophrenia from a control theory viewpoint. In N. Sebanz, & W. Prinz (Eds.), *The Disorders of Volition* (pp. 87–118). Cambridge, MA: MIT Press.

Quilty-Dunn, J., & Mandelbaum, E. (2018). Against dispositionalism: Belief in cognitive science. *Philosophical Studies, 175*(9), 2353–2372.

Randall, F., Corcoran, R., Day, J., & Bentall, R. (2003). Attention, theory of mind, and causal attributions in people with persecutory delusions: A preliminary investigation. *Cognitive Neuropsychiatry, 8*(4), 287–294.

Ratcliffe, M., & Wilkinson, S. (2015). Thought insertion clarified. *Journal of Consciousness Studies, 22*(11–12), 246–269.

Sass, L. (1992). *Madness and Modernism: Insanity in the Light of Modern Art, Literature, and Thought.* New York: Basic Books.

Sass, L. & Parnas, J. (2003). Schizophrenia, consciousness, and the self. *Schizophrenia Bulletin, 3*(29), 427–444.

Shinn, A. K., Heckers, S., & Öngür, D. (2013). The special treatment of first rank auditory hallucinations and bizarre delusions in the diagnosis of schizophrenia. *Schizophrenia Research, 146*(1–3), 17–21.

Spence, S. A., Brooks, D. J., Hirsch, S. R., Liddle, P. F., Meehan, J., & Grasby, P. M. (1997). A PET study of voluntary movement in schizophrenic patients experiencing passivity phenomena. *Brain, 120*(11), 1997–2011.

Stephens, G. L., & Graham, G. (1994). Self-consciousness, mental agency, and the clinical psychopathology of thought insertion. *Philosophy, Psychiatry, & Psychology, 1*(1), 1–10.

Stephens, G. L., & Graham, G. (2000). *When Self-Consciousness Breaks.* Cambridge, MA: MIT Press.

Stone, T., & Young, A. (1997). Delusions and brain injury: The philosophy and psychology of belief. *Mind and Language, 12*, 327–64

Udachina, A., Varese, F., Myin-Germeys, I., & Bentall, R. (2014). The role of experiential avoidance in paranoid delusions: An experience sampling study. *British Journal of Clinical Psychology, 53*(4), 422–432.

Wilson, K., & Luciano, C. (2002). Terapia de Aceptación y Compromiso: un tratamiento conductual orientado a los valores [Acceptance and Commitment Therapy: A behavioral therapy oriented to values]. Madrid: Pirámide.

Wittorf, A., Giel K., Hautzinger, M., Rapp, A., Schönenberg, M., Wolkenstein, L., Zipfel, S., Mehl, S., Fallgatter, A., Klingberg, S. (2012). Specificity of jumping to conclusions and attributional biases: A comparison between patients with schizophrenia, depression, and anorexia nervosa. *Cognitive Neuropsychiatry, 17*(3), 262–286.

11
Thought Insertion as a Persecutory Delusion

Peter Langland-Hassan

11.1. Introduction

Thought insertion is the delusion that an outside agent has inserted thoughts into one's mind. Most existing explanations of the nature and aetiology of thought insertion begin by identifying a peculiar feature of the thoughts reported as 'inserted'. This approach makes sense if we think of thought insertion as a particular kind of *experience* a person might have—one with an unusual content or phenomenology that leaves the thinker with the odd impression that his own thoughts are someone else's. The most common such proposal is to hold that, normally, we experience a 'sense of agency', or a feeling of having agential *control*, over our thoughts, the absence of which—in pathology—leads to reports of thought insertion (Carruthers, 2012; Frith, 1992; Langland-Hassan, 2008; Proust, 2006). Another approach appeals to the unwelcome content of the thoughts, with sufferers of thought insertion refusing to endorse as their own some of their more upsetting, accusatory, or rationally incongruous thoughts (Graham & Stephens, 2000; Pickard, 2010; Vosgerau & Newen, 2007). Other theories invoke more esoteric thought properties, such as Parrott's (2017) proposal that thought insertion results from one having a sense that one's state of awareness is not ordinary first-person awareness.

Despite these differences, such accounts typically agree that there is more to be explained in thought insertion than the unusual phenomenological features of the (putatively) inserted thoughts. No matter how odd one's own thoughts might appear, after all, it will remain a poor explanation of that oddity to conclude that someone else has (somehow) inserted *their* thoughts into one's mind. Thus, theorists typically invoke an additional factor in explaining the formation and maintenance of such delusional beliefs—such as an inability to properly weigh evidence, or a tendency to jump to conclusions—that, in concert with the oddity of an experienced thought, may generate the delusion that another agent has inserted thoughts into one's mind (Coltheart, 2010; Davies & Coltheart, 2000; Davies, Coltheart, Langdon, & Breen, 2001).

I will follow Davies et al. (2001), McKay et al.(2005), and Coltheart et al. (2007, 2011) in calling this style of explanation a *two-factor* account, a style of explanation that has been extended to a variety of other delusions. On the broadest characterization of a two-factor view, delusions are to be explained by appeal to two distinct abnormalities working in tandem. The first is 'what initially prompts the delusional belief and is responsible for the content of that delusion' (Coltheart et al., 2007, p. 292). This is often, though not always, held to be an anomalous experience of some kind.[1] The second factor, conceived as a deficit in belief-evaluation, is 'what prevents the person from rejecting the belief in the light of the very strong evidence against it' (Coltheart et al., 2007, p. 292). Davies et al. (2001) and Coltheart et al. (2007, 2011) argue that a wide variety of so-called 'monothematic' delusions are amenable to this form of explanation. A monothematic delusion, on their understanding, is one whose subject-matter is tightly limited in scope—such as that one's family members have been replaced by imposters (as occurs in the Capgras delusion) or that one is being followed by friends or family members in disguise (as in the Fregoli delusion). On the classic two-factor account of the Capgras delusion, it is proposed that normal autonomic affective response to familiar faces are suppressed, and that this abnormal suppression serves as the first factor—that which gives rise to the specific claim that one's family member has been replaced by an imposter—while a general impairment in updating and revising beliefs in the light of conflicting evidence constitutes the second factor, explaining why the unusual belief is not revised in the light of contrary evidence (Coltheart et al., 2007, 2011).

Because it is the express role of the first factor to explain the specific content of a delusion, two-factor theories are less well suited to explaining delusions in a context where the patient has many delusions on many different topics—what are known as 'polythematic' delusions. While it is possible, in principle, to appeal to different two-factor explanations to account for each delusion such an individual has on a distinct topic (see, e.g., Coltheart et al., 2011, p. 293), such manoeuvring will appear ad hoc, suggesting an unlucky confluence of distinct delusion-causing mechanisms in a patient where a single

---

[1] On a the most general of two-factor accounts, the first factor may be subconscious or motivational in nature—such as a desire for self-preservation. McKay, Langdon, and Coltheart (2005) even propose that in some cases 'there are multiple relevant first-factor sources', raising the possibility that the first factor—understood entirely generally as that which explains the content of the delusion—is in fact several factors working in tandem. (Thanks to a reviewer for emphasizing this flexibility in two-factor accounts.)

underlying pathology is more likely. Thus, despite the relative popularity of two-factor accounts in explaining thought insertion, there remains a *prima facie* tension in extending them to this specific delusion, as thought insertion occurs almost invariably in patients with schizophrenia, where polythematic delusions are the norm (Mullins & Spence, 2003).

This is one reason that I want to chart an alternative path in this chapter, despite the fact that I have in the past been among those developing and defending two-factor accounts of thought insertion (with a focus on the first factor (Langland-Hassan, 2008, 2016)). It is not that I view two-factor accounts of thought insertion as dead in the water. I simply think that they face challenges strong enough to warrant considering alternatives. The thesis I will defend in their place is that thought insertion is better viewed as a type of persecutory delusion. Persecutory delusions are delusions to the effect that one is under threat of harm because others intend for one to be harmed (Freeman, 2007). If this assimilation on the right track, two-factor accounts of thought insertion may nevertheless succeed, if they can be extended to persecutory delusions. Yet, to date, two-factor theorists have had little to say about how persecutory delusions may be explained in their terms, even if persecutory delusions are the most common form of delusion in psychosis, occurring in over 70% of those experiencing their first psychotic symptoms (Freeman & Garety, 2014).[2] This is likely because persecutory delusions are characteristic of psychiatric illnesses, such as schizophrenia, where the kinds polythematic delusions ill-suited to explanation by two-factor accounts are common. Nevertheless, persecutory delusions also occur in medical conditions with well-understood aetiologies, such as Alzheimer's (Bassiony & Lyketsos, 2003), and in cases of traumatic brain injury (Fujii & Ahmed, 2002).

A key difference between the view of thought insertion I will propose and existing two-factor accounts is that the present view does not posit any unusual *experiential* feature shared by all and only the thoughts that are reported as inserted. We should no more expect to discover an anomalous experience distinctive to thought insertion, I will propose, than we should one that causes all and delusions about spy agencies (however common the latter may be). To be sure, there could be very general anomalous experiences of a type that gives rise to many different persecutory delusions, and which, in some cases, may help to explain why a delusion concerning secret service agencies has arisen. But we would be spinning our wheels in seeking a particular type of

---

[2] McKay, Langdon, and Coltheart's (2005) generalized two-factor account, which allows for motivational factors to constitute the first factor, is the best suited two-factor view (of which I am aware) for explaining persecutory delusions; yet they do not explicitly extend the view to persecutory delusions.

anomalous experience specific *only* to secret service delusions. Similarly, I will suggest, were we to gather up all the thought episodes that trigger reports of thought insertion, there will be no phenomenological or content-related feature they share that would unify them and, in so doing, serve to explain why they generated the delusion that thoughts have been into one's mind (*as opposed to* a delusion with some other persecutory content).

In short, I propose a reorientation away from the question of 'what sort of experience would lead someone to think that another's thoughts have been inserted into their mind?' and towards the more general question of, 'what would lead a person to form irrational beliefs to the effect that others intend to harm him (where claims of thought insertion are just one manifestation of such)?' (See Ratcliffe & Wilkinson (2015) for a similar reorientation.) This reorientation—which sees thought insertion most fundamentally as a kind of (delusional) belief, and not an abnormal type of experience—is at odds with at least one standard definition of thought insertion. The Schedules for Clinical Assessment in Neuropsychiatry (SCAN)—formerly known as the Present State Examination (PSE-10)—is a set of clinical tools endorsed by the World Health Organization for the diagnosis of psychiatric symptoms. The SCAN includes thought insertion in Section 18 under 'experiences of thought interference and replacement of will', where it is noted that 'experiences of thoughts being inserted into the respondents' minds are … rated here' (Wing et al., 1990). In the SCAN, all forms of delusion—including 'paranoid' (and persecutory) delusions—are diagnosed separately, in accordance with procedures outlined in its Section 19. Thus, according to the SCAN, thought insertion is not itself a delusion, but, rather, a kind of pathological *experience*—not unlike a hallucination that may, but need not, lead to delusions.

However, the idea that thought insertion is best viewed as an experience and not as a kind of (delusional) belief is not universally endorsed. In an influential review article on how thought insertion has been approached in psychiatry, Mullins and Spence (2003) note that, unlike the symptom of thought broadcast, thought insertion 'has developed a reliable definition' (p. 293). Ironically, however, they cite two contradictory definitions in support of said reliability. The first, taken from the Schedules for the Assessment of Positive Symptoms (SAPS) (Andreasen, 1984), holds that thought insertion occurs when 'the subject believes that thoughts that are not his own have been inserted into his mind'. By this commonly used assessment tool, simply having the delusional belief that thoughts have been inserted into one's mind is sufficient for having the symptom of thought insertion. The second definition, pulled from Wing et al.'s (1983) predecessor to the SCAN, describes thought insertion as occurring when 'the subject experiences thoughts which are not his own intruding into his mind'. This definition allows for thought insertion to occur (as a pathological 'experience') in the absence of delusional beliefs, even if it is unlikely to be reported when there is not a corresponding delusion. It also allows for someone to have the delusion that someone has inserted thoughts into their minds without in fact experiencing the symptom of thought insertion.

My working hypothesis will be that the first definition of thought insertion is preferable: to have the symptom of thought insertion is nothing other than to have a delusional belief that some of one's thoughts are not one's own and have been inserted into one's mind by someone else. Further, I will argue that this delusional belief is, in most cases, best viewed as a persecutory delusion. The plan in what follows is to motivate this approach, in Section 11.2, by explaining some of the challenges faced by two-factor theories of thought insertion. Then, in Section 11.3, I will offer independent evidence—including numerous first-person accounts from people suffering thought insertion—for viewing thought insertion as a persecutory delusion. I will also consider and rebut the objection that, because thought insertion does not cluster under the same factor with persecutory delusions in principal component analyses (Paolini, Moretti, & Compton, 2016), it should not be viewed as a form of persecutory delusion. Part of this rebuttal will appeal to the considerable variability in the kinds of delusions individual patients present with over time. Section Four concludes by discussing some of the means for treating thought insertion that become available on the hypothesis that thought insertion is a form of persecutory delusion. The ultimate value of the present proposal will indeed hang on the efficacy of treating persecutory delusions and thought insertion with similar interventions.

11.2. Challenges for Two-factor Accounts of Thought Insertion

The first challenge for any two-factor account of thought insertion is to say something comprehensible about the first factor. Thoughts that patients report as inserted are said to have acquired a phenomenology of *alienness* or of *otherness*. What do we mean by this? To start, it seems we need to know what it is in the normal case that makes thoughts seem as though they are one's own, such that this normal sense of ownership might get disrupted in psychosis. The first and most obvious answer may be that we have introspective access to the thought. By 'introspective access' I mean that form of privileged and peculiar (Byrne, 2005) access each person has to (many of) her own thoughts, and that others lack, whatever the ultimate mechanisms underlying that access.

However, people suffering from thought insertion presumably have that sort of access to the thoughts they deem inserted, yet still conclude that the introspected thoughts are not their own. This has led many to suppose that it is instead a sense of being the agent, or causal source, of an introspected thought that has gone missing (Campbell, 1999; Frith, 1992; Gallagher, 2000; Proust, 2006). The problem—now frequently remarked—is that it is not very clear what it is, in general, to feel like the agent of one's thoughts. Sure, thinking may at times be difficult. We may have a sense of working at it, or of trying to keep it on course. But most are also familiar with thoughts coming effortlessly, randomly, and even against one's will. We might try, but fail, to stop thinking about some disturbing or annoying topic, for instance. If this is what it is to lack a sense of agency over a thought, the phenomenon is not anomalous or pathological. Nor does it tend to raise suspicions that some other agent is doing the thinking. Thus, it is not clear how a lack of such a sense of agency could play an explanatory role as a first factor in two-factor accounts. Moreover, the normal feeling of lacking control over one's thoughts can rise to pathological levels—as in obsessive-compulsive disorder—without those suffering it having any phenomenological impression that someone else is the agent of their thinking (Graham & Stephens, 2000; Langland-Hassan, 2008; Parrott, 2017). What, then, does the pathological sense of 'alienness' or 'otherness'—the putative first factor in two-factor accounts of thought insertion—consist in?

This is where I entered the debate some years ago, building on influential theories of Frith (1992), Blakemore et al. (2002), and others to offer a version of the comparator account of thought insertion (Langland-Hassan, 2008, 2016). On this style of view, schizophrenic symptoms of passivity and alien control result from a disruption in the prediction and comparison mechanisms that help to guide ordinary perception and action. An influential view of motor control holds that, when we act on the environment, a copy of the motor command is sent to a cognitive system (known as a 'forward model') that generates a prediction of the sensory consequences of carrying out the command (Miall, Weir, Wolpert, & Stein, 1993; Wolpert, Miall, & Kawato, 1998). That prediction is then compared to actual sensory feedback. If there is a match, one is left with a sense of having successfully carried out the intended action. If there is not a match, an error signal is generated that alerts one to adjust the motion or reattempt the action. This error signal, whatever its phenomenological upshot, could be associated with unexpected intervention by other agents, as such interventions may often be the cause of prediction errors. An advantage of this approach is that it builds on an architecture for sensorimotor control that has considerable independent support. Further, people with schizophrenia have been shown to have a variety of motor and perceptual deficits over and above thought insertion that mesh with the hypothesis that people with schizophrenia have general problems with sensorimotor self-monitoring (Blakemore, Wolpert, & Frith, 1998; Frith, 2012).

While some have argued that comparator-style accounts cannot be extended to thought insertion precisely because thinking is not a motor process (Campbell, 1999; Synofzik, Vosgerau, & Newen, 2008), this scepticism can be resisted. Speaking and hearing are sensorimotor processes, elements of which are exploited in acts of inner speech (i.e., of talking to oneself silently, 'in the head'). If episodes of inner speech are the relevant 'thoughts' that seem not to be one's own, then we have a way of uniting the 'sense of otherness' corresponding to the first factor in two-factor accounts of thought insertion to the kinds of sensorimotor self-monitoring mechanisms invoked by comparator theories—even if *other kinds* of thoughts are not well-viewed as sensorimotor processes. Further, we can expect this sort of disruption in the sense of agency to be categorically different than the lack of agency attending ordinary unwilled and undesired thoughts. I have filled in the details of this inner-speech-related proposal elsewhere (Langland-Hassan, 2008, 2016). The key move is to assimilate thought insertion onto a single experiential spectrum with auditory verbal hallucinations (AVHs), which are one of the most common and disruptive symptoms of schizophrenia. Both AVHs and thought insertion can then be seen as symptoms resulting from a failure to appropriately monitor (or 'filter', or 'attenuate', in my terms) one's own inner speech. Episodes with higher degrees of sensory character, and which seem to come from outside the head, may be more likely to be reported as AVHs, while episodes that are low in sensory character and that seem to emanate from within the head may be more likely reported as inserted thoughts. In either case, they could be symptoms that occur due to disruptions in the ordinary subconscious mechanisms that serve to filter and attenuate self-generated inner speech signals, through prediction and comparison processes involved in the generation of ordinary speech (and reused in the case of inner speech).

In my view, this remains a promising approach to explaining thought insertion, *if* one is committed to articulating a two-factor account. It has the advantage of assimilating thought insertion to the more commonly reported and studied phenomenon of AVH. It also avoids positing entirely *sui generis* mechanisms or phenomenological elements and, instead, builds on a well-supported framework for understanding how sensorimotor control works in healthy individuals (and how it becomes disrupted in people with schizophrenia). However, my project here is to say what I find lacking in this approach.

First, to assimilate thought insertion to AVHs—and to find an impaired sensorimotor process at work—we need to assume that cases of thought insertion really are mis-monitored episodes of inner speech and not some other form of thought. Yet there is, at present, relatively little empirical data that directly supports (or undermines) this assumption. It certainly *could be* that most or all episodes that get reported as inserted thoughts are aberrant episodes of inner speech. But it is equally possible that they are not. Due in part to its relative infrequency, there are no neuroimaging studies of people suffering from thought insertion that correlate reports of thought insertion with activation of the language areas underlying inner speech (such as Broca's and Wernicke's areas). By contrast, there are numerous such studies with respect to AVHs (Allen, Aleman, & Mcguire, 2007; Allen et al., 2012; Shergill, 2003; Shergill et al., 2000).

Other forms of evidence remain possible, however. For instance, if a patient reports that their inserted thoughts occur in a particular spoken language (such as English), this is good reason to conclude that their language-production mechanisms are involved in their generation (Langland-Hassan, 2018). Such a conclusion would, in turn, warrant applying theories of sensorimotor self-monitoring to thought insertion. However, current clinical assessments of thought insertion do not ask patients whether their inserted thoughts occur in a particular language. Suitable data is therefore lacking. Alternatively, should we find that a person's experiences of thought insertion suddenly dissipate upon their having a stroke that disables language-production areas, or if their inserted thoughts are modulated by transcranial magnetic stimulation (TMS) to language areas, this would be reason to think that thought insertion is impaired (or 'mis-monitored') inner speech. On the other hand, if the experience of thought insertion continued despite the loss—or temporary impairment—of language abilities, this would be reason to think that sensorimotor approaches cannot be extended to thought insertion. Yet, to my knowledge, there are no existing reports that trend in either direction.

Aside from the challenges in experimentally discriminating the first factor in thought insertion, the approach is further weighted by a commitment to a second factor—some additional deficit in belief evaluation that leads people to move from a merely unusual phenomenology to the delusional belief that someone else has (per *impossible*) inserted thoughts into their minds. It is commonly recognized that this reasoning deficit must be only partial, or intermittent. People experiencing thought insertion—and with schizophrenia more generally—do not form delusional beliefs about the nature of *every* unusual experience they might have, after all. Nor are they completely unable to weigh evidence and form reasonable conclusions in experimental reasoning tasks. For instance, while people suffering delusions have been shown not to gather as much evidence as healthy individuals before generating a hypothesis (Colbert, Peters, & Garety, 2010; Fine et al., 2007), their delusional beliefs tend to remain fixed even when they are forced to encounter a large amount of disconfirming evidence from friends and caregivers. Thus, the reasoning deficit that would lead one to adopt and then *maintain* such an unusual hypothesis appears more profound than a tendency to gather less evidence before forming an opinion. Moreover, data concerning the jumping-to-conclusions bias and its correlation with the experience of delusions is decidedly mixed, with one cross-study meta-analysis finding no correlation between decreased data gathering and the concurrent possession of delusions (Ross et al., 2015).

A two-factor theorist can instead propose that those suffering delusions only reason poorly on certain topics. However, when the reasoning deficit corresponding to the second factor is fine-tuned to give rise only to delusions with a certain range of contents, it begins to subsume the work of the first factor. For instance, if I only reason in pathological ways when the topic is the control of my own thoughts and actions, there is no need to appeal to an anomalous (first factor) experience to explain the resulting (mental-control-related) delusion. The view will have collapsed into a one-factor account, where the one factor is a content-specific reasoning deficit.

This points to a general tension in all two-factor accounts: if the second-factor reasoning deficit is entirely domain general—i.e., not restricted to any particular contents or subject matter—then, given the seriousness of that deficit, we should expect a person with one delusion to have very many delusions on many different topics, formed in response to ordinary odd thoughts that (in the non-delusional) are quickly dismissed.[3] In short, we should not expect to find the very monothematic delusions that two-factor accounts seem best equipped to explain. On the other hand, if the second-factor reasoning deficit is not domain general and is instead limited to certain topics or subject matters, then we have no need for the first factor, whose only role was to explain the content of the delusion.

---

[3] Coltheart et al. (2011) offer a response to this objection, proposing that the belief-revision capacity is 'impaired but not abolished', which allows it to reject odd ideas that only occur sporadically. They suggest that it is only when faced with a persistent first factor—a continuous anomalous experience, say—that the impaired belief revision capacity is unable to overcome the delusional belief. However, this wrongly predicts that patients experiencing Capgras will give up their delusion when their spouse is not present (and, thus, when they are not experiencing the abnormal affect related to a lack of autonomic response to familiar faces). Further, continuously high levels of stress and anxiety are relatively commonplace in everyday life and, in a person with an impaired (domain general) ability to evaluate beliefs, ought to generate a panoply of delusions on multiple topics as coping strategies.

The difficulties in articulating an experimentally tractable first factor for thought insertion, combined with the tensions inherent in two-factor views more generally (as applied both to polythematic and monothematic delusions), give reason to shift focus from trying to describe the distinctive anomalous experience (or thought content) responsible for thought insertion to the question of what it is that makes a person susceptible to (possibly polythematic) delusions in general. When we shift focus in this way, the thesis that thought insertion is just one form of persecutory delusion gains plausibility, for reasons we will now explore.

11.3. The Persecutory Content of Inserted Thoughts

As earlier remarked, persecutory delusions are by far the most common form of delusion in schizophrenia, marked by the concern that one is under a threat of harm from others. People with persecutory delusions tend to believe they are under constant surveillance: their phones are tapped, homes bugged, computers hacked. They are being followed by cars on the road and monitored by satellites. On an intuitive level, having another person's thoughts in one's mind—feeling as though someone else is *using* one's thoughts to think— would constitute a similar, if more profound, invasion of privacy. To fear that someone else's thoughts are in one's mind is to fear that the last and most solid privacy wall has been breached and that one is not free from persecution even within the confines of one's own mind. In short, to believe that one has had thoughts inserted into one's mind by some other agent is a very short step from believing that one is being persecuted. Or so one might propose.

However, it is not immediately obvious from the small number of cases of thought insertion quoted (and requoted) in the literature that those experiencing thought insertion view themselves as under threat. There is, for instance, the man quoted by Mellor (1970, p. 17) who explains that 'the thoughts of Eamonn Andrews come into my mind. There are no other thoughts there, only his'. We do not, from this snippet, get a clear sense of whether the patient feels harmed or threatened by the thoughts (or by Mr Andrews). There is also the patient quoted by Frith (1992, p. 66) who says that 'thoughts are put into my mind like 'Kill God' ... they come from this chap, Chris. They are his thoughts'. While 'Chris' is described amiably as a 'chap', the order to kill God is not a friendly piece of advice. Arguably, the patient feels persecuted by having such thoughts forced upon him.

The ambiguity in these brief reports warrants a search for more (and more detailed) reports of thought insertion, from which we might more clearly assess whether inserted thoughts are indeed viewed, by those suffering them, as a kind of persecution. Publicly available online discussions among people with schizophrenia provide a rich source of such data, even if it must be taken with a grain of salt due to our inability to confirm the sincerity of the reports. I offer them here as evidence suggestive of a common theme, rather than as proof thereof. What follow are several first-person accounts pulled from the public discussion boards at Schizophrenia.com and Crazyboards.org, two websites aimed at fostering supportive conversation among those suffering from schizophrenia and other forms of mental illness. The accounts—only a handful of which I reproduce here—were retrieved from these discussion boards by using 'thought insertion' as a search term to narrow topics. As we will see, there is a strong persecutory theme throughout.

I've been having this feeling that maybe this person that I know is inserting thoughts into my head or controlling them. Now I feel like my life isn't my own anymore and that I'm forever cursed to live with that person manipulating my mind (from *Fleur2576*).[4]

Alien is evil spirit living in my head and he puts his thoughts into my head. When he puts these in my head I suddenly have a thought that's in my head but it didn't come from me—its foreign . . . It's definitely not mine and causes irritation and distress (from EarthChild).[5]

Now I have voices and inserted thoughts reminding me all day long that I'm going to be tortured after death forever (from Rei26, *Schizophrenia.com*[6]).

I have intrusive thoughts and inserted thoughts. Not sure what the difference is except inserted thoughts seem foreign or inserted and not from me, but are 'inserted' in my head from an external source like ET, chip, AI, God, quantum physics, parallel universes, past lives, etc. Knowledge that comes from no-where, but it's hard to get at and prove and makes me miserable (from johnnyboy 1[7]).

---

[4] Retrieved on 5 May 2022 from https://forum.schizophrenia.com/t/thought-insertion-thought-control-by-a-person/244626
[5] Retrieved on 10 February 2021 from https://forum.schizophrenia.com/t/whats-the-difference-between-intrusive-thoughts-and-inserted-thoughts/220352/26
[6] Retrieved on 10 February 2021 from https://forum.schizophrenia.com/t/psychosis-as-a-distorting-mirror/196472/3
[7] Retrieved on 10 February 2021 from https://forum.schizophrenia.com/t/whats-the-difference-between-intrusive-thoughts-and-inserted-thoughts/220352/26

People from my past constantly interfere with my mind and insert things into it. It used to be manageable but it's becoming less so. Hoping Clozapine wipes out all of this nonsense, as it's driving me crazy" (from Joker, *Schizophrenia.com*[8]).

(Replying to Joker) "Yes, I've had this as well @Joker. It's almost as if they're really talking to you and it's not a good feeling, as usually it's kinda menacing—at least for me' (from Schztuna, *Schizophrenia.com*[9]).

Annette, my main voice, even when silent inserts thoughts in my head and takes thoughts from my head. I am in her control. Puppet in her hands. Just a toy in her hands. Anyone else feeling the same? (from Om_Sadasiva[10])

I am going through some of the same stuff like thought insertion and a lot of fake memories. And it seems like whatever spirit it's taking a lot of time and effort to mess with me. Also says I am gonna be tortured after death just for smoking (from Jesse25, *Schizophrenia.com*[11]).

I have rarely had images that are especially vivid, involuntary and strange and seem to come out of nowhere a few of them seemed to be another person's thoughts, memories or experience ... two of them involved puppets ... someone was or was at least attempting to manipulate my mind, this experience was unpleasant and fortunately isolated in my case (bobhope 74, from *Crazyboards*[12]).

I don't hear voices very often, but I have experienced thought insertion. I thought the thoughts were being inserted by the sun. I felt like they were distinctly NOT my own thoughts. They felt foreign, and it sometimes hurt when they were inserted and I would flinch and bang my head to get them out. They were thoughts I would never have on my own. It was horrible (from Parapluie, on *Crazyboards*[13]).

For the past few weeks, I have been getting severe thought insertion. It has been telling me dangerous things and scary things. There are times where it is so bad

---

[8] Retrieved on 6 May 2022 from https://forum.schizophrenia.com/t/thought-insertion/260837/5 .
[9] Retrieved on 6 May 2022 from https://forum.schizophrenia.com/t/thought-insertion/260837/5 .
[10] Retrieved on 10 February 2021 from https://forum.schizophrenia.com/t/thought-insertion-thought-withdrawal/101687
[11] Retrieved on 10 February 2021 from https://forum.schizophrenia.com/t/inserted-thoughts/178478/3. I have made several corrections to obvious typos in this post.
[12] Retrieved on 10 February 2021 from https://www.crazyboards.org/topic/68230-thought-insertion-something-in-your-mind/?tab=comments#comment-716274
[13] Retrieved on 10 February 2021 from https://www.crazyboards.org/topic/68230-thought-insertion-something-in-your-mind/?tab=comments#comment-716274

that I nearly break down in tears. Some of it is from the government and some is from aliens from another galaxy ... they enjoy controlling me and sending me scary thoughts. They tell me it is better if I kill myself quickly instead of the slow and painful death they promise me ... The thought insertion is different than voices as it isn't audible. But it is stronger than my own thoughts. So, what do I do? (from FireBird at *Crazyboards.com*[14]).

We should put ourselves in the shoes of a clinician treating these individuals. Clearly, we can identify such patients as suffering from the symptom of thought insertion. Should we also conclude that they have persecutory delusions? On the one hand, they appear to satisfy the standard criteria for such. Each seems to have an irrational belief to the effect that 'harm is occurring, or is going to occur', because a 'perceived persecutor has the intention to cause harm' (Freeman & Garety, 2004, p. 13). This would suggest that the reports qualify them as having both thought insertion and persecutory delusions—that, often enough, having the former suffices for having the latter. On the other hand, the symptom of thought insertion is classed separately from persecutory delusions. As noted, the SCAN diagnostic system includes all delusions in an entirely distinct diagnostic class from pathological 'experiences' such as thought insertion. And while the also popular SAPS diagnostic system classifies thought insertion as a delusion, it lists thought insertion as a different type of delusion than persecutory delusions—not a possible subtype thereof. A clinician using either diagnostic system will thus most likely respond to the reports just mentioned by simply diagnosing thought insertion and not a persecutory delusion. And, indeed, from symptom correlation studies, we can see that most reports of thought insertion appear not to be coded additionally as persecutory delusions. For instance, Peralta and Cuesta (1999) found only a .13 correlation between (what they term) Schneiderian 'bizarre' delusions (which includes thought insertion) and paranoid delusions (which includes persecutory delusions). While statistically significant, it is a far weaker correlation than one would expect if many reports of thought insertion were also coded as paranoid delusions. Consider also the many principal component analyses that have been used to look for significant clusters of symptoms among schizophrenia patients (Ellersgaard et al., 2014; Kimhy et al., 2005; Paolini et al., 2016; Vázquez-Barquero et al., 1996). These studies use statistical methods to investigate which symptoms tend to appear together in clusters, in hopes of revealing an underlying causal basis for such clusters. For instance, the SAPS

---

[14] Retrieved 21 February 2012 from https://www.crazyboards.org/topic/23396-severe-thought-insertion/?tab=comments#comment-288579.

contains descriptions of 34 distinct schizophrenic symptoms. However, these symptoms 'load' onto three, four, or five factors—depending on which meta-analysis one consults—meaning that we can identify three or so symptom clusters where to have one symptom in the cluster makes it more likely that one will have another symptom in the cluster, and less likely that one has a symptom in another cluster. In all of these studies, thought insertion tends to cluster with other 'Schneiderian first rank', symptoms, such as thought broadcasting, delusions of control, and thought withdrawal, while *not* clustering with persecutory delusions (which themselves cluster on another factor with delusions of reference) (Ellersgaard et al., 2014; Paolini et al., 2016).

This might seem to challenge the hypothesis that thought insertion is well-viewed as a species of persecutory delusion. After all, if thought insertion is itself a persecutory delusion, we should expect patients reporting thought insertion to have other persecutory delusions as well, and thus for thought insertion to cluster with persecutory delusions. However, we have also noted the possibility that artificial divisions in how the most commonly used diagnostic systems group symptoms could lead clinicians to exclusively diagnose thought insertion in contexts where patients clearly satisfy criteria for having persecutory delusions in addition. This, too, could plausibly prevent the symptoms from clustering together on a single factor in principal component analyses.

Which explanation for the failure of thought insertion to cluster with persecutory delusions should we favour? Is there a deep underlying difference between the two symptoms, or is the appearance of such an artefact of arbitrary classification criteria? Striking evidence for the latter can be found in numerous studies that have shown relatively little longitudinal stability in the content and type of delusions had by patients with schizophrenia (Appelbaum, Robbins, & Vesselinov, 2004; Ellersgaard et al., 2014; Jørgensen & Jensen, 1994; Sinha & Chaturvedi, 1990). For instance, Ellersgaard et al. (2014) examined clinical reports of 411 patients with schizophrenia spectrum disorders and delusions at four different time periods: initial exam, one year, two years, and five years later. The patients' delusions were in all cases scored according to the SAPS criteria. When looking only at symptoms coded on the first clinical visit, thought insertion again clustered separately from persecutory delusions. However, looking *across* visits, the researchers found 'delusional themes being just as likely to change as to stabilize', and that 'delusional themes do not necessarily reappear during consecutive psychotic episodes' and 'are, in fact, likely to change' (p. 347). They noted 'frequent shifts' where 'patients shifted between ... delusional themes of FRSs [i.e., first rank Schneiderian symptoms, such as thought insertion] or 'mind reading' and persecution or reference'

(p. 346). Patients who were not diagnosed with persecutory delusions on a first visit often presented with such delusions later, with delusions of persecution being 'frequent at all three follow-up points' and 'not only in patients having these delusions at baseline' (i.e., at first visit) (p. 343). More generally, 'the majority of patients with a certain predominant delusion at a follow-up point did not have this delusion as predominant at baseline' (p. 343).

A similar instability in the content of delusions over time is reported by others. Jørgensen and Jensen (1994) found that less than half of patients maintained an earlier delusion from one follow-up point to another. Likewise, in a population of 262 patients who were treated multiple times for delusions, Appelbaum et al. (2004) found that most showed variation in the content of their primary delusion over time. They note that 'delusions appear to be more fluid over relatively short periods of time than has been suggested by many classic descriptions and contemporary formulations' (Appelbaum et al., 2004).

In short, having delusions concerning a certain subject matter during a first assessment does not reliably predict that one's delusions will have the same subject matter at follow-up. This suggests that there is no deep aetiological difference between delusions with different contents—at least, not among those with psychosis. Whatever pathological processes lead to delusions with one subject matter can be expected to lead to delusions with another. Thus, while the SAPS, for instance, allows clinicians to diagnose 12 different forms of delusion—differentiating them by contents such as 'religious delusions', 'delusions of guilt or sin', 'delusions of reference', 'thought insertion', 'persecutory delusions', and 'delusions of being controlled'—these different categories may not track correspondingly different underlying processes. At the same time, the simple fact that a diagnostic system includes distinct places to rate each 'form' of delusion may lead clinicians to treat a patient's report as evidence for only one type of delusion. This may occur even though some reports—such as that one is forced to have distressing thoughts to 'kill God'—could plausibly qualify one as having many forms of delusion, including thought insertion, religious delusion, persecutory delusion, delusion of being controlled, delusions of sin, and delusions of mind reading (all of which are coded separately on the SAPS).

The especially odd content of Schneiderian First Rank delusions such as thought insertion and thought broadcasting further fuel a tendency to see (and code) them as categorically distinct from other delusions. Standard persecutory delusions—such as that one is being followed by the FBI—cite events of a sort that actually occur. By contrast, Schneiderian First Rank delusions are patently bizarre and involve events that seem, to many, to be impossible. The oddity of such delusions intuitively suggests a correspondingly bizarre basis in experience (though I have challenged that intuition). If, at one visit, a patient remarks most adamantly about experiencing inserted thoughts or thought broadcasting, this may lead the clinician to assign less significance to the fact that the patient is simultaneously voicing persecutory delusions. Indeed, as one reads through a large variety of thought insertion reports on patient bulletin boards, it is hard to see any reason why thought insertion would *not* highly correlate with persecutory delusions *other than* that they are treated by many clinicians as mutually exclusive. In each one of the patient reports quoted, there is material that warrants ascribing a persecutory delusion, such as that, for EarthChild, 'Alien is an evil spirit living in my head' that 'causes irritation and distress', or that, for Rei26, inserted thoughts are 'reminding me all day long that I'm going to be tortured after death'; or that, for FireBird, the government and aliens 'enjoy controlling me and sending me scary thoughts'.

These reports leave open the possibility that, at a subsequent visit, the patient will be troubled by delusions that are less patently bizarre. Their responses during that clinical assessment may focus instead on the comparatively pedestrian theme that their employer is spying on them. They will then be diagnosed with persecutory delusions, even if, properly understood, persecution has remained a theme across multiple visits.

To consider a possible objection (raised by a reviewer for this volume) one might worry that labelling reports of thought insertion as persecutory delusions is only plausible given an overly broad and theoretically unhelpful conception of what it is to be a persecutory delusion. Of course, the traditional category of 'persecutory delusion' is already broad, encompassing delusions with many different contents. The complaint, in this case, is that we would need to understand it in *even broader* terms to bring thought insertion into the fold. For instance, the reviewer rightly notes that simply feeling as though one is harmed by the (putatively) inserted thoughts is not enough to render the delusion persecutory, as one may feel harmed by the sting of a doctor's needle, despite not feeling persecuted by the doctor (this is the reviewer's example). To feel persecuted, one must, in addition, think that someone else intends one harm and that this intention is guiding their actions. Yet it seems quite clear, from the quotes provided, that patients invariably *do* think that another agency intends to harm them through the insertion of the thoughts. The very idea that the thoughts are described as *inserted*—as opposed to merely *caused*—by another entity clearly implies intent; and in no case does the patient suggest that the resulting harm is an accidental by-product of the insertion.

A related worry may be that, if we include thought insertion among the persecutory delusions, the category will have become trivially broad, as we will have equal grounds for assimilating other delusions to that class—including delusions of alien control, and even the Capgras and Fregoli delusions. After all, it is not hard to see how these may also be conceived as examples of believing that some other agent intends one harm. In response, the longitudinal fluidity of delusional themes in individual patients suggests that we may indeed be warranted in collapsing the traditional boundaries between many delusion 'types', instead identifying a general susceptibility to persecutory delusions as the single underlying pathology. Of course, whether or not we are correct to lump delusions in these ways will turn on the question of whether doing so leads to better theories and more effective interventions, in the long term. I will expand on this point in the next, concluding section.

First, however, it should be granted that not *all* reports of thought insertion will be well-viewed as persecutory delusions; nor is the present thesis that all episodes of thought insertion are persecutory delusions—only that the vast majority are. In reading many descriptions of thought insertion on *Schizophrenia.com* and *Crazyboards.org,* I came upon one where the writer described his inserted thoughts in wholly positive terms:

> My 'voices' are inserted thoughts. I can identify who the 'speaker' is even though I can't 'hear' anything. Do you actually 'hear' auditory voices? or do you get your voices via inserted thoughts? I like my voices and miss them. I don't get them that much anymore since I got the Invega shot. My 'voices' are comforting, reassuring and validating so it's no fun when they go away (from non-average at Schizophrenia.com[15]).

Interestingly, non-average goes on to explain that they suffer from 'delusions of grandeur', which constitute another common form of delusion in psychosis, distinguished from persecutory delusions. Specifically, non-average reports being monitored constantly by scientists and spy agencies as part of an important brain study (while also showing some degree of insight into the delusional nature of these beliefs). Just as the themes of being spied upon can appear in both persecutory and grandiose delusions, so, too, can the theme of having thoughts inserted into one's mind. In neither case need we suppose that there is a particular type of phenomenal experience responsible for each type of report.

---

[15] Retrieved on 6 May 2022 from https://forum.schizophrenia.com/t/hearing-voices-vs-inserted-thoughts/249426

11.4. Treating Thought Insertion as a Multi-Componential Persecutory Delusion

An advantage of viewing thought insertion as a persecutory delusion is that one avoids the explanatory demand of providing an account of the distinctive anomalous experience, or unusual phenomenology, that gives rise to such delusions. Like believing that one's neighbour wishes one ill, or that aliens, or the FBI, plan to cause one harm, believing that someone has inserted thoughts into one's mind is, typically, an expression an underlying propensity for persecutory delusions. There may well be anomalous experiences of a kind that are causally implicated in such delusions. But it would be a mistake to put too fine a point on them—to suggest that, if only we too had such an experience, we would understand why it generated the delusional belief (which, again, is the key explanatory role of the 'first factor' in two-factor accounts).

The most important upshot of this analysis, however, lies in the kinds of treatments and interventions it suggests. If most or all cases of thought insertion are persecutory delusions, treatments already shown successful for persecutory delusions may be effective in the treatment of thought insertion as well. For instance, Daniel Freeman and colleagues have advanced a multi-component account of the causal bases for persecutory delusions (Freeman, 2007, 2016; Freeman et al., 2015; Freeman & Garety, 2014). In a 2016 overview of his theory, Freeman explains that 'debates about delusions being caused by either one or two factors are outdated', and holds instead that 'many contributory factors are implicated in persecutory delusions', and that 'it is most certainly not a matter of one or two causes' (Freeman, 2016, p. 686). Nor, he argues, should we think they are caused by the same combination of causes in each situation. According to Freeman, when we identify causally relevant elements to a delusion, we are identifying insufficient but non-redundant parts of an unnecessary but sufficient condition (an 'INUS condition') for the delusion (Freeman, 2016, p. 686). Each such cause 'only increases the probability of the delusion occurring'. Freeman's model synthesizes results across a wide spectrum of studies to identify six core processes centrally involved in the development and persistence of persecutory delusions: worry, negative self-beliefs, anomalous experiences, sleep dysfunction, reasoning bias, and safety behaviours (p. 687).

We see in Freeman's account the familiar anomalous experiences and reasoning biases of many two-factor accounts. Yet they are placed in a broader context where other features, such as a 'worry thinking style', are equally likely to lie at the root of a persecutory delusion. Freeman and colleagues (2015) showed that persecutory delusions were significantly decreased by means of cognitive behavioural therapy (CBT) aimed at counteracting worry, comparing a patient group who paired such therapy with standard treatment to a control patient group who received only ordinary treatment. Further, it is known that most patients suffering persecutory delusions tend to sleep poorly. Freeman proposes that disrupted sleep can maintain paranoia in several ways, including elevating negative emotion, mood dysregulation, and anomalous perceptions, while limiting cognitive resources available for revising initial interpretations of ambiguous situations (Freeman, 2016, p. 687). A separate review of 66 studies has indeed found sleep dysfunction to be a contributing cause of delusions generally (Reeve, Sheaves, & Freeman, 2015).

This all suggests a very different approach to treating thought insertion than that encouraged by two-factor theories. As we saw earlier, many two-factor theories invoke disrupted sensorimotor self-monitoring mechanisms as necessary contributors to the experience of thought insertion. From that theoretical standpoint, intervening on thought insertion seems to require remedying these sensorimotor irregularities. By contrast, in viewing thought insertion as a persecutory delusion, we have reason to think that intervening on a worrying thinking style, or facilitating better sleep, may equally likely provide substantial relief. More generally, because persecutory delusions are by far the most diagnosed form of delusion—and therefore most easily studied—assimilating thought insertion as a subclass instantly allows a large amount of data and research to be applied to the treatment of this symptom. The ultimate value and interest of the present proposal will indeed hinge on how successful therapeutic approaches to persecutory delusions are when applied to those suffering from thought insertion.

References

Allen, P., Aleman, A., & Mcguire, P. K. (2007). Inner speech models of auditory verbal hallucinations: evidence from behavioural and neuroimaging studies. *International Review of Psychiatry, 19*(4), 407–415.

Allen, P., Modinos, G., Hubl, D., Shields, G., Cachia, A., Jardri, R., et al. (2012). Neuroimaging auditory hallucinations in schizophrenia: From neuroanatomy to neurochemistry and beyond. *Schizophrenia Bulletin, 38*(4), 695–703.

Andreasen, N. C. (1984). *Scale for the Assessment of Positive Symptoms (SAPS)*. Iowa City: University of Iowa.

Appelbaum, P. S., Robbins, P. C., & Vesselinov, R. (2004). Persistence and stability of delusions over time. *Comprehensive Psychiatry, 45*(5), 317–324.

Bassiony, M. M., & Lyketsos, C. G. (2003). Delusions and hallucinations in Alzheimer's disease: review of the brain decade. *Psychosomatics, 44*(5), 388–401.

Blakemore, S. J., Wolpert, D. M., & Frith, C. D. (1998). Central cancellation of self-produced tickle sensation. *Nature Neuroscience*, *1*, 635–640.

Blakemore, S. J., Wolpert, D. M., & Frith, C. D. (2002). Abnormalities in the awareness of action. *Trends in Cognitive Science*, *6*, 237–241.

Byrne, A. (2005). Introspection. *Philosophical Topics*, *33*(1), 79–104.

Campbell, J. (1999). Schizophrenia, the space of reasons, and thinking as a motor process. *The Monist*, *82*(4), 609–626.

Carruthers, G. (2012). The case for the comparator model as an explanation of the sense of agency and its breakdowns. *Consciousness and Cognition*, *21*(1), 30–45.

Colbert, S. M., Peters, E., & Garety, P. (2010). Jumping to conclusions and perceptions in early psychosis: Relationship with delusional beliefs. *Cognitive Neuropsychiatry*, *15*(4), 422–440.

Coltheart, M. (2010). The neuropsychology of delusions. *Annals of the New York Academy of Sciences*, *1191*(1), 16–26.

Coltheart, M., Langdon, R., & McKay, R. (2007). Schizophrenia and monothematic delusions. *Schizophrenia Bulletin*, *33*(3), 642–647.

Coltheart, M., Langdon, R., & McKay, R. (2011). Delusional belief. *Annual Review of Psychology*, *62*(1), 271–298.

Davies, M., & Coltheart, M. (2000). Pathologies of belief. *Mind and Language*, *15*, 1–46.

Davies, M., Coltheart, M., Langdon, R., & Breen, N. (2001). Monothematic delusions: Towards a two-factor account. *Philosophy, Psychiatry, & Psychology*, *8*(2), 133–158.

Ellersgaard, D., Mors, O., Thorup, A., Jørgensen, P., Jeppesen, P., & Nordentoft, M. (2014). Prospective study of the course of delusional themes in first-episode non-affective psychosis. *Early Intervention in Psychiatry*, *8*(4), 340–347.

Fine, C., Gardner, M., Craigie, J., & Gold, I. (2007). Hopping, skipping or jumping to conclusions? Clarifying the role of the JTC bias in delusions. *Cognitive Neuropsychiatry*, *12*(1), 46–77.

Freeman, D. (2007). Suspicious minds: The psychology of persecutory delusions. *Clinical Psychology Review*, *27*(4), 425–457.

Freeman, D. (2016). Persecutory delusions: a cognitive perspective on understanding and treatment. *Lancet Psychiatry*, *3*(7), 685–692.

Freeman, D., Dunn, G., Startup, H., Pugh, K., Cordwell, J., Mander, H., et al. (2015). Effects of cognitive behaviour therapy for worry on persecutory delusions in patients with psychosis (WIT): a parallel, single-blind, randomised controlled trial with a mediation analysis. *The Lancet Psychiatry*, *2*(4), 305–313.

Freeman, D., & Garety, P. (2014). Advances in understanding and treating persecutory delusions: A review. *Social Psychiatry and Psychiatric Epidemiology*, *49*(8), 1179–1189.

Freeman, D., & Garety, P. A. (2004). *Paranoia: The Psychology of Persecutory Delusions*. Hove and New York: Psychology Press.

Frith, C. D. (1992). *The Cognitive Neuropsychology of Schizophrenia*. Hove: Lawrence Erlbaum.

Frith, C. D. (2012). Explaining delusions of control: The comparator model 20 years on. *Consciousness and Cognition*, *21*, 52–54.

Fujii, D., & Ahmed, I. (2002). Characteristics of psychotic disorder due to traumatic brain injury: An analysis of case studies in the literature. *The Journal of Neuropsychiatry and Clinical Neurosciences*, *14*(2), 130–140.

Gallagher, S. (2000). Self-reference and schizophrenia: A cognitive model of immunity to error through misidentification. In D. Zahavi (Ed.), *Exploring the Self: Philosophical and Psychological Perspectives on Self-Experience* (pp. 203–239). Philadelphia, PA: John Benjamins.

Graham, G., & Stephens, G. L. (2000). *When Self-Consciousness Breaks*. Cambridge, MA: MIT Press.

Jørgensen, P., & Jensen, J. (1994). How to understand the formation of delusional beliefs: A proposal. *Psychopathology, 27*(1–2), 64–72.

Kimhy, D., Goetz, R., Yale, S., Corcoran, C., & Malaspina, D. (2005). Delusions in individuals with schizophrenia: Factor structure, clinical correlates, and putative neurobiology. *Psychopathology, 38*(6), 338–344.

Langland-Hassan, P. (2008). Fractured phenomenologies: Thought insertion, inner speech, and the puzzle of extraneity. *Mind & Language, 23*(4), 369–401.

Langland-Hassan, P. (2016). Hearing a Voice as one's own: Two views of inner speech self-monitoring deficits in schizophrenia. *Review of Philosophy and Psychology, 7*(3), 675–699.

Langland-Hassan, P. (2018). From introspection to essence: The auditory nature of inner speech. In P. Langland-Hassan & A. Vicente (Eds.), *Inner Speech: New Voices* (p. 71). Oxford: Oxford University Press.

McKay, R., Langdon, R., & Coltheart, M. (2005). 'Sleights of mind': Delusions, defences, and self-deception. *Cognitive Neuropsychiatry, 10*(4), 305–326.

Mellor, C. S. (1970). First rank symptoms of schizophrenia. *British Journal of Psychiatry, 117*, 15–23.

Miall, R. C., Weir, D. J., Wolpert, D. M., & Stein, R. C. (1993). Is the cerebellum a Smith Predictor? *Journal of Motor Behavior, 25*, 203–216.

Mullins, S., & Spence, S. A. (2003). Re-examining thought insertion. *The British Journal of Psychiatry, 182*(4), 293.

Paolini, E., Moretti, P., & Compton, M. T. (2016). Delusions in first-episode psychosis: Principal component analysis of twelve types of delusions and demographic and clinical correlates of resulting domains. *Psychiatry Research, 243*, 5–13.

Parrott, M. (2017). Subjective misidentification and thought insertion. *Mind & Language, 32*(1), 39–64.

Peralta, V., & Cuesta, M. J. (1999). Diagnostic significance of Schneider's first-rank symptoms in schizophrenia. Comparative study between schizophrenic and non-schizophrenic psychotic disorders. *British Journal of Psychiatry: The Journal of Mental Science, 174*, 243–248.

Pickard, H. (2010). Schizophrenia and the epistemology of self-knowledge. *European Journal of Analytic Philosophy, 6*(1), 55–74.

Proust, J. (2006). Agency in schiophrenia from a control theory viewpoint. In N. Sebanz, & W. Prinz (Eds.), *Disorders of Volition* (pp. 87–118). Cambridge, MA: MIT Press.

Ratcliffe, M., & Wilkinson, S. (2015). Thought insertion clarified. *Journal of Consciousness Studies, 22*(11–12), 246–269.

Reeve, S., Sheaves, B., & Freeman, D. (2015). The role of sleep dysfunction in the occurrence of delusions and hallucinations: A systematic review. *Clinical Psychology Review, 42*, 96–115.

Ross, R. M., McKay, R., Coltheart, M., & Langdon, R. (2015). Jumping to conclusions about the beads task? A meta-analysis of delusional ideation and data-gathering. *Schizophrenia Bulletin, 41*(5), 1183–1191.

Shergill, S. S. (2003). Engagement of brain areas implicated in processing inner speech in people with auditory hallucinations. *The British Journal of Psychiatry, 182*(6), 525–531.

Shergill, S. S., Bullmore, E., Simmons, A., Murray, R. M., & McGuire, P. K. (2000). Functional anatomy of auditory verbal imagery in schizophrenic patients with auditory hallucinations. *American Journal of Psychiatry, 157*, 1691–1693.

Sinha, V. K., & Chaturvedi, S. K. (1990). Consistency of delusions in schizophrenia and affective disorder. *Schizophrenia Research, 3*(5–6), 347–350.

Synofzik, M., Vosgerau, G., & Newen, A. (2008). Beyond the comparator model: A multifactorial two-step account of agency. *Consciousness and Cognition, 17*(1), 219–239.

Vázquez-Barquero, J. L., Lastra, I., Nuñez, M. J. C., Castanedo, S. H., & Dunn, G. (1996). Patterns of Positive and Negative Symptoms in First Episode Schizophrenia. *British Journal of Psychiatry, 168*(6), 693–701.

Vosgerau, G., & Newen, A. (2007). Thoughts, motor actions, and the self. *Mind and Language, 22*, 22–43.

Wing, J., Babor, T., Brugha, T., Burke, J., Cooper, J., Giel, R., et al. (1990). SCAN. Schedules for Clinical Assessment in Neuropsychiatry. *Archives of General Psychiatry, 47*(6), 589.

Wing, J., Cooper, J., & Sartorius, N. (1983). *Present State Examination* (9 ed.). Cambridge: Cambridge University Press.

Wolpert, D. M., Miall, R. C., & Kawato, M. (1998). Internal models in the cerebellum. *Trends in Cognitive Science, 2*, 338–347.

SECTION 3
BRAIN, MIND, AND CONTEXTS OF CARE

Experimental and Therapeutic Approaches to TI

12
Experimental Approaches to Understanding Thought Insertion

Elisa Brann, Eamonn Walsh, Mitul A. Mehta, David A. Oakley, and Quinton Deeley

12.1. Introduction

Thought insertion (TI), the experience and belief that certain thoughts are not one's own but have been inserted into the mind by an external agent, is a psychotic phenomenon that has been reported as occurring in 6–30% of patients diagnosed with schizophrenia (Idrees et al., 2010; Marneros, 1984; Mellor, 1970; Sartorius et al., 1986; Thorup et al., 2007). TI involves a loss of the sense of both control and ownership of thought. It is inherently linked to an attribution that the thought originates with an external agent, resulting in a sense of 'ego permeation' by the thought (Mullins & Spence, 2003). Loss of the sense of ownership differentiates TI from the closely related psychotic symptom of influenced thinking in which thought processes are experienced as controlled from outside but for which ownership is retained. The ego permeation of both symptoms distinguishes them from obsessions i.e., repetitive intrusive thoughts which are nevertheless typically experienced as originating in the patient's own mind (Mullins & Spence 2003).

The loss of control and ownership, and 'ego permeation', of TI is shared with other 'alien control' phenomena such as alien control of movement (also termed 'delusions of control' in psychosis). Loss of control and ownership, and ego permeation, of self-generated mental contents also extend to perception in experiences of auditory verbal hallucinations among other 'first rank symptoms' of schizophrenia (Mullins & Spence, 2003).

While symptoms such as TI, alien control of movement, and auditory verbal hallucinations are strongly associated with schizophrenia they are not pathognomic of the condition, as they also occur in other psychiatric disorders such as bipolar disorder (Soares-Weiser et al., 2015). They are also observed in the general population—in other words, people experience these alterations in self-experience without distress, disability, or care-seeking in their everyday lives (Johns et al., 2014; Wiles et al., 2006).

Non-pathological instances of TI and related alterations in self-experience include culturally influenced dissociative phenomena linked to practices such as spirit possession, mediumship, and shamanism, which have been widely reported across different cultures and periods of history (Rouget, 1985; Seligman et al., 2008; Taves, 2006; Vitebsky, 2001). These phenomena are associated with culturally sanctioned attributions of alien control of thought, speech, or movement by supernatural agents (such as spirits or deities), in which a human intermediary is often viewed as a vehicle through which a supernatural agent communicates or reveals information to a human audience. Any account of TI as a symptom of psychopathology should ideally be able to explain its relationships with other closely related phenomena in both pathological and non-pathological settings.

TI, as a named psychiatric symptom, has mainly been researched as a feature of psychopathology. Studies using phenomenological and epidemiological methods have delineated the experiential characteristics and psychopathological associations of TI and related phenomena (e.g., Mullins & Spence, 2003). This approach dates to the foundations of psychiatry at the start of the twentieth century through the clinical and phenomenological descriptive observation of individual psychiatrists (Bleuler, Kraeplin, Jaspers, Schneider) (Oyebode, 2018) to quantitative studies using questionnaires in larger samples (Idrees et al., 2010; Thorup et al., 2007).

Ethnographic and qualitative studies of alterations in self-experience in religious and other cultural settings have helped understand their attributed significance and biographical and cultural contexts (e.g., Rouget, 1985; Seligman et al., 2008; Taves, 2006; Vitebsky, 2001). In the language of descriptive psychopathology, these experiences variously involve TI, hallucinations, alien control of movement, narrowing or loss of consciousness, and amnesia—among other possible changes in aspects of experience. These studies provide insights into TI and related phenomena. However, their methods are not in themselves able to identify the cognitive and brain processes underlying or motivating TI and related phenomena.[1] Indeed, despite their centrality to both pathological and normal variations in experience, few studies have sought to investigate TI and related phenomena experimentally to identify their underlying mechanisms.

---

[1] We note here that ethnographic and historical methods are increasingly being brought into dialogue with cognitive psychology and neuroscience to account for altered self-experience in religious settings—e.g., Deeley (2018, 2019); Luhrmann (2012); Luhrmann et al. (2021); Taves (2016).

Experimental approaches to psychopathological phenomena aim to identify components of complex experiences which can be linked to underlying causal processes by controlled manipulation of psychological or neurophysiological variables. Neurophysiological methods such as brain imaging (e.g., functional magnetic resonance imaging, fMRI, and electroencephalography, EEG) or neuromodulation techniques (e.g., transcranial magnetic stimulation, TMS), can help to identify brain processes contributing to specific alterations of experience in psychopathology and health. Experimental studies of alien control and related phenomena have mainly been conducted in people with psychopathology, although some studies have been undertaken in healthy participants. As we will see, these studies are potentially mutually informative.

The most frequently studied symptoms of psychosis have been auditory verbal hallucinations (for reviews see: Ćurčić-Blake et al., 2017; David, 1999; Ford et al., 2012; Zmigrod et al., 2016) as they are experienced by approximately 70% of people diagnosed with schizophrenia (Sartorius et al., 1986). Compared to other psychotic symptoms, however, TI remains largely unstudied. This is likely the result of a number of general challenges to experimental studies of psychotic symptoms, as well as obstacles specific to TI. In this chapter we describe these challenges and an approach to addressing them. We outline a series of recent experiments modelling TI and related alien control phenomena in healthy participants using direct verbal suggestion and neuroimaging (Oakley et al., 2020). The experiments illustrate an experimental approach to phenomenology as well as neuroscience. We discuss what has been learned from these experiments and propose possible avenues of investigation of TI and related phenomena.

12.2. Challenges of Studying Thought Insertion Experimentally

12.2.1. Psychotic phenomena are temporally unpredictable

All psychotic phenomena, including TI, share the feature of being temporally unpredictable; it is difficult to predict *when* they are about to occur. This presents a particular problem for approaches to their study relying on symptom capture, a naturalistic experimental method in which neuroimaging measures the brain 'state' as a phenomenon takes place. As a result, most experimental studies of psychotic symptoms have tended to focus on the individual's propensity to have the experience, so-called 'trait' studies (Ford et al., 2012).

The design of a trait study may consist of comparing a particular neurophysiological feature between two groups, the experimental group that experiences the psychotic symptom and the control group that does not. For example, Maruff and colleagues (2005) compared grey matter volume in patients diagnosed with schizophrenia who experienced passivity (including TI) and those who did not. They observed that passivity, as a trait, is associated with reduced grey matter volume of the right inferior parietal lobe. While trait studies can be useful for identifying general associations between psychotic symptoms and brain behaviour or structure, they do not directly assess the brain behaviour associated with the experience itself.

Although less frequent due to its challenging nature, symptom capture has been successfully used to study brain activity accompanying particular psychotic phenomena. Most examples of this are of auditory verbal hallucinations (for reviews see Ford et al., 2012; van Lutterveld et al., 2011); to the best of our knowledge, no patient studies exist that reliably capture the brain basis of TI (see Brann et al. for a review, in preparation).

A common paradigm employed for symptom capture of auditory verbal hallucinations involves the participant pressing a button to indicate the onset of their hallucination, thereby enabling the experimenter to lock the timing of the event to neuroimaging data (Hubl et al., 2007). This approach is confounded by the introduction of self-monitoring, movement preparation, and execution of the task.

12.2.2. Psychotic phenomena can be difficult to distinguish

Another challenge facing the experimental study of psychotic symptoms is that they can be difficult to accurately distinguish from one another. Identifying instances of TI can be particularly problematic, often requiring careful examination by a skilled interviewer (Badcock, 2016). This is due in part to TI and auditory verbal hallucinations sharing similar phenomenological features. Both phenomena involve language and are experienced as being intrusive, with a reduced sense of control and ownership linked to an attribution that they are generated by an external agent. Having an auditory sensory quality has intuitively been considered a hallmark of auditory verbal hallucinations; however, the characterization of 'soundless voices' has challenged this idea (McCarthy-Jones et al., 2014). Conversely, TI is sometimes described as being similar to an 'internal voice' (Mullins & Spence, 2003). This underlines the need for careful phenomenological assessment and explicit, consistent definitions of symptoms.

Similarly, the accurate identification of TI requires the use of a suitable psychometric measure. A recent systematic review of the neurophysiological basis of passivity (Brann et al., in preparation) found that common measures used to characterize the presence of psychotic symptoms for research purposes do not explicitly characterize TI. For example, the Positive and Negative Syndrome Scale (PANSS) (Kay et al., 1987), commonly used for measuring the severity of positive symptoms (PANSS-positive) such as TI and auditory verbal hallucinations in people with schizophrenia, allocates a subscale to audio visual hallucinations specifically, whereas the categorization of TI is not well defined; being usually included within the delusion subscale alongside primary delusions and delusional perception. As a result, the widespread use of the PANSS-positive to characterize psychosis in clinical research has rendered the presence of TI largely invisible. Remedying this issue would require other measures that provide a more detailed phenomenological account of symptoms of TI, such as the Scale for Assessment of Positive Symptoms (SAPS; Andreasen, 1984).

Another issue related to distinguishing psychotic phenomena is that they often occur together or are in close temporal association (Breier & Berg, 1999). For instance, Nayani and David (1996) observed reports of TI in 39% of individuals who experienced auditory verbal hallucinations. TI has also been documented alongside other psychotic symptoms, such as delusions of control (Waters et al., 2009). Such co-occurrence can make it difficult to isolate TI within experimental settings, underlining the need for careful phenomenological assessment.

12.2.3. Thought insertion increases with illness severity

Another challenge when attempting to capture TI specifically is its relationship to illness severity. Clinical experience suggests that TI is more common in patients with severe illness, although this has not been directly assessed—most likely because of the widespread use of the PANNS, which fails to adequately account for the experience. When patients are severely unwell there are several practical and theoretical challenges when conducting experimental research. Patients may be unwilling or unable to cooperate with the demands of the task. There may also be ethical concerns associated with engaging patients in experiments that may be delusionally interpreted, which in turn affects the validity of such studies, or for which they may be unable to give informed consent due to the loss of 'reality testing'.

Neuroimaging studies of patients are also likely to be accompanied by a number of confounds that potentially affect brain structure or function. For example, antipsychotic medications may alter brain structure and function (Hawkins et al. 2021; Vita et al., 2015). Patients with schizophrenia are likely to smoke more cigarettes than healthy controls (Allen et al., 2012) and are more likely to have a co-occurring substance use disorder, most frequently alcohol and/or cannabis abuse (Dixon, 1999). Neurodevelopment prior to the emergence of first-rank symptoms of psychosis is different compared to the general population in many people with psychosis (Pantelis et al., 2005). People with psychosis are, and have been, exposed to greater psychosocial stressors and adversities compared to the general population (Lukoff et al., 1984; Shevlin et al., 2008). Disease progression may also confound observations due to associated changes in brain structure and function. For instance, grey matter abnormalities have been shown to be more extensive for patients in the chronic stage of illness compared to first-episode schizophrenia (Chan et al., 2011). Disease progression is also associated with changes in brain function. For example, measures of mismatch negativity, an event-related potential measured using EEG, have been shown to be approximately 47% reduced in patients with chronic illness compared to those with first-episode schizophrenia (Salisbury et al., 2002). In summary, several factors affecting brain structure, and function, and behaviour in patients with schizophrenia potentially confound interpretation of brain measurement during TI and related first-rank symptoms.

12.3. Experimentally Suggested Thought Insertion

One solution to address these challenges in studying TI and allied phenomena is to reproduce them experimentally using suggestion in hypnotically responsive healthy participants. This approach allows experimental neurophenomenology—eliciting specific alterations in experience—combined with measurement of concomitant brain activity. This approach has been adopted in a series of studies of alien control phenomena, including TI, which we outline here. First, we consider the nature of hypnosis and suggestibility and how it might be used experimentally to explore phenomenology.

12.3.1. Creating new experiences using hypnosis and suggestion

The recognition of suggestion as a psychological process was closely linked to the derivation of hypnosis from earlier healing practices (Deeley, 2016). Animal magnetism, the immediate precursor of hypnosis, originated in the work of Anton Mesmer (1734–1815) who believed a subtle magnetic force permeating the universe could be manipulated to produce healing (Ellenberger, 1994). Some of his successors arrived at a more psychological and contemporary concept of suggestion along with other ideas and practices which were then incorporated into hypnosis (Binet & Féré, 1891; Ellenberger, 1994; Janet, 1907). Before then, other forms of ritual healing practices such as exorcism involved unintentionally suggestive verbal and nonverbal stimuli (Deeley, 2016). Notably, the practices from which hypnosis derived involved the production or removal of alterations in subjectivity and agency—such as the ritual management of possession states or the healing convulsive 'crisis' of animal magnetism.

While the association of hypnosis with the paranormal and entertainment has led to scepticism and ambivalence in some medical and scientific circles, an alternative arc has seen hypnosis employed as a secular method of medical treatment and object of scientific inquiry (Kihlstrom, 2013; Milling, 2008; Deeley, 2016). Since the turn of the millennium, there has been substantial growth in researching the application of hypnosis in the areas of psychology, medicine, social science, and neuroscience (Halligan & Oakley, 2014).

The British Psychological Society definition of hypnosis describes it as an interaction between one person, the 'hypnotist', and another person or other people, the 'subject(s)'. In this interaction, the hypnotist attempts to influence the subjects' thinking, perceptions, feelings, and behaviour by asking them to concentrate on ideas and images that may evoke the intended effects (Heap et al., 2001). The verbal communications that the hypnotist uses to achieve these effects are termed 'suggestions'. The 'classic suggestion effect' entails those responses elicited by suggestions that are experienced as involuntary and effortless (Heap et al., 2001).

Hypnotic suggestibility as a measure refers to the number of suggestions that an individual responds to after the administration of a standard set of test suggestions, such as the Harvard Group Scale of Hypnotic Susceptibility (Shor & Orne, 1963) or the Stanford Scale of Hypnotic Susceptibility (Weitzenhoffer & Hilgard, 1962). Not all individuals respond to hypnotic suggestion in the same way. When measured using standardized protocols, hypnotic suggestibility appears to be a normally distributed trait (Oakley et al., 2020). While most individuals respond to hypnotic suggestion to some extent, a small subpopulation of 'virtuosos' respond particularly well.

These highly suggestible individuals have been shown to be capable of having vivid perceptual experiences in response to suggestion (Bryant & Mallard, 2003), involving distinct cognitive and brain processes. For instance, the use of hypnosis as an intervention for pain has been shown to be effective across a range of suggestibility scores (Milling, 2008). However, compared to low hypnotically suggestible individuals, analgesic suggestions significantly modulated experiences of pain intensity and unpleasantness in highly suggestible individuals. The suggestions also modulated cortical responses triggered by the pain stimuli, which may reflect a specific processing ability of highly suggestible individuals when allocating cognitive control resources (Valentini et al., 2013).

Suggestions can also be used to create psychosis-like experiences. For instance, experiences of passivity are routinely induced within standardized protocols (Bowers, 1993; Shor & Orne, 1963). Both 'ideomotor' and 'challenge' suggestions result in participants experiencing a loss of control over their movements. The concept of an 'ideomotor action' rests on the idea that seeing, imagining, or thinking about a movement has the capacity to produce that movement via cognitive and brain processes that are outside the individual's subjective awareness (Gauchou et al., 2012). An everyday example would be unknowingly mirroring a watched or imagined behaviour of another person (Bargh & Chartrand, 1999). A participant may receive a suggestion that their 'eyelids are getting heavier and closing', and consequently may experience their eyes closing involuntarily, even if they attempt to resist it.

Conversely, 'challenge' suggestions are slightly less readily experienced (Oakley et al., 2020) and result in the participant being unable to control their body in response to a 'challenge' posed by the hypnotist. For example, the participant may receive the suggestion that their 'arm is becoming more and more stiff—like a bar of iron ... test how stiff and rigid it is now, try to bend it'. In response they are unable to bend their arm despite attempting with effort to do so.

Some of the most difficult hypnotic suggestions to respond to are categorized as 'cognitive', and can include complex experiences, which in standardized assessments of hypnotic suggestibility include auditorily hallucinating a fly/mosquito or hearing music. The ability to experience this kind of suggestion has been shown to moderately positively correlate with suggestibility

(Oakley et al., 2021). In other words, individuals who are more suggestible are more likely to be able to achieve such effects in response to suggestion.

12.4. Experimental Approaches to Suggestion

Targeted suggestions administered to a participant within an experimental setting allow features of an experience to be precisely specified, creating different experimental conditions which can then be compared. The use of a predefined script of 'experimental suggestions' also ensures that suggestions administered across participants are identical. The use of experimental suggestion to model psychosis-like experiences allows many of the challenges of capturing such phenomena to be circumvented. For instance, specific phenomena can be elicited and then observed in isolation and on command at a specific point in time. The use of healthy participants with no history of psychiatric illness means that brain measurement is free of potential confounds such as effects of disease on brain structure and function, and other factors such as medication or other substances. Symptoms can be modelled and captured in a safe and controlled way.

12.4.1. The foundations of experimental approaches to suggestion

The last twenty years has seen a series of behavioural and neuroimaging studies that have used experimental suggestion to explicitly model different aspects of passivity phenomena, culminating in the development of a paradigm to evoke experiences of TI. The earliest example of this approach is a pioneering study by Blakemore and colleagues (Blakemore et al., 2003) involving six healthy highly suggestible individuals who underwent positron emission tomography (PET) imaging during a simple movement task while in hypnosis.

Four counterbalanced experimental conditions included an 'active movement' condition in which the participant was given suggestions that they should move their arm up and down smoothly; a 'passive movement' condition during which the participant was informed that their arm would be moved by the experimenter using a pulley system; a 'deluded passive movement' condition that was designed to mimic the passivity experienced by a patient with delusions of control—during this condition the participant was given a suggestion that their arm would be moved up and down by the pulley system, when in fact it was not; and a final 'rest' condition that served as a baseline control, in which the participant was told to remain still and rest their arm.

Participants were asked to rate the 'voluntariness' of their movement during each condition on a scale from 1 (voluntary and self-generated) to 100 (involuntary and externally generated). The investigators observed that participants experienced the deluded passive movements as being highly involuntary (Fig. 12.1). While there was no difference in the participants' observed movements during the active movement and deluded passive movement conditions, the active movement condition was experienced as being significantly more voluntary. When asked, none of the participants felt that the movement in either the passive movement or deluded passive movement conditions was voluntary or self-generated. In other words, although movement in the deluded passive movement condition was entirely self-generated, it was attributed to an external cause and experienced as involuntary.

The neuroimaging results demonstrated significantly higher activations in the left pre-motor cortex, bilateral parietal cortex (right parietal operculum and left inferior parietal cortex) and bilateral cerebellum during the deluded passive movement condition, when participants attributed their own movements to an external source, compared to the active movement condition when movements were correctly attributed to the self. Based on this observation, the authors concluded that altered functioning of this cerebellar-parietal network resulted in self-produced actions being experienced as externally driven. Specifically, they interpreted their results in the context of changes in central monitoring. The concept of central monitoring, which originates from theories of motor control (Feinberg, 1978), posits that the brain processes self-generated movement by way of prediction. This involves the use of two cognitive models, an inverse and forward model, that work in tandem (Wolpert, 1997). The former involves the generation of a motor command to achieve a desired action, while the latter entails that an internal copy of the motor command, referred to as an 'efference copy' (or 'corollary discharge'), is used to predict the changes in movement that will occur as a consequence of the intended action.

The forward output model (Fig. 12.2; usually abbreviated to the 'forward model') (Miall et al., 1993) predicts the sensory consequences of motor commands, which are compared with the actual consequences of movement based on sensory feedback (reafference). A close match between predicted and actual sensory feedback leads to attenuation of the sensation of movement. At a neural level, this would be associated with reduced activation of brain regions involved in sensory processing of a given type of movement. Discrepancies

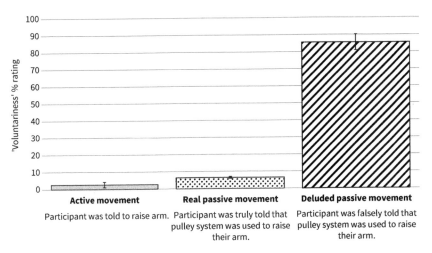

Figure 12.1 Overview of experimental conditions (control 'rest' condition not shown). Graph of ratings of voluntariness of movement across the different experimental conditions, y-axis scale: 0% (voluntary) to 100% (involuntary). Error bars depict standard deviations. Figure based on results reported in Blakemore et al. (2003).

between predicted and actual movement lead to more salient sensory feedback linked to increased activity in relevant brain regions. These discrepancies can be used, for example, to correct movement 'online', but also to distinguish self-produced and externally produced movements. In this model dysfunction of the comparator mechanism leading to a sensory discrepancy between the outcome of the two models results in an abnormal prediction error and experiences of loss of motor control (Haggard, 2017).

This proposed dysfunction of the comparator mechanism has been hypothesized to underlie the loss of control experienced in psychotic symptoms of movement (Frith, 2005; Frith & Done, 1989). This stems from observations that, compared to other patients diagnosed with schizophrenia, patients with passivity of movement show impaired motor performance in the absence of visual feedback and impaired recall of their own motor acts. This suggests a problem with integrating feedforward predictions about the sensory consequences of an intended movement with afferent sensory feedback, which would otherwise be used to fine-tune movement performance and aid its recollection (Frith & Done, 1989; Mlakar, Jensterle, & Frith, 1994).

During the 'deluded passive movement' condition in the study by (Blakemore et al., 2003), participants were still able to perform the movements and this involved activation of similar brain areas to normal

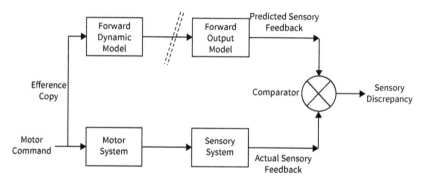

Figure 12.2 The forward model of motor control (Miall et al., 1993), which predicts and compares the sensory consequences of motor commands with a goal state. Discrepancies in this comparison can result in the feeling that a movement has been externally controlled. This theoretical model has been extended more recently to human thought (Frith, 2005). The dashed lines signify an imbalance or break in the system, which leads to a neural discrepancy resulting in delusions of control of movement and thought. It has been proposed that experimental suggestion may operate on the same neural mechanism (dashed lines; Blakemore et al., 2003).

movement (i.e., right sensorimotor cortex, premotor cortex, SMA and insula, bilateral basal ganglia and parietal operculum and left cerebellum), thereby demonstrating intact functioning of the motor system. However, participants experienced a loss of control in this condition which in terms of the 'forward' model, indicates that the experimental suggestions given to the participants prevented motor intentions from reaching the forward output model. They propose that this is mediated by top-down signals from the prefrontal cortex, which was activated only in this condition. In this case, the forward output model would no longer be able to make an accurate prediction of the sensory consequences of the movement. Nevertheless, this raises the question of whether the failure to attenuate sensory processing of what in reality is self-generated movement during the 'deluded passive condition' is responsible for the feeling of loss of agency, or only a heightened sensory awareness of movements as a by-product of altered sense of agency due to other causes. Subsequent studies that have employed a similar approach using experimental suggestion have investigated a range of closely related changes in the control, ownership, and awareness of thought and movement, and are relevant to the question of what underpins the sense of agency, as discussed next.

12.4.2. Modelling psychiatric and cultural possession phenomena with suggestion

TI and related symptoms combine several changes in experience and its interpretation. For instance, TI involves loss of control and ownership of thought linked to an attribution that it has been inserted by another agent. As noted above, it is possible for each of these components to vary; in influenced thinking ownership of thought is retained but not control or self-origination while in obsessions, control is lost but ownership and self-origination are retained. In alien control of movement, control of movement is attributed to an external agent, whereas in 'anarchic' or 'alien' hand following medial frontal or corpus callosal lesions, the experience of loss of control for apparently purposive hand movements may not be accompanied by an attribution that some other agent is responsible for the movements (Spence, 2002). Similarly, in non-epileptic seizures involuntary movements typically occur without attributions of external agentive control (and approximately 50% of these episodes occur with reduction or loss of awareness) (Brown et al., 2011).

The source of alien control of thought and movement can also be attributed to machines, referred to as 'technical' delusions of control in the case of movement (Kristensen, 2018). A distinction can therefore be made between alien control phenomena involving *external personal control* (involving an agent), and *external impersonal* control (involving a machine). In practice, however, machines are frequently understood as the means through which a maleficent agent exercises control of thought or actions. Nevertheless, technical delusions of control also raise the question of what cognitive and neural processes might be involved in the formation of a delusion of technical (impersonal) alien control per se, to the extent that representations of impersonal alien control may dominate aspects or phases of the experience of involuntary movement in a person suffering a technical delusion of control. These attributions of personal and impersonal alien control in the case of psychosis can be contrasted with spirit possession or mediumship which posit *internal personal alien control* whereby a possessing supernatural agent assumes control of the person from within.

These closely related variations in the control, ownership, and causal attributions of thought and movement were investigated using targeted suggestion, phenomenological inquiry, and functional magnetic resonance imaging (fMRI) in 15 highly suggestible participants (Deeley et al., 2014). The experimental design illustrates the potential for suggestion to produce specific, stepwise changes in experience and test hypotheses about underlying cognitive and neural processes.

During the task participants were required to move a joystick with their right hand in response to instructions. After each experimental condition they were asked to self-rate depth of hypnosis on a 0 (not hypnotized) to 10 (fully hypnotized) scale, and also rate perceived control, ownership, and awareness of hand movements on a 0 to 10 Likert scale. Semi-structured interviews about the experiences accompanying each experimental condition were conducted after the completion of the experiment and the reversal of hypnosis.

In condition (i), the normal alert state, brain activity during normal voluntary hand movement was measured. Following a hypnotic induction procedure, (ii) brain activity during the experience of normal voluntary hand movement was measured as a control to contrast with subsequent conditions conducted during hypnosis. In (iii) a suggestion for involuntary movement was made, but without a causal attribution. This modelled alien hand, or non-epileptic seizures (in which involuntary movements occur) without loss of awareness. In (iv) a suggestion for involuntary movement with loss of awareness was made. This modelled non-epileptic seizures (in which involuntary movements occur with reduced awareness) and other similar dissociative automatisms (Deeley et al., 2013).

The next three experimental conditions most closely modelled alien control phenomena because all involved suggestions for specific causal attributions. In this phase, the 'Engineer' was introduced as someone who was conducting experiments on limb movement by operating a machine. In (v) the 'external impersonal' condition, it was suggested that the movements of the participant's hand were being remotely controlled by a malfunctioning machine that operated autonomously. The suggestion contained the following information, which also illustrates the type of wording used for a suggestion:

> 'When you hear the word 'MOVE' you will have the experience of your right hand being remotely controlled by a machine, resulting in the joystick being moved to the right and then to the left once each time. The remote-control machine is however malfunctioning due to an error and the Engineer who created the machine left no instructions on how to correct this error. The machine error causes your hand to move every time there is an instruction to move; there is no apparent purpose to these movements which you have no control over, they are simply the product of machine error. You will have no control over when your right hand is going to move, this is controlled by the machine, but you will be clearly aware of the movement of your hand and of the joystick when it occurs.'

This condition modelled a 'technical' delusion of control involving *external impersonal control* and served as a control condition for two *personal alien control* conditions.

In (vi) the *external personal control* condition, participants were given the suggestion that their hand movements were controlled by a machine operated by the Engineer. This was a direct experimental model of a typical delusion of control, in which movements are remotely controlled by an external agent.

In (vii), the *internal personal alien control* condition it was suggested that the Engineer had taken over the participant's mind from within and was able to control their hand movement accordingly. This condition was designed to model cultural accounts of spirit possession, in which the possessing supernatural agent assumes control of the person from within. The wording was partly based on an informant account of possession by a *Zar* spirit among the Hofrayati people of Northern Sudan (Boddy, 1988). The suggestion included the following information to produce a sense of attenuation of the normal self and replacement by another self. Note here that this includes 'ego permeation' by the Engineer who now controls the participant from within—in other words, the thoughts of the Engineer, another agent, have been inserted into the subjective awareness (the 'mind') of the experimental participant. This, then, was the first experimental production of experiences of TI using suggestion. The gender of the Engineer was matched to that of the participant:

> 'When he/she assumes control of your hand movements, you lose your normal sense of who you are, and all the associations of your normal life fade away. Instead of your usual thoughts and feelings, you find yourself aware of the thoughts and feelings of the Engineer—his/her interest in the research, his/her desire for the experiment to succeed, his/her thoughts of how impressed his/her colleagues will be by his/her research. You can no longer tell any difference between yourself and the Engineer, so that you share all of his/her thoughts and feelings, and also his/her sense of controlling the movements of your hand. There is a feeling of being calm and relaxed throughout.'

The suggestions resulted in realistic, vivid subjective experiences of the intended effects (Box 12.1), and significant reductions in feelings of control and ownership of hand movements (Fig. 12.3). Compared to the condition of impersonal external control of hand movement (attributed to remote control by a malfunctioning machine), suggestions for external personal and internal personal alien control were associated with an increase in functional connectivity between the primary motor cortex (M1, a key movement implementation

Box 12.1 Comparison of qualitative descriptions of psychotic phenomena from highly suggestible individuals using experimental suggestion and patient experiences

Experience	Patient	Highly suggestible individual
Alien control of movement (also termed 'delusions of control' in psychosis)	'When I reach my hand for the comb it is my hand and arm which move, and my fingers pick up the pen, but I don't control them ... I sit there watching them move, and they are quite independent, what they do is nothing to do with me ... I am just a puppet who is manipulated by cosmic strings. When the strings are pulled my body moves and I cannot prevent it.' (1)	'[there were] two steps. 1) Engineer put sticks through my stomach up to my left and right brain and made my hand move. 2) After that the engineer took over "me".' (2)
Thought insertion	'I look out of the window and I think the garden looks nice and the grass looks cool, but the thoughts of Eamonn Andrews come into my mind. There are no other thoughts there, only his ... He treats my mind like a screen and flashes his thoughts on to it like you flash a picture.' (1)	'It was like I didn't have a say, my mind was empty and they [the words] just came ... It felt different to the other block [in which the participant had been given suggestions for an auditory verbal hallucination], that felt more heard ... I thought things I wouldn't normally think.' (3)
Auditory Verbal Hallucination	'One voice, deep in pitch and roughly spoken, repeatedly said "G.T. is a blood paradox", and another higher in pitch said, "He is that, he should be locked up". A female voice occasionally interrupted, saying "He is not, he is a lovely man"' (1)	'... it was like hearing my own voice outside my body ... at the time I didn't know who's voice it was, at the time it was someone else.' (3)

(1) (Mellor, 1970)
(2) (Deeley et al., 2014)
(3) unpublished data

region), and the anterior pre-frontal cortex (BA10, a prefrontal region supporting the representation of agency and of self in relation to others) (U. Frith & Frith, 2003; Vogeley et al., 2004). Compared to both personal alien control conditions, impersonal control of movement was associated with increased activity in brain regions involved in error detection (anterior cingulate cortex, BA 32; Craig, 2009) and object imagery (left middle temporal gyrus) (Dennis et al., 2012). There were no significant differences in brain activity, and minor differences in M1 connectivity, between the external and internal personal alien control conditions.

These results demonstrate that experiences of loss of control and ownership of movement can be elicited by suggestion, and that brain regions which may support representations of independent agents can be functionally coupled to motor systems. This potentially explains how it is possible for control of movement to be experienced as reassigned to another agent. Also, compared to the experience of normal voluntary control of movement, involuntary movement

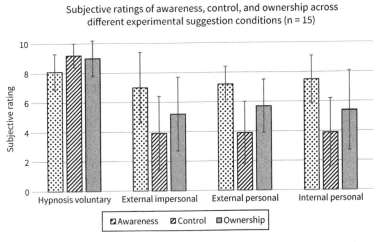

Figure 12.3 Mean subjective ratings (0–10 scale) for 'awareness', 'control', and 'ownership' for the voluntary movement condition under hypnosis (condition ii), and three experimental conditions: external impersonal (condition v, attribution of alien control of movement to external machine); external personal (condition vi, attribution of alien control of movement to an external agent, 'the Engineer'); and internal personal (condition vii, attribution of alien control to an external agent who has entered their mind, modelling spiritual possession). Error bars depict standard deviation. Perceived control and ownership were significantly reduced for experimental conditions compared to control but did not differ between experimental conditions. For awareness, there was no overall difference between all four conditions. Figure from Deeley et al. (2014).

was associated with reduced functional connectivity between motor planning brain regions (supplementary motor area, SMA) and regions involved in movement execution (e.g., premotor areas, M1, and the primary somatosensory cortex, S1). This indicates a possible neural mechanism by which involuntary movements (e.g., movements accompanied by a loss of the usual sense of control) can occur, which can be attributed to different causes (e.g., impersonal control by a machine or personal control by an agent). Finally, reduced awareness of hand movement was associated with decreased activity in brain areas involved in bodily awareness (BA 7) and sensation (insula), suggesting a mechanism for the loss of awareness sometimes reported in association with episodes of possession or other types of involuntary behaviour (Deeley et al., 2013; Boddy, 1988).

Overall, the findings indicate that a loss of perceived self-control of movement can be embedded in a range of complex experiences supported by distinct brain mechanisms. The findings caution against generalization about single cognitive processes or brain systems underpinning different experiences of loss of self-control of movement. Nevertheless, similar experiences (such as loss of motor control linked to attributions of external and internal alien control) appear to engage similar brain regions.

12.4.3. Modelling thought insertion and alien control of movement with suggestion

The initial studies described in the previous sections involved simple actions (arm or joystick movements) rather than more complex motor behaviour coupled with thought insertion—as for example occurs in experiences of inspired or revealed writing in addition to instances of psychopathology. Writing involves the integration of thought content and hand movement. Reports of inspired or automatic writing indicate that it can involve experiences of external control of thought, and/or loss or control of hand movement (analogous to the symptoms of 'thought insertion' and 'alien control of movement', respectively, in schizophrenia). Walsh and colleagues (Walsh et al., 2015) conducted an fMRI study with 18 highly suggestible individuals, using a novel writing paradigm. Writing involves the composition of verbal thoughts, followed by the use of skilled hand movements to write the words down (Beeson, 2004; Sage & Ellis, 2004). A 'sentence completion task' required participants to think of a suitable ending to a pre-recorded sentence stem. Following this, they were cued to write down the sentence ending they had thought of.

The two primary experimental conditions involved targeted suggestions for TI and alien control of movement.

In the case of TI, individuals were given the suggestion that a short suitable sentence ending would be inserted into their mind by 'the Engineer', who returned after their previous role in the prior study employing a joystick (Deeley et al., 2014). For alien control of movement, it was suggested that the Engineer would initiate and control the movements of their hand—'just hold onto the pen; the rest will happen by itself'. These were contrasted with control conditions during which the participant was told they had full control of their thoughts and movements, and another control condition in which they were told to simulate the experience of the Engineer while retaining normal control. Table 12.1 provides an overview of the suggestions given and the respective phenomenological changes in the locus of control. A third condition contained a suggestion for both TI and alien control of movement, with suggestions for loss of awareness. This modelled complex automatisms as they occur in dissociative psychopathology and certain types of automatic writing (Walsh et al., 2017).

Following each condition, participants were asked to rate on a scale from 0 (representing the least) to 10 (representing the most) how much control and ownership they felt they had over their thoughts in regard to the sentence endings and their subsequent handwriting movements. Awareness of thought and movement were also rated (Walsh et al., 2017).

The results of the study showed that during suggestions of TI, participants' ratings of control and ownership of thought were reduced relative to the voluntary condition, while the movement component of that condition was unaffected. During suggestions of alien control of movement, the reverse was true, i.e., there were reduced ratings for control and ownership of the movement component, but not for the thought component (Fig. 12.4). Similar observations were made when comparing the experimental conditions with the simulation condition, indicating that the subjective experience of TI and alien control of movement were subjectively compelling.

12.4.4. Experimental findings from studies of automatic writing and their implications for theoretical models of thought insertion and alien control of movement

The results of the automatic writing study showed that brain activations during normal thought and writing movements were largely non-overlapping,

Table 12.1 Overview of the experimental conditions relating to alien control, the suggestions used, and locus of control with respect to thought and movement components of the task. Taken from (Walsh et al., 2015)

		Locus of control	
Condition	Suggestion instruction	Thought component	Movement component
Voluntary	'When you hear the sentence stem, your job is to quickly think of a short simple suitable ending and then hold it in your mind and wait for the first tone. When you hear this tone, write down the short simple ending to the sentence that you held in your mind. Once you hear the second tone stop writing immediately.'	Self	Self
Thought insertion	'When you hear the sentence stem, you will have the experience that an engineer has composed and then inserted a short simple suitable ending to the sentence into your mind. This happens immediately after the sentence stem, and before the 1st tone is heard—when you hear the 1st tone, recall the engineer's short simple ending to the sentence and write it down in your normal handwriting—however, the engineer has no control over your movements.'	Alien	Self
Alien control of movement	'When you hear the sentence stem, then think of a short simple suitable ending to the sentence, hold it in your mind, and wait for the first tone. When you hear this tone, you will have the experience of the movements of your right hand being initiated and controlled by an engineer; these movements cause the marker to write down the sentence ending which you kept in mind, each time. Just hold the marker, the rest will happen by itself—however, the engineer cannot control your thoughts, only your hand movements when writing. You and you alone, think of the endings to each sentence and only you hold these in your mind.'	Self	Alien

Table 12.1 Continued

		Locus of control	
		Thought component	Movement component
Condition	Suggestion instruction		
Simulation	'As you write, maintain your normal handwriting, but this time and this time only, just pretend that the movements of your right hand are being initiated and controlled by an engineer. You and you alone, cause the marker to move, no one else.'	Self	Self

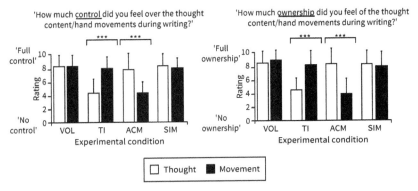

Figure 12.4 Mean control and ownership ratings for voluntary writing (VOL), during suggestions of thought insertion (TI) and alien control of movement (ACM) experiences, and instructions for simulation of alien control of movement (SIM). Error bars depict standard deviations. Note the double dissociation for the thought and movement components of writing for control and ownership ratings, in both the thought insertion and alien control of movement conditions. Significant difference is indicated by ***. Figure from Walsh et al. (2015).

as were those during TI and alien control of movement. This is in keeping with the view that thought is different from movement at both a phenomenological and neural level. Specifically, the experience of TI was not associated with increased activity in regions involved in self-monitoring as predicted by comparator or forward models of motor control. TI was instead associated with reduced activity in language production regions rather than overactivation of cerebellar and parietal regions. This is consistent with the critique of the forward model, that thoughts, unlike movements, do not have well defined sensorimotor characteristics that could inform feedforward inhibition of self-monitoring systems. By contrast, previous findings of parietal cortical and cerebellar activation during alien control (Blakemore et al., 2003) were confirmed and extended by showing these to be restricted to movement preparation and implementation respectively (Walsh et al., 2015).

While TI and alien control of movement were associated with distinct changes in brain activity, both experiences involved a reduction in activity of left supplementary motor cortex (SMA). This pre-motor brain region, located at the midline surface of the dorsomedial frontal cortex, is an essential part of the motor system known for its role in the organization of motor acts (for review see: Nachev et al., 2008). In particular, it has been shown to play a role in self-initiated action (Haggard & Whitford, 2004) as well as action inhibition (Sumner et al., 2007). The SMA is functionally connected with both motor and language networks (Bathla et al., 2019). Taken together these findings suggest that SMA is a high-level executive system involved in the control and ownership of movement and thought (Peck et al., 2009). Applied to alien control of movement, this executive control interpretation suggests that a lack of sensory suppression associated with increased cerebellar-parietal activations may underlie an altered sensory quality of unexpected movements, but not the loss of the sense of their control and ownership. Rather, in the present model this is the result of reduced activation of the SMA given its proposed role in mediating the sense of control and ownership of movements as well as thoughts.

Both alien control of movement and TI were also associated with reductions in functional connectivity of the left SMA, albeit with different respective connectivity patterns. This highlights how the consistent reduction in SMA activity underpinning loss of control and ownership appears to be task and modality dependent (see dashed lines in Fig. 12.2). A more complete cognitive account of alien control phenomena must therefore accommodate specific features of each phenomenon—for example, whether thought or movement is affected. Finally, loss of awareness for TI and alien control of movement was associated with reduced activation in a predominantly left-sided posterior cortical network, including BA 7 (superior parietal lobule and precuneus), and posterior cingulate cortex, involved in self-related processing and awareness of the body in space (Walsh et al., 2017). These findings partly replicate the previous finding of reduced awareness of the simpler hand movement of a joystick during suggested involuntary hand movement and loss of awareness, in which there was decreased activity in brain areas involved in bodily awareness (parietal regions of BA 7, BA 40, and insula) (Deeley et al., 2013).

12.5. Limitations of the Experimental Suggestion Approach

A potential limitation of the use of suggestion to model TI and related phenomena is the assumption that experiences produced by suggestion are fully comparable to those of patients and psychologically healthy individuals (including cultural practitioners such as mediums, shamans, or other religious practitioners). Investigating the relationship between types of experience in different individuals and groups requires careful comparative phenomenology as well as the application of comparable brain measurement approaches. The identification of brain processes mediating specific changes in experience in the 'noisier' data sets of patient groups or cultural practitioners can potentially be informed by experimental modelling. For example, data obtained from experimental modelling with suggestions can be used to generate hypotheses about brain activation involved in psychopathology. This involves testing for the presence of specific patterns of brain activity derived from the use of suggestion to produce discrete alterations in experience in healthy participants (such as the brain correlates of TI or alien control of movement respectively). Patterns of brain activity associated with aspects of altered experience in healthy participants helps to constrain interpretation of brain measurements of analogous experiences in patients and cultural practitioners.

Nevertheless, similarities in components of experience and underlying brain processes should not be taken to imply that all aspects of experience and brain activity are shared between people with psychosis, cultural practitioners, and people who respond to suggestions for TI and related phenomena. For example, in the case of culturally influenced automatic writing, implicit suggestive processes based on social modelling and implicit learning may produce similar changes in experience and brain function to the use of direct verbal suggestions in highly hypnotically responsive individuals (Walsh et al., 2014). This could be directly tested in future studies with practitioners of automatic writing or other types of cultural practitioner, or in patients to try and reduce episodes of TI. In the case of patients with psychosis, alien control phenomena such as TI and alien control of movement may be underpinned by alterations in the function and connectivity of regional brain networks as modelled in studies using suggestion. However, in patients with psychosis the altered function and connectivity of regions and networks identified in studies using experimental suggestion may arise from dysregulation of executive and other brain systems associated with abnormal brain anatomy and neuromodulatory systems (Fornito et al., 2009), rather than the effects of some form of prior belief or suggestion. Nevertheless, proposals about a cross-modal role of the SMA in control and ownership of thought and movement, and the contribution of disrupted sensory suppression effects to the sensory quality rather than the sense of control of movements, are relevant to the proximate (immediate) changes in brain activity underpinning alien control phenomena in patients with psychosis even if the distal influences vary between individuals and groups.

12.6. Conclusions

In this chapter we have described the challenges facing the experimental study of TI and related phenomena. These include the fact that within the context of psychosis TI and other alien control phenomena are sporadic and cannot easily be captured within experimental settings. Psychotic phenomena are also often difficult to distinguish and often co-occur when presenting in patients. Finally, TI in particular may be associated with illness severity, making the assessment of patients difficult. The novel experimental approach of applying suggestion to model TI and related alien control phenomena provides a way of circumventing these challenges. Initial studies adopting this method have clearly demonstrated that experiences of TI and alien control of movement can be reliably produced and combined with brain measurement techniques in healthy participants (Deeley et al., 2014; Walsh et al., 2015). The derivation of hypotheses from experimental modelling in healthy individuals can inform analysis of data acquired in future studies which investigate the phenomenology and underlying neurocognitive mechanisms of alien control phenomena across the full range of their manifestations—including people with psychosis and psychologically healthy cultural practitioners such as spiritualist mediums.

References

Allen, P., Modinos, G., Hubl, D., Shields, G., Cachia, A., Jardri, R., Thomas, P., Woodward, T., Shotbolt, P., Plaze, M., & Hoffman, R. (2012). Neuroimaging auditory hallucinations in schizophrenia: from neuroanatomy to neurochemistry and beyond. *Schizophrenia Bulletin*, 38(4), 695–703.

Andreasen, N. C. (1984). *Scale for the Assessment of Positive Symptoms (SAPS)*. Iowa City: University of Iowa.

Badcock, J. C. (2016). A neuropsychological approach to auditory verbal hallucinations and thought insertion grounded in normal voice perception. *Review of Philosophy and Psychology, 7*(3), 631–652.

Bargh, J. A., & Chartrand, T. L. (1999). The unbearable automaticity of being. American Psychologist, 54(7), 462–479.

Bathla, G., Gene, M. N., Peck, K. K., Jenabi, M., Tabar, V., & Holodny, A. I. (2019). Resting state functional connectivity of the supplementary motor area to motor and language networks in patients with brain tumors. *Journal of Neuroimaging, 29*(4), 521–526.

Beeson, P. M. (2004). Remediation of written language. *Topics in Stroke Rehabilitation, 11*(1), 37–48.

Binet, A., & Féré, C. (1891). *Animal Magnetism (Vol. 60)*. Trübner: Kegan Paul, Trench, and co.

Blakemore, S. J., Oakley, D. A., & Frith, C. D. (2003). Delusions of alien control in the normal brain. *Neuropsychologia, 41*(8), 1058–1067.

Boddy, J. (1988). Spirits and selves in Northern Sudan: The cultural therapeutics of possession and trance. *American Ethnologist, 15*(1), 4–27.

Bowers, K. S. (1993). The Waterloo-Stanford Group C (WSGC) scale of hypnotic susceptibility: Normative and comparative data. *International Journal of Clinical and Experimental Hypnosis, 41*(1), 35–46.

Breier, A., & Berg, P. H. (1999). The psychosis of schizophrenia: Prevalence, response to atypical antipsychotics, and prediction of outcome. *Biological Psychiatry, 46*(3), 361–364.

Brown, R. J., Syed, T. U., Benbadis, S., LaFrance, W. C., & Reuber, M. (2011). Psychogenic nonepileptic seizures. *Epilepsy and Behavior, 22*(1), 85–93.

Bryant, R. A., & Mallard, D. (2003). Seeing is believing: The reality of hypnotic hallucinations. *Consciousness and Cognition, 12*(2), 219–230.

Chan, R. C. K., Di, X., McAlonan, G. M., & Gong, Q.-Y. (2011). Brain anatomical abnormalities in high-risk individuals, first-episode, and chronic schizophrenia: An activation likelihood estimation meta-analysis of illness progression. *Schizophrenia Bulletin, 37*(1), 177–188.

Craig, A. D. (2009). How do you feel—now? The anterior insula and human awareness. *Nature Reviews Neuroscience, 10*(1), 59–70.

Ćurčić-Blake, B., Ford, J. M., Hubl, D., Orlov, N. D., Sommer, I. E., Waters, F., Allen, P., Jardri, R., Woodruff, P. W., David, O., Mulert, C., Woodward, T. S., & Aleman, A. (2017). Interaction of language, auditory and memory brain networks in auditory verbal hallucinations. *Progress in Neurobiology, 148*, 1–20.

David, A. S. (1999). Auditory hallucinations: Phenomenology, neuropsychology and neuroimaging update. *Acta Psychiatrica Scandinavica Supplementum, 99*(Suppl 395), 95–104.

Deeley, Q. (2016). Hypnosis as therapy for functional neurologic disorders. Handbook of Clinical Neurology, 139, 585–595.

Deeley, Q. (2018). Neuroanthropology: Exploring relations between brain, cognition, and culture. In A. K. Petersen, I. S. Gilhus, L. H. Martin, J. S. Jensen, & J. Sørensen (Eds.), *Evolution, Cognition and the History of Religion: A New Synthesis* (pp. 380–396). Brill: Koninklijke.

Deeley, Q. (2019). Revelatory experiences: meanings, motives, and causes. Religion, Brain and Behavior, 9(3), 284–291.

Deeley, Q., Oakley, D. A., Walsh, E., Bell, V., Mehta, M. A., & Halligan, P. W. (2014). Modelling psychiatric and cultural possession phenomena with suggestion and fMRI ScienceDirect. *Cortex, 53*(1), 107–119.

Deeley, Q., Walsh, E., Oakley, D. A., Bell, V., Koppel, C., Mehta, M. A., & Halligan, P. W. (2013). Using hypnotic suggestion to model loss of control and awareness of movements: An exploratory fMRI study. *PLoS ONE, 8*(10), e78324.

Dennis, N. A., Bowman, C. R., & Vandekar, S. N. (2012). True and phantom recollection: An fMRI investigation of similar and distinct neural correlates and connectivity. *NeuroImage, 59*(3), 2982–2993.

Dixon, L. (1999). Dual diagnosis of substance abuse in schizophrenia: prevalence and impact on outcomes. *Schizophrenia Research, 35*, S93–100.

Ellenberger, H. M. (1994). *The Discovery of the Unconscious: The History and Evolution of Dynamic Psychiatry*. New York: Fontana Press.

Feinberg, I. (1978). Efference copy and corollary discharge: implications for thinking and its disorders. *Schizophrenia Bulletin, 4*(4), 636–640.

Ford, J. M., Dierks, T., Fisher, D. J., Herrmann, C. S., Hubl, D., Kindler, J., Koenig, T., Mathalon, D. H., Spencer, K. M., Strik, W., & van Lutterveld, R. (2012). Neurophysiological studies of auditory verbal hallucinations. *Schizophrenia Bulletin, 38*(4), 715–723.

Fornito, A., Yücel, M., Patti, J., Wood, S. J., & Pantelis, C. (2009). Mapping grey matter reductions in schizophrenia: An anatomical likelihood estimation analysis of voxel-based morphometry studies. *Schizophrenia Research, 108*(1–3), 104–113.

Frith, C. D. (2005). The self in action: Lessons from delusions of control. *Consciousness and Cognition, 14*(4), 752–770.

Frith, C. D., & Done, D. J. (1989). Experiences of alien control in schizophrenia reflect a disorder in the central monitoring of action. *Psychological Medicine, 19*(2), 359–363.

Frith, U., & Frith, C. D. (2003). Development and neurophysiology of mentalizing. *Philosophical Transactions of the Royal Society B: Biological Sciences, 358*(1431), 459–473.

Gauchou, H. L., Rensink, R. A., & Fels, S. (2012). Expression of nonconscious knowledge via ideomotor actions. *Consciousness and Cognition, 21*(2), 976–982.

Haggard, P. (2017). Sense of agency in the human brain. *Nature Reviews Neuroscience, 18*(4), 196–207.

Haggard, P., & Whitford, B. (2004). Supplementary motor area provides an efferent signal for sensory suppression. *Cognitive Brain Research, 19*(1), 52–58.

Halligan, P. W., & Oakley, D. A. (2014). Hypnosis and beyond: Exploring the broader domain of suggestion. *Psychology of Consciousness: Theory, Research, and Practice, 1*(2), 105–122.

Hawkins, P. C. T., Zelaya, F. O., O'Daly, O., Holiga, S., Dukart, J., Umbricht, D., & Mehta, M. A. (2021). The effect of risperidone on reward-related brain activity is robust to drug-induced vascular changes. *Human Brain Mapping, 42*(9), 2766–2777.

Heap, M., Alden, P., Brown, R. J., Naish, P. L. N., Oakley, D. A., Wagstaff, G. F., & Walker, L. J. (2001). *The Nature of Hypnosis: Report Prepared by a Working Party at the Request of the Professional Affairs Board of the British Psychological Society*. London: British Psychological Society.

Hubl, D., Koenig, T., Strik, W. K., Garcia, L. M., & Dierks, T. (2007). Competition for neuronal resources: How hallucinations make themselves heard. *British Journal of Psychiatry, 190*(JAN.), 57–62.

Idrees, M., Khan, I., Sarwar, R., & Irfan, M. (2010). Frequency of first rank symptoms in patients of schizophrenia: A hospital-based study. *Gomal Journal of Medical Sciences, 8*(1), 8–11.

Janet, P. (1907). *The Major Symptoms of Hysteria: Classics of Psychiatry & Behavioral Sciences Library*. New York: Division of Gryphon Editions.

Johns, L. C., Kompus, K., Connell, M., Humpston, C., Lincoln, T. M., Longden, E., Preti, A., Alderson-Day, B., Badcock, J. C., Cella, M., Fernyhough, C., McCarthy-Jones, S., Peters, E., Raballo, A., Scott, J., Siddi, S., Sommer, I. E., & Larøi, F. (2014). Auditory verbal hallucinations in persons with and without a need for care. *Schizophrenia Bulletin, 40*(Suppl_4), S255–S264.

Kay, S. R., Fiszbein, A., & Opler, L. A. (1987). The positive and negative syndrome scale (PANSS) for schizophrenia. *Schizophrenia Bulletin, 13*(2), 261–276.

Kihlstrom, J. F. (2013). Neuro-hypnotism: Prospects for hypnosis and neuroscience. *Cortex, 49*(2), 365–374.

Kristensen, S. (2018). Technical delusions in schizophrenia: A philosophical interpretation. *Philosophy, Psychiatry, & Psychology, 25*(3), 173–181.

Luhrmann, T. M. (2012). *When God Talks Back: Understanding the American Evangelical Relationship with God.* New York: Knopf.

Luhrmann, T. M., Weisman, K., Aulino, F., Brahinsky, J. D., Dulin, J. C., Dzokoto, V. A., Legare, C. H., Lifshitz, M., Ng, E., Ross-Zehnder, N., Smith, R. E., & Designed, R. E. S. (2021). Sensing the presence of gods and spirits across cultures and faiths. *Proceedings of the National Academy of Sciences of the United States of America, 118*(5), 2016649118.

Lukoff, D., Snyder, K., Ventura, J., & Nuechterlein, K. H. (1984). Life events, familial stress, and coping in the developmental course of schizophrenia. *Schizophrenia Bulletin, 10*(2), 258–292.

Marneros, A. (1984). Frequency of occurrence of Schneider's first rank symptoms in schizophrenia. *European Archives of Psychiatry and Neurological Sciences, 234*(1), 78–82.

Maruff, P., Wood, S. J., Velakoulis, D., Smith, D. J., Soulsby, B., Suckling, J., Bullmore, E. T., & Pantelis, C. (2005). Reduced volume of parietal and frontal association areas in patients with schizophrenia characterized by passivity delusions. *Psychological Medicine, 35*(6), 783–789.

McCarthy-Jones, S., Trauer, T., Mackinnon, A., Sims, E., Thomas, N., & Copolov, D. (2014). A new phenomenological survey of auditory hallucinations: Evidence for subtypes and implications for theory and practice. *Schizophrenia Bulletin, 40,* 231–235. doi:10.1093/schbul/sbs156

Mellor, C. S. (1970). First rank symptoms of schizophrenia: I. The frequency in schizophrenics on admission to hospital II. Differences between individual first rank symptoms. *The British Journal of Psychiatry, 117,* 15–23.

Miall, R. C., Weir, D. J., Wolpert, D. M., & Stein, J. F. (1993). Is the cerebellum a smith predictor? *Journal of Motor Behavior, 25*(3), 203–216.

Milling, L. S. (2008). Is high hypnotic suggestibility necessary for successful hypnotic pain intervention? *Current Pain and Headache Reports, 12*(2), 98–102.

Mlakar, J., Jensterle, J., & Frith, C. D. (1994). Central monitoring deficiency. *Psychological Medicine, 24*(August), 557–564.

Mullins, S., & Spence, S. A. (2003). Re-examining thought insertion. *The British Journal of Psychiatry, 182*(4), 293–298.

Nachev, P., Kennard, C., & Husain, M. (2008). Functional role of the supplementary and pre-supplementary motor areas. Nature *Reviews Neuroscience, 9*(11), 856–869.

Nayani, T. H., & David, A. S. (1996). The auditory hallucination: A phenomenological survey. *Psychological Medicine, 26*(01), 177.

Oakley, D. A., Walsh, E., Lillelokken, A. M., Halligan, P. W., Mehta, M. A., & Deeley, Q. (2020). United Kingdom norms for the Harvard group scale of hypnotic susceptibility, form a. *International Journal of Clinical and Experimental Hypnosis, 68*(1), 80–104.

Oakley, D. A., Walsh, E., Mehta, M. A., Halligan, P. W., & Deeley, Q. (2021). Direct verbal suggestibility: Measurement and significance. *Consciousness and Cognition, 89,* 103036.

Oyebode, F. (2018). *Sims' Symptoms in the Mind: Textbook of Descriptive Psychopathology E-Book.* London: Elsevier Health Sciences.

Pantelis, C., Yücel, M., Wood, S. J., Velakoulis, D., Sun, D., Berger, G., Stuart, G. W., Yung, A., Phillips, L., & McGorry, P. D. (2005). Structural brain imaging evidence for multiple pathological processes at different stages of brain development in schizophrenia. *Schizophrenia Bulletin, 31*(3), 672–696.

Peck, K. K., Bradbury, M., Psaty, E. L., Brennan, N. P., & Holodny, A. I. (2009). Joint activation of the supplementary motor area and presupplementary motor area during simultaneous motor and language functional MRI. *Neuroreport, 20,* 487–91.

Rouget, G. (1985). *Music and Trance: A Theory of the Relations Between Music and Possession*. Chicago, IL: University of Chicago Press.

Sage, K., & Ellis, A. W. (2004). Lexical influences in graphemic buffer disorder. *Cognitive Neuropsychology, 21*(2–4), 381–400.

Salisbury, D. F., Shenton, M. E., Griggs, C. B., Bonner-Jackson, A., & McCarley, R. W. (2002). Mismatch negativity in chronic schizophrenia and first-episode schizophrenia. *Archives of General Psychiatry, 59*(8), 686–694.

Sartorius, N., Jablensky, A., Korten, A., Ernberg, G., Anker, M., Cooper, J. E., & Day, R. (1986). Early manifestations and first-contact incidence of schizophrenia in different cultures: A preliminary report on the initial evaluation phase of the WHO Collaborative Study on Determinants of Outcome of Severe Mental Disorders. *Psychological Medicine, 16*(4), 909–928.

Seligman, R., Laurence, A. E., Kirmayer, J., Seligman, R., & Kirmayer, L. J. (2008). Dissociative experience and cultural neuroscience: Narrative, metaphor and mechanism. *Culture, Medicine, and Psychiatry, 32*, 31–64.

Shevlin, M., Houston, J. E., Dorahy, M. J., & Adamson, G. (2008). Cumulative traumas and psychosis: An analysis of the national comorbidity survey and the British Psychiatric Morbidity Survey. *Schizophrenia Bulletin, 34*(1), 193–199.

Shor, R. E., & Orne, E. C. (1963). Of the Harvard Group scale of hypnotic susceptibility, form A1. *International Journal of Clinical and Experimental Hypnosis, 11*(1), 39–47.

Soares-Weiser, K., Maayan, N., Bergman, H., Davenport, C., Kirkham, A., Grabowski, S., & Adams, C. (2015). First rank symptoms for schizophrenia. *Cochrane Database of Systematic Review, 1*, CD010653.

Spence, S. A. (2002). Alien motor phenomena: A window on to agency. *Cognitive Neuropsychiatry, 7*(3), 211–220.

Sumner, P., Nachev, P., Morris, P., Peters, A. M., Jackson, S. R., Kennard, C., & Husain, M. (2007). Human medial frontal cortex mediates unconscious inhibition of voluntary action. *Neuron, 54*(5), 697–711.

Taves, A. (2006). Where (fragmented) selves meet cultures. *Culture and Religion, 7*(2), 123–138.

Taves, A. (2016). *Revelatory Events*. Princeton, NJ: Princeton University Press.

Thorup, A., Petersen, L., Jeppesen, P., & Nordentoft, M. (2007). Frequency and predictive values of first rank symptoms at baseline among 362 young adult patients with first-episode schizophrenia. Results from the Danish OPUS study. *Schizophrenia Research, 97*(1–3), 60–67.

Valentini, E., Betti, V., Hu, L., & Aglioti, S. M. (2013). Hypnotic modulation of pain perception and of brain activity triggered by nociceptive laser stimuli. *Cortex, 49*(2), 446–462.

van Lutterveld, R., Sommer, I. E. C., & Ford, J. M. (2011). The neurophysiology of auditory hallucinations—a historical and contemporary review. *Frontiers in Psychiatry, 2*(MAY), 1–7.

Vita, A., De Peri, L., Deste, G., Barlati, S., & Sacchetti, E. (2015). The effect of antipsychotic treatment on cortical gray matter changes in schizophrenia: Does the class matter? A meta-analysis and meta-regression of longitudinal magnetic resonance imaging studies. *Biological Psychiatry, 78*(6), 403–412.

Vitebsky, P. (2001). *Shamanism*. Norman, OK: University of Oklahoma Press.

Vogeley, K., May, M., Ritzl, A., Falkai, P., Zilles, K., & Fink, G. R. (2004). Neural correlates of first-person perspective as one constituent of human self-consciousness. *Journal of Cognitive Neuroscience, 16*(5), 817–827.

Walsh, E., Mehta, M. A. A., Oakley, D. A. A., Guilmette, D. N. N., Gabay, A., Halligan, P. W. W., & Deeley, Q. (2014). Using suggestion to model different types of automatic writing. *Consciousness and Cognition, 26*(1), 24–36.

Walsh, E., Oakley, D. A., Halligan, P. W., Mehta, M. A., & Deeley, Q. (2015). The functional anatomy and connectivity of thought insertion and alien control of movement. *Cortex, 64,* 380–393.

Walsh, E., Oakley, D. A., Halligan, P. W., Mehta, M. A., & Deeley, Q. (2017). Brain mechanisms for loss of awareness of thought and movement. *Social Cognitive and Affective Neuroscience, 12*(5), 793–801. https://doi.org/10.1093/scan/nsw185

Waters, F., Price, G., Dragović, M., & Jablensky, A. (2009). Electrophysiological brain activity and antisaccade performance in schizophrenia patients with first-rank (passivity) symptoms. *Psychiatry Research, 170*(2–3), 140–149.

Weitzenhoffer, A. M., & Hilgard, E. R. (1962). *Stanford Hypnotic Susceptibility Scale, Form C* (Vol. 27). Consulting Psychologists Press. http://socrates.berkeley.edu/~kihlstrm/PDFfiles/Hypnotizability/SHSSC Script.pdf

Wiles, N. J., Zammit, S. G., Bebbington, P., Singleton, N., Meltzer, H., & Lewis, G. (2006). Self-reported psychotic symptoms in the general population: Results from the longitudinal study of the British National Psychiatric Morbidity Survey. *British Journal of Psychiatry, 188*(JUNE), 519–526.

Wolpert, D. M. (1997). Computational approaches to motor control. *Trends in Cognitive Sciences, 1*(6), 209–216.

Zmigrod, L., Garrison, J. R., Carr, J., & Simons Jon S. (2016). The neural mechanisms of hallucinations: A quantitative meta-analysis of neuroimaging studies. *Neuroscience and Biobehavioral Reviews, 69,* 113–123.

13
What Can Magic and Science Tell Us About the Experience of Thought Insertion?

Alice Pailhès, Jay Olson, and Gustav Kuhn

13.1. Introduction

The conjuring techniques in performance magic allow us to experience things that we believe to be impossible (Kuhn, 2019). Throughout history, conjurers have learnt to use clever psychological tricks to create compelling illusory phenomena that violate our understanding of the world (e.g., psychic powers, violations of the laws of physics). Magicians have developed a wide range of tricks that allow them to push the limits of what their audiences believe is possible. Among other things, they often proclaim that they can insert specific thoughts into people's minds or unconsciously manipulate their behaviour. This form of magic is known as *mentalism*, and the context of such performances varies widely. For example, some performers attribute the effects to paranormal and psychic abilities while others frame it as psychological skills such as reading body language or using subtle suggestion techniques. Mentalism is the genre of magic that most often plays with the concept of thought insertion. In some instances, the magician genuinely influences and manipulates their spectator's thoughts, while in others they simply provide the illusion of thought insertion (Cole, 2020; Pailhès & Kuhn, 2021b). In recent years, scientists have started to systematically investigate the psychological mechanisms that underpin these magic tricks as well as the impact that they have on people's minds (Kuhn, 2019; Kuhn, Amlani, & Rensink, 2008; Pailhès & Kuhn, 2021a; Rensink & Kuhn, 2015). Understanding the cognitive mechanisms by which magicians can manipulate people's thoughts provides new insights into the nature of human cognition (Pailhès & Kuhn, 2021a). Moreover, researchers have started to implement conjuring techniques within their own experimental settings to learn more about the impact that this form of mind control and thought insertion has (Olson et al., 2016). In these instances, the experimenter/performer relies on secret methods that mimic the appearance of thought insertion, rather than genuine thought insertion. In this chapter, we start by outlining some of the principles magicians use to insert thoughts into the spectator's mind and to covertly influence choices. In the second part, we examine the benefits of using magic to mimic thought insertion in non-clinical populations and discuss results from novel paradigms using magic as a tool to provide the illusion of a thought-inserting machine. In the final section, we explore common conjuring principles that are used to mimic thought insertion and how these could be applied in future research procedures.

13.2. Thought Insertion Through Forcing

Magicians have developed a wide range of psychological tricks that allow them to manipulate their audiences' experience of the world (Kuhn, 2019). Some of these tricks rely on misdirecting people's perceptual experiences, while others involve manipulating people's thought processes. The latter processes are of particular interest here, as many of them involve inserting thoughts into people's mind. Let us examine a typical magic trick that might involve such thought insertion. The magician asks you to pick a card, and even though you have the experience of a free selection, the magician is able to predict this choice by influencing your decision. This principle, known as *forcing*, refers to any technique that allows conjurers to covertly influence a person's choices, or the outcome of this choice (Pailhès & Kuhn, 2021a; Pailhès, Rensink, & Kuhn, 2020). There are two key components that must be fulfilled for a force to be considered successful. First, the force must influence a person's choice towards a predetermined outcome. In some instances, the magician can guarantee that the spectator will choose a particular item, while in other instances they will simply increase the probability that a particular item is selected. Second, the spectator must be unaware of how their choice has been influenced. Magic relies on people being unaware of the true cause of an effect, and forcing techniques therefore rely on covertly influencing a person's decision, or the impact that their decision has on the outcome.

Let us now examine how forces can result in the insertion of the thought. There are two different ways in which the thought insertion can be operationalized. In the most direct way, the magician will influence the card that will come to your mind, and thus the forcing principle will have a direct impact on your mental representation. The second process involves indirect manipulations of thoughts. Here you are asked to physically select an item and the magician covertly influences this decision process, which results in the spectator thinking of the predetermined outcome. For example, the magician may ask you to physically select a playing card, and this selected card represents your thought. Unbeknown to the spectator, the physical selection process has either been covertly influenced (e.g., through the physical positioning of the presented items), or the selection does not have a direct impact on the outcome (e.g., using a deck in which all cards are identical). In both instances, the spectator ends up with the erroneous thought that they have selected a random playing card or item. Let us now examine these two forms of thought insertion in turn.

We have recently developed a psychologically based taxonomy of forcing that examines the psychological mechanisms that underpin all forcing techniques. This taxonomy is largely based on one central distinction regarding the target of influence (Pailhès et al., 2020). *Outcome forces* are forces in which the spectator makes a free choice, but the choice does not have an impact on the outcome of the decision. For example, the spectator picks a random card, but the magician secretly switches the card for another card. A large number of forcing principles fall within this category (Cole, 2020; Pailhès & Kuhn, 2020b; Pailhès, Kumari, & Kuhn, 2020) and the end product results in people erroneously believing that they were in control over the item that they chose. Another way of providing such an illusion might be through the use of the Equivoque, also called the magician's choice. In this technique, the magician uses ambiguous language to get the spectator to end with a predetermined outcome (Fig. 13.1). For instance, the magician might want to use red cards and say, 'We will proceed by elimination. Red or black?'. If the spectator says 'red', the magician keeps the red cards, and if the spectator says 'black', the magician does exactly the same thing while saying something like 'alright, let's remove the black!'. Results from scientific experiments show that this technique is very powerful to produce the illusion that the participants have control over the outcome item (Pailhès, Kumari, et al., 2020).

Decision forces are forcing principles in which the magicians directly influence your decision. Many of these forces rely on exploiting systematic cognitive biases that allow the magician to predict and influence your decision processes. Although you may feel that you were in control of your decision, many of the choices we make are highly predictable. Some of these decision forces directly involve manipulating thought processes, while others involve manipulating the physical behaviours that are responsible for making the decision.

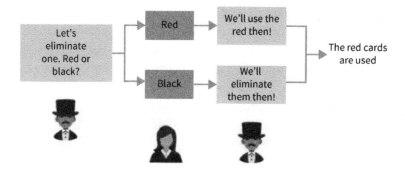

Figure 13.1 Example of an Equivoque in which the magician forces the outcome of using red cards by using ambiguous language in his question. Thanks to this procedure, the spectator's choice has no impact on the outcome of the trick, which is predetermined before the performance.

One such principle that we have investigated in the lab is the principle for priming. The idea of using unconscious stimuli to influence people's thoughts and behaviours has long attracted public and scientific interest (DeCoster & Claypool, 2004; Lucas, 2000; Newell & Shanks, 2014; Van den Bussche, Van den Noortgate, & Reynvoet, 2009). This idea has also been applied to magic, in the form of *priming forces*—techniques in which the magician alters the tendency of the spectator to name a target object. Conjurers typically use both verbal and nonverbal primes to influence decisions. For instance, we have investigated the Mental Priming force (Pailhès & Kuhn, 2020a), which relies on subtle hand gestures and key words to prime people to think of the Three of Diamonds. In this force, the magician declares that they will try to mentally transmit the identity of a playing card to the spectator, and then asks them to follow some instructions while imagining different things. For example, the magician gestures a diamond shape while asking participants to imagine a screen in their mind, or quickly draws little '3's in the air while asking them to imagine the numbers on the card (Fig. 13.2). Results showed that 18% of participants choose the Three of Diamonds, compared to a baseline of 2% given 52 cards. Nearly 40% of participants chose threes of any suits. Most importantly, these participants were oblivious to the fact that they were manipulated and reported that the card had simply popped into their mind.

Another popular way of biasing a person's decision is to increase the saliency of target items (i.e., the extent to which they visually stand out from their surroundings), making them more likely to be chosen. These forcing principles are well documented in the magic literature (Annemann, 1933; Banachek, 2002; Jones, 1994) and some have been studied empirically.

What Can Magic and Science Tell Us About TI? 229

Figure 13.2 Mental Priming Force's four nonverbal primes to influence participants to think about the Three of Diamonds: 1) primes the diamond's shape; 2) primes the number three by drawing little '3's with the index finger in the corners of the card; 3) prime three suits/symbols in the centre of the card by pointing three fingers; and 4) prime three suits on the card by pointing three times at the imaginary suits and using the keywords 'boom-boom-boom', verbally priming three suits.

Olson et al. (2015) tested a popular force known as the visual saliency force, in which the magician flips through a deck of cards and asks the spectator to visually select one of them. Unbeknown to the spectator, the target card was shown slightly longer than the others, thus becoming more salient. In a live performance, almost all participants (98%) chose the target card while being unaware that their choice had been influenced and feeling completely free in their choice. Again, this provides an effective way of 'implanting' a thought into the spectator's mind.

Some decision forces are based on the use of reverse psychology, misrepresenting the magicians' true desires to influence the spectator's choice towards a target card or object. A famous example of this type of force is Dai Vernon's five card mental force (Banachek, 2002; Hugard, 1974), which consists in choosing five specific cards and pushing the spectator to be suspicious about them so that they end up choosing the 'least obvious' card, predetermined by the performer. We have recently investigated this technique and found that reverse psychology plays a significant role in the success of this force (Pailhès & Kuhn, 2023).

Decision forces also often exploit stereotypical behaviour, or population stereotypes (French, 1992; Marks & Kammann, 1980), using the fact that when presented with a specific situation or question, most people choose and answer the same thing. In this case, the magician tries to influence the spectator's choice by presenting a specific set of options among which one is most commonly chosen. For example, if asked to name a number between 1 and 10, people are most likely to name 7 (Banachek, 2002; French, 1992). Although such techniques are not 'inserting thoughts' as such, the magicians can make use of such knowledge to present the different options in such a way that one will be more likely to be the chosen one.

Finally, a common way for magicians to influence the spectators' decision and force a particular item is by restricting the number of options that they can consider. These restrictions can be verbal (e.g., 'don't take number 3, it's too obvious'), perceptual (e.g., making only one card visible), or physical (e.g., pushing a card under the spectator's finger when he/she is reaching out to grab one). Forcing allows magicians to influence people's choices and in doing so provides the opportunity to insert the idea that they have freely chosen a particular item in their mind. In most instances, this form of mind control occurs indirectly, by getting people to physically select an object that represents a thought. It is important to note that many of the forcing principles in which spectators are simply asked to mentally select an object are far from perfect, and even though they can bias a person's decision, the magician does not have full control over their thought. In the next section we will examine how magicians can provide the illusion that they have full control of their audience's thoughts and mimic this ability of inserting thoughts into their audience's mind.

13.3. Why Use Magic to Mimic Thought Insertion

Forcing allows magicians to covertly influence a person's thoughts. A force is only effective if the spectator feels that their decision was free and that they are oblivious to the principles that have been used to influence this decision. There are, however, instances in which magicians want you to believe that they have influenced your thoughts when in reality they had no way of controlling them (Cole, 2021; Pailhès & Kuhn, 2021b). For example, in a card trick the magician might ask you to pick a card after which they reveal how they have

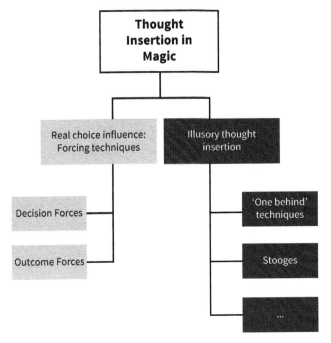

Figure 13.3 Principles of thought insertion in magic. Some techniques, called forcing (discussed in the first section of the chapter), focus on influencing the spectators' choice or the outcome of this choice. Other techniques simply mimic thought insertion and give the illusion that the performer influenced the spectator's thought process (see third section).

unconsciously influenced choice. In this instance your choice was indeed free, and the magician may use a different method to discover the identity of the playing card and simply pretended to have influenced you to choose it (Fig. 13.3). This form of magic has become very popular in recent years, and the principles are being used to study the psychological impact that such illusions of thought insertion have on an individual's beliefs and experiences.

Psychological research has shown that people often erroneously believe they have full control over their actions and thoughts. For example, studies using hypnosis or Ouija boards reveal that people can have control over their behaviours while feeling they do not (Connors, 2015; Gauchou, Rensink, & Fels, 2012). Conjuring techniques provide a new perspective and experimental tool to examine this discussion—what happens when people think that a machine, or another person, is able to influence their thoughts? Some of these mentalism principles allow us to simulate thought insertion phenomena. Other researchers have attempted to mimic thought insertion with hypnosis. For example, Walsh and colleagues (Walsh et al., 2015) told people under hypnosis that an engineer would insert thoughts into participants' brains through the use of a brain scanner. The participants were asked to write sentences while the machine ostensibly influenced them; participants often reported that the thoughts seemed to be inserted into their head and their hand wrote them without their apparent control. The benefit of such techniques is that they allow researchers to mimic clinically relevant phenomena in healthy populations, who are often more accessible and avoids some of the ethical issues of studying vulnerable populations. One of the downsides of such techniques is that they only work for highly hypnotizable individuals, which are a minority of the population.

While neuroimaging and brain stimulation methods are on the rise, neuroscientific techniques are attracting the curiosity from both scientists and popular media. Neuroenchantment—the fascination with brain science at the expense of critical thinking abilities—is born, with a tendency to overestimate the present state of skills and knowledge that science holds about the brain (Ali, Lifshitz, & Raz, 2014; Thibault et al., 2018). Olson and colleagues recently investigated whether it was possible to make people believe that a machine was influencing their thoughts and mental choices (Olson et al., 2016). Using a mentalism trick combined with an inactive fMRI machine, the researchers created a novel deceptive paradigm. They told participants that they were taking part in a study to examine how a brain scanner could read thoughts and influence their mind. Although the machine looked and sounded like a functioning scanner, it was completely inactive throughout the experiment. Participants had to lie into the mock scanner and were asked to do two tasks: a *mind-reading* task, and a *mind-influencing* one. For the mind-reading task, participants chose any two-digit number. After this, the machine allegedly analysed their brain recording to infer which number they chose, and the participants could see the technician writing it on a sheet of paper containing the machine's output. Next, participants exited the scanner, and the experimenter, holding the paper with the output, asked them which number they chose. After they responded, he showed the output, revealing that the machine guessed the right number. In the 'mind influencing' task, the protocol was reversed (Fig. 13.4). The researcher told the participants that the machine was programmed to influence their thoughts and insert a specific number into their mind. This time, the experimenter pretended to write down the number the scanner would 'transmit' before the participant was asked to choose it. Then, as before, the subject had to silently choose a two-digit number, while the machine was 'influencing them'. After this, using the same technique, the experimenter asked which number the participant chose and showed on his clipboard that it was matching with the machine's predicted number.

After each of these tasks, participants rated how much control they felt over their thoughts and choice of numbers. Participants felt significantly less sense of control over their thoughts when they believed that the machine was influencing their mind than only reading it. These results were replicated in a second experiment, also showing that the majority of subjects felt a range of physical and mental symptoms resulting in the machine's influence. Participants reported feeling things such as numbers 'popping in' their head, voices dragging them from a number to the other, feeling 'some kind of force' or even being stuck on one number.

These studies are the first to have used magic as a way to simulate thought insertion, and both quantitative and qualitative results show that the majority of people were convinced that the machine was controlling their thoughts. This belief resulted in a distorted sense of agency expressed differently among participants, and the study demonstrates the usefulness of magic techniques in scientific experiments. Pilot data from our research programme and using a similar procedure suggest that the alleged proof provided by the magic technique (i.e., showing the matching number) seems to be a significant factor contributing to the observed effects. Here, it seems that the deceiving method allows participants to be more confident in the procedure and enhance their expectations of what the machine is capable of doing to their brain activity.

This type of paradigm, much like the ones using hypnosis (Connors, 2015; Walsh et al., 2014), allows researchers to model symptoms of mental disorders and explore the loss of agency over thoughts with a high level of control in non-clinical populations. Likewise, it opens several possibilities for future

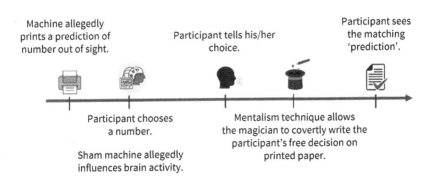

Figure 13.4 Representation of a mind-influencing task mimicking thought insertion. The magician/experimenter uses a gimmick to covertly write the participant free choice after they have named it.

research. If it is possible to make participants believe that a machine can read and influence thoughts, it might extend to inserting other phenomena such as memories, judgements, or emotions. Adapting established techniques from magic and mentalism performances offers a powerful way to create experimental methods that can simulate thought insertion. The next section will examine different means of achieving these various thought insertions.

13.4. How to Mimic Thought Insertion with Magic

Magicians, and especially mentalists, have a great number of techniques that give the illusion that they can control and influence spectators' mental processes. Mentalism is a branch of magic that involves creating illusions of highly developed mental skills or paranormal abilities. In these performances, the performer may appear to make use of things such as precognition, hypnosis, telepathy, or mind control techniques. For example, magicians may give the illusion that they influence a person's thoughts through telepathy or psychological priming. However, several principles can be used to provide such an illusion of thought insertion. Some of them are very simple and risk-free for the performers, while others are a lot more elaborate or do not guarantee a hundred per cent success rate.

13.4.1. 'One behind' choice techniques

The most commonly used techniques to mimic thought insertion rely on either switching a prediction so that it fits the spectator's thought, or by using a special writing gimmick that allows the magician to covertly write the selected item *after* the spectator told what they were (freely) thinking about (Corinda, 1961). These techniques allow magicians to give an illusion of thought insertion despite the spectator being in full control over their choice.

Let us examine the one behind principle in more detail and what it would look like in practice. The magician might perform a trick as follows: The performer states that they will try to mentally insert a thought into the spectator's mind. The performer then selects a card from a deck and inserts it into an envelope which they give to the spectator. The magician then explains that this card represents a prediction about the choice that the spectator is about to make. The spectator is then asked to think of a playing card and the magician falsely claims that they are using their special powers to influence their thought process, after which the spectator names the card. The performer reveals that the prediction in the envelope matches the card they have just thought about, providing 'proof' of their thought insertion powers. In reality, the magician simply switched the card in the envelope for one that matched the prediction, thus providing false proof. There are many other ways in which the prediction can be switched but they all essentially rely on the same principle. Other techniques allow magicians to covertly write a spectator's free choice after they have said it out loud—this is what was used in the studies described in the previous section (Olson et al., 2016), and the same type of effect can be easily done with any other prediction beyond merely two-digit numbers.

13.4.2. Use of stooges

One of the simplest ways of creating illusions of thought insertion is by using confederates, or stooges—magicians' associates pretending to be spectators. In this case, although the person involved in the performance does not experience the illusion, the rest of the audience does indirectly, and the possibilities are endless. The magician and stooge simply have to agree on specific answers and choices before the show and mimic a performance in which the conjurer successfully inserts a thought in the spectator's/stooge's mind. Scientific experiments frequently use this principle: a lot of psychological studies work thanks to the use of confederates (Olson & Raz, 2021). For instance, Asch's well-known work on social conformity could not have been possible without the use of stooges pretending to give obvious incorrect answers to pressure real participants to do it as well (Asch, 1951). Following this idea, it would therefore be possible for instance to use one or several confederates to mimic thought insertion in front of genuine participants, and then investigate whether this can lead them to experience a loss of agency over their thoughts and choices when they believe it is their turn to experience thought insertion.

13.5. Concluding Remarks

Magicians have developed a great number of techniques that either allow them to insert thoughts into their audience's minds or produce the illusion of thought insertion. Empirical research and new theoretical perspectives on these principles are providing new insights into the ease by which our thought processes can be manipulated. These conjuring techniques also provide novel and powerful tools to mimic thought insertion, and recent psychological research has already provided promising results. Diverse methods—more or less costly and sophisticated—can be used and easily implemented in experimental research to simulate thought insertion in non-clinical populations. By adapting magicians' techniques to experimental settings, we can answer important questions regarding agency over thoughts, and uncover psychological processes involved in thought insertion phenomenon.

References

Ali, S. S., Lifshitz, M., & Raz, A. (2014). Empirical neuroenchantment: From reading minds to thinking critically. *Frontiers in Human Neuroscience, 8*, 357.

Annemann, T. (1933). *202 Methods of Forcing*. London: L. Davenport.

Asch, S. E. (1951). Effects of group pressure upon the modification and distortion of judgments. In H. Guetzkow (Ed.), *Groups, Leadership and Men: Research in Human Relations* (pp. 177–190). Lancaster, UK: Carnegie Press.

Banachek. (2002). *Psychological Subtleties 1*. Houston, TX: Magic Inspirations.

Cole, G. G. (2020). Forcing the issue: No psychology in the magician's choice. *Consciousness and Cognition, 84*, 103002.

Cole, G. G. (2021). Who's fooling whom in the science of magic? *Proceedings of the National Academy of Sciences., 118*(3), e2019540118.

Connors, M. H. (2015). Hypnosis and belief: A review of hypnotic delusions. *Consciousness and Cognition, 36*, 27–43.

Corinda, T. (1961). *Thirteen Steps to Mentalism*. New York: Tannen Magic Inc.

DeCoster, J., & Claypool, H. M. (2004). A meta-analysis of priming effects on impression formation supporting a general model of informational biases. *Personality and Social Psychology Review, 8*(1), 2–27.

French, C. C. (1992). Population stereotypes and belief in the paranormal: Is there a relationship? *Australian Psychologist, 27*(1), 57–58.

Gauchou, H. L., Rensink, R. A., & Fels, S. (2012). Expression of nonconscious knowledge via ideomotor actions. *Consciousness and Cognition, 21*(2), 976–982.

Hugard, J. (1974). *Encyclopedia of Card Tricks*. (J. Hugard, Ed.). New York: Dover Publications.

Jones, L. (1994). *Encyclopedia of Impromptu Card Forces*. H&R Magic Books.

Kuhn, G. (2019). *Experiencing the Impossible: The Science of Magic*. Cambridge, MA: MIT Press.

Kuhn, G., Amlani, A. A., & Rensink, R. A. (2008). Towards a science of magic. *Trends in Cognitive Sciences, 12*(9), 349–354.

Lucas, M. (2000). Semantic priming without association: A meta-analytic review. *Psychonomic Bulletin and Review, 7*(4), 618–630.

Marks, D., & Kammann, R. (1980). The psychology of the psychic. *The American Journal of Psychology, 93*(4), 748–749.

Newell, B. R., & Shanks, D. R. (2014). Unconscious influences on decision making: A critical review. *Behavioral and Brain Sciences, 37*(1), 1–19.

Olson, J. A., Amlani, A. A., Raz, A., & Rensink, R. A. (2015). Influencing choice without awareness. *Consciousness and Cognition, 37*, 225–236.

Olson, J. A., Landry, M., Appourchaux, K., & Raz, A. (2016). Simulated thought insertion: Influencing the sense of agency using deception and magic. *Consciousness and Cognition, 43*, 11–26.

Olson, J. A., & Raz, A. (2021). Applying insights from magic to improve deception in research: The Swiss cheese model. *Journal of Experimental Social Psychology, 92*, 104053.

Pailhès, A., & Kuhn, G. (2020a). Influencing choices with conversational primes: How a magic trick unconsciously influences card choices. *Proceedings of the National Academy of Sciences, 117*(30), 17675–17679.

Pailhès, A., & Kuhn, G. (2020b). The apparent action causation: Using a magician forcing technique to investigate our illusory sense of agency over the outcome of our choices. *Quarterly Journal of Experimental Psychology, 73*(11), 1784–1795.

Pailhès, A., & Kuhn, G. (2021a). Mind control tricks: Magicians' forcing and free will. *Trends in Cognitive Sciences, 25*(5), 338–341.

Pailhès, A., & Kuhn, G. (2021b). Reply to Cole: Magic and deception—do magicians mislead science? *Proceedings of the National Academy of Sciences, 118*(3), e2022099118.

Pailhès, A., & Kuhn, G. (2023). Don't read this paper! Reverse psychology in a magician forcing technique. *Journal of Performance Magic, 7*(1). doi: https://doi.org/10.5920/jpm.1264.

Pailhès, A., Kumari, S., & Kuhn, G. (2020). The magician's choice: Providing illusory choice and sense of agency with the Equivoque forcing technique. *Journal of Experimental Psychology: General, 150*(7), 1358–1372.

Pailhès, A., Rensink, R. A., & Kuhn, G. (2020). A psychologically based taxonomy of magicians' forcing techniques. *Consciousness and Cognition, 86*, 103038.

Rensink, R. A., & Kuhn, G. (2015). A framework for using magic to study the mind. *Frontiers in Psychology, 5*, 1508.

Thibault, R. T., Veissière, S., Olson, J. A., & Raz, A. (2018). Treating ADHD with suggestion: Neurofeedback and placebo therapeutics. *Journal of Attention Disorders, 22*(8), 707–711.

Van den Bussche, E., Van den Noortgate, W., & Reynvoet, B. (2009). Mechanisms of masked priming: A meta-analysis. *Psychological Bulletin, 135*(3), 452.

Walsh, E., Mehta, M. A., Oakley, D. A., Guilmette, D. N., Gabay, A., Halligan, P. W., & Deeley, Q. (2014). Using suggestion to model different types of automatic writing. *Consciousness and Cognition, 26*, 24–36.

Walsh, E., Oakley, D. A., Halligan, P. W., Mehta, M. A., & Deeley, Q. (2015). The functional anatomy and connectivity of thought insertion and alien control of movement. *Cortex, 64*, 380–393.

14

Generalized Internal Model of Mental Representations

Thought Insertion, Mental Agency, and the Cerebellum

Kentaro Hiromitsu and Tomohisa Asai

14.1. The Generalized Internal Model Principle

Modern researchers in some areas should be familiar with the concept of 'model' or 'control'. For such researchers, it is natural that humans have so-called *systems* and can *regulate* anything if that representation has been learned as the model. Although this innovative notion remains controversial (e.g., Morasso et al., 2015), the good regulator theorem is powerful and practical in many cases (Conant & Ashby, 1970). A typical example is motor control, where our brain controls our own body. The learned representation (the relationship between the motor outflow and the sensory inflow) is called the internal model, which further includes coupled submodules (i.e., the inverse and forward models for each representation; see Haruno et al., 2001).

For learning, the models require prediction errors (Miall & Wolpert, 1996). That error (the distance between the output of the model and the actual outcome) could update the parameters in a model such that the desired goal state would be achieved in a trial-and-error manner (presumably, in a simple energy-minimization principle such as the free energy theory; Apps & Tsakiris, 2014). We can easily imagine that once learned (e.g., riding my bicycle), these parameters are largely effective in a similar situation (e.g., riding a friend's bicycle). However, it is not possible to return to the state before learning to ride a bicycle. These inverse and forward prediction errors in any representation might be understandable in Bayesian subjective probability as the common frame (Asai et al., 2019). Therefore, the internal model now emerges as a bidirectional function between the self and the world. We may call this the 'generalized' internal model principle.

The cerebellum is thought to be responsible for the internal model in a narrow sense (Wolpert et al., 1998), while the cerebral cortex is more oriented toward the actual input and output as a 'sensorium' (i.e., sensory space) where the 'wiring' could be dense and complicated in order to make an arbitrary correspondence to the external situation. For this purpose, the cerebellum only maintains the reduced dimensional space of the actual sensorium as the model or function. The simple structure of the cerebellum serves as an anatomical dimension-reducer that may mediate hierarchical prediction errors between the self and the world (Teufel & Fletcher, 2020) (Fig. 14.1). If the internal model, embedded within the cerebellum, is generalized in order to communicate between the self and the world as the gateway (i.e., wrapper function since the 'language' should be different), we may believe that mental activity such as thought has its own internal model, where an abstract object is being controlled in a multidimensional space, even without visible output such as motor control (Jones & Fernyhough, 2007).

Indeed, Ito generalized the internal model principle for any other higher mental representations (Ito, 2008). In a sense, all of our physical or mental activities are summarized as controlling something practical or abstract in a multidimensional space. As a result, we may feel like controlling many things with subjective experiences such as 'I am controlling the object or outcome' or

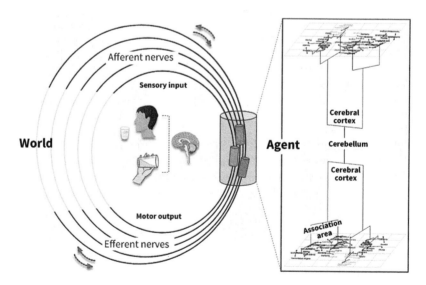

Figure 14.1 Illustrative summary of the current chapter.
Humans as an agent have a vitally 'closed system' with the world. Our brain is only one of the convergent points of this bidirectional flow, wherein the cerebellum may be a further converging region of the cerebral cortex as a 'sensorium'.

'I have the power to affect the world'. This so-called *sense of agency* has been empirically examined in various settings (e.g., general motor behaviours, button press and its reaction, virtual bodily movement, phantom-limb movement, speech production and inner speech, and associative thought or memory) (Asai, 2015, 2016a; Imaizumi et al., 2014; Sugimori et al., 2011, 2013) and suggests 'agency over anything' if we can minimize the prediction error in that representation. With regard to *thought* specifically, even the average person has illusional agency (sometimes fabulation in choice blindness) and behaves as a fortune teller in a specific situation (Bear et al., 2017; Bear & Bloom, 2016). Accordingly, the aim of this chapter is to suggest that *thought insertion* is a form of learning disorder, which should entail an atypical agency experience in terms of the generalized internal model principle.

14.2. Aberrant Agency

The agency theory was originally developed as the self-monitoring theory and was introduced to explain schizophrenic symptoms (Gallagher, 2004), particularly Schnider's first-rank disorders or simply positive symptoms including delusions and hallucinations (Frith, 2005). The initial notion was that we have a 'surveillance system' over our own mental state, the disorder of which could reduce the sense of agency, for example 'this is not me (not my own action, voice, or thought)'. After this classical theory encountered the internal model principle in motor control, the *comparator model* was suggested for such a self-other attribution mechanism (Synofzik et al., 2013). Accordingly, schizophrenic positive symptomatology is called 'external misattribution' (e.g., Costafreda et al., 2017). On the contrary, healthy people exhibit 'self-serving bias' under the same empirical situations ('this should be me or mine') (Wetzel, 1982), which facilitates learning through errors by minimizing the *self-attributed* prediction error. Therefore, this error-assignment capability (e.g., continuous 'activation function' between self-other boundaries) is indeed essential for adaptive learning in general. That is, the *self-prior* is observed in a healthy adaptive population, while *non- or others-prior* might be observed in patients with schizophrenia, as discussed next.

If we take other-attributions whenever we detect part of the prediction error in our internal model, it would be difficult to update the model because the error is not of our doing. If we believe that this is not our body when the body is not moving exactly as we want, we do not want to move that body anymore because it belongs to someone else. This situation could be 'catalepsy', the clinical observation of no-will-to-act. In contrast to this reduced agency, enhanced agency is also observed in patients with schizophrenia, including expansive delusions. Although this superficially opposite attribution style for patients has been a point of discussion (Haggard et al., 2003), the non-prior account (we refer to this as a 'flattened slope') would entail the 'self is other, other is self' attribution under the blurry self-other boundary (Asai, 2016b). In this sense, patients may have a non-biased naïve view of the self and the world, while healthy people have a self-convenient prior for these elements (i.e., ecological adaptation).

However, another possibility has also been discussed. Namely, over/under self-attribution (enhanced/reduced association between the self and the world) is context-dependent; therefore, both are concomitant. In this regard, why a specific 'other' inserts into patients' minds is an important research question to be solved. Although some neurological disorders, such as Huntington's disease, involve involuntary movements, patients generally do not believe that those movements are caused by others, but that this is not their own willed action. Thus, the reduced agency is not the same as external misattribution. The *others-prior* hypothesis can be further distinguished from the *non-prior* hypothesis. Patients with schizophrenia should have a context-dependent 'specific other' prior in this sense. For future studies, examining the schizophrenic 'mind perception' (Gray et al., 2011) of all nature (Hebart et al., 2020) is a practical approach for this purpose because patients with schizophrenia tend to perceive others in auditory or visual meaningless noises (e.g., Merckelbach & van de Ven, 2001, c.f., Powers et al., 2017).

Thus far, we have introduced two explanations that seem contrasting but could be concomitant for schizophrenic self-other/world discrimination: the boundary is *generally flattened* and is *locally steep* (Fig. 14.2). Therefore, patients' self-other representations are essentially weak, as many empirical studies have suggested, but they have specific illusory others in their minds. Their delusions/hallucinations are known to be environment-congruent (e.g., 'the KGB is spying on me' for Russian patients). At this stage it is still a speculative hypothesis, but it is suspected that the cerebellum is where the generalized internal model has been atypically learnt (Andreasen & Pierson, 2008). In the following section, the essential architecture of the cerebellum is introduced and we present our preliminary findings regarding the relationship between cerebellar lesions and aberrant agency (i.e., thought insertion), once aside from schizophrenia.

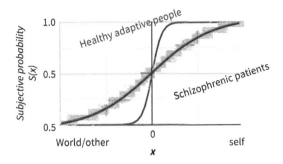

Figure 14.2 Schizophrenic aberrant agency.
The self-other boundary for patients with schizophrenia and healthy adaptive people is depicted as simple sigmoid curves. Patients' 'activation function' could be globally flattened but locally steep as it is unsmooth, and therefore less optimized.

14.3. Internal Models in the Cerebellum

14.3.1. The structure and function of the cerebellum

The cerebellum is located at the base of the human brain (Fig. 14.3A) and its volume accounts for approximately 10% of the total volume of the whole brain. Nevertheless, the cerebellum has 78% of the surface area of the cerebral cortex since the surface of the cerebellar cortex is much more tightly folded than the cerebral cortex (Sereno et al., 2020). The structure comprises a series of highly regular repeating units, each of which has the same microcircuit (Kandel et al., 2013). Of all of the cells in the cerebellum, Purkinje cells are thought to be the most functionally important because they provide the sole output for the cerebral cortex. They receive two major inputs: one from climbing fibres and one from parallel fibres. Climbing fibres originate from the inferior olive and send information to the Purkinje cells. This information processing is demonstrated to be related to motor learning (Nguyen-Vu et al., 2013). Parallel fibres relay sensory information from various pre-cerebellar nuclei. Information relayed to parallel fibres via climbing fibres is critical for associative learning in mice (ten Brinke et al., 2015). Thus, these two fibres are crucial and associated with function, particularly (motor) learning, which is based on the system of internal models.

According to the above-mentioned information processing in terms of motor learning, dysfunctions due to cerebellar damage result in a lack of

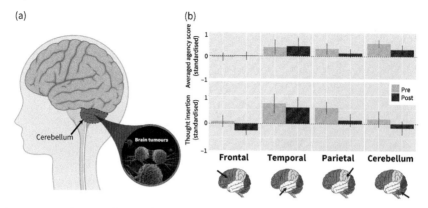

Figure 14.3 Schematic figure of a cerebellum with brain tumours and the results of the subjective ratings for the sense of agency and thought insertion before and after tumour resection in the brain tumour patients

A. Schematic figure of the cerebellum with brain tumours. B. The results of the Embodied Sense of Self Scale (ESSS; Asai et al., 2016) scores for the 'agency' subfactor (upper panel) and 'thought insertion' item (lower panel) before and after tumour resection. The horizontal axis indicates the brain regions affected by the tumours. The number of patients in each region was as follows: frontal, 34; temporal, 12; parietal, 29; and cerebellum, 22. The lesion areas are indicated by arrows. The vertical axis indicates the standardized scores for the agency subfactor and thought insertion item, which were calculated based on healthy age-matched controls. A higher score indicates an anomalous state. The dotted lines indicate the baseline (i.e., healthy controls) and error bars denote the standard error.

coordination and disruption of the accuracy of movement. Specifically, cerebellar damage induces a set of symptoms, including ataxia, posture disorders, gait disorders, hypotonia, limb coordination error, oculomotor deficits, etc. The set of symptoms reflect the dysfunctions of the cerebellum, involving disruption of the error detection of signals when an incoming stimulus from the environment does not match the prediction by the internal state. However, more complicated symptoms manifesting as cognitive and emotional deficits are reported in patients with cerebellar damage, suggesting that information processing within the cerebellum alone is not sufficient to explain such symptoms. Thus, we need to consider this from the perspective of the interaction between the cerebral cortices and the cerebellum.

14.3.2. Cerebro-cerebellar interactions: Is the cerebellum a mirror of the cerebral cortex?

Although researchers have long considered that the cerebellum is only involved in movement coordination, Schmahmann and Sherman first proposed the cerebellum's role in cognition and emotion as cerebellar cognitive affective syndrome (Schmahmann & Sherman, 1998). Starting with this publication, the relevance of higher brain function with the cerebellum has rapidly attracted academic interest. Clinical and neuroimaging studies support this view that the cerebellum is involved in cognition and emotion, such as linguistic, executive, visuo-spatial, and emotional control functions (Koziol et al., 2014). The association between the cerebellum and higher brain function has been explained by the interaction between the cerebellum and cerebral cortex. Specifically, anatomical and functional connectivity with the cerebral regions has been demonstrated in many studies. Anatomically, the cerebellum receives input from cortices via the pons and projects back to similar areas via the thalamus, forming a closed loop (Sokolov et al., 2017). The cerebellar output reaches the primary motor cortex and the premotor, prefrontal, and posterior parietal areas of the cerebral cortex (Bostan et al., 2013). In terms of functional connection, resting state functional magnetic resonance imaging (fMRI) revealed that the dentate nucleus of the cerebellum has temporal correlations with the frontal and parietal regions (Allen et al., 2005; Habas et al., 2009). At the network level, the cerebellum participates in the default mode, salience, and executive control networks (Habas et al., 2009). A meta-analysis of imaging studies reporting cerebellar activation demonstrated that language functions were right-lateralized and visuospatial functions were left-lateralized, indicating the mirroring of functional lateralization of the cerebellar hemispheres to some extent. The anatomo-functional consistency in terms of cerebello-cerebral interactions suggests that the cognitive and affective symptoms due to cerebellar damage can be regarded as a dysfunction in these connections.

Beyond the connections between the cerebellum and cerebral cortices, the cerebro-cerebellar interactions posit a hypothesis that the cerebellum is a mirror of the cerebral cortex. One potential reason for the similar anatomical and functional architecture between the cerebellum and the cerebrum is that the cerebellum is the alternative organ of the cerebrum. For example, individuals with hydranencephaly, in which the cerebral cortex is destroyed *in utero* but the cerebellum appears to be normal, exhibit a full range of instinctual emotions (Solms, 2013). Moreover, the volume of the cerebellar regions connected to the prefrontal cortex is larger in humans than in other species (Balsters et al., 2010), implying that evolutionary expansion of cerebellar regions may have contributed to the evolution of higher cognitive functions in humans. Ito also claims that the cerebellum contributes to the control of mental activities, such as thought, based on the concept of internal models in the cerebellum, which was demonstrated by a series of studies started in the 1990s (Ito, 2008). In the next section, we explore the functions of the cerebellum more deeply by focusing on the internal models from the notion that the cerebellum is a mirror of the cerebellar cortex.

14.3.3. Internal models in the cerebellum

The internal model is the term developed for motor control (Wolpert et al., 1995). When we move our own arm, the movements are supported by neural mechanisms that can calculate the motor commands necessary for realizing intended motions and predict sensorimotor feedback from the motor commands before the movements are executed. Reducing the mismatch between the prediction and actual feedback allows us to move our own body rapidly and smoothly. This model is considered to be realized in neural processes and is called the internal model; neuroimaging research has evidenced the existence of this internal model (Imamizu et al., 2000). In this research, two types of cerebellar activity were observed when participants learned how to use a novel tool (i.e., a computer mouse with a rotated cursor position). One was decreasing activity in which the intensity was correlated with the size of the error made by the participants. The other was increasing activity in which the intensity reflected the acquired internal model because it remained after learning. These results indicate that the cerebellum acquires internal models of objects in the external world (i.e., tools). A subsequent study showed that prefrontal and parietal areas are involved in the predictive and postdictive switching of internal models, suggesting that the prediction of outcomes from the motor commands due to internal models plays a crucial role in the postdictive switching of internal models in order to minimize the mismatch between the prediction and outcomes by comparing the internal models (Imamizu et al., 2004). The internal models are considered to be updated and switched by the cerebral cortices, allowing us to act automatically in daily life. Moreover, a recent study suggested that information regarding reward in the cerebellum is related to sensorimotor learning (Kostadinov et al., 2019). The climbing fibres of the cerebellar cortex were found to modulate their activity in response to the reward, and this modulation was stronger when the reward was surprising or unexpected. This implies that the internal models in the cerebellum may contribute to our higher function, such as reward, to minimize the prediction errors and to maximize the utility of our action.

Based on the conceptual framework and neuroscience research, we can apply the internal models from motor learning to cognitive functions. Ito postulated the hypothesis on thoughts as an analogy to the motor learning that occurs when the prefrontal cortex acts as the controller manipulating an idea from the temporoparietal cortex as a controlled object (Ito, 2008; Koziol et al., 2014). This hypothesis is consistent with previous research demonstrating the switching role of cortical regions (i.e., the frontal and parietal lobes) in the internal models in the cerebellum (Imamizu et al., 2004). The importance of this hypothesis is that the autonomy of our thoughts can be explained by internal models. Once the internal models regarding thoughts are represented in the cerebellum, we can proceed without awareness, with 'intuition'. Thus, the extension of the internal models to higher cognitive functions, such as thinking, leads to the understanding of the mechanisms of clinical symptoms in people with psychiatric diseases (e.g., schizophrenia) or brain damage. In the following section, we focus on patients with brain damage exhibiting an anomalous sense of self, including thoughts inserted from the point of view of internal models.

14.4. Internal Models for Thought: Sense of Agency Over Metal Representation

A person with cerebellar damage exhibits numerous symptoms regarding movement, as described earlier. Such deficits can be explained by the disruption of the error detection of signals when an incoming stimulus from the environment does not match the prediction by the internal models. This mismatch between the prediction and the actual feedback is known to modulate the feeling of causing one's own actions, or of being an agent, which is called *a sense of agency* and is one of the elements of the sense of self (Gallagher, 2000). If there is almost no mismatch in the internal model, we attribute our own action to the self. In contrast, if there is a mismatch, we attribute our own actions to the non-self (e.g., others). Accordingly, we can be an agent of our own actions and the internal models underpin our senses of self. Although the mechanisms generating the sense of agency are based on implicit processes such as internal models, and this implicit level can be measured by objective indices (e.g., intentional binding paradigm), we cannot determine whether it actually exists until we reflect it. For example, when we press a button and a light turns on, we interpret the outcome (i.e., a shining light) as being caused by our own action (i.e., pressing a button). In this situation, although a sense of causality for the outcome may be automatic (or so-called *pre-reflective*), we need to be consciously aware of who the agent of the action is in order to recognize the causality. That is, not until we are consciously aware of this sense of causality, do we recognize the causal effect of our own action on an outcome. In this regard, the sense of agency has a dimension of subjectivity, and this dimension is often called the judgement of agency (Synofzik et al., 2008).

The subjective aspects of the sense of agency, which is measured by the self-administered questionnaire (Asai et al., 2016), were disrupted in patients with brain tumours (Hiromitsu et al., 2018). After curative tumour resection, the sense of agency in the patients with left hemispheric lesions recovered to the level of healthy individuals, suggesting that brain lesions are associated with an anomalous sense of agency. However, we did not investigate the role of specific brain regions in the sense of agency. Previous research has suggested that the sense of agency can be attributed to specific regions in the brain, such as certain frontal areas, the insula, the posterior parietal areas, and the cerebellum (David et al., 2008). In terms of the relationship between the brain regions associated with the sense of agency and the internal models, there is a possibility that patients with cerebellar damage experience disruption of the sense of agency. We examined the influence of cerebellar brain tumours (Fig. 14.3A) on the subjective aspect of the sense of agency which might be represented in the cerebellum for healthy individuals (Kanayama et al., 2017). The results indicated that patients with cerebellar tumours achieved lower scores for the sense of agency (a subfactor of the Embodied Sense of Self Scale (ESSS); Asai et al., 2016) after surgery (Fig. 14.3B). Interestingly, the score for a specific item in the ESSS relating to thought insertion (i.e., '*No matter how hard I concentrate, unrelated thoughts intrude upon my thinking*') was lower after surgery in patients with cerebellar tumours (Fig. 14.3B). Moreover, the same tendency was observed in patients with frontal and parietal lobe tumours. The results support the hypothesis that not only the sense of agency, but also the thought can be interpreted with the internal models in the cerebellum and its association cortices (i.e., the frontal and parietal cortices). The abstract aspect of our psychological functions, such as thought, can be interpreted from the perspective of the internal models in relation to the function of the cerebellum and related areas in the cerebrum.

As we explored the roles of various brain areas in the sense of agency, including thought insertion, the internal models may play a crucial role in thought insertion. As Ito described, it is possible to apply the internal models from motor learning to cognitive functions (i.e., generalized internal models). It has been proposed that some hierarchical models of the sense of agency can be applied not only to movements, but also to thoughts (Synofzik et al., 2008). Based on these claims, the crucial aspect of thoughts in terms of the internal models is autonomy. As mentioned earlier, once the internal models regarding thoughts are represented in the cerebellum, they allow us to proceed with thoughts without awareness and with intuition. If this is the case, we can explain the manifestation of thought insertion in patients with psychiatric diseases such as schizophrenia in terms of the internal models. Indeed, patients with cerebellar tumours reported a sensation of thought insertion before surgery, but such sensation did not persist after surgery. We can interpret the results as a disorder of learning via an internal model. It is possible that the cerebellar lesions induce a loss of the sensation of control over the thought, which is automatically obtained via the internal model. This view supports the notion of 'agency over anything' as a generalized internal model.

Acknowledgement

This work was supported by JSPS KAKENHI Grant Numbers 20J00669 to KH, and 19H01777 and 20H04094 to TA.

References

Allen, G., McColl, R., Barnard, H., Ringe, W. K., Fleckenstein, J., & Cullum, C. M. (2005). Magnetic resonance imaging of cerebellar-prefrontal and cerebellar-parietal functional connectivity. *NeuroImage, 28*(1), 39–48.
Andreasen, N. C., & Pierson, R. (2008). The role of the cerebellum in schizophrenia. *Biological Psychiatry, 617*(2), 156–159.
Apps, M. A. J. J., & Tsakiris, M. (2014). The free-energy self: A predictive coding account of self-recognition. *Neuroscience and Biobehavioral Reviews, 41*, 85–97.
Asai, T. (2015). Feedback control of one's own action: Self-other sensory attribution in motor control. *Consciousness and Cognition, 38*, 118–129.
Asai, T. (2016a). Agency elicits body-ownership: Proprioceptive drift toward a synchronously acting external proxy. *Experimental Brain Research, 234*(5), 1163–1174.
Asai, T. (2016b). Self is 'other', other is 'self': Poor self-other discriminability explains schizotypal twisted agency judgment. *Psychiatry Research, 246*, 593–600.
Asai, T., Imaizumi, S., & Imamizu, H. (2019). The self as a generative, teleological, and subjective prior: Mutually-modulated temporal agency. *bioRxiv*, 519934.

Asai, T., Kanayama, N., Imaizumi, S., Koyama, S., & Kaganoi, S. (2016). Development of embodied sense of self scale (ESSS): Exploring everyday experiences induced by anomalous self-representation. *Frontiers in Psychology, 7*, 1005.

Balsters, J. H., Cussans, E., Diedrichsen, J., Phillips, K. A., Preuss, T. M., Rilling, J. K., et al. (2010). Evolution of the cerebellar cortex: The selective expansion of prefrontal-projecting cerebellar lobules. *NeuroImage, 49*(3), 2045–2052.

Bear, A., & Bloom, P. (2016). A simple task uncovers a postdictive illusion of choice. *Psychological Science, 27*(6), 914–922.

Bear, A., Fortgang, R. G., Bronstein, M. V., & Cannon, T. D. (2017). Mistiming of thought and perception predicts delusionality. *Proceedings of the National Academy of Sciences of the United States of America, 114*(40), 10791–10796.

Bostan, A. C., Dum, R. P., & Strick, P. L. (2013). Cerebellar networks with the cerebral cortex and basal ganglia. *Trends in Cognitive Sciences, 17*(5), 241–254.

Conant, R. C., & Ross Ashby, W. (1970). Every good regulator of a system must be a model of that system. *International Journal of Systems Science, 1*(2), 89–97.

Costafreda, S. G. G., Brébion, G., Allen, P., Mcguire, P. K. K., Fu, C. H. Y. H. Y., Costafreda, S. G. G., et al. (2017). Affective modulation of external misattribution bias in source monitoring in schizophrenia. *Psychological Medicine, 38*(2008), 821–824.

David, N., Newen, A., & Vogeley, K. (2008). The 'sense of agency' and its underlying cognitive and neural mechanisms. *Consciousness and Cognition, 17*(2), 523–534.

Frith, C. (2005). The neural basis of hallucinations and delusions. *Comptes Rendus—Biologies, 328*(2), 169–175.

Gallagher, S. (2000). Philosophical conceptions of the self: Implications for cognitive science. *Trends in Cognitive Sciences, 4*(1), 14–21.

Gallagher, S. (2004). Neurocognitive models of schizophrenia: A neurophenomenological critique. *Psychopathology, 37*(1), 8–19.

Gray, K., Jenkins, A. C., Heberlein, A. S., & Wegner, D. M. (2011). Distortions of mind perception in psychopathology. *Proceedings of the National Academy of Sciences of the United States of America, 108*(2), 477–479.

Habas, C., Kamdar, N., Nguyen, D., Prater, K., Beckmann, C. F., Menon, V., et al. (2009). Distinct cerebellar contributions to intrinsic connectivity networks. *The Journal of Neuroscience: The Official Journal of the Society for Neuroscience, 29*(26), 8586–8594.

Haggard, P., Martin, F., Taylor-Clarke, M., Jeannerod, M., & Franck, N. (2003). Awareness of action in schizophrenia. *Neuroreport, 14*(7), 1081–1085.

Haruno, M., Wolpert, D. M., & Kawato, M. (2001). Mosaic model for sensorimotor learning and control. *Neural Computation, 13*(10), 2201–2220.

Hebart, M. N., Zheng, C. Y., Pereira, F., & Baker, C. I. (2020). Revealing the multidimensional mental representations of natural objects underlying human similarity judgements. *Nature Human Behaviour, 4*(11), 1173–1185.

Hiromitsu, K., Asai, T., Saito, S., Shigemune, Y., Hamamoto, K., Shinoura, N., et al. (2018). Measuring the sense of self in brain-damaged patients: A STROBE-compliant article. *Medicine, 97*(36), e12156.

Imaizumi, S., Asai, T., Kanayama, N., Kawamura, M., & Koyama, S. (2014). Agency over a phantom limb and electromyographic activity on the stump depend on visuomotor synchrony: A case study. *Frontiers in Human Neuroscience, 8*(July), 545.

Imamizu, H., Kuroda, T., Yoshioka, T., & Kawato, M. (2004). Functional magnetic resonance imaging examination of two modular architectures for switching multiple internal models. *The Journal of Neuroscience: The Official Journal of the Society for Neuroscience, 24*(5), 1173–1181.

Imamizu, H., Miyauchi, S., Tamada, T., Sasaki, Y., Takino, R., Pütz, B., et al. (2000). Human cerebellar activity reflecting an acquired internal model of a new tool. *Nature, 403*(6766), 192–195.

Ito, M. (2008). Control of mental activities by internal models in the cerebellum. *Nature Reviews. Neuroscience, 9*(4), 304–313.

Jones, S. R., & Fernyhough, C. (2007). Thought as action: Inner speech, self-monitoring, and auditory verbal hallucinations. *Consciousness and Cognition, 16*(2), 391–399.

Kanayama, N., Asai, T., Nakao, T., Makita, K., Kozuma, R., Uyama, T., Yamane, T., Kadota, H., & Yamawaki, S. (2017). Subjectivity of the anomalous sense of self is represented in gray matter volume in the brain. *Frontiers in Human Neuroscience, 11*, 232.

Kandel, E. R., Schwartz, J. H., Jessell, T. M., Siegelbaum, S., & Hudspeth, A. J. (2013). *Principles of Neural Science* (5th ed.). New York: McGraw-Hill.

Kostadinov, D., Beau, M., Blanco-Pozo, M., & Häusser, M. (2019). Predictive and reactive reward signals conveyed by climbing fiber inputs to cerebellar Purkinje cells. *Nature Neuroscience, 22*(6), 950–962.

Koziol, L. F., Budding, D., Andreasen, N., D'Arrigo, S., Bulgheroni, S., Imamizu, H., et al. (2014). Consensus paper: The cerebellum's role in movement and cognition. *Cerebellum, 13*(1), 151–177.

Merckelbach, H., & van de Ven, V. (2001). Another white Christmas: Fantasy proneness and reports of 'hallucinatory experiences' in undergraduate students. *Journal of Behavior Therapy and Experimental Psychiatry, 32*(3), 137–144.

Miall, R. C., & Wolpert, D. M. (1996). Forward models for physiological motor control. *Neural Networks: The Official Journal of the International Neural Network Society, 9*(8), 1265–1279.

Morasso, P., Casadio, M., Mohan, V., Rea, F., & Zenzeri, J. (2015). Revisiting the body-schema concept in the context of whole-body postural-focal dynamics. *Frontiers in Human Neuroscience, 9*, 83.

Nguyen-Vu, T. D. B., Kimpo, R. R., Rinaldi, J. M., Kohli, A., Zeng, H., Deisseroth, K., et al. (2013). Cerebellar Purkinje cell activity drives motor learning. *Nature Neuroscience, 16*(12), 1734–1736.

Powers, A. R., Mathys, C., & Corlett, P. R. (2017). Pavlovian conditioning-induced hallucinations result from overweighting of perceptual priors. *Science, 357*(6351), 596–600.

Schmahmann, J. D., & Sherman, J. C. (1998). The cerebellar cognitive affective syndrome. *Brain: A Journal of Neurology, 121*(Pt 4), 561–579.

Sereno, M. I., Diedrichsen, J., Tachrount, M., Testa-Silva, G., d'Arceuil, H., & De Zeeuw, C. (2020). The human cerebellum has almost 80% of the surface area of the neocortex. *Proceedings of the National Academy of Sciences of the United States of America, 117*(32), 19538–19543.

Sokolov, A. A., Miall, R. C., & Ivry, R. B. (2017). The cerebellum: Adaptive prediction for movement and cognition. *Trends in Cognitive Sciences, 21*(5), 313–332.

Solms, M. (2013). The conscious id. *Neuropsychoanalysis, 15*(1), 5–19.

Sugimori, E., Asai, T., & Tanno, Y. (2011). Sense of agency over thought: External misattribution of thought in a memory task and proneness to auditory hallucination. *Consciousness and Cognition, 20*(3), 688–695.

Sugimori, E., Asai, T., & Tanno, Y. (2013). The potential link between sense of agency and output monitoring over speech. *Consciousness and Cognition, 22*(1), 360–374.

Synofzik, M., Vosgerau, G., & Newen, A. (2008). Beyond the comparator model: A multifactorial two-step account of agency. *Consciousness and Cognition, 17*(1), 219–239.

Synofzik, M., Vosgerau, G., & Voss, M. (2013). The experience of agency: An interplay between prediction and postdiction. *Frontiers in Psychology, 4*, 1–8.

ten Brinke, M. M., Boele, H. -J., Spanke, J. K., Potters, J. -W., Kornysheva, K., Wulff, P., et al. (2015). Evolving models of Pavlovian conditioning: Cerebellar cortical dynamics in awake behaving mice. *Cell Reports, 13*(9), 1977–1988.

Teufel, C., & Fletcher, P. C. (2020). Forms of prediction in the nervous system. *Nature Reviews Neuroscience, 21*(4), 231–242.

Wetzel, C. G. (1982). Self-serving biases in attribution: A Bayesian analysis. *Journal of Personality and Social Psychology, 43*(2), 197–209.

Wolpert, D. M., Ghahramani, Z., & Jordan, M. I. (1995). An internal model for sensorimotor integration. *Science, 269*(5232), 1880–1882.

Wolpert, D. M., Miall, R. C., & Kawato, M. (1998). Internal models in the cerebellum. *Trends in Cognitive Sciences, 2*(9), 338–347.

15

Metacognitive Treatment in Patients with Thought Insertion

Susana Ochoa and Helena García-Mieres

15.1. What is Metacognition?

Metacognition is cognition about cognition, thinking about thinking. It involves two major components: monitoring, the capacity of observing one's own cognitive processes, and control, the ability to modify these cognitive processes (Flavell, 1979; Nelson & Narens, 1990). Many of the symptoms of schizophrenia suggest malfunctions of metacognition. Particularly, thought insertion ('thoughts are put into my mind') and delusions of control, involves a failure in the process of metacognition, when thinking about cognitive processes. Thought insertion can be the result of an impairment in self-monitoring of one's own cognitive processes and disruption of integrative functions of cognition. If integrative functions are disrupted, there is a failure to incorporate prior outputs from a different cognitive task and integrate them into a novel cognitive schema. Therefore, the patient would experience this unintegrated novel cognitive schema as not belonging to his/her consciousness (Patniyot, 2021). Thus, the patients would feel that their thoughts, and, as a consequence, their actions, are no longer under their own control (Farrer & Franck, 2007). This metacognitive process is necessarily explicit, as it involves creating experiential units, that is, conscious of what oneself is thinking.

Although our ability to introspect is limited, we as humans like to reflect upon our experiences and actions, and to discuss these reflections with other people. By these discussions, we develop explicit accounts of the world and ourselves, and our experiences can be altered (Frith, 2012b). This basic principle enables the viability of metacognitive-based therapy to treat thought insertion. In this sense, patients with psychosis lack insight and experience difficulties in describing their experiences to others, and their beliefs and experiences are less influenced by what others say. This has important implications for social functioning, as reaching consensus with others is a basic component of our social world. Finally, thought insertion reflects a dysfunction of the metacognition process about reflection of states of the self ('these are not my thoughts') (Frith, 2012a).

In this chapter we will present two metacognitive approaches for the treatment of thought insertion. The first is Metacognitive Training developed by Steffen Moritz and Todd Woodward (Moritz & Woodward, 2007a, b). The second is Metacognitive Reflection and Insight Therapy (MERIT), developed by the team of Paul Lysaker (Indianapolis, United States) (Lysaker & Klion, 2017). Each section contains the following main components: the definition of metacognition and the description of the therapeutic approach, the conceptualization of thought insertion within this approach, a brief review of studies showing efficacy of this therapy in the treatment of psychosis and metacognitive-related processes, and a presentation of therapeutic tools to use in treatment with a patient suffering thought insertion, accompanied by a clinical case.

15.2. Metacognitive Training for Treating Thought Insertion

15.2.1. Metacognitive Training (MCT)

The metacognitive concept underlying Metacognitive Training (MCT) is based on the improvement of awareness of cognitive biases more prevalent in people with psychosis. The main aim is to increase knowledge and detection of these biases, and increase insight and self—awareness of them in order to modify and to change the interpretation of situations in daily life. Being aware of these biases could act as prophylaxis for a new psychotic episode by the attenuation of positive symptoms of psychosis, especially delusions. The final purpose is to change the 'cognitive infrastructure' of delusional ideation, including thought insertion delusion.

MCT for psychosis is a low-threshold approach based on a cognitive behavioural intervention combined with psychoeducation. The intervention is based on a normalizing approach in which those cognitive biases more frequent in people with psychosis are discussed in an illustrative and entertained way. There are two formats of MCT: in group (MCT) or individual (MCT+). MCT consists of 8 therapeutic units and 2 complementary sessions developed during weekly or bi-weekly sessions lasting between 45 and 60 minutes. The material available for the MCT programme is made up of power-point presentations. Each unit contains abundant therapeutic material that includes psychoeducational information, exercises, case examples, demonstrations and worksheets. Seven of the therapeutic units address cognitive deviations and errors that are frequently seen in problem-solving in schizophrenia, involved in the formation and maintenance of delusions (Moritz & Woodward, 2007a; Moritz & Woodward, 2007b; Freeman, 2007). These sessions work on attributional style, jumping to conclusions (JTC), bias against disconfirmatory evidence (BADE), overconfidence in memory errors, emotional recognition, Theory of Mind (ToM), and depression. Recently, two complementary sessions covering self-esteem and self-stigma have been added, although it is recommended that they be included in the treatment.

The MCT + treatment includes ten therapeutic sessions in which cognitive biases are similarly addressed but in an individual context. The first two sessions focus on explaining the concept of metacognition and the evaluation of the patient's clinical history in order to mark the objectives of the intervention. The third session works with the illness model, during which the aims are to identify vulnerability, triggers and aggravating and protective factors. The following sessions cover cognitive biases, such as those related to attributional style, memory biases, JTC, and BADE. The final sessions are addressed towards working on self-esteem and the prevention of relapses.

The MCT therapy is freely available in 37 languages (www.uke.de/mct) and versions of the program have been developed for other disorders (depression, borderline personality, obsessive-compulsive disorders, among others). MCT is addressed towards people with schizophrenia or schizophrenia spectrum disorders, however it can also be applied to patients with other diagnoses who have displayed positive symptoms (delusions, ideas of reference, though insertion). Only those patients who show inappropriate behaviour are recommended to be excluded from the group intervention.

15.2.2. Studies about the effectiveness of MCT

MCT has been demonstrated to be a successful psychological intervention to reduce positive symptoms, especially delusions. Moreover, MCT is effective in improving cognitive insight and other cognitive biases, cognitive functioning, self-esteem and quality of life in schizophrenia (Moritz & Woodward, 2007a, b; Moritz et al., 2011; Moritz et al., 2013; Moritz et al., 2014; Briki et al., 2014; Andreou et al., 2017). One of the most relevant studies described a latent effect of MCT (Moritz et al., 2014), finding that the effects in reduction of symptoms remain over 3 years after the treatment. Additionally, MCT therapy has a high level of tolerability, being described by patients as more enjoyable than other therapies as well as useful for daily life (S. Moritz et al., 2011).

Only two studies have explored the moderators' variables of MCT. The first, by Moritz et al., 2018, found that people with severe symptoms, higher levels of anxiety, and low self-esteem and quality of life are more able to improve with MCT. The second, by Leanza et al., 2020, based on MCT+, found that the patients with low self-esteem and JTC bias are those who benefit more.

Several meta-analyses have demonstrated the benefits of MCT over symptoms, especially positive symptoms, in schizophrenia spectrum disorders (Eichner & Berna, 2016; Jiang et al., 2015; Liu et al., 2018; Philipp et al., 2019). Similarly, the meta-analyses performed by Lopez-Morinigo et al., 2020 found that MCT is a good psycho-therapeutical approach to improving cognitive insight in people with psychosis. These results are of great interest considering that cognitive insight is a core variable in the metacognition process, allowing the improvement of self-reflectiveness (recognizing and accepting one's own failures) and the reduction of self-certainty (overconfidence in one's own judgements and attributions) (Beck et al., 2004).

Recently, our research group has led a study to demonstrate the effectiveness of MCT in people with first-episode psychosis. Our results show that MCT improves cognitive insight, psychotic symptoms, social cognition, and irrational beliefs [removed for review]. In addition, we found positive results on the improvement of cognitive insight starting from the third session of MCT (Birulés et al., 2020). Interestingly, we have also found that women benefit more from MCT than from the psychoeducational approach than men, in terms of general symptoms, cognitive insight and social cognition, which suggests that MCT is a gender-sensitive intervention (Salas-Sender et al., 2020).

In summary, the main results of MCT outlined here found that this intervention is effective for the treatment of positive symptoms and for improving cognitive insight. We can therefore consider MCT as an attractive option for the treatment of patients with thought insertion delusion.

15.2.3. The treatment of thought insertion using MCT

As Ratcliffe and Wilkinson (2015) suggest, thought insertion involves an error of identification, that is, the patient is aware of the thought but fails to recognize it as their own. In this sense, the thought insertion disorder is related to metacognition, given that it involves thinking about one's own thoughts.

MCT is addressed towards improving self-reflectiveness about processes of thoughts, and to sow doubt in the patient about their non-adaptative beliefs related to cognitive biases. Thought insertion is a kind of delusion related directly to metacognition of one's own thoughts, where patients feel that their thoughts are implemented by others or by outside forces.

As noted above, MCT can be delivered in group or individual format. While MCT + allows us to better adapt the intervention to the specific problems lived by the patient, MCT in a group format can be of great help, in particular for the treatment of thought insertion and its consequences, because of the effect on the group. A range of approaches should always be considered in the use of MCT for people with thought insertions. We should avoid intellectual activism, our interest is not centred in changing patients' delusions, refuting their ideas with intellectual reasoning. In MCT we expect that the patient could be able to think about their thoughts and modify their beliefs about them. From our intervention we should only plant the seed of doubt about the possibility of recognizing these thoughts as their own, as previously noted.

Similarly, thought insertion disorder can be a part of the patient's identity that they prefer to not recognize as their own, because this could affect their self-esteem. We should help to increase the self-esteem of patients, and to be aware of their identity apart from their psychotic symptoms. It is therefore important to work with their strengths and resiliency factors, as this can improve their self-esteem and help them to build a better identity of themselves.

MCT works with the idea of normalization, as cognitive biases included in therapeutic sessions are present in the general population too. Indeed, this is an important point to raise about thought insertion, that in some cases all of us may perceive particular thoughts as not being our own. An example of this could be when you experience the idea of jump when you are on the border of a cliff. But crucially, the certainty with which an idea is held, and the repercussions of behaviour associated with this idea, determine the difference between pathological and not pathological. MCT tries to help patients using the idea of a continuum of these experiences. The important thing to remark is that when such experiences are not adaptive and patients suffer as a result, we should attempt to treat them. We are not interested in modifying thought insertions themselves; rather, we should help the patient to see the consequences of their behaviour related to them. For instance, a patient may think that their mother is inserting thoughts of 'you are worthless'. From the MCT perspective we could help the patient doubt this thought, by considering other options and perspectives, and most importantly, by helping them not react to in an extreme manner.

In MCT, as in other cognitive behavioural therapies, we can make use of reality. This technique can be used in order to help a patient test their beliefs.

The results could help the patient to re-evaluate the situation and the feelings associated with thought insertion. Socratic discussion could be of help also to modify internal conflicts associated with inserted thoughts. After a Socratic discussion, the patient could arrive at new conclusions about these thought insertions, generated jointly with the therapist. Finally, one of the most important messages of MCT is to be able to understand others and to put ourselves in their place. Sometimes the patient has a person (mother, father, friend, sibling) in whom they fully trust. The question: 'What do you think your sister thinks about this?' could help them to take some distance and modify their thought or behaviour associated to this inserted thought.

15.2.4. Clinical example: The case of Simone

Simone is a single Caucasian-American female in her late 50s with a long history of involvement in psychiatric services (Hamm & Leonhardt, 2016). At the time of referral to her therapist, Simone had been placed on court commitment to treatment, which for the last several years had consisted of requirements to follow prescribed pharmacological treatment, as well as placement in a residential facility. Per available clinical history, Simone had continuously experienced prominent delusions and hallucinations. For many years, Simone had demonstrated profound functional impairments. With prompting, she would come into the common areas for meals, but remained socially isolative. Simone refused to participate in community outings, citing beliefs about 'demons' that would destroy her if she stepped outside of the facility. She engaged minimally in activities of daily living such as personal hygiene, and then typically only reluctantly after repeated prompting by staff.

Knowledge of Simone's psychosocial history is sparse. For her part, Simone offered only a highly fragmented and impoverished personal narrative. She also has consistently endorsed a range of claims about her life associated with numerous delusional beliefs. She reported that she is hundreds of years old. She reported that she invented jokes, bread, and candy. In addition to these claims, Simone expressed several persecutory beliefs, including maintaining a range of claims about demons causing her harm and tenaciously endorsing the belief that staff members regularly poison her meals. She reported having maintained some factory work during a portion of her life, but her account of this tended to be so fragmented and intertwined with grandiose and persecutory claims that it is difficult to discern much of her work history. Her descriptions of her educational experiences are quite fragmented and clouded by delusions.

Case formulation: Simone showed a long history of tenaciously held delusions, daily hallucinations, and disorganized thought. There was a marked loss of the sense of personal agency, with Simone attributing almost every decision to the direction of supernatural beings that spoke to her. She was aware of having thoughts, but she stated that she did not have thoughts of her own. Summarizing, Simone not only appears to have experienced prolonged schizophrenia, but her degree of disability and her long history of reluctance to engage in treatment would likely be considered through conventional models of treatment as a poor candidate for psychotherapy, due to being 'treatment resistant'.

15.2.5. Treatment of Simone with MCT

Simone could be treated with the MCT in a group or with the MCT+. In both cases, the sessions could be addressed by working with the cognitive biases present in this case.

- The first session, based on attributional style, works with the causality of several events. Simone may feel that the cause of the thought insertions are demons or supernatural beings that are trying to implant their thoughts into her mind. Alternatively, she might be sure that an antenna in the building is transmitting thoughts to her. Crucially, the thought is attributed to others or to strange, supernormal situations, rather than to her personally. During the MCT therapy we would work on becoming aware of multiple causalities to events, and discuss several options and possibilities with different degrees of probability.
- Two sessions of the group MCT are based on JTC bias. Here we would help the patient identify those situations where she is not considering all the available information and makes hasty decisions without enough evidence. This part of the treatment serves to help the patient stop and think about a given situation, in order to delay or avoid non-adaptive behaviour related to a delusional thought. In the case of Simone, the aim would be for her to doubt the origin of delusional thoughts, and therefore stop inadequate behaviour.
- The third session is based on BADE. In this session we would talk about this bias, and how one sometimes clings to one's beliefs despite the fact that there is evidence to the contrary. In this session we would not work directly with the experience of the patient with demons or supernatural

beings. Rather we would study related situations, such as conspiracy theories. The idea would be to create doubt about Simone's experiences, by examining other situations in which the falsity of thoughts can clearly be identified.

Another bias that should be worked on is overconfidence in memory, using examples that demonstrate that memory is fallible and subject to false memories. Because Simone may have the belief that all of her memories related to her symptoms are certain, our goal would be to sow the seeds of doubt regarding the events in the past that may be related to her thought insertion symptoms.

- Two sessions are addressed to improving the patient's understanding of their own emotions, and of the minds and feelings of others (emotional recognition and ToM). Working with emotions could help the patient understand their own emotions better and to regulate their behaviour when certain emotions arise. Understanding that others may act in a particular way for multiple reasons could reduce the JTC bias. Likewise, it could help Simone decrease attributions of events to others.
- Three sessions (one and two complementary) focus on depression, self-esteem and self-stigma. The work on emotions and self-esteem is essential as the patient's identity may be based on her delusions, raising the possibility that she might not accept thoughts contrary to these delusions as this would be contrary to her idea of self. Therefore, if we can help the patient identify her strengths, she will be able to build her identity on this basis and consequently reduce the importance of her delusional thoughts.

In MCT+ another important part of the therapy is the prevention of relapses. While in the MCT group we work on prevention with the entire group, MCT+ allows us to directly address the individual problems of our patient.

15.3. The MERIT Approach for Treating Thought Insertion

The MERIT therapeutic approach uses metacognition as a global or 'umbrella' term (Semerari et al., 2003), that is, as an integrative or synthetic concept to describe the general ability of a person to form representations of their own, and of others', mental states. Metacognition then involves the abilities to create, revise, or rethink ideas about what is believed, felt, dreamt, imagined, and pretended by oneself and others. These abilities allow humans to make sense of our own dilemmas, to understand our own intentions and the intentions of others, and to finally adapt to our world (Semerari et al., 2003).

Metacognition can be divided into four components: Self-reflectivity, Understanding others' minds, Decentration, and Mastery. In the MERIT approach, these components are assessed by a clinician in the context of a narrative provided by the patient about their own life events and illness difficulties, by using the Metacognitive Assessment Scale Abbreviated (MAS-A, (Lysaker et al., 2005). This scale was adapted from the original Metacognitive Assessment Scale of Semerari (2003) for the particular context of people with psychosis. Detailed explanations of how to score metacognition using this scale are available in its manual (Lysaker, Buck, & Hamm, 2011).

In the following we present a description of the major components of metacognition:
- Self-reflectivity: the ability to identify and think about one's own thoughts, desires, emotions and feelings, their interrelationships, and their effect on one's own behaviour both in the present and over time.
- Understanding others' minds: the ability to identify and reflect on the thoughts, intentions, and feelings of other people, their interrelationships, and their influence on understanding the behaviour of others.
- Decentration: the ability to understand that one is not the centre of the world, that there are many different ways of understanding reality, and that facts can result from multiple and complex factors.
- Mastery: the ability to integrate intersubjective information on a wide range of psychological problems, and the ability to use this information to face, in an adaptive way, the psychological and social problems that the person encounters in their life.

15.3.1. Metacognition and thought insertion

Related to what was previously noted in the background of this chapter, the component of metacognition particularly relevant to thought insertion is the domain of self-reflectivity. The self-reflectivity scale is divided into nine hierarchical levels that represent more complex levels of this domain at each step. This ability reflects, on its lowest level, a capacity to identify thoughts as one's own, while subsequent levels evidence a growing capacity to understand complex personal narratives in which a complex set of intentions, thoughts and feelings interact. Table 15.1 shows a brief description of each level.

According to the levels described in Table 15.1, particular attention for thought insertion is required in the lower levels: S0, S1, S2, and S3:

- S0—This level reflects that the person is not aware that they are experiencing any mental activity, so the person does not explicitly know that he or she is having any thoughts or ideas. People at this level may be patients suffering from catatonia, or with an extremely disorganized language.
- S1—The person knows that he/she has ideas or experiences, but is not aware or certain that these are their own thoughts or experiences. Examples of persons who might be awarded this score are those experiencing thought insertion or who have a deeply impaired sense of personal boundaries such that they cannot distinguish internal from external stimuli. The description of experiencing thoughts that belong to a witch would be an example of functioning at this level.
- S2—This level suggests participants are experiencing themselves as having mental activities which are their own. Utterances such as 'I had a thought that …' 'I thought that I saw,' or 'one thing that occurred to me was …' would all suggest an experience of having mental activities that are one's own.
- S3—This level reflects that participants are able to recognize and distinguish a variety of different kinds of cognitive operations that they experience. Participants functioning at this level may notice different operations including thinking, planning, remembering, imagining, fantasizing, dreaming, desiring, deciding, foreseeing, and show some degree of awareness of how these are different from one another. Evidence of meeting this level can sometimes be found in utterances such as 'I hoped that …' 'I remembered that …' and 'I expected that …' In cases where participants mention only one or possibly even just two different cognitive operations, a half point might be most appropriate to award.

In sum, following this approach, a person experiencing thought insertion would have the lowest levels of self-reflectivity, being scored in the S1 level. Following the principles of MERIT (Lysaker & Klion, 2017), the psychological treatment will imply that the therapist will have to adapt his/her intervention to this level of self-reflectivity, and the therapist will need to use techniques that stimulate the metacognitive capacity of the patient in order to proceed to subsequent levels (S2, then S3, and next S4). We explain how to boost this metacognitive capacity in the next sections.

Table 15.1 Description of levels of self-reflectivity

S0	The person is not aware that they have mental states
S1	The person is conscious that they have mental states and that these thoughts are of representational nature
S2	The person knows that they are an autonomous being and that their thoughts are their own
S3	The person can name and distinguish between different mental operations (e.g., thinking, remembering, imagining, desiring, deciding, anticipating)
S4	The person can name, and distinguish between, different emotions (e.g., anger, sadness, happiness, grief, anxiety)
S5	The person can recognise that their ideas about themself are subjective and fallible, and have changed or may change over time
S6	The person can recognise that what they expect, think and wish may not match with what happens in reality
S7	The person can formulate a representation of themself within at least one narrative episode. This episode can be described and the person can describe the mental activities that happened and interrelated in that episode
S8	The person is able to recognize a psychological pattern over time, through connecting at least two narrative episodes, describing how the narrative episodes involve similar themes and relationships between different mental activities such as thoughts and feelings
S9	The person is able to recognize psychological patterns across their life, synthesizing multiple narrative episodes into a coherent and complex narrative which integrates different modes of cognitive and/or emotional functioning

15.3.2. Efficacy of MERIT on improving metacognition and symptomatology in psychosis

As MERIT is a therapy that was developed and manualized recently, studies proving its efficacy have emerged in the last few years. For the case of clinical trials, two randomized controlled trials, have demonstrated an acceptance rate for MERIT of more than 66% of patients with psychosis, with participation in MERIT also leading to metacognitive and clinical improvements (de Jong et al., 2019; Vohs et al., 2018). In another clinical trial, a version of MERIT that focused on social skills training (MOSST) showed that the group receiving MOSST had unique improvements in metacognitive capacity, in social functioning, and in disturbing behaviours (Inchausti et al., 2018). Similar rates of improvement and participation in treatment were also reported in an open trial of a 12-week version of MERIT (de Jong et al., 2016) and 1–2 years of metacognitively focused, individual psychotherapies offered to 11 persons with schizophrenia that followed the elements of MERIT. We note that a three-year follow-up of participants of this trial showed that the improvements in metacognition and functioning were maintained (for a review of these trials, see Lysaker et al., 2020).

Qualitative studies have also offered evidence of the usefulness of MERIT. Patients who received MERIT were more likely to describe how the treatment helped them develop a deeper sense of personal agency and enabled them to use their unique, personal history to make sense of their challenges and emotional pain (de Jong et al., 2019; Lysaker et al., 2020). Finally, many detailed case studies of patients in clinical settings have illustrated how MERIT can be used with patients with widely varying and often quite complex clinical presentations. Hamm and Lysaker (2018) have suggested a three-stage process that synthesize the findings of these case studies: (1) a sense of agency emerged, (2) followed by the development of a more coherent sense of self, followed by (3) action and management of one's own recovery. These clinical cases include conditions such as severe negative symptoms, substance abuse, disorganization, emotional distress, and lack of insight (for a review of these cases and their references, see Lysaker et al., 2020).

Finally, the efficacy of MERIT on specifically improving thought insertion has been demonstrated in several clinical cases (Hamm & Leonhardt, 2016; Lysaker et al., 2007; Lysaker & Gumley, 2010). These cases are used in the following section to illustrate with specific techniques how a therapist can treat thought insertion following the principles of MERIT.

15.3.3. The treatment of thought insertion using the MERIT approach

People experiencing thought insertion will have the lowest level of metacognitive capacity when reflecting about the self. At this level, the sense of the self is highly fragmented and the personal sense of agency in thoughts is profoundly diminished. These problems lead to an internal experience of confusion (resulting from this lack of coherence among thoughts), as well as a feeling of impotence ('I am not the owner of my thoughts'). Following the principles of MERIT, the therapist will have to assess the metacognitive capacity of the patient before starting the intervention, but also at each session, to ensure that he or she is tailoring the intervention to the metacognitive level of the patient (Lysaker & Klion, 2017).

MERIT is guided by basic conceptual principles rather than highlighting a particular combination of techniques. For patients with thought disorder, the aim is to recapture their personhood, which is achieved by helping the patient to identify his/her own mental states, those of others, and to synthesize that information into subsequently more complex representations of themselves (and others). Therapy is viewed as a platform to assist clients to evolve, to use this storied account to make meaning of their experiences, and to allow clients to perceive themselves as active agents in the world, which includes being active agents of their thoughts (Lysaker & Gumley, 2010).

Therapy of patients with thought insertion may initially be based on the following guidelines (Lysaker et al., 2011):

a) Building rapport with the patient.
b) Adopt a therapeutic non-hierarchical relationship. Role of consultant rather than expert.
c) Elicit personal narratives.
d) Make direct reflections about the ownership of the thoughts that the patient communicates while eliciting his/her personal narrative.
e) Once they recover the agency and ownership of their thoughts, connect with emotional experiences linked to their personal narratives.

We illustrate this using as previously the case of Simone.

15.3.4. Treatment of Simone with MERIT

15.3.4.1. Building rapport with Simone

The therapist dedicated the first sessions to ask Simone about her subjective experiences. Examples of these questions were how she spent her day, or how long she had been at the residence. The mandates of the residential staff were that they requested the therapist for ideas to facilitate that Simone to engage in activities and follow their recommendations. The therapist avoided aligning directly with these mandates, as this would not have been efficient to establish good rapport with Simone. During the first sessions it is important to focus on building this rapport, and to avoid focusing entirely on symptomatology (Hamm & Leonhardt, 2016).

15.3.4.2. Adopt a therapeutic non-hierarchical relationship

We try to avoid a paternalistic or 'health expert' role with the patients, instead opting to attempt to reduce the hierarchical dynamic and to try to establish a 'consultant' role as a therapist. This role can be transmitted, for instance, by making direct and honest reflections about the apparent difference between the thoughts of the therapist and the thoughts of the patient. For example, Simone sometimes claimed that the therapist did not understand her delusions or did not believe her at all. In this case, the therapist was able to directly state that he wanted to understand her, but there were times when he was not able to. These kinds of reflections made Simone feel more relaxed and open to talking during sessions.

15.3.4.3. Elicit personal narratives

One way of reducing the space that delusions have in the mind of the patient is by requesting descriptions of narratives of significant life events for the patient. Requesting these narratives for patients with thought disorder needs to adapt to their current high level of thought disorganization. As these patients have a very low level of metacognition, their personal narratives are often quite impoverished and fragmented; that is, they are often unable to formulate an articulated story of themselves. The adaptation can be made by making brief and descriptive-level questions about simple episodes. For the case of Simone, Simone believed that she was constantly harassed and intruded upon by demons, but she also could briefly remember that when she was young, she had enjoyed the music of Bob Dylan. At this point, the therapist inquired about her favourite songs of this singer, called up one of these songs on YouTube and played it for Simone. This helped with the emergence of positive effects, and also stimulated more narratives related to times in Simone's life in which she had enjoyed these songs. These narratives could shift into explanations very coloured with delusions, but another tool here can be to gently redirect back toward descriptive aspects of the episode in question.

15.3.4.4. Make direct reflections about the ownership of the thoughts that the patient communicates while eliciting their personal narrative

Patients with thought disorder are not truly aware that they have thoughts of their own, nor differentiate between cognitive operations (level S1 of self-reflectivity). Therefore, it is key to assist them at this point by sharing observations of their demonstrated cognitive operations, and by focusing the attention of the patient to the events that occur inside their mind to increase their awareness of them. This can be done using the following kind of verbalizations: 'You are thinking that …'; 'You have the idea that …'; 'You are having a memory of …'; 'You wish that …', 'You are having the thought that …'. These basic reflections highlight the patient's cognitive functions happening at that moment. As an illustration, when Simone said: 'I liked making carrot cake when I was younger', the therapist noted: 'You are remembering that you liked to make carrot cakes when you were younger'. When Simone said: 'The demons are angry and not to be trusted', the therapist noted: 'You are angry', 'You may feel that you are someone not to be trusted'.

15.3.4.5. Once they recover the agency and ownership of their thoughts, they connect with emotional experiences linked to their personal narratives

Once the patient is able to identify and distinguish among their cognitive operations, it is time to try to lift their metacognitive capacity to S4, that is, to name and differentiate emotions. This can be done by using clarifying questions, informational questions, empathy, reflection, and refocusing while constructing the relevant narrative episodes of the patient. The interpersonal connectedness built on the therapeutic alliance is another crucial component to ensure the development of the appropriate context for the identification of emotions.

More detailed explanations and illustrations on how to intervene at the level of self-reflectivity can be consulted on the published conceptual model of the key tasks and processes (Lysaker et al., 2011), in the MERIT manual (Lysaker & Klion, 2017), and in the case illustrations reported here (Lysaker et al., 2007, 2020; Lysaker & Gumley, 2010).

15.4. Conclusion

MCT and MERIT conceptualize treating metacognition as a pathway to improve thought disorder, though both approaches face different angles (Moritz & Lysaker, 2018). MCT focuses on metacognitive experience, on awareness of mental processes, like by challenging and replacing dysfunctional explicit metacognitive beliefs, or by sowing the seeds of doubts regarding the certainty of their own beliefs (including their delusional beliefs of thought insertion). In contrast, MERIT focuses on larger senses of identity, in metacognitive knowledge about oneself and others. Its main target is to develop the capacity for self-reflectivity for assisting the person in moving towards recovery of thought insertion. MCT and MERIT have in common the final aim of leading patients to become aware of thinking processes, and obtaining a complete experience of themselves as a human being in the world with a richer and more coherent sense of the self and personal narrative.

References

Andreou, C., Wittekind, C. E., Fieker, M., Heitz, U., Veckenstedt, R., Bohn, F., & Moritz, S. (2017). Individualized metacognitive therapy for delusions: A randomized controlled rater-blind study. *Journal of Behavior Therapy and Experimental Psychiatry, 56*, 144–151.

Beck, A. T., Baruch, E., Balter, J. M., Steer, R. A., & Warman, D. M. (2004). A new instrument for measuring insight: The Beck Cognitive Insight Scale. *Schizophrenia Research, 68*(2–3), 319–329.

Birulés, I., López-Carrilero, R., Cuadras, D., Pousa, E., Barrigón, M., Barajas, A., Lorente-Rovira, E., González-Higueras, F., Grasa, E., Ruiz-Delgado, I., Cid, J., de Apraiz, A., Montserrat, R., Pélaez, T., Moritz, S., & Ochoa, S. (2020). Cognitive insight in first-episode psychosis: Changes during metacognitive training. *Journal of Personalized Medicine, 10*(4), 253.

Briki, M., Monnin, J., Haffen, E., Sechter, D., Favrod, J. Ô., Netillard, C., Cheraitia, E., Marin, K., Govyadovskaya, S., Tio, G., Bonin, B., Chauvet-Gelinier, J. C., Leclerc, S., Hodé, Y., Vidailhet, P., Berna, F., Bertschy, A. Z., & Vandel, P. (2014). Metacognitive training for schizophrenia: A multicentre randomised controlled trial. *Schizophrenia Research, 157*(1–3), 99–106.

de Jong, S., van Donkersgoed, R. J. M., Aleman, A., van der Gaag, M., Wunderink, L., Arends, J., Lysaker, P. H., & Pijnenborg, M. (2016). Practical implications of metacognitively oriented psychotherapy in psychosis. *The Journal of Nervous and Mental Disease, 204*(9), 713–716.

de Jong, S., van Donkersgoed, R. J. M., Timmerman, M. E., aan het Rot, M., Wunderink, L., Arends, J., van Der Gaag, M., Aleman, A., Lysaker, P. H., & Pijnenborg, G. H. M. (2019). Metacognitive reflection and insight therapy (MERIT) for patients with schizophrenia. *Psychological Medicine, 49*(2), 303–313.

Eichner, C., & Berna, F. (2016). Acceptance and efficacy of metacognitive training (MCT) on positive symptoms and delusions in patients with schizophrenia: A meta-analysis taking into account important moderators. *Schizophrenia Bulletin, 42*(4), 952–962.

Farrer, C., & Franck, N. (2007). Self-monitoring in schizophrenia. *Current Psychiatry Reviews, 3*(4), 243–251.

Flavell, J. H. (1979). Metacognition and cognitive monitoring: A new area of cognitive-developmental inquiry. *American Psychologist, 34*(10), 906–911.

Freeman, D. (2007). Suspicious minds: The psychology of persecutory delusions. *Clinical Psychology Review, 27*(4), 425–457.

Frith, C. D. (2012a). Explaining delusions of control: The comparator model 20 years on. *Consciousness and Cognition, 21*(1), 52–54.

Frith, C. D. (2012b). The role of metacognition in human social interactions. *Philosophical Transactions of the Royal Society B: Biological Sciences, 367*(1599), 2213–2223.

Hamm, J. A., & Leonhardt, B. L. (2016). The role of interpersonal connection, personal narrative, and metacognition in integrative psychotherapy for schizophrenia: A case report. *Journal of Clinical Psychology, 72*(2), 132–141.

Hamm, J. A., & Lysaker, P. H. (2018). Application of integrative metacognitive psychotherapy for serious mental illness. *American Journal of Psychotherapy, 71*(4), 122–127.

Inchausti, F., García-Poveda, N. V., Ballesteros-Prados, A., Ortuño-Sierra, J., Sánchez-Reales, S., Prado-Abril, J., Aldaz-Armendáriz, J. A., Mole, J., Dimaggio, G., Ottavi, P., & Fonseca-Pedrero, E. (2018). The effects of metacognition-oriented social skills training on psychosocial outcome in schizophrenia-spectrum disorders: A randomized controlled trial. *Schizophrenia Bulletin, 44*(6), 1235–1244.

Jiang, J., Zhang, L., Zhu, Z., Li, W., & Li, C. (2015). Metacognitive training for schizophrenia: a systematic review. *Shanghai Archives of Psychiatry, 27*(3), 149–157.

Leanza, L., Studerus, E., Bozikas, V. P., Moritz, S., & Andreou, C. (2020). Moderators of treatment efficacy in individualized metacognitive training for psychosis (MCT+). *Journal of Behavior Therapy and Experimental Psychiatry, 68*, 101547.

Liu, Y. C., Tang, C. C., Hung, T. T., Tsai, P. C., & Lin, M. F. (2018). The efficacy of metacognitive training for delusions in patients with schizophrenia: A meta-analysis of randomized controlled trials informs evidence-based practice. *Worldviews on Evidence-Based Nursing, 15*(2), 130–139.

Lopez-Morinigo, J.-D., Ajnakina, O., Martínez, A. S.-E., Escobedo-Aedo, P.-J., Ruiz-Ruano, V. G., Sánchez-Alonso, S., Mata-Iturralde, L., Muñoz-Lorenzo, L., Ochoa, S., Baca-García, E., & David, A. S. (2020). Can metacognitive interventions improve insight in schizophrenia spectrum disorders? A systematic review and meta-analysis. *Psychological Medicine, 50*(14), 2289–2301.

Lysaker, P. H., Buck, K. D., Carcione, A., Procacci, M., Salvatore, G., & Dimaggio, G. (2011). Addressing metacognitive capacity for self reflection in the psychotherapy for schizophrenia: A conceptual model of the key tasks and processes. *Psychology and Psychotherapy: Theory, Research and Practice, 84*(1), 58–69.

Lysaker, P. H., Buck, K. D., & Hamm, J. A. (2011). *Metacognition Assessment Scale: A Brief Overview and Coding Manual for the Abbreviated Version*. Indianapolis, IN: Indiana University School of Medicine.

Lysaker, P. H., Buck, K. D., & Hammoud, K. (2007). Psychotherapy and schizophrenia: An analysis of requirements of individual psychotherapy with persons who experience manifestly barren or empty selves. *Psychology and Psychotherapy: Theory, Research and Practice, 80*(3), 377–387.

Lysaker, P. H., Carcione, A., Dimaggio, G., Johannesen, J. K., Nicolo, G., Procacci, M., & Semerari, A. (2005). Metacognition amidst narratives of self and illness in schizophrenia: associations with neurocognition, symptoms, insight and quality of life. *Acta Psychiatrica Scandinavica, 112*(1), 64–71.

Lysaker, P. H., & Gumley, A. (2010). Psychotherapeutic and relational processes and the development of metacognitive capacity following five years of individual psychotherapy: A case study of a person with psychotic symptoms. *Psychosis, 2*(1), 70–78.

Lysaker, P. H., & Klion, R. (2017). *Recovery, Meaning-Making, and Severe Mental Illness: A Comprehensive Guide to Metacognitive Reflection and Insight Therapy* (1st ed.). Oxford: Routledge.

Lysaker, P. H., Minor, K. S., Lysaker, J. T., Hasson-Ohayon, I., Bonfils, K., Hochheiser, J., & Vohs, J. L. (2020). Metacognitive function and fragmentation in schizophrenia: Relationship to cognition, self-experience and developing treatments. *Schizophrenia Research: Cognition, 19*, 100142.

Moritz, S., Kerstan, A., Veckenstedt, R., Randjbar, S., Vitzthum, F., Schmidt, C., Heise, M., & Woodward, T. S. (2011). Further evidence for the efficacy of a metacognitive group training in schizophrenia. *Behaviour Research and Therapy, 49*(3), 151–157.

Moritz, S., & Lysaker, P. H. (2018). Metacognition: What did James H. Flavell really say and the implications for the conceptualization and design of metacognitive interventions. *Schizophrenia Research, 201*, 20–26. https://doi.org/10.1016/j.schres.2018.06.001

Moritz, S., Menon, M., Andersen, D., Woodward, T. S., & Gallinat, J. (2018). Moderators of symptomatic outcome in metacognitive training for psychosis (MCT). Who benefits and who does not? *Cognitive Therapy and Research, 42*(1), 80–91.

Moritz, S., Veckenstedt, R., Andreou, C., Bohn, F., Hottenrott, B., Leighton, L., Köther, U., Woodward, T. S., Treszl, A., Menon, M., Schneider, B. C., Pfueller, U., & Roesch-Ely, D. (2014). Sustained and 'sleeper' effects of group metacognitive training for schizophrenia a randomized clinical trial. *JAMA Psychiatry, 71*(10), 1103–1111.

Moritz, S., Veckenstedt, R., Bohn, F., Hottenrott, B., Scheu, F., Randjbar, S., Aghotor, J., Köther, U., Woodward, T. S., Treszl, A., Andreou, C., Pfueller, U., & Roesch-Ely, D. (2013). Complementary group Metacognitive Training (MCT) reduces delusional ideation in schizophrenia. *Schizophrenia Research, 151*(1–3), 61–69.

Moritz, S., & Woodward, T. S. (2007a). Metacognitive training for schizophrenia patients (MCT): A pilot study on feasibility, treatment adherence, and subjective efficacy. *German Journal of Psychiatry, 10*(3), 69–78.

Moritz, S., & Woodward, T. S. (2007b). Metacognitive training in schizophrenia: from basic research to knowledge translation and intervention. *Current Opinion in Psychiatry, 20*(6), 619–625.

Nelson, T. O., & Narens, L. (1990). Metamemory: A theoretical framework and new findings. Psychology of Learning and Motivation, 26, 125–173.

Ochoa, S., López-Carrilero, R., Barrigón, M. L., Pousa, E., Barajas, A., Lorente-Rovira, E., González-Higueras, F., Grasa, E., Ruiz-Delgado, I., Cid, J., Birulés, I., Esteban-Pinos, I., Casañas, R., Luengo, A., Torres-Hernández, P., Corripio, I., Montes-Gámez, M., Beltran, M., De Apraiz, A., ... Moritz, S. (2017). Randomized control trial to assess the efficacy of metacognitive training compared with a psycho-educational group in people with a recent-onset psychosis. *Psychological Medicine, 47*(9), 1573–1584.

Patniyot, N. S. (2021). Deficits in access consciousness, integrative function, and consequent autonoetic thinking in schizophrenia. *Medical Hypotheses, 155*, 110664.

Philipp, R., Kriston, L., Lanio, J., Kühne, F., Härter, M., Moritz, S., & Meister, R. (2019). Effectiveness of metacognitive interventions for mental disorders in adults—a systematic review and meta-analysis (METACOG). *Clinical Psychology & Psychotherapy, 26*(2), 227–240.

Ratcliffe, M., & Wilkinson, S. (2015). Thought insertion clarified. *Journal of Consciousness Studies: Controversies in Science & the Humanities, 22*(11–12), 246–269.

Salas-Sender, M., López-Carrilero, R., Barajas, A., Lorente-Rovira, E., Pousa, E., Barrigón, M. L., Grasa, E., Ruiz-Delgado, I., González-Higueras, F., Cid, J., Aznar, A., Pélaez, T., Birulés, I., Moritz, S., The Spanish Metacognition Study Group, & Ochoa, S. (2020). Gender differences in response to metacognitive training in people with first-episode psychosis. *Journal of Consulting and Clinical Psychology, 88*(6), 516–525.

Semerari, A., Carcione, A., Dimaggio, G., Falcone, M., Nicolò, G., Procacci, M., & Alleva, G. (2003). How to evaluate metacognitive functioning in psychotherapy? The metacognition assessment scale and its applications. *Clinical Psychology & Psychotherapy, 10*(4), 238–261.

Vohs, J. L., Leonhardt, B. L., James, A. V., Francis, M. M., Breier, A., Mehdiyoun, N., Visco, A. C., & Lysaker, P. H. (2018). Metacognitive reflection and insight therapy for early psychosis: A preliminary study of a novel integrative psychotherapy. *Schizophrenia Research, 195*, 428–433.

SECTION 4
BEYOND THE PHENOMENON

Thought Insertion and the Nature of Thinking

16
Thought Insertion and Commitment

Jordi Fernández

16.1. Introduction

There is a certain idea about introspection which seems, on the face of it, quite attractive. This is the idea that being aware of having, or occupying, some mental state and being aware of that mental state as one's own are one and the same thing. Natural as it is, this idea is challenged by the thought insertion delusion, in which subjects claim to have thoughts which are not theirs.[1] In these subjects' mental life, occupying some mental state and owning that mental state seems to have been pulled apart as separate experiences, and one of them seems to be missing from the subjects' phenomenology.[2] In order to understand thought insertion, then, we need to understand, first, the experience of a conscious state as being one's own.[3] I draw on the literature on self-knowledge to offer a proposal about the nature of this experience. The experience of owning a conscious state to which one can be committed is, I suggest, the experience of being committed to that state. This view can help us account for the disownment of thoughts in thought insertion. For there seem to be some signs that thought insertion subjects miss the experience of being committed to the thoughts that they disown. To motivate this explanation of thought insertion further, I describe how the explanation can also be applied to other mental disorders in which subjects disown some of their conscious states. I consider, in particular, the case of disowned memory, and the case of anarchic hand

---

[1] One might think that there is no challenge here, since the just-mentioned idea about introspection concerns mental states whereas thought insertion seems to concern mental events. Hereafter, I will construe states as properties, and events as property exemplifications (Kim, 1976). Thus, the point that, in thought insertion, a subject claims to have a thought which is not theirs should be understood as the point that the subject claims to instantiate a certain property (the property of thinking something) even though, in some sense, that property is not their own. Hence the conflict.

[2] For the purposes of this discussion, the notion of a subject's experience should be understood as a state wherein some state of affairs is presented to the subject as being the case. Thus, the notion of experience, as used here, will not be a factive notion. A subject may experience something that is not, in fact, the case. I will be assuming that whether the subject believes what they experience or not depends on whether the subject trusts, or takes at face value, the content of their experience.

[3] In what follows, I will use the notion of a state that one is 'aware of', and the notion of a state which is 'conscious', interchangeably. Hopefully this will cause no confusion.

syndrome. The conclusion is that thought insertion is an instance of a more general phenomenon; the phenomenon of lacking the experience of commitment for mental states to which we should be committed when we become aware of them.

16.2. Thought Insertion

Thought insertion is a mental condition in which the subject claims to be aware of the fact that some of the thoughts that they are having are not their own thoughts. Instead, they are other people's thoughts taking place in their minds. In the psychiatric literature, this condition is considered one of the 'first rank' symptoms of schizophrenia (see Schneider, 1959). Here are some examples of reports from subjects with thought insertion:

Report 1
'I look at the window and I think that the garden looks nice and the grass look cool, but the thoughts of Eamonn Andrews come into my mind. There are no other thoughts there, only his ... He treats my mind like a screen and flashes thoughts onto it like you flash a picture.' (Mellor, 1970, p. 17)

Report 2
'Thoughts come into my head like "Kill God". It's just like my mind working, but it isn't. They come from this chap, Chris. They're his thoughts.' (Frith, 1992, p. 66)

Report 3
'It's like a thought as it comes in ... a thought is very light really, inspirational ... it's a light feeling where you feel as though I'm actually thinking it ... or you're receiving it rather ... it's just a thought but it feels logical say ... it feels pretty normal or fits with what I suspect, [I] wonder if that's me ... it felt like a piece of information.' (Hoerl, 2001, p. 190)

Report 4
'As I walked along, I began to notice that the colors and shapes of everything around me were becoming very intense. And at some point, I began to realize that the houses I was passing were sending messages to me: *Look closely. You are special. You are especially bad. Look closely and you shall find. There are many things you must see. See. See.* I didn't hear these words as literal sounds, as though the houses were talking and I were hearing them; instead, the words just came into my head—they were ideas I was having. Yet I instinctively knew they were not *my* ideas.

They belonged to the houses, and the houses had put them in my head.' (Saks, 2007, p. 27)

Report 5
'I have never read nor heard them; they come unasked; I do not dare to think I am the source but I am happy to know of them without thinking them. They come at any moment like a gift and I do not dare to impart them as if they were my own.' (Jaspers, 1963, p. 123)

Report 6
'One evening the thought was given to me electrically that I should murder Lissi.' (Mullis & Spence, 2003, p. 295)

The general structure of reports of thought insertion seems to be, then, the following. On the one hand, the subject with thought insertion claims to be aware of the fact that they are having a certain thought. On the other hand, the subject claims that the thought in question is not their own. The reports are puzzling because, on the face of it, it is hard to understand what it could mean for the relevant thought not to be the subject's own given that, by the subject's own admission, they are having that thought.

To make sense of reports with this puzzling structure, one might raise two questions about thought insertion. We may refer to them as the 'what-question' and the 'why-question' about thought insertion. The what-question is: What do subjects with thought insertion experience? What are they trying to express when they disown some of their thoughts? The why-question is: Why do these subjects have the unusual experience in question? What causes them to have that experience? The what-question about thought insertion is more basic than the why-question because, unless we have a firm grasp on what it is like for these subjects to have thought insertion, it is hard to see how we could begin to investigate the causes of their experience. In what follows, therefore, I will concentrate on the what-question about thought insertion. I intend to remain neutral on what the correct answer to the why-question is.

16.3. Ownership as Commitment

Normally, if a subject is aware of having some thought, then, they experience that thought as being their own or, to put it differently, they experience being the owner of the thought. If I am aware of thinking that the garden looks nice, for example, then I will normally experience the thought that the garden looks nice as being my own. The point does not apply to thought exclusively, but to any conscious state. Thus, if I am aware of remembering that my last family holiday happened at a beach, for instance, then I will normally experience the memory of that family holiday as being my own. And, similarly, if I am aware of typing this essay on my computer keyboard, then I will normally experience that action as being my own. We may call this experience, an 'experience of ownership'.

The fact that thought insertion subjects disown some of their conscious thoughts suggests that this is not true of them. That is, it suggests that, for some of their thoughts, they are aware of having those thoughts, but they do not experience those thoughts as being their own. The reasoning here is that if thought insertion subjects do lack the experience of those thoughts as being their own, then it makes sense that they disown the relevant thoughts. For, by disowning them, they are simply taking at face value their experience of those thoughts when they make reports such as 1–6 above. This diagnosis, however, does not provide us with an answer to the what-question about thought insertion, unless we are able to specify what it is for one to experience a thought as being one's own in the first place. That is our task in this section.

There is a certain notion in the literature on self-knowledge which may be helpful for illuminating the nature of the experience of ownership. Consider the following aspect of the self-attribution of thoughts. Normally, if a subject is aware of having some thought, then they become especially related to the thought that they attribute to themselves in that they experience being committed to that thought. What exactly does 'committed' mean here? In general, a subject's commitment to a conscious state is an experience wherein the subject takes the state in question to be fitting, merited, or appropriate. In the case of thought, for example, a subject is committed to a thought that they are aware of having in the sense that they regard the content of that thought as being correct. Thus, if I am aware of thinking that the garden looks nice, then I will thereby accept that the garden looks nice. I will, in that sense, experience being committed to the thought that the garden looks nice.[4]

It is worth considering the extent to which commitment may be the by-product of self-knowledge through awareness. On the one hand, the

---

[4] For discussion, see (Moran, 2001, pp. 88–94) and (Fernández, 2013, pp. 166–172). The experience of commitment to a thought that one attributes to oneself may not arise in a situation in which one self-attributes the thought by relying on testimony, reasoning, or behavioural evidence, as it happens in psychological therapy, for example. Thus, the claim that a subject experiences being committed to a thought that they attribute to themselves needs to be restricted to those situations in which the subject's self-attribution of the thought is the result of the subject being aware of the fact that they have the thought (or, equivalently, it is the result of the fact that the thought is a conscious thought).

experience of commitment does seem to arise when a subject is aware of having propositional attitudes other than thought. Thus, if a subject is aware of wanting a beer, for example, then they will thereby regard their desire for a beer as being fitting, that is, they will take the beer to be desirable. Similarly, if a subject is aware of intending to grab a pen, then they will take their intention to be appropriate, that is, they will regard the grabbing of the pen as something to be brought about by them. On the other hand, however, the experience of commitment does not seem to generalize to all the kinds of mental states that a subject could be aware of having. If a subject is aware of having an itch, for example, then it does not seem that the subject will thereby take that itch to be appropriate. Similarly, if a subject is aware of being depressed, then it does not seem that the subject will thereby regard that depression as being fitting. Self-knowledge through awareness, therefore, seems to be necessary for commitment, but it does not seem to be sufficient for it.

The notion of commitment can help us illuminate the notion of owning a thought, or being the owner of a thought. My contention is that the experience of owning a thought, which we normally have when we are aware of having that thought, is the experience of being committed to the relevant thought. In other words, the proposal is that what it takes for a subject to experience a thought as their own, when they are aware of having that thought, is to regard the content of that thought as being correct. We can refer to this view as the 'ownership as commitment view'.

In what follows, I will propose that the ownership as commitment view delivers a satisfactory answer to the what-question about thought insertion. Two kinds of considerations will be offered in support of this proposal. Firstly, I will argue that the proposed answer accommodates some of the details in reports 1–6 above; details which concern the 'inserted' thoughts as being, in a certain sense, informationally neutral. Secondly, I will argue that the proposed answer has considerable explanatory power. For it can be extended to two other conditions in which subjects also disown some of their conscious states; a disorder of memory and a disorder of action. Let us consider the two steps in this line of reasoning in more detail now.

16.4. Thought Without Commitment

The ownership as commitment view can help us account for why subjects with thought insertion disown the 'inserted' thoughts that they are aware of having. The view contends that the experience of ownership and the experience of commitment for those thoughts are one and the same experience.

The reason why this reductive identification is helpful is that there seem to be some indications that, when subjects with thought insertion are aware of having their 'inserted' thoughts, they do not experience being committed to those thoughts. If this is correct, then the ownership as commitment view offers a simple answer to the what-question about thought insertion: What it is like for subjects with thought insertion to be aware of their 'inserted' thoughts, one may claim, is to be aware of having thoughts to which the subjects are not committed. How plausible, then, is the idea that subjects with thought insertion do not experience being committed to their 'inserted' thoughts?

The main reason for thinking that subjects with thought insertion do not experience being committed to the thoughts that they disown is that, in some reports of thought insertion, subjects refer to their 'inserted' thoughts in ways which suggest that those thoughts are not experienced by them as the kinds of mental states to which commitment applies. Consider report 1, for example. The subject describes the thought that the garden looks nice and the grass looks cool as a 'picture' flashed onto a screen. Likewise, in report 3, the subject refers to their thought as a 'piece of information'. And, in report 4, the subject refers to the thought that they are especially bad as an 'idea'. This is the kind of language that you would expect thought insertion subjects to use while expressing their 'inserted' thoughts if, despite being aware of those thoughts, they were unable to commit to them. You would expect them to speak of their 'inserted' thoughts as ideas, pictures, or pieces of information. For these expressions suggest that the mental states that these subjects are aware of having are not being experienced by them as mental states which need to match the world in any way: Attending to a mental picture does not need to elicit the sense that the pictured state of affairs is the case. Entertaining an idea in one's mind does not need to bring with it the feeling that the content of that idea is the case. And holding a piece of information in one's mind does not need to be accompanied by the feeling that the content of that information actually obtains. But if subjects with thought insertion do not experience their 'inserted' thoughts as belonging to the kinds of mental states which need to match the world, then it seems that thought insertion subjects will not experience being committed to those thoughts.

The proposed account of why subjects with thought insertion disown their 'inserted' thoughts in spite of the fact that they are aware of having those thoughts, then, is that the experience of owning those thoughts is identical with the experience of being committed to them.[5] And, when subjects

---

[5] Notice that the issue of whether thought insertion patients lack an experience of ownership for their disowned thoughts and the issue of what that experience amounts to are separate issues. George Graham and Lynn Stephens, for example, agree that patients with thought insertion do not experience their

with thought insertion are aware of having their 'inserted' thoughts, they miss the experience of being committed to those thoughts. At this point, a reasonable concern about the proposed account may arise. One may worry that the evidential basis for this account is extremely narrow. After all, it is built on some details from just a few reports of thought insertion. For that reason, it is worth considering whether the account of thought insertion based on the ownership as commitment view can be extended to explain other mental disorders in which subjects disown some of their conscious states. If it can, then the fact that the ownership as commitment view has a broader explanatory power which extends beyond thought insertion will lend support to its proposed account of the delusion. In the next two sections, I intend to show that the proposed account of thought insertion can indeed be extended to two other mental disorders in which the disownment of conscious states takes place; a disorder of memory and a disorder of action.

16.5. Memory Without Commitment

The general structure of thought insertion reports makes them interestingly similar to reports from a different disorder; a disorder in which a subject disowns some of their own memories. We may refer to it, accordingly, as 'disowned memory'. There seems to be only one case of disowned memory. This is the case of patient RB who, due to head trauma sustained during a bicycle accident, appears to be aware of having episodic memories, but disowns some of those memories. The following are reports from patient RB illustrating his condition:

> Report 7
> 'I was remembering scenes, not facts ... I was recalling scenes ... that is ... I could clearly recall a scene of me at the beach in New London with my family as a child. But the feeling was that the scene was not my memory. As if I was looking at a photo of someone else's vacation.' (Klein & Nichols, 2012, p. 686)

'inserted' thoughts as their own. But they propose that the experience of ownership which is missing when they are aware of those thoughts is the experience of carrying out those thoughts, or being the agents who are doing the thinking (Graham & Stephens, 2000, p. 154). In (Fernández, 2010), I argue that this proposal does not sit easily with the fact that we routinely lack the experience of carrying out, or being the agents of, our perceptual beliefs, and yet we continue to experience those beliefs as being ours.

Report 8

'My memories of having been at MIT I did not own. Those scenes of being at MIT were vivid, but they were not mine.' (Klein & Nichols, 2012, p. 686)

Report 9

'I can see the scene in my head. I'm studying with friends in the lounge at my residence hall. I am able to re-live it. I have a feeling... a sense of being there, at MIT, in the lounge. But it doesn't feel like I own it. It's like I'm imagining, re-living the experience but it was described by someone else.' (Klein & Nichols, 2012, p. 687)

Notice that the structure of these reports is parallel to the structure of reports from subjects with thought insertion: Just like subjects with thought insertion claim to be having some thoughts, and they also claim that those thoughts are not theirs, patient RB claims to be having some memories, and he also claims that those memories are not his. This similarity between the two types of reports suggests that it may be possible to offer an explanation of RB's experience which is analogous to the account of thought insertion proposed above. The explanation proceeds in three steps.[6]

The first step in an explanation of patient RB's experience is to point out that RB seems to be lacking an experience of ownership for some of his memories. This is suggested by the fact that patient RB disowns the relevant memories. If RB does not experience those memories as being his own, then this explains why he claims that they are not his. By disowning the memories to which he is referring in reports 7–9 above, RB is merely accepting the way in which he experiences those memories. This diagnosis, however, falls short of an explanation of RB's experience, unless we can specify what it is for one to experience a memory as one's own to begin with.[7]

The second step in an explanation of RB's experience is to appeal to the ownership as commitment view to spell out what it is for one to experience a memory as one's own. Let us recall that, in general, a subject's commitment

---

[6] As in the case of thought insertion, one might raise both a what-question and a why-question about RB's experience: What is RB experiencing? And why is he having that unusual experience? By 'an explanation of RB's experience', I am referring to an answer to the what-question about RB, and not to an answer to the why-question about him. My interest here only concerns the nature of the experience that he may be trying to express in his reports. I intend to remain neutral on what the causes of that experience may be.

[7] As in the case of thought insertion, the issue of whether RB lacks an experience of ownership for his disowned memories and the issue of what that experience amounts to are separate issues. Stanley Klein and Shaun Nichols, for instance, agree that RB lacks a sense of ownership when he is aware of the memories that he disowns. But they propose that RB's missing sense of ownership amounts to 'a sense of numerical personal identity with the past person' (Klein & Nichols, 2012, p. 689). In (Fernández, 2023), I argue that this proposal does not square with two types of details in RB's reports; RB's references to himself as the person who was at the remembered scenes, and RB's references to the sense of 're-living' the remembered scenes, and of 'being there' when he remembers them.

to a conscious state is an experience wherein the subject regards the state in question as fitting, merited, or appropriate. This general idea suggests a natural application to the specific case of memory: A subject is committed to a conscious memory when they regard that memory as being correct, that is, they take the remembered state of affairs to have been the case in the past. It seems that, in normal circumstances, we are committed to the memories that we are aware of having. Thus, if I am aware of remembering that my last family holiday happened at a beach, then, normally, I will regard the memory in question as being correct, that is, I will accept that my last family holiday happened at that beach. The proposal being put forward in the ownership as commitment view is that the experience of regarding the memory of that family holiday as being correct, and the experience of the memory as being my own, are one and the same experience.

Now, if RB disowns some of his conscious memories because he lacks an experience of ownership for those memories, and if the experience of owning a memory amounts to the experience of being committed to it, then it seems to follow that RB must not experience being committed to the memories that he disowns. The third step in the explanation of RB's experience consists in highlighting those details in RB's reports which seem to confirm this prediction. There are two such details.

In order to describe the experience that RB is having when he is aware of remembering the scene at the beach in New London, he uses, in report 7, the analogy of looking at a photograph; a photograph of someone else's vacation.[8] This is what you would expect if RB did not experience being committed to the memory of the scene at the beach in New London. For if RB were looking at a photograph of the scene instead of remembering it, then it would not thereby feel to RB as if the scene had happened in the past. And this failure to regard the memory of the scene at the beach in New London as being correct is precisely what it means for RB not to be committed to it. Similarly, in order to describe the experience that RB is having when he is aware of remembering the scene at the MIT study lounge, he uses, in report 9, the analogy of imagining the scene. This is what you would expect if RB did not experience being committed to the memory of the scene at the MIT study lounge. For if RB was imagining the scene, then it would not thereby feel to RB as if the scene had happened in the past. And this failure to regard the memory of the scene at the MIT study lounge as being correct is precisely what it means for RB not to be committed to it.

---

[8] In (Klein, 2012, p. 493), Stanley Klein claims that RB described his memory by saying, instead, 'As if I am looking at a movie of someone else's vacation'. As far as I can see, the point that I am making will apply whether the analogy used by RB was that of looking at a photograph or that of looking at a movie.

It seems, therefore, that there is some evidence suggesting that patient RB does not experience being committed to the memories that he disowns. But if this is correct, then it seems that the account of the thought insertion delusion proposed by the ownership as commitment view does generalize to disowned memory. And this, in turn, means that the explanatory power of the proposed account of thought insertion extends beyond that particular delusion; a consideration which seems to count in favour of the account.

16.6. Action Without Commitment

The general structure of thought insertion reports also makes them interestingly similar to reports from yet another disorder; a disorder in which the subject disowns some of their actions. This is a condition which is associated with lesions to the frontal lobe of the brain, and which is referred to as 'anarchic hand' syndrome in the neurological literature (see Della Sala et al., 1991). A subject with an anarchic hand appears to carry out actions with one of their hands, in the minimal sense that their hand performs movements which seem to be goal-directed. A subject with an anarchic hand also acknowledges that the hand in question is their own hand. But they claim that the actions performed by that hand are not the subject's own. Instead, the subject attributes the relevant actions to the hand itself, as if it had a will of its own. In fact, the subject is typically unable to inhibit the movements of their 'anarchic' hand. The following are two reports of anarchic hand cases:

Report 10
'For example, at one point it was noted that the patient had picked up a pencil and had begun scribbling with the right hand. When her attention was directed to this activity, she reacted with dismay, immediately withdrew the pencil, and pulled the right hand to her side using the left hand. She then indicated that she had not herself initiated the original action of the right arm. She often reacted with dismay and frustration at her inability to prevent these unintended movements of the right arm. She experienced a feeling of dissociation from the actions of the right arm, stating on several occasions "it will not do what I want it to do".' (Goldberg et al., 1981, pp. 684–685)

Report 11
'For example, JC and his spouse reported that the right hand reached for light switches, repeatedly pressed buttons on the television remote control, and groped for his left hand or face during sleep. JC expressed distress over the actions of the

right hand and reported, "the hand does what it wants to" and "it has a mind of its own"." (Giovannetti et al., 2005, p. 77)

Notice that there is a similarity between thought insertion and anarchic hand: In the same way in which the subject with thought insertion claims to have some thoughts, and they also claim that those thoughts are not their own, the patient with anarchic hand claims to have a hand which is performing some actions, and they also claim that the hand's actions are not their own. This similarity between the two conditions suggests that it may be possible to extend the account of thought insertion built upon the ownership as commitment view to offer an explanation of anarchic hand as well. The explanation proceeds, once again, in three steps.[9]

The first step in an explanation of anarchic hand is to point out that patients with anarchic hand seem to be lacking an experience of ownership for some of their actions. This is suggested by the fact that they disown those actions. If JC, for example, does not experience the action of reaching for the light switch as being his own, then this explains why he does not attribute it to himself. By disowning the action of reaching for the light switch, he is simply taking at face value the way in which he experiences that action. This diagnosis, however, falls short of an explanation of the experience of having anarchic hand, unless we can specify what it is for a subject to experience an action as being their own in the first place.

The second step in an explanation of anarchic hand is to deploy the ownership as commitment view to specify what it is for one to experience an action as one's own. Let us recall that, in general, a subject's commitment to a conscious state is an experience wherein the subject regards the state in question as fitting, merited, or appropriate. This general idea suggests a natural application to the specific case of action: A subject is committed to a conscious action when they regard that action as being fitting, that is, they regard the goal of that action as being intended by them. It seems that, in normal circumstances, we are committed to the actions that we are aware of performing. Thus, if I am aware of reaching for the light switch, then, normally, I will regard the action as being fitting. That is, I will take the state of affairs wherein I am touching the light switch to be something that I intend to be the case. The proposal being put forward in the ownership as commitment view is that the experience of

---

[9] As in the cases of thought insertion and disowned memory, one might raise both a what-question and a why-question about anarchic hand: What is the patient with anarchic hand experiencing? And why are they having that unusual experience? By 'an explanation of anarchic hand', I simply mean an answer to the what-question about anarchic hand.

regarding the reaching action as fitting, and the experience of the action as being my own, are one and the same experience.

Now, if patients with anarchic hand disown some of their conscious actions because they do not have an experience of ownership for those actions, and if the experience of owning an action is the experience of being committed to it, then it seems to follow that patients with anarchic hand must not experience being committed to the actions that they disown. The third step in the explanation of anarchic hand consists in highlighting a feature of the condition which seems to confirm this prediction. It seems that if a subject qualifies as having anarchic hand syndrome, then the subject's actions performed by their 'anarchic' hand are, as far as the subject is concerned, not intended, or not wanted, by them. This is one of the features which, in the neurological literature, is considered characteristic of the syndrome.[10] And, judging by some reports of anarchic hand cases, it does seem that patients with anarchic hands do not regard themselves as having the intention, or the desire, to pursue the goal at which their 'anarchic' hand's action is aimed. Thus, in report 10, the subject says, of their hand, 'it will not do what I want it to do'. Similarly, in report 11, JC says, of their hand, that it 'does what it wants to'. It seems, therefore, that patients with anarchic hands regard the goals of their actions as unintended, or unwanted, by them. But if patients with anarchic hands regard the goals of their actions as unintended, or unwanted, by them, then, on the notion of commitment to action specified above, these patients count as not being committed to the relevant actions.

The upshot seems to be that the account of the thought insertion delusion which stems from the ownership as commitment view can indeed be extended, not only to disowned memory, but also to anarchic hand syndrome. This fact lends further plausibility to the proposed account of thought insertion, as it enhances its explanatory power.

16.7. Conclusion

The picture which starts to emerge, at this point, is that of thought insertion as a particular instance of a broader phenomenon; the phenomenon of lacking a sense of ownership for one's own conscious states. It seems that the notion of

---

[10] See, for example, Della Sala et al. (1991, p. 1113) and Della Sala (2009, p. 37). The important differences between the notions of intention and desire, which seem to be used equivalently to characterize anarchic hand syndrome, will not concern us in this discussion. For the version of the ownership as commitment view which applies to the ownership of actions can be formulated in terms of either notion.

commitment can be utilized to explain this feature of different mental disorders, and the thought insertion delusion is a prominent disorder among them. But if one can account for the thought insertion delusion, and for other disorders, by construing the experience of owning a conscious state as the experience of being committed to it, it is only because, in the disorders concerned, the subject does not experience being committed to the relevant conscious states. Thus, the scope of the proposed explanation of thought insertion, which appeals to the ownership as commitment view, will only extend as far as the notion of commitment can be stretched.

Consider, then, a mental state for which it is not plausible to think that, in virtue of being aware of occupying that state, a subject will thereby regard the state as being fitting, or appropriate. A hallucination, or a dream (assuming that one can be aware of one's own dreams as one is dreaming), may be a state of this kind. As mentioned, a sensation, or a generalized mood, may be a state of this kind as well. More generally, any conscious state which is lacking in success conditions will be a state for which it is implausible to think that, in virtue of being aware of occupying that state, a subject will thereby regard the state as being fitting, or appropriate. And, therefore, it will be a state to which the property of commitment does not apply. Our sense of ownership for states of this kind cannot be explained, then, by the ownership as commitment view. And, therefore, any mental disorder involving the disownment of these states will be left outside of the scope of the account of thought insertion proposed here.

A different limitation of the ownership as commitment view concerns the issue of control over one's own thoughts. In cases of intrusive thought, for example, a subject claims to persistently have an unwanted, and typically negative, thought (Rachman, 1981). The ownership as commitment view cannot explain why the subject with intrusive thoughts lacks control over those thoughts. It makes, however, a prediction with regards to the subject's experience of ownership over those thoughts. It predicts that, in those cases in which the subject regards the intrusive thought that they are aware of having as false, then the subject will experience the thought at issue as not being theirs, in much the same way in which the subject with thought insertion experiences the 'inserted' thought as not being theirs. Two interesting questions suggest themselves at this point. One of them is whether subjects with intrusive thoughts regard those unwanted thoughts as being true or false. The other one is whether a subject must always attribute an alien origin to a thought just by virtue of experiencing it as not being their own. We will, however, not be able to pursue these questions as part of our discussion here.

What the thought insertion delusion seems to teach us, in the end, is not only that the sense of ownership for a conscious state can come apart from the sense that one is occupying that state. It is also that, in the case of thought, that sense of ownership amounts to looking at the world, as it were, from the perspective of that thought. It may be possible to be aware of having a thought without regarding that thought as one's own. But the lesson to draw from our discussion seems to be that it is not possible for one to regard a conscious thought as being correct without regarding that thought as being one's own.

References

Della Sala, S. (2009). Anarchic hand. In T. Bayne, A. Cleeremans, & P. Wilken (Eds.), *The Oxford Companion to Consciousness* (pp. 37–39). Oxford: Oxford University Press.

Della Sala, S., Marchetti, C., & Spinnler, H. (1991). Right-sided anarchic (alien) hand: a longitudinal study. *Neuropsychologia, 29*, 1113–1127.

Fernández, J. (2010). Thought insertion and self-knowledge. *Mind & Language, 25*, 66–88.

Fernández, J. (2013) *Transparent Minds: A Study of Self-Knowledge*. Oxford: Oxford University Press.

Fernández, J. (2023). The ownership of memories. In M. Guillot, & M. García-Carpintero (Eds.), *The Sense of Mineness* (pp. 343–362). Oxford: Oxford University Press.

Frith, C. (1992). *The Cognitive Neuropsychology of Schizophrenia*. Hillsdale, NJ: Erlbaum.

Giovannetti, T., Buxbaum, L., Biran I., & Chatterjee, A. (2005). Reduced endogenous controlling alien hand syndrome: evidence from naturalistic action. *Neuropsychologia, 43*, 75–88.

Goldberg G., Mayer N., & Toglia J. (1981). Medial frontal cortex and the alien hand sign. *Archives of Neurology, 38*, 683–686.

Graham, G., & Stephens, G. L. (2000). *When Self-Consciousness Breaks: Alien Voices and Inserted Thoughts*. Cambridge, MA: MIT Press.

Hoerl, C. (2001). On thought insertion. *Philosophy, Psychiatry and Psychology, 8*, 189–200.

Jaspers, K. (1963). *General Psychopathology*. Manchester: Manchester University Press.

Kim J. (1976). Events as property exemplifications. In M. Brand, & D. Walton (Eds.), *Action Theory* (pp. 310–326). Dordrecht: Springer.

Klein, S. (2012). The self and its brain. *Social Cognition, 30*, 474–518.

Klein, S., & Nichols, S. (2012). Memory and the sense of personal identity. *Mind, 121*, 677–702.

Mellor, C. S. (1970). First rank symptoms of schizophrenia. I. The frequency of schizophrenics on admission to hospital. II. Differences between individual firstrank symptoms. *British Journal of Psychiatry, 117*, 15–23.

Moran, R. (2001). *Authority and Estrangement: An Essay on Self-Knowledge*. Princeton, NJ: Princeton University Press.

Mullins, S., & Spence, S. (2003). Re-examining thought insertion. Semi-structured literature review and conceptual analysis. *British Journal of Psychiatry, 182*, 293–298.

Rachman, S. (1981). Unwanted intrusive cognitions. *Advances in Behaviour Research and Therapy, 3*, 89–99.

Saks, E. (2007). *The Centre Cannot Hold: A Memoir of my Schizophrenia*. London: Virago.

Schneider, K. (1959). *Clinical Psychopathology*. New York: Grune & Stratton.

17
Thought Insertion and the Ontology of Thinking

Johannes Roessler

17.1. The No Subject View

The complaint that thoughts are being inserted into one's mind looks, at first sight, unintelligible. We do not ordinarily seem to conceive of thoughts as items that can be placed or put (or, as one patient put it, flashed) into minds or heads. So it is natural to think that we have no real understanding of the content of the delusion. Put bluntly, we don't really know what patients are talking about. This is a natural reaction, but, according to the dominant view, it is too hasty. On reflection, and drawing on philosophical discussions of the ownership of thoughts, we can articulate intelligible truth conditions for patients' statements. That is not say, of course, that patients are right to attribute the thoughts they experience as alien to others (as they usually, though not invariably, do: see Henriksen et al., 2019). They *are* right about two things, though. They are talking about mental events they correctly identify as thoughts. And they are right, furthermore, that there is a sense in which the question of the 'ownership' of a thought is not settled by one's awareness that the thought takes place in one's own mind. Here are three statements from articles that promote this sort of interpretation (the first quote is from the paper that pioneered the interpretation, the second from an influential article that helped to disseminate it, the third from one of the many recent contributions in which the interpretation is taken for granted)[1]:

> The patient (...) reports that an alien thought occurs in her mind, but insists that it is not she who thinks the thought. (Stephens & Graham, 1994, p. 7)

---

[1] See also e.g., Peacocke (2008), Bortolotti and Broome (2009), Pickard (2010), Martin and Pacherie (2013), Sousa and Swiney (2013), Sollberger (2014), Pedrini (2015), Seeger (2015), Gallagher (2015), Fernández (2010). (The last contribution differs from the standard view in taking thought insertion to be about belief states rather than thoughts conceived as events.)

The schizophrenic seems to find himself with first-person knowledge of a token thought which was formed by someone else. (Campbell, 1999, p. 620)

How could anyone really think that thoughts woven into their stream of consciousness belonged to someone else? (Parrott, 2017, p. 40)

There may be a subtle difference of opinion as regards the condition that needs to be satisfied for 'a thought' to be fully *one's own thought*. Stephens and Graham take this to be a matter of oneself 'thinking' the thought. For Campbell, the critical question is who 'forms' (or 'generates') the thought. Parrot's formulation seems to be neutral on how to specify the full-ownership-conferring relation. Still, it seems to be agreed on all hands that it is possible to be aware of 'a thought' without being aware of the thought's owner, in a sense of 'ownership' that is to be distinguished from ownership of the mind in which 'the thought occurs'. Let's call this the No Subject view.

In recent work on thought insertion, the No Subject view has often been uncritically assumed, as if it were so much common sense. One source of the view's popularity, I think, is a certain analysis of the familiar phenomenon of unwelcome or intrusive or disturbing thoughts. As Harry Frankfurt wrote in a discussion that inspired Stephens and Graham's interpretation of thought insertion, 'to some of the thoughts that occur in our minds, as to some of the events in our bodies, we are mere passive bystanders' (p. 59). The notion of an impersonal or 'subjectless' awareness of a 'thought' may seem to capture precisely the 'spectatorial' character of our relation to certain thoughts—thoughts with which we may not, as Frankfurt puts it, 'identify' ourselves. If this is right, then the No Subject really may *be* so much common sense. Its credentials can be established by reflection on cases of 'ordinary alienation', quite independently of its potential to shed light on a bizarre delusion such as thought insertion.

Nevertheless, there are grounds for suspicion about the No Subject view. One is that its advocates are notably cagey about what is involved in being aware, impersonally, of a 'thought'. Campbell speaks of thoughts as things we 'encounter in consciousness' (1999, p. 615). But how is that metaphor to be cashed out? Furthermore, formulations of the No Subject view can seem to equivocate on the term 'thought'. Thoughts are being treated in the same breath as mental events and as the objects or contents of such events. Is this merely carelessness or is it indicative of something more serious? And there is a question whether the No Subject view may not falsify the phenomenology of what I called ordinary alienation. Consider the first sentences of a recent publication entitled *Overcoming Unwanted Intrusive Thoughts. A CTB-based Guide for Getting Over Frightening, Obsessive, or Disturbing Thoughts*:

Have you ever stood on the edge of a train platform, minding your own business, and then, suddenly out of the blue, had the brief thought, *I could jump off and die!* Or have you been struck by the passing thought, *Hey, I could push that guy onto the tracks!* (Winston & Seif, 2017, p. 1)

On the No Subject view, 'encountering' such thoughts may involve no awareness of who is their thinker. Since tokens of the first person refer to whoever is using them, one should, as a consequence, be uncertain as to *who* is thought to be able to jump off (or push). Having such thoughts would be akin to hearing a voice while being uncertain as to who is speaking. That seems implausible. While the thoughts in question can be disturbing, it is not uncertainty over the reference of 'I' that creates anxiety (quite the reverse). My first aim in what follows is to substantiate these worries. The No Subject view, I argue, not only misrepresents our ordinary conception of thoughts and thinking (making it unwise to rely on the view in interpreting patients' statements); there are reasons to doubt its coherence. I also wish to suggest that closer attention to the ontology of thinking can provide a more helpful perspective on alienation, both of the 'ordinary' variety and the pathological kind manifested by the delusion of thought insertion.

17.2. Equivocal Thoughts

Start with two distinctions common in philosophical discussions of thoughts and thinking. (I am drawing in particular on Zeno Vendler's *Res Cogitans*; Vendler, 1972).[2] First, we need a distinction between the activity of thinking about something and the sorts of events that tend to occur as part of that activity. The former is arguably not an event—something that occurs or happens at a particular time—but a process, unfolding over a period of time. Correlatively, thinking about something does not fall within the ontological category of particulars. 'Olive is thinking about her summer holiday' does not entail the existence of an event of Olive's thinking about her holiday. (For one thing, Olive's activity may be ongoing.) However, engaging in the activity of thinking about something is typically, and perhaps necessarily, bound up with the occurrence of attendant events. As part of her activity, it occurred to Olive that Cornwall could be wet in August, and she reluctantly concluded that Switzerland was not an option. These facts seem to entail the existence

---

[2] See also O'Shaughnessy (2000), ch. 6 and pp. 324–325.

of particular events, for example it's occurring to Olive that Cornwall can be wet in August. Following Vendler, we might call such events 'mental acts'. This brings us to the second distinction we need: between a mental act and its object or content. The same proposition—that it can be wet in Cornwall in August—can be the object of different kinds of mental acts, and the object of mental acts on the part of different thinkers. It is something Nasya conjectured, Victor discovered, and that occurred to Olive and Yousif.

Where do *thoughts* fit into this schema? There are clearly two candidates: we might call 'thoughts' the objects of such events as form part of the process of thinking; or the events themselves. I briefly go over the case for each candidate in turn.

(a) It is surely natural to conceive of thoughts as *things we think*, in a sense of 'think' that is something of an umbrella term for different kinds of mental acts: Nasya, Victor and Olive all may be said, in their different ways, to think the thought that Cornwall can be wet in August. To think something, in that distinctive sense, is not the same as engaging in the activity of thinking *about* something. Nor does it entail believing what one thinks.[3] Thinking a thought can be quite non-committal. It might be a matter, for example, of mooting a proposition for further consideration. (More on this next.) I will not try to settle the large question here of what thoughts, conceived as things we think, are. But I want to mention two key features the answer would need to accommodate. First, thoughts can be true or false.[4] Second, they are can be shared. For example, thoughts can be expressed by the use of speech. As Vendler observes, '(i)t does not take mind-reading to acquaint oneself with somebody else's thought; ordinary reading or listening is enough' (Vendler, 1972, pp. 36–37). And of course different thinkers may, quite independently of each other, happen to think the same thought.

(b) We can distinguish two routes to the notion of 'occurrent thoughts', thoughts conceived as mental events 'woven into the stream of consciousness'. It might be said that the notion captures ordinary usage. And it might be said that we need the notion to articulate the

---

[3] There is a common use of 'think', of course, that does have this implication. As Ryle observed, 'it is a vexatious fact about the English language that we use the verb 'to think' both for the beliefs and opinions that a man has, and for the pondering and reflecting that a man does [...].' (1971, p. 392)

[4] A wider use of the term would allow that thoughts can be reported not just by the use of 'that' clauses following a verb of some mental act, but also by the use of oratio recta. For example, a schizophrenic patient reported the thought: 'Kill God!' In this broader sense, thoughts may include not just propositions—things that can be true or false—but commands, questions, imprecations, etc. Still, the second feature holds: the same thought, in this broad sense, can be the object of many thinkers' mental acts of directing, asking, or cursing.

phenomenology of what Frankfurt calls 'mental passivity'. Re ordinary usage: thoughts are said to cross our minds, to arrest our attention, or to strike us out of the blue, etc.; and a natural way to interpret these and related constructions, so one might argue, is that they reflect a conception of thoughts as events. Re mental passivity: suppose Frankfurt is right that to some of our thoughts 'we are mere passive bystanders'. If we are spectators, there must be something for us to spectate, viz. (one might argue): events that happen in our minds.

I will later raise some misgivings about (b), but for now, let's assume that the notion of an 'occurrent thought' captures part of our ordinary thinking about thoughts. My question is whether the No Subject view is right that being aware of the occurrence of a thought may leave one in the dark as to who (if anyone) is doing the thinking. I start from this observation: one commonality among diverse formulations of the No Subject view is that they equivocate between a conception of thoughts as mental events and a conception of thoughts as things we think. After some illustrative examples, I spell out the charge of equivocation, and then offer a diagnosis.

Here is Frankfurt: 'It is not incoherent, despite the air of paradox, to say that a thought that occurs in my mind may or may not be something that *I think*' (Frankfurt, 1988, p. 59). Here are Stephens and Graham: 'The patient (...) reports that an alien thought occurs in her mind, but insists that it is not she who thinks the thought' (Stephens & Graham, 1994, p. 7). And here is Parfit: Descartes (in the context of the Second Meditation, in which, Parfit maintains, he should not have claimed to be aware of the existence of a thinker) 'could have claimed instead: "This is a thought, therefore at least one thought is being thought"' (Parfit, 1984, pp. 224–225). In the first two passages, an *occurrent thought* is said to be something someone may *think*. The third passage is at least suggestive of such a reading, on the natural assumption that the thought mentioned in the conclusion ('at least one thought is being thought') is supposed to be the self same thought referred to in the premise ('this thought'—where 'this' is presumably intended as a sort of introspective demonstrative, referring to a concurrent mental event).

'Thoughts' are expected to do double duty in these passages. They are things that happen, and they are the things we think (or at least *may* think) when such things happen. It should then be intelligible to speak of Olive thinking the event that happened when she started to ponder her holiday. Indeed, 'thoughts' would be peculiarly self-reflexive: when a thought occurs, what is being thought is that very (occurrent) thought. That cannot be right: the object of Olive's occurrent thought is *that Cornwall can be wet in August*—*something* that is not an event. The problem, then, may be put this way: people do not think events.[5] The objects or contents of the mental acts we perform as part of the process of thinking about something are not things that happen.[6]

Can we formulate the No Subject view in a way that is free of equivocation? Here is a start: we might say that in being aware of an occurrent thought woven into one's stream of consciousness, one is aware of an event that involves the thinking (in the umbrella sense) of a thought. For example, one may be aware of the event of affirming or conjecturing or mooting or realizing that Cornwall can be wet in August. Note, though, that by introducing the *object* of an occurrent thought we simultaneously seem to introduce its *subject*: the event of affirming (etc.) something is the event of *someone* affirming something. For one thing, such acts are moves in the game of giving and asking for reasons. They invite specific 'reason-seeking' questions, questions addressed to the subject of the mental act. For example, someone's act of mooting that p might be greeted with the query: why do you take that p to be a relevant observation? This would seem to put paid to the idea of a wholly impersonal articulation of our awareness of occurrent thoughts. For example, it would seem to impugn Parfit's claim that 'we could fully describe our thoughts without claiming that they have thinkers' (1984, p. 224) Still, there may seem to be room for a more modest brand of the No Subject view. The suggestion may be this: one can be aware (in the way in which we are aware of the sorts of events implicated in the activity of thinking about a particular matter) of someone's affirming or mooting something, without being aware that it is oneself who is affirming/mooting it.

There is a sense, of course, in which that sort of awareness is utterly commonplace. In listening to someone, or in reading an article, we are aware that someone is affirming or mooting various propositions. Suppose that, unbeknownst to one, the speaker or writer is none other than oneself. This is not quite what the No Subject view needs, however. The problem is that the awareness one enjoys in such a case is simply the experience of listening or reading, rather than an experience we would naturally describe as an awareness of an

---

[5] This is intended to echo a remark of Jennifer Hornsby's: 'people do not do events.' Her point was that 'actions', as the word is ordinarily used in English, are things we do, and that philosophers therefore need to be careful to distinguish actions in the ordinary sense—'things we do'—from actions conceived in the way that has become standard in the philosophy of action: as events. In her example, one thing Anna did was *write the word 'blue'*. As Hornsby points out, 'such a thing as *write the word blue* [...] is repeatable; it is not a particular' (Hornsby, 1999, pp. 623–624).

[6] The notion of a 'token thought' encourages the idea that occurrent thoughts relate to things we think in the way in which a particular event relates to a type it instantiates. But things we think of are not even *types of* events.

occurrent thought. One may well be aware of an act of affirming or mooting here, but not *in the way* in which we are aware of such acts when they occur as part of our activity of thinking about something. What we would need, to make sense of the modest variant of the No Subject view, is a case in which

(i) one is aware of the occurrence and content of an act of (e.g.) affirming or mooting something;
(ii) one's awareness is not a matter of observation: that is, it's not by looking or listening or in some other way attending to someone's overt performance of the act that one knows *what* is being affirmed or mooted; for in such a case, one's experience would be that of hearing or seeing or in some other way observing someone thinking something, rather than an experience of an 'occurrent thought';
(iii) one is not aware of *oneself* performing the act.

Can these conditions be jointly satisfied? The problem I see here develops from an observation about the propriety of the question, 'How do you know?' We would ordinarily regard the question as off-key in response to *first-person* self-ascriptions of acts of thinking (as we would in response to first-person self-ascriptions of attitudes or intentional actions). But we would take it that any other attributions of acts of thinking are in principle open to that question. This gives rise to a dilemma for the No Subject view. If the putative awareness of a mental act is a case of knowledge that is immune to the request for an account of how one knows, then it must be first-person awareness of oneself (e.g.) mooting or affirming something—in violation of condition (iii). If one's knowledge of the mental act *is* subject to the demand for a source, one's awareness must play a certain epistemic role: it must be a matter of observing and so finding out that someone is mooting or affirming something. It would need to involve something like an act of perceptual (or quasi-perceptual) attention, enabling one to detect the occurrence of the mental act. There would be room for questions such as these: 'Are you sure you got the content of the mental act right? Are you confident it is an act of affirmation rather than merely a case of mooting something?' In other words, one's awareness would be an experience of (in some way) observing what someone is thinking—in violation of condition (ii). Phrases such as 'introspectively encountering a thought' conceal this issue. They encourage the assumption that one can be aware of an act of thinking *in the way* in which we are ordinarily aware of our own acts of thinking, without being aware of oneself as the subject of the act. The trouble is that by subtracting the first-person content of the awareness, we are turning the awareness into an experience, not of a 'thought', but of observing someone thinking, akin to the experience we have when we listen to each other's speech acts.

To summarize, the 'thoughts' that figure in the No Subject tradition seem to be a mongrel: they are supposed to be things that are *thinkable* but also *happen*. When we disentangle these elements, we can see that there is a substantive challenge confronting the No Subject view, a challenge that—possibly as a result of the tendency to equivocate on 'thoughts'—has not received the attention it would deserve. What is not clear is that we can provide a coherent articulation of the idea that one can be aware of the occurrence of mental act in the way in which we are ordinarily aware of our own mental acts, without being aware of (oneself) thinking something.[7] The challenge has an immediate bearing on the standard interpretation of thought insertion. If we cannot make sense of the assumption that 'thoughts' can be introspectively 'encountered' (in a way that involves no awareness of oneself as their thinker) we can hardly expect to make rational sense of the delusion, relying on that assumption.

There is more to be said about the challenge, but at this point I want to turn to another, more basic question raised by the standard interpretation. Should we interpret the 'thoughts' patients complain of as (in the philosophers' jargon) 'occurrent' or 'token' thoughts? I want to make a case for a negative answer. The negative answer, however, will be part of a positive proposal. Drawing on work by Josef Parnas and his colleagues, I will suggest that the delusion is best understood as the end point of a pathological process of self-alienation, a central aspect of which is the progressive 'reification' of thoughts (= things we think).

17.3. Thoughts and Thinkings

The category of events has been a cornerstone of post-Davidsonian philosophy of mind. But it is worth reminding ourselves that Davidson, for one, did not assume that there are idiomatic English expressions to pick out the sorts of events he was interested in. For instance, Davidson's illustrative list of mental events (in the first sentence of his eponymous essay) starts with 'perceivings'

---

[7] One complication is that thinking about something may involve imagining conversations. Could there be cases in which it is indeterminate whether imagining someone telling one 'Cornwall can be wet in August' amounts to mooting a proposition as part of one's activity of thinking about something or *merely* to an imagined conversation about the weather? I suppose there may be such cases (say, in a state of reverie)—but they will not be clear-cut examples of being aware of a thought without being aware of thinking.

and 'rememberings'. That seems a sensible choice of terminology. 'Perceptions' and 'memories', for example, would have been inapt. Now suppose we wish to add to Davidson's list a term referring to such events as occurred in Olive's and Nasya' stream of consciousness. Adopting Davidson's policy, we might label them thinkings. Or should we say that, in this case, a more idiomatic alternative is at hand: thoughts?

Straight off, the evidence for an affirmative answer to that question may seem overwhelming. Recall the examples of intrusive thoughts I quoted earlier: have you ever had the 'brief/passing thought'? And recall Frankfurt's point: there are 'thoughts that strike us unexpectedly out of the blue; and thoughts that run willy-nilly through our heads' (Frankfurt, 1988, p. 59). Again, consider an example of Anscombe's: 'The thought: "it is my duty" kept hammering away in my mind until I said to myself "I can do no other" and so signed' (Anscombe, 1957, p. 11). And think of the myriad adjectives we naturally reach for in characterizing our own and others' thoughts: tormenting, soothing, untimely, predictable, and so on. Is it not obvious that we must be talking about mental events here: in particular, about their temporal profile ('brief'), their phenomenology ('kept hammering away') and our cognitive relation to them (striking 'expectedly out of the blue')?

I want to argue that it is not obvious. There is, first of all, strong counterevidence. The thought: 'it is my duty' is something that can be true or false, as it the thought: 'I could push that guy onto the tracks!' If there is a completely general characteristic of thoughts, as we ordinarily conceive them, it is that they can be identified by the use of a that-clause or scare quotes. (Sometimes only the latter will do: see note 4.) If that is right, then thoughts, as ordinarily conceived, are not mental events but the objects or contents of certain mental events. Having, or being struck by, a thought is a matter of thinking something. 'I had the passing thought: "I could push that guy onto the tracks"' is equivalent to 'I found myself suddenly (and perhaps casually) thinking: "I could push that guy onto the tracks."' You may qualify the thought as 'passing' but you nevertheless take it to be something that you think—and that others may think as well. (In fact, if the guide from which the quote is taken is reliable, most of us have done so at some point.)

Furthermore, on closer inspection, the case for construing thoughts as events looks weak. True, we speak of thoughts striking us. But is it *events* that strike us? Surely not: the sorts of things that—literally—strike us ('hit forcibly') are persisting objects; paradigmatically: people. The same may be said of 'hammering away' ('work hard and persistently'). This encourages a general, parsimonious hypothesis: we consistently conceive of thoughts as things we think (not as events), but there is a tendency to bring out salient features of our mental lives—in particular, of the kinds of mental acts involved in thinking—by projecting them on to the things we think. We might label this a matter of 'reifying' thoughts: we treat them metaphorically as things that have duration and causal powers, for example. Unexpectedly finding oneself thinking something becomes 'being struck by a passing thought' or a 'thought crossing one's mind'. Being disturbed or repelled by one's thinking certain things is a matter of experiencing 'intrusive' thoughts.

This last example touches on what Frankfurt calls 'mental passivity'. On his analysis, 'occurrent thoughts' are internal to our experience in such cases: we find ourselves confronted by 'a thought' without having a sense of thinking something. Here is an alternative account. We can be surprised, puzzled, and disturbed by things we think, giving us a sense of being, in Frankfurt's phrase, 'passive bystanders' to our thinking. Still, what we find surprising or puzzling is something we do, viz. thinking—e.g., affirming or mooting—some thought. Such acts can be spontaneous and unbidden. They may not be embedded in an intentional activity of thinking about something (though they *may* be embedded in an involuntary such activity, in the sense of 'involuntary' in which you may involuntarily imagine a tune you can't get out of your system). One reason for preferring this analysis to Frankfurt's is that sufferers from intrusive thoughts often find the experience distressing precisely because they find *themselves* thinking these thoughts. Connectedly, when intrusive thoughts involve tokens of the first person (as they often do) usually the subject unhesitatingly takes the thought to be about themselves. That suggests that an awareness of thinking the thought is part of the experience. Frankfurt makes much of what he sees as an analogy between thoughts and bodily movements: a thought occurring in my mind, he suggests, need not be something *I think*, just as an 'event occurring in my body may or may not be something that *I do*' (1988, p. 60). It is debatable whether events occurring in my body are *ever* something that I do (see note 5), but in any case, the analogy is surely forced. There simply is no equivalent, in the case of thoughts, of being proprioceptively or visually aware of a spasmodic twitch.[8]

I have raised doubts about two assumptions that underpin the standard interpretation of thought insertion. In the last section, I challenged the intelligibility of a 'subjectless' awareness of an 'occurrent thought'. In this section, I have questioned the very idea of an 'occurrent thought'. If we abandon these

---

[8] The closest we seem to get to this would be the experience of seeming to hear a voice in one's head. But hallucinating is not the same thing as thinking. Note that the standard interpretation does not say that patients mistake an auditory experiences of someone expressing a thought for the occurrence of a 'thought' in their mind.

assumptions, it becomes difficult to sustain a distinction that has routinely been made in the literature on thought insertion between two senses of ownership: a minimal sense in which a thought is my thought simply in virtue of occurring in my mind vs. a richer sense in which a thought is my thought only it if meets a further condition, such as my thinking (Stephens and Graham) or 'generating' (Campbell) the thought. If thoughts are things we think, rather than mental events of which we may be introspectively aware, then presumably *my* thoughts are things I think. It would then seem as puzzling as ever what patients might have in mind when they talk about thoughts that are not theirs. I want to end by approaching this issue from a different perspective, one that gives a vital role to the psychological and temporal context of the delusion.

17.4. Thought Insertion Without 'Occurrent Thoughts'

A useful starting point is a diatribe Josef Parnas and his colleagues have recently launched against (as they see it) philosophers of mind dabbling in psychopathology. A major problem with recent work on thought insertion, they contend, is that much of it is conducted by authors who lack 'any comprehensive familiarity with clinical psychopathology' and rely 'only on a few examples that are constantly recycled in the literature' (Henriksen, Parnas, & Zahavi, 2019, p. 4). Partly as a result of this, there is tendency to distort the delusion by 'decontextualizing' it. We can distinguish two aspects of the context that, according to Henriksen et al., goes missing when philosophers of mind construct theories of thought insertion. First, schizophrenic delusions are manifestations of a global 'reorganization' or 'transformation' of consciousness (Parnas & Sass, 2001, p. 101), characterized by such things as a 'diminished presence of the world', 'solipsism', and an 'altered experiential framework'. It is only by relating a delusion to the 'Gestalt' in which it is 'embedded' that we can begin to understand it. Call this the psychological context. Second, thought insertion is described as an 'end phenomenon': roughly, the delusion marks the end of the line of a process of 'increasing self-alienation', starting long before the onset of psychosis.[9] Only in the light of the preceding stages of the process is it possible to understand the delusion. Call this the temporal context.

---

[9] Henriksen, Parnas, and Zahavi (2019, p. 6). They attribute the term 'end phenomenon' to Klosterkötter (1988).

Let's set aside for a moment the question of *why* patients believe what they do, and focus on the question of *what* it is they believe. Attention to the temporal context of the delusion provides a distinctive and I think illuminating perspective on this question. There is much evidence that a concern with ownership of thoughts *predates* the formation of the delusion. During the prodromal phase of schizophrenia patients often describe their state of mind in terms that are closely related to the delusion they (typically) go on to develop but that do not evoke the same kind of bafflement. One key difference is that, at this stage, the disconcerting characterization of their state of mind occurs within the scope of an 'as if …' operator. They might say, for example, 'my thinking felt strange, as if it didn't have to be any longer I myself who was thinking' or 'it seems to me as if it is not me who generates these ideas'.[10] Now, one way to interpret the difference between such 'as if' beliefs and the subsequent delusion would be as different kinds of responses to patients' evidence, in a broad sense of 'evidence'. For example, we might say that there is an abnormal phenomenology of thinking, of a kind that can rationalize—can make seem plausible—the denial of ownership of 'thoughts'. The idea would be that during the prodromal phase, patients describe that experience by reference to the claim it rationalizes, without *making* that claim. Post-psychosis, they make it.

That 'evidential' interpretation is not mandatory, however. Consider this flowery description of a sun-set: 'it looks as if the sun is sinking into the sea'. To get the idea here we do not need to think there is evidence that the sun will sink into the sea, or even to understand what would constitute such evidence. The statement is quite unlike 'it looks as if it is going to rain', used as a way of registering the presence of evidence that rain is imminent. We might say that the scene is described by likening the sun to something that can (be seen to) sink into the sea.[11] Parnas and Sass characterize patients' 'as if' statements as 'metaphorical' (Parnas & Sass, 2001, p. 109). A good example of what they have in mind is one patient's statement that he felt 'as if' his interlocutor somehow 'invaded him' (ibid). It is of course not easy to say what is involved in understanding such a statement, but it seems clear that to understand it we do not need to grasp what it would mean to be (literally) invaded by an interlocutor, or to recognize the patient's experience as something that would provide intelligible evidence for such a claim.

---

[10] Klosterkötter (1988, pp. 110–111, my translation); Parnas and Sass (2001, p. 106).
[11] I borrow the example (and this gloss on it) from Martin (2010).

If we look at the content of patients' 'as if' descriptions of their thinking, taking into account the wider narratives of which they form part, we may note three themes, corresponding to the threefold distinction I made at the beginning of section 17.2: patients' reflections concern (a) the activity of thinking about something, (b) the things they think, and (c) the mental acts involved in thinking about something.

Re (a): the first example—'my thinking felt strange, as if it didn't have to be any longer I myself who was thinking'—is preceded by a catalogue of impairments in the patient's ability to think about something: she had problems concentrating, there were frightening lapses of short term memory, disabling her from carrying out everyday activities; when thinking about something she would often experience a blank ('the thread was cut off') or would suddenly find herself thinking about unrelated matters. In addition to (in the words of the second patient) a lack of 'mastery' over the course of one's cogitations, there are other, harder-to-articulate alterations, summarized by Parnas et al. under the heading of feeling 'distanced' from one's thinking. The first patient tries to capture these changes in the following terms: 'it was as if someone no longer thought himself, as if he were prevented from doing his own thinking'.[12]

Re (b): patients extend their concern with ownership to the objects of their thinking. For example: 'I had the impression that everything I think isn't necessarily my own ideas'.[13]

Re I: I suggested earlier that we sometimes 'reify' thoughts (= the things we think), by treating them as object with causal powers, where this affords an indirect characterization of our mental acts (as in 'being struck by a passing thought'). Some of the patients' descriptions of their thinking are naturally understood in this way. Consider this phrase: 'it is as if it's not me who generates these thoughts'.[14] Patients are surely not complaining here of a lack of originality in their thinking. Rather, they speak of thoughts as if they were objects with passive causal powers, capable of being 'generated'. Likening thoughts to things that can be 'generated' (and are not generated by oneself) may be a way of articulating what is strange about their thinking these thoughts, including the sense of lacking mastery and feeling 'distanced'.[15]

---

[12] 'Es war, wie wenn einer gar nicht mehr selber denkt, an seinem eigenen Denken gehindert wird.' (Klosterkötter, 1988, p. 110).
[13] See Klosterkötter (1988, p. 110).
[14] 'Patients also often report that certain thoughts may feel as if they weren't generated by the patients themselves.' (Henriksen et al., 2019, p. 6)
[15] It is tempting to interpret the use of the phrase 'generating thoughts' in the recent philosophical literature (e.g., in Campbell, 1999) as an import from schizophrenic patients' 'metaphorical' employment of the phrase.

In the light of all this, let us return to the two kinds of reaction to reports of thought insertion I mentioned at the outset: sheer bafflement as to what patients might be talking about vs confidence that (armed with the No Subject view) it is possible to make sense of these beliefs. One thing that has emerged is that the two reactions are not exhaustive. Suppose we understand the delusion as developing from patients' prodromal 'as if' reflections. Specifically, suppose that, with the onset of psychosis, patients are disposed to take at face value propositions they previously used to articulate their state of mind in broadly metaphorical terms. This would enable us to comprehend what patients have in mind, without thinking of the delusion's content in terms that would invite a rationalizing explanation. A sense of the bizarre would be retained.[16] (Compare our reaction to someone who *believes* that all the world's a stage.)

But can reflection on the delusion's context shed light on *why* patients believe what they do? Part of the reason work in the tradition of 'phenomenological psychopathology' (such as Parnas's and his colleagues') has had little impact on the philosophy of mind, I think, is that it can seem as if this work confines itself to making connections among symptoms and so placing them in their (psychological and temporal) contexts, without attempting a causal explanation of a delusion. Ultimately, the phenomenologists may seem to be committed to a view of schizophrenic delusions as 'incomprehensible', as not being open (in Jaspers' terms) to any form of 'genetic' psychological understanding. Correlatively, if we think some such understanding must surely be possible, it may seem as if there is really no serious alternative to a broadly rationalizing explanation, one that seeks to make sense of the delusion by reference to aspects of the patients' situation that can seem to provide evidence for it.

That diagnosis, I want to suggest, underestimates the resources of the phenomenological approach. Parnas' and his colleagues' work does provide materials for a certain kind of 'genetic' understanding of the delusion, viz. in two parts. The first part is an account of the prodromal 'as if' belief. This is not a delusion, let alone a bizarre one. We can surely make sense of the belief, as an attempt to articulate strange and distressing experiences. The attempt may of course itself be coloured by the patient's emerging schizophrenic state of mind. Perhaps only someone peculiarly susceptible to the general theme of being

---

[16] For Parnas, that point is crucial. He draws a sharp distinction between two kinds of delusions. 'Empirical delusions' are stubborn, irrational beliefs that, however, have intelligible truth conditions and are informed by a sense of the relevant reasons. 'Bizarre' or 'autistic-schizophrenic delusions' are insulated from the space of reasons and their content is elusive; they present themselves as 'a subjective revelation that needs no evidence from the shared empirical world in order to become valid' (Parnas, 2004, p. 157). I discuss the distinction in more detail in Roessler (2013).

'influenced', or being no longer one's familiar self, would tend to describe their experiences in terms such as (a)–(c). Alternatively, those themes may themselves be rationally intelligible in the light of patients' experience. In any case, it is the second part that moves beyond a sense-making explanation. And it is here that what I called the psychological context of the delusion—the state of consciousness in which it is 'embedded'—plays a distinctive non-rational role. Parnas and Sass speak of a 'delusional transformation', characterized by a fundamentally altered experience of self (a form of 'solipsism') and world (the construction of a 'delusional world'). As I suggested earlier, a relevant aspect of that 'transformation' may be that patients are now disposed to take at face value ideas that previously figured in the context of a metaphorical 'as if' description.[17] How is this to be understood? An austere version of the two-part story might simply say that the disposition to do so is one facet of the cluster of tendencies that constitute the delusional state of consciousness. But there may be ways of rendering the disposition intelligible by reference to more basic elements of the cluster. If the schizophrenic 'transformation' of consciousness is marked by a 'subjectivization' of reality—a quasi-solipsistic inability to distinguish the objective world from the way things strikes one (Parnas & Sass, 2001; Parnas, 2004)—it may be unsurprising if patients fail to retain a grip on the metaphorical character of their prodromal musings under the heading of ownership.

These sketchy remarks suggest an alternative diagnosis of the disagreement between post-Heideggerian 'phenomenological psychopathology' (exemplified by the work of Parnas and his colleagues) and post-Davidsonian philosophy of mind (exemplified by the standard interpretation of thought insertion). It is not that the former confines itself to describing the delusion as part of a pattern, whereas the latter seeks a causal explanation. Rather, the key difference is that the causal explanation provided for by the former makes essential use of the notion of a state of consciousness—something that is altogether missing from the latter. In part, the disagreement here may reflect a more general dispute about the reality and explanatory value of 'states of consciousness'. One way to understand that dispute is this. In post-Davidsonian philosophy of mind, psychological explanations are taken to turn on causal relations among mental events or 'token' mental states. But suppose we think of such explanations as making essential reference to subjects' exercise of

---

[17] Another aspect is that patients often embellish things by attributing the thoughts of which they complain to specific individuals, or alleging that the thoughts are 'generated' by them. Klosterkötter refers to this as the phase of 'concretization', typically reflecting the patient's individual circumstances and experiences. See Klosterkötter (1988, p. 251).

relevant capacities, say intellectual, perceptual, or practical capacities. That would invite the thought that there is a difference between merely having a capacity and being in a state in which one is able to exercise it (in which the capacity is 'capacitated'). And it would make room for the thought that the availability of a 'rationalizing explanation' is not a basic given of human psychology but conditional on the satisfaction of an enabling condition: only if the subject is in a state of wakeful consciousness (rather than, say, in a state of sleep, drunkenness, or insanity) can her actions and attitudes be explained, directly, by reference to the exercise of her rational capacities.[18]

17.5. Conclusion

By way of summary, let me distinguish three tendencies to 'reify' thoughts (things we think) that have figured in my discussion. A mild form of reification can be observed in some of the ways we ordinarily talk about our thinking. Thoughts are said to *act* on us in various ways: they cross our minds, arrest our attention, etc., where this is used to bring out certain features of the mental acts involved in thinking the thoughts, say their spontaneity or their absorbing character. The tendency can also take a pathological form, implicated in several symptoms of schizophrenia. For example, patients sometimes 'describe their thoughts in physical terms, as if possessing an object-like spatial quality' or 'locate them spatially ("my thoughts feel mainly in the right side of the brain")' (Parnas & Sass 2001, p. 107). Thought insertion is another example of this: patients treat thoughts as if they were not the content of their thinking but something that could be 'generated', or even inserted into someone's mind. Yet another form of reification is in evidence in recent philosophical work on ownership of thoughts. Thoughts are conceived here as particulars we 'encounter' or introspectively 'access'. And we are supposed to be able to 'access' thoughts without having much of an idea as to *whose* thoughts they are. I have argued that this view is not supported by the first, mild form of reification, and that it offers no help in understanding the second, pathological form.

---

[18] The most detailed discussion of the nature and explanatory value of states of consciousness is Brian O'Shaughnessy's *Consciousness and the World*. For an illuminating Aristotelian perspective on this, see Crowther (2018).

Acknowledgements

For extremely helpful comments on a draft of this chapter, I would like to thank Lucy Campbell, Tom Crowther, Naomi Eilan, Alexander Greenberg, Christoph Hoerl, Hemdat Lerman, Guy Longworth, Eylem Özaltun, Jack Shardlow, and Matt Soteriou. I am also grateful to an anonymous referee for valuable comments and suggestions.

References

Anscombe, E. (1957). *Intention*. Oxford: Blackwell.
Bortolotti, L., & Broome, M. (2009). A role for ownership and authorship of thoughts in the analysis of thought insertion. *Phenomenology and the Cognitive Sciences, 8*, 205–224.
Campbell, J. (1999). Schizophrenia, the space of reasons, and thinking as a motor process. *The Monist, 82*, 609–25.
Crowther, T. (2018). Experience, dreaming and the phenomenology of wakeful consciousness. In F. Dorsch & F. Macpherson (Eds.), *Phenomenal Presence* (pp. 252–282). Oxford: Oxford University Press.
Fernández, J. (2010). Thought insertion and self-knowledge. *Mind & Language, 25*(1), 66–88.
Frankfurt, H. (1988). Identification and externality. In H. Frankfurt (Ed.), *The Importance of What We Care About: Philosophical Essays* (pp. 58–68). Cambridge: Cambridge University Press.
Gallagher, S. (2015). Relations between agency and ownership in the case of schizophrenic thought insertion and delusions of control. *Review of Philosophy and Psychology, 6*(4), 865–879.
Henriksen, M. G, Parnas, J., & Zahavi, D. (2019). Thought insertion and disturbed for-me-ness (minimal selfhood) in schizophrenia. *Consciousness and Cognition, 74*, 1–9.
Hornsby, J. (1999). Anomalousness in action. In L. Hahn (Ed.), *The Philosophy of Donald Davidson* (pp. 623–636). Chicago, IL: Open Court.
Klosterkötter (1988). *Basissymptome und Endphänomene der Schizophrenie*. Berlin: Springer.
Martin, M. (2010). What's in a look? In B. Nanay (Ed.), *Perceiving the World* (pp. 160–225). Oxford: Oxford University Press.
Martin, J., & Pacherie, E. (2013). Out of nowhere: Thought insertion, ownership and context-integration. *Consciousness and Cognition, 22*(1), 111–122.
O'Shaughnessy, B. (2000). *Consciousness and the World*. Oxford: Oxford University Press.
Parfit, D. (1984). *Reasons and Persons*. Oxford: Oxford University Press.
Parnas, J., & Sass, L. (2001). Self, solipsism, and schizophrenic delusions. *Philosophy, Psychiatry, & Psychology, 8*, 101–120.
Parnas, J. (2004). Belief and pathology of self-awareness. *Journal of Consciousness Studies, 11*, 148–161.
Parrott, M. (2017). Subjective misidentification and thought insertion. *Mind & Language, 32*(1), 39–64.
Peacocke, C. (2008). *Truly Understood*. Oxford: Oxford University Press.
Pedrini, P. (2015). Rescuing the 'loss-of-agency' account of thought insertion. *Philosophy, Psychiatry, & Psychology, 22*(3), 221–233.

Pickard, H. (2010). Schizophrenia and self-knowledge. *European Journal of Philosophy, 6*, 55–74.

Roessler, J. (2013). Thought insertion, self-awareness, and rationality. In K. W. M. Fulford, M. Davies, R. Gipps, G. Graham, & J. Sadler (Eds.), *The Oxford Handbook of Philosophy and Psychiatry* (pp. 658–672). Oxford: Oxford University Press.

Ryle, G. (1971). *Collected Papers Vol. II*. New York: Barnes and Noble.

Seeger, M. (2015). Authorship of thoughts in thought insertion: What is it for a thought to be one's own?. *Philosophical Psychology, 28*(6), 837–855.

Sollberger, M. (2014). Making sense of an endorsement model of thought-insertion. *Mind & Language, 29*(5), 590–612.

Sousa, P., & Swiney, L. (2013). Thought insertion: Abnormal sense of thought agency or thought endorsement?. *Phenomenology and the Cognitive Sciences, 12*(4), 637–654.

Stephens, G. L., & Graham, G. (1994). Self-consciousness, mental agency, and the clinical psychopathology of thought insertion. *Philosophy, Psychiatry, & Psychology, 1*, 1–12.

Vendler, Z. (1972). *Res Cogitans*. Ithaca, NY: Cornell University Press.

Winston, S., & Seif, M. (2017). *Overcoming Unwanted Intrusive Thoughts*. Oakland, CA: New Harbinger Publications.

Index

For the benefit of digital users, indexed terms that span two pages (e.g., 52–53) may, on occasion, appear on only one of those pages.

absence, awareness of 17–18
Acceptance and Commitment Therapy (ACT) 160–61
action without commitment 282–84
acts of consciousness 85–86
adaptive agency 49–51
affect
   affective framing of affordance 47–48, 49–50, 51, 54
   belief maintenance and revision 155
affordances 43
   affective framing 47–48, 49–50, 51, 54
   disclosure 49–52
   field of 45–46
   landscape of 45
   mental affordances 48–53
   solicitations and mental actions 44–49, 51
agency
   adaptive 49–51
   depression 50
   judgement of 247–48
   OCD 50
   phenomenology 154–55
   sense of agency 52–53, 81, 90–91, 154–55, 159, 177, 240–42, 247–49
   soundless voices 69–70
alien control 4–5, 51–52, 161–66, 175–76, 207–13
anarchic hand 207, 282–84
antipsychotic medication 200
apophany 14–15
'as if' statements 298–300
attention, selective 46–47, 54–55, 106
attribution
   attributional biases 164–65
   external attribution 161–66
   external misattribution 241
   misattribution of inner speech 62, 66–72
   of salience 121–22

auditory cortex, atypical connectivity 109
auditory processing streams 107–8
auditory-verbal hallucinations 3–4, 17–18, 101–12
   cognition 104–7
   co-occurrence of symptoms 199
   imagery 146
   inner speech 144–46, 177–78
   neural processing 107–9
   perception 104–7
   phenomenology 102–4
   top-down processing 140–41
authorship, sense of 104–7, 154–55
automatic processing 31
automatic writing 212–16
awareness of absence 17–18

Bayesian inference 35–36, 107, 114–15, 120–21, 122
'becoming sensory' 17–18, 27–28, 30–31, 34
beliefs
   belief-negative models 9
   belief-positive models 8–9
   cognitive processes of belief change 156
   emotions 155
   thought insertion as beliefs 15, 115–16
   see also delusional beliefs
Beringer, K. 34–35
Berze 32
bias
   attributional 164–65
   cognitive 120, 164–66
   externalizing 164–65
   jumping to conclusions 119–20, 165–66, 179
   personalizing 165
   phenomenology 37–38
   reasoning 165–66
   self-serving 164–65, 241

Binswanger, L. 28
Birchwood, M. 29–30
Blankenburg, W. 31, 32
bodily attunement 52–53

Capgras delusion 136, 137, 172
case examples 33–34, 37, 258–60, 265–67
central monitoring 204
cerebellum 239–41, 242, 243–47, 248
cerebral cortex, *see* cortex
Chadwick, P. 29–30
cognition
 auditory-verbal hallucinations 104–7
 automatic processing 31
 belief change 156
 biases 120, 164–66
 impairments 119–20, 164
 models 8–9, 29–30, 204
 phenomenology 37–38
 processes 31, 146
Coltheart, M. 172
commitment 273–86
 action without 282–84
 memory without 279–82
 ownership as 275–77
 thought without 277–79
common sense 31
comparator model 141, 176–77, 204–5, 241
compartmentalization 157–60
confederates 235
consciousness, acts of 85–86
content view 152–53, 155–57
context
 contextual coherence 69
 decontextualization 62–63, 127–28, 297
 experiential context 63, 116–18
 recontextualization 51–52, 127–28
Corlett, P. R. 125–26, 140–41
corollary discharge 204
cortex
 auditory cortex connectivity 109
 auditory processing streams 107–8
 cerebellar interactions 245–46
 grey matter changes 198, 200
 motor cortex 108–9
 supplementary motor area 108–9, 216

Davidson, D. 157–58
Davies, M. 172
decision forces 227–30

decontextualization 62–63, 127–28, 297
deficit accounts 115–16, 152
delusional atmosphere xxiii–xxiv, 22, 113, 116–17, 124–25
delusional beliefs
 belief-negative models 9
 belief-positive models 8–9
 cognitive models 8–9
 doxastic account 8–9, 11, 115–16
 DSM-5 definition 8–9
 first-rank symptoms 10–11
 reality 22–23
 schizophrenia-spectrum psychoses 8–9
 thought insertion as 11–15
 thought interference symptoms as 13
 truth 22–23
delusional mood 36, 124–25
delusional transformation 300–1
demand character 45–46
depression, agency 50
Diagnostic and Statistical Manual of Mental Disorders (DSM-5) 8–9
Dings, R. 51
disease progression 200
disowned memory 279–82
dissociability problem 124–25
dissonance 163
dopaminergic system 36, 55, 121–22
dorsal processing stream 107, 108
double-bookkeeping 11, 19–20
doxastic framework 8–9, 11, 115–16

Early Heidelberg School of Psychiatry 30–31, 34–35, 115–16
efference copy 204
ego-boundaries 10–11, 12–13, 16–17, 162–63
ego-dystonic thinking 69, 156, 159–60
Ellersgaard, D. 184–85
emotions, beliefs 155
enactivism 16, 44–45
endorsement account 18–19
entitlement 54
equivocal thoughts 289–94
equivoque 227
error-prediction models 114–15, 120–27, 135, 136, 239, 241–42
 imagistic prediction errors 137–41, 146
event-related potentials 200
events, thoughts as 294–97

executive control model 108
experiences
  agency and ownership 82–83
  avoidance 160–61
  context 63, 116–18
  experiential evidence 84–86
  features of thought insertion 173–75
  passivity 90–91
experimental studies 195–223
  alien control 207–13
  automatic writing 212–16
  challenges of 197–200
  confounding factors 200
  distinguishing symptoms from one another 198–99
  experimental suggestion using hypnosis 200–16
  illness severity 199–200
  limitations 217–18
  temporal unpredictability of symptoms 197–98
explanationist accounts 18–19
expressions of states 87
external attribution 161–66
externalizing bias 164–65
external misattribution 241

false beliefs 13
Fernyhough, C. 71, 117–18
first-person authority 83–90
first-rank symptoms 10–11, 30–31
five card mental force 229–30
Fletcher, P. C. 125–26
forcing 226–30
forward model 108, 176–77, 204–6
Frankfurt, H. 288
Freeman, D. 188–89
functional magnetic resonance imaging (fMRI) 207–13, 245

Gallagher, S. 80, 154–55
Gibson, J. J. 43, 44
Gipps, R. G. 16
Graham, G. 156–57
Gray, D. M. 17
grey matter 198, 200
Gruhle, H. W. 30–31, 32

hallucinations
  inner speech-based 61
  leading to delusions 9
  memory-based 61
  see also auditory-verbal hallucinations
hearing voices, see auditory-verbal hallucinations
heterogeneity
  imagery 143–44
  thought insertion 20–21
hybrid theory 135–50
hypersalience 119–20
hypervigilance 61
hypnosis 200–16, 231–32

identification 17
ideomotor action 202
illness severity 199–200
imagery
  inner speech 66–67, 143–44, 146
  prediction errors 137–41, 146
immunity to error through misidentification 79
inference 8–9, 35–36, 107, 114–15, 120–21, 122
inhibitory failure, inner speech 118
inner speech 117–18
  auditory-verbal hallucinations 144–46, 177–78
  condensation 70–71
  contextual coherence 69
  direct vs. indirect mode of address 68
  expansion 70–71
  experiential context 63
  hallucinations 61
  imagery 66–67, 143–44, 146
  individual differences 66
  inhibitory failure 118
  inner speech acts 64
  linguistic 66–67
  mere acts of inner speech 64
  processing 118
  soundless voices 62, 66–72
  as thinking 64–66
  thought insertion 62, 66–72, 143–46
  transparency 68
  type of speech act 67–68
inquisitive clinician 22
internal model
  cerebellum 239–41, 242, 243–47, 248
  of thought 247–49
introspection 162–63, 175–76, 273–74

Index

inverse model 204
irrationality 157–58

James, W. 15
Jaspers, K. 29, 31–32
judgement of agency 247–48
jumping to conclusions 119–20, 165–66, 179

Kant, I. 105–6
ketamine 125–26
Kiverstein, J. 45–46
Kusters, W. 32, 93

language
   disturbances 50–51
   games 87–88
   inner speech 66–67
   processing 178

magic 225–37
   forcing 226–30
   magician's choice 227
   mentalism 225–26, 234
   mimicking thought insertion 230–35
   'one behind' choice technique 234–35
   stooges (confederates) 235
maintenance of delusions 125–26
Mathys, C. 140–41
Mayer-Gross, W. 33–35
McClelland, T. 48–49
memory
   memory-based hallucinations 61
   without commitment (disowned memory) 279–82
mental action/acts 44–49, 51, 289–90
mental affordances 48–49, 52–53
   disclosure 49–52
mental events 294–96
mentalism 225–26, 234
mental passivity 290–91, 296
mental priming force 228
mescaline experiments 34–35
metacognition xxxiii, 253–54
Metacognitive Assessment Scale Abbreviated (MAS-A) 261
Metacognitive Reflection and Insight Therapy (MERIT) 260–67
Metacognitive Training 254–60
mismatch negativity 200
Miyazono, K. 124–25

monothematic delusions 172
motivational approaches 152–53, 155–57
motor control
   modelling 212–16
   sensorimotor processes 176–78
motor cortex 108–9
Mullins, S. 174–75
multimodal physicality 31–33

narrative interconnectedness 142
Natorp, P. 94–95
neural processing 107–9
neurocomputational model 35–37
neurodevelopment 200
neuroenchantment 232–33
neuropsychiatric models 115–20
No Subject view 288, 292–94

obsessive-compulsive disorder (OCD)
   agency 50
   content-thought disorder 152–53
   ego-dystonic thinking 159–60
   experiential avoidance 161
   external attribution 161–66
   mental affordances 51–52
occurrent thoughts 290–91, 297–302
Olson, J. A. 232–33
omnipotence 29–30
'one behind' choice technique 234–35
ontology
   ontologically impossible experiences 19–20
   thinking 287–304
open-minded clinician 22
otherness 175–77
outcome forces 227
ownership
   as commitment 275–77
   predating delusions 298
   sense of 53–54, 80, 81, 82, 90–91, 104–7, 154–55

pain, analgesic effects of hypnosis 202
paradoxes of subjectivity 92–96
Parnas, J. 297
passivity
   experiences 90–91
   mental passivity 290–91, 296
   thought insertion as a passivity phenomenon 10–11, 17–18

Pawar, A. V. 32
perceptual processes 104–7, 146
persecutory delusions
  cognitive biases 165
  multi-component account 188–89
  nonclinical populations 9
  thought insertion and 11–12, 173–75, 180–89
perseverance of delusions 125–26
personal account 3–6
personalizing bias 165
phenomenology
  agency in thought insertion 154–55
  auditory-verbal hallucinations and thought insertion overlap 102–4
  bias 37–38
  cognition 37–38
  enactivism 44
  error-prediction models 123–24
  first-person authority 84–86, 89–90
  neurocomputational model of psychosis 35–37
  phenomenological psychopathology 21, 300
  prodromal stage of psychosis 162–64
  self-disturbance 30–31, 37–38
  self-experience 79–81
  thinking 64–66
physicality of thought insertion xxiv, 28
  imaginary 29–30
  multimodal 31–33
Positive and Negative Syndrome Scale (PANSS) 199
power relationships 29–30
Powers, A. R. 140–41
prediction-error model 114–15, 120–27, 135, 136, 239, 241–42
  imagistic prediction errors 137–41, 146
predictive coding 35–36, 114–15, 120–21, 138–39, 146
primary motor cortex 108–9
priming forces 228
psychological immune system 156
Purkinje cells 243

Ramstead, M. 45, 46
reality 22–23
reality monitoring 104, 139–40
reasoning
  biases 165–66
  deficits 178–79

recontextualization 51–52, 127–28
refrigerator light problem 65
reifying thoughts 295–96, 299
reverse psychology 229–30
Rietveld, E. 45–46
Rules 4
Ryle, G. 65

salience
  aberrant salience hypothesis 55, 122–23, 127–28
  attribution of 121–22
  hypersalience 119–20
  visual salience force 228–29
Sartre, J.-P. 65
Sass, L. 53, 93
Scale for Assessment of Positive Symptoms (SAPS) 174–75, 199
Schedules for Clinical Assessment in Neuropsychiatry (SCAN) 14, 174
schizophrenia
  cognitive abnormalities 119–20, 164–66
  delusional beliefs 8–9
  ego-boundaries 16–17
  experiential context 116–18
  first-rank symptoms 10
  language disturbances 50–51
  metaphors of self 28
  ontologically impossible experiences 19–20
  paradoxical nature of symptoms 15
  personal account 3–6
  philosophy and 77–98
  self-disturbance 30–31
  unworlding 53–54
selective attention 46–47, 54–55, 106
selectivity of inserted thoughts 151–52
self-conscious 16–21, 105
self-disturbance
  multimodal physicality 31–33
  phenomenology 30–31, 37–38
  thought insertion as 30–31
self-experience, phenomenology 79–81
self-monitoring 137–38, 141–43, 177–78
self-serving bias 164–65, 241
sense of agency 52–53, 81, 90–91, 154–55, 159, 177, 240–42, 247–49
sense of authorship 104–7, 154–55
sense of involvement 162–63

sense of ownership 53–54, 80, 81, 82, 90–91, 104–7, 154–55
sense of subjectivity 154–55
sensorimotor processes 176–78
Simone (case example) 258–60, 265–67
sleep dysfunction 188–89
smoking 200
solicitations 44–49, 51
soundless voices 17–18, 59–75
   inner speech misattribution 62, 66–72
   mechanism 61
   same phenomenon as thought insertion 59–60, 61–63, 66–72
Space Aliens 4–5
spatial perception of voices 108
Spence, S. A. 32, 174–75
spontaneity 106
standard approach 154
Stephens, G. L. 156–57
stereotypical behaviour 230
Sterzer, P. 35–36, 122, 142
stooges 235
subjective privilege 84
subjectivity
   paradoxes of 92–96
   sense of 154–55
   sense of agency 247–48
substance misuse 200
supplementary motor area 108–9, 216
symptom capture 198

technical delusions 207
temporal factors
   association of psychotic symptoms 199
   unpredictability of psychotic symptoms 197–98
thalamus hyperactivity 109
thinking/thought
   activity of thinking 106, 289–90

ego-dystonic 69, 156, 159–60
equivocal thoughts 289–94
first-person authority 83–90
inner speech as 64–66
internal models 247–49
No Subject view 288, 292–94
occurrent thoughts 290–91, 297–302
ontology 287–304
phenomenology 64–66
priors 122–23
reifying thoughts 296, 299
thought broadcasting 4, 10–11, 12–13, 32
thought echo 10–11, 12–13
thoughts as events 294–97
thoughts as things that happen 291–92
thoughts as things we think 290, 291–92
thought withdrawal 10–11, 12–13, 32
twelve categories 106
without commitment 277–79
top-down theory 138–39, 140–41, 159, 205–6
trait studies 197–98
truth 22–23
two-factor theory 135, 136, 172–73, 175–80

uncertainty xxiii–xxiv, 125–26
unworlding 53–54

ventral processing stream 107–8
visual salience force 228–29
vulnerability to psychosis 165
Vygotsky, L. S. 71, 117–18

Wilkinson, S. 61
Wittgenstein, L. 87–92

Young, G. 105–6

Zahavi, D. 80, 84–85, 86